Alphabet to Internet

Media in Our Lives

Second Edition

Alphabet to Internet

Media in Our Lives

Second Edition

Irving Fang

Rada Press
St. Paul, MN

ISBN 978-1-933011-01-1

Library of Congress Cataloging-in-Publication Data

Fang, Irving E.
 Alphabet to Internet : media in our lives / Irving Fang. -- 2nd ed.
    p. cm.
 Includes bibliographical references and index.
 ISBN 978-1-933011-01-1
 1. Mass media--History. I. Title.
 P90.F264 2012
 302.2309--dc23
    2011046553

Printed in the United States of America

Rada Press, Inc.
1277 Fairmount Avenue
St. Paul, MN 55105-2702

phone: 651-645-3304
email: info@radapress.com
www.radapress.com

BOOK DESIGN BY RON-MICHAEL PELLANT
COVER DESIGN ON PAPYRUS BY DAISY PELLANT

TEXT SET IN GARAMOND AND OPTIMA

Table of Contents

Acknowledgments

I would like to thank Marvin Petal, Philip Tichenor and Rachel Fang, who edited the manuscript with discerning eyes and supportive voices. Margaret Price, Ron-Michael Pellant and Daisy Pellant offered their sound advice and help that is much appreciated. Kristin Harley provided the index.

Irving Fang, Ph.D., a former journalist, has worked at Reuters and ABC News. He is also an emeritus professor of the School of Journalism and Mass Communication, University of Minnesota. Among his books on broadcast news skills and communication history are *Those Radio Commentators!*, *Television and Radio News*, *A History of Mass Communication: Six Information Revolutions* and a series of eleven books, *The Story of Communication*, for younger readers. He has lectured in several countries of Europe, Africa and Asia, including a Fulbright professorship in the Philippines.

Introduction

As this book was being written, governments in power for decades collapsed. Their dictators fled. In the streets the young people danced and the old people laughed. Clutched in their fingers were their weapons, Mobile phones.

Some observers called these uprisings "social media revolutions," "Facebook revolutions" or "Twitter revolutions." New communication technologies were the magnets that pulled together the dense masses into city squares. At home, viewers gathered around television sets to watch the street demonstrations in other countries and hear the news of the end of autocrats, seeing events unfold on cross-border programs brought in by satellite dishes. Salma Said, a 26-year-old Egyptian woman activist, said she had been arrested, kicked, groped and pepper-sprayed. "Two years ago I just got disappointed in organized groups and left it and discovered this world of Twitter and blogs," she said. "We work with Twitter aggregators, web designers, techno geeks."[1]

"Flash Mobs"

We live in an era of "flash mobs." (Like a flash flood it suddenly appears in force.) Rage goes viral and angry people cluster. Information running through social networks and cell phones directs them. In 2011, fueled by Twitter, Facebook, YouTube, email, camera phones and mimeographed leaflets, pent-up fury exploded against government corruption, widespread unemployment and rising prices. With messages fed into cell phones in every other hand, daily street riots brought down the governments of Egypt and Tunisia. Threats spread to governments across the Middle East and North Africa. The United States saw flash mobs in several of its own cities robbing stores and causing havoc. However, in London days of Twitter-fueled riots and looting were followed by ordinary citizens organizing via Twitter to protect their neighborhoods.

Governments control choke points—the ISPs through which electronic messages pass. When the Egyptian government shut down the internet and cell phone links for five days, ordinary Egyptians turned to the plentiful television satellite dishes, dial-up modems and land lines to reach ISPs in other countries. Security police could confiscate their mobiles but the video was already on its way around the world.[2] *Seeing* what others were watching informed the protestors. *Knowing* that others watched cheered them and drove them on.

Enemies of democracy also network. After a fanatic Florida pastor oversaw the burning of a Qur'an, the news that raced across the Muslim world led to deadly anti-American riots in Afghanistan. Pictures of the 2009 Tehran demonstrations that turned bloody were fed to the outside by phones despite efforts by the Iranian government. A cell captured the street death of 26-year-old Neda Agha-Soltan, the student whose picture as she lay dying became an icon for protest.

Mobile media were in the thick of things. The Occupy Wall Street movement in 2011, spreading to cities across the United States and to other countries, had its own media center. It funneled images snapped on camera phones of Occupy movements worldwide to YouTube, Facebook, and traditional media. At the same time Facebook and Twitter messages urged worldwide demonstrations. The 2011 urban riots in England and the French urban riots of 2005 were strung together by cell phones, texting and the internet. The combination of street organization and cheap technology proved so efficient that the French government and police in 2005 hardly knew what hit them or how to stop it. During the global disputes about the Iraq War that started in 2003, armies of antiwar protesters were summoned to the streets of Western capitals by email and cell phone instant messaging.

News racing from city to city and to journalists who have immediate access to the outer world overwhelms governments trying to control the information. Historically, protesters have been weaker than government forces. Cell phones to some extent level the field. The days of workers starting revolutions by taking over factories are long gone. So are the days of seizing radio stations and, in the immediate post-Soviet Union days, television stations. Today the messages pour out through many avenues.

If we look back across the centuries we find many examples of how media have influenced political action. Tom Paine's pamphlet *Common Sense* and Harriet Beecher Stowe's novel *Uncle Tom's Cabin* spring to mind. This book identifies others.

Mass and Personal

Each new medium has penetrated the lives of individuals and societies. To say that communication media have been a factor in the course of history is not a deterministic point of view, for many factors have played their part. The point made on these pages is that mediated communication has been a significant and, today, an expanding element of historic change. Mediated communication can be defined as both *mass* and *personal* communication using a physical medium. In fact, because mass and personal media use the same tools and sometimes have the same goals, their distinctions have eroded. The inclusive term is *mediated communication*. Because so much of our daily life is spent with it, we should know how it affects us. Besides asking what mediated communication does *for* us, we should also ask what mediated communication does *to* us.

Mediated communication — using external means to carry information — has been part of human life since the start of recorded history. Almost by definition, recorded history requires media and itself uses such media as alphabets and paper. The term includes every means of communication listed in this book's table of contents, and more. The communication can be as broad as showing the world the moon landing or as personal as helping a family member reach a decision. Modern technology has enmeshed as never before what is mass and what is personal.

In 2011 Japanese were informing relatives and friends around the world via Facebook, Twitter and a special Google service that they had survived the 9.0 earthquake and tsunami As images of the horrors filled YouTube and moved on to television, social media removed the pain of not knowing. Reporters interviewed both victims and experts via a video telephone service, Skype. The mass communication ability to inform on a global scale and the personal communication ability of one person to reach another even on a global scale became intertwined. Social networks are both mass and personal communication. So is email. Postal services have enabled both mass and personal communication at least since Benjamin Franklin mailed out his first catalog for scientific and academic books in 1744. Today when disaster strikes, CNN trolls for witnesses who took pictures.

The Sources of Our Values

Mediated communication has a push-pull effect, pushing us apart but keeping us tethered to family and friends, to home and sometimes to workplace. It helps us to stay in contact with one another while also contributing to our physical separation. The internet is just one of the latest catalysts for our new reality. Soldiers serving in Afghanistan or Iraq can receive digital pictures daily from their families and friends using camera phones. Or talk to the family via Skype or FaceTime. When children travel they stuff DVD movies and portable gaming systems into their carry-on backpacks. If they move to another country their parents now have nightly podcasts of American radio and television newscasts to keep them up to date about events at home.

At some level, humans have had media for centuries to accompany life's changes. Communication media are so tangled up in our existence that we give little thought to these connections or to living without them. Yet societies are both subtly and profoundly affected by media. So is individual behavior. Values and culture once came entirely through the family, the church, the community, the school. Values came from people you knew and saw. This changed when the Industrial Revolution brought mass media. Advertising, newspapers, magazines and the novel introduced the standards of people who lived far away. Immigration, driven in part by communication, has led to cities bulging with the signs and sighs of many cultures. Personal advice now also comes from the newspaper column and the television screen.

With the integration of each new medium, life became different for those who used the medium. Because you are reading these words it is likely that you will spend more time today with mediated communication—in some of its many forms—than doing anything else, including sleeping. If you decide to test this, you can use the stopwatch feature of your smartphone or a real stopwatch. Click it if you wake to a clock radio or turn on the TV. Click it at the breakfast table if you read a newspaper or the back of the cereal box. Click for the car radio and the billboards you glance at. Click for phone calls. Click for the letter you are writing, because mediated communication runs in both directions and you will be using the technology of an alphabet and the postal service. Continue to click as warranted throughout the day until you finally turn out the light. Add up the times tomorrow.

Much of our use of media is routine and habitual, baked into our lives. If you read a morning newspaper, do you read it at breakfast, always starting at the same section, such as the sports page, the comics or the obits? When you flip your car's ignition switch, does your radio come on, always tuned to the same station? When you arrive at work, do you start with the same blogs or news reports as you did yesterday? How about your television viewing? You may know it's Tuesday because your favorite show is on tonight; on Tuesdays if you don't have DVR you stay home. If a popular news anchor changes her hairstyle, she can be sure some viewers will complain, for the change has intruded into *their* expectations, *their* routine.

Adapting to Our Tools

A perception exists that to succeed in romance or business today we must use the latest tools of mediated communication, or at least be able to talk about them with familiarity. We adapt ourselves to media imperatives. We carry devices everywhere. We respond to the ringing tones wherever and whenever. We sometimes watch what our friends watch just so that we can talk about it. We learn the jargon. We adjust. Not to put too fine a point on it, we as a society create mediated communication that alters how we spend our days, how we live our lives, how we relate to others. That way, we may succeed. Darwin never taught a clearer lesson.

History has repeatedly demonstrated the capacity that communication media have to affect our lives. Each new medium has brought in its wake a pattern of change distinct to that medium. Yet many media encountered opposition along the way to general acceptance, a grudging recognition that change was not always welcome. While certain elements of change are common to several media—such as separating us from our immediate surroundings—each medium creates its own pattern, its own signature of human behavior.

Century by century, and now year by year, media have become enmeshed in our lives. Whether it is reading, watching television, listening to music, working on the computer, or internet surfing, a significant part of our attention each day is spent apart from other people. The more time spent with mediated communication, the less time remains for the direct contact that was once a social dynamic.

Whether it is talking on the telephone, writing email, using a pen to send a greeting card, connecting via Facebook, or Skyping, we are still not in direct contact. What we are doing satisfies our needs and gives us some degree of pleasure, but there are differences. For all their benefits, media bring unintended consequences. We employ media instead of living the simpler life that is frequently praised, but infrequently chosen. Few of us since Henry David Thoreau would truly prefer the simple life of *Walden*.

As we take note of all the media that have come along, do we see common factors among them? Or common trends? Are there commonalities among such advances as the adoption of a phonetic alphabet, the inventions of photography and the telegraph and today's mobile phones, web pages and blogs? Let us recognize some common effects of mediated communication both old and new:

• Because of mediated communication, everyone's potential knowledge base has expanded from what one person can be expected to know. It is now boundless. The most educated scholars a few years ago could not have dreamed of the amount of information so readily at hand everywhere.

• Mediated communication has led to new means of education and to libraries holding ever more information remote from the here and now. If we can store information, we can reflect upon the past and build upon that information. We can share it systematically. This happens every day.

• We use mediated communication to take our attention from the *here* to connect to the *there*. The *there* now can be anywhere on Earth at any time in history. The philosopher Martin Heidegger observed that "everything is equally far and equally near." This can affect not only the information and entertainment we choose to receive, but where we choose to live and other factors central to our lives.

• The more we use media the more we separate ourselves from those physically close to us and from our surroundings. In this way mediated communication separates as it connects.

• Information, misinformation and opinions come from people we don't know. Interest grows in what is distant. From its ancient beginnings, mediated communication has enabled individuals to access information that they come to deeply believe from people they would never meet, people separated by distance, by generation and by culture and experience.

• Time and attention spent with mediated communication are not spent in other ways. There is always a trade-off.

• Words, pictures and sounds that we bring in occupy our attention. They often drive out silence and any deep thought that accompanies silence.

• Respect for the knowledge of elders, a vital part of every traditional society, diminishes with the arrival of competing, distant standards. In a heavily mediated world, the accumulated wisdom of family and community elders loses value and may become superfluous. Nothing new here. Early printed books brought knowledge that competed with the acquired wisdom of parents and the local elders.

• As new inventions and new methods diffuse into society, the number and variety of our choices of information and entertainment grows. Life becomes more complex.

• *Personal* communication uses the expanded tools of *mass* communication. Email users, for example, are certainly aware that *mass* communication intrudes into a means of *personal* communication. As noted, the truly descriptive term is *mediated communication.*

• The expansion of the personal into the mass has weakened the economic underpinnings of traditional mass communication.[3] In the several ways that we read, hear and view information, the industrial model of mass communication is breaking apart. And national borders matter less.

• Beyond population growth the number of information producers increases. They use an increasing variety of media and reach more and more information consumers. This was true in the 15th century when Gutenberg began printing. It is true today. When available to everyone, mediated communication has a leveling effect even if real equality remains out of reach.

• The more educated we are, the more we rely on mediated communication. It is an essential part of becoming a specialist. The content that we choose, of course, determines what we know.

• The effort to convince others continues to increase. With the transmission of knowledge has come persuasion, using every means of communication to that end. One of the commonalities of all media is their use to convince message receivers to share the views of the senders.

• Even where it is not fully available to everyone, mediated communication of every type is used by rulers to maintain their power and by specialists to retain their influence. Those who gain added power and influence by holding the levers of mediated communication may withhold them from those who want to share them. This pattern has ancient roots.

• The entire history of communication has been spotted with efforts to limit, censor, or punish those who would say what those in power did not want them to say. Efforts at control never flag. Yet even in dictatorships more information is sent and received than ever before. Witness the Syrian government effort in 2011 and 2012 to bar journalists from entering the country and the killing of journalists in a number of dictatorships.

• In a mediated world, talent trumps individual expression. We are provided with professional entertainment at the expense of family closeness. Before the phonograph and certainly before broadcasting took hold, enjoyment in the home often came from family members reading, telling stories, playing a musical instrument or singing to one another. Little remains in a heavily mediated household.

• Today we never have to separate ourselves from media. As our portable communication tools shrink, thin, add functions and power and capacity, they attach to us like the shirt we put on each day. What cannot walk down the street with us now: songs? news? novels? games? work files? blogs? phone and even visual contacts? All of that can, and more. We never need to be parted from our distant connections.

• Those who can afford media always have an important advantage. Media require not only the hours to use them but also the working hours to pay for them. Owning or using media takes time and money.

Changes That Media Brought

The chapters that follow examine how our lives have been affected by the adoption of new means of communication. These are just some of the changes that have made the deepest impact. They should be obvious to us, but it doesn't hurt to remind ourselves of them:

Writing stores most of mankind's knowledge and allows that knowledge to be unlimited by memory. Writing carries thought across the centuries and across the lands and oceans. It makes progress and our civilization possible. Nations with significant illiterate populations are at a disadvantage. The scattered tribes that cling to an oral culture eke out a bare existence.

Printing broadens the spread of information and the pleasure to be found in reading. It makes mass education and democracy possible even if all nations do not practice it. It has expanded science and medicine and every other field of knowledge. It has also expanded commerce, the rule of law, and almost every field of human activity.

The mails for centuries have carried that information, bringing us both personal and commercial messages. Where postal services are weak, the spread of information is stunted. Where they are strong, nations benefit.

The telegraph stitched together distant communities and connected individuals with information that they could share and that arrived almost instantly. It made railroads safer. Its role has diminished only because it is the parent of the telephone, radio and the other ways we transmit messages.

The telephone has brought familiar voices to people who are separated by events that have altered their lives. What makes loved ones special flies through the wires, and now through the air. The telephone saves lives by giving us a means to summon help. Because it makes life safer and more pleasant, many of us keep a telephone by our side day and night. Yet the same phone that can keep us physically independent from others, like parents, can also, if we want, pull us into a flash mob that overwhelms police efforts at control. And phones that snap and twitter images of violence sometimes send crowds into inflamed, destructive riots.

Recording brings us entertainment of a quality we could not otherwise encounter. It holds the music that is an expression of every culture. It retains memories that delight us as the years roll by, connecting us to distant times and places and people who mattered to us.

Photography has enriched our memories and our awareness and has shown us scenes that we could not personally witness. Although photographs today can be altered, most photos for most people still fit the saying that seeing is believing. Photos also remind us of past times, and that is important. When people are forced to flee a home because of fire or flood, what they may clutch in their hands is a photo album.

Movies have given people everywhere the realities and stories that have become part of our lives. To see a film, literacy doesn't matter. We recognize movie stars much more readily than those who govern us. To appreciate the impact that the motion picture has, we have only to consider the nature and direction of censorship and outright bans. Today it is not only easier to own movies but it is also easier to make them.

Radio, immediately within reach, has kept us company with information and entertainment no matter where we are. It can be a companion from the moment we wake, through each day's commute, and as we fall asleep. In remote places where no other communication is available, radio remains a dependable servant. Before broadcasting, radio was known for its wireless capacity to connect ships and distant places.

Television keeps us company with news and a variety of entertainment so compelling that people all over the world spend hours with it each day. More television sets than people reside in the average American home. Visitors may come into our homes and go, events may occur that demand attention, but for many viewers the TV stays on.

The computer as a tool of communication assists our work and our study. It extends our reach in every direction and reduces our need for transportation. It stores data and calculates far better than our minds can. It helps us to publish books and produce films. It provides the physical underpinning of the internet and email.

The internet opens up as much of the world to us as we want. It leads us into new areas of knowledge at the touch of a button. The more educated you are the more likely to use the internet. The unfolding social networks are a part of the astonishing communication revolution that is now underway.

Video games are the new way that we entertain and challenge ourselves. Many people, especially but not only younger people, never tire of such a challenge. The games allow us to interact with a means of professionally created entertainment. They reflect human values and human desires, not all of which are matters of pride.

Persuading others to a point of view or to take an action has always been part of life, and certainly of communication. Advertising and propaganda are ever with us. They take many forms, overt or subtle, including public relations. Persuasion via mediated communication has a considerable role in modern warfare and both political and religious conflict.

Year by year the amount of mediated communication in our lives increases both in what we are able to send and what we receive. In all these ways and in many other ways we are different because of our means of communication. The tools of communication have accompanied us in our journey across the centuries. Let us examine the specific changes that each brought to human life. We start with writing.

1. Writing

In most conflicts pitting an oral culture against a written culture, the literates win a lopsided victory. Non-literates may have enjoyed a more admirable culture, such as the Native Americans who encountered the arriving European immigrants, but time and again, they ended up enslaved or dead. The illiterate Vikings and Mongols did well, but the peoples who left writing behind them have influenced the future far more than the efficient warriors who once shook worlds. Today, the remaining non-literate communities have no more power than the literate world grants them. The few pockets of oral culture that survive do so by the sufferance of the literate.

Writing, the use of symbols to express thought and set information down, is as old as recorded history because, of course, that is how history was recorded. Speech and gesture preceded writing, but distance limited their reach. Cave paintings preceded writing, as did engraved marks on bones and antlers, but the meaning of their messages is mostly lost to us today. Native American smoke signals were limited. African drums—the original telegraph—may have been there ahead of writing, but, remarkable as they could be, what they transmitted and how far they could send a message were also limited. However, the scratches on Sumerian jars, Babylonian clay tablets, Egyptian stone and papyrus, Chinese silk and Indonesian lontar leaves started a process that continues with the public library, the newspaper on your doorstep, Internet blogs and what's on TV tonight.

In literate societies, many individuals who lack literacy in the language of their community wish they had it. Some non-literate, oral societies still in existence in remote corners of the world manage well enough without writing as long as they are left alone by the always more powerful possessors of writing.

Still, a few people, like Socrates, disparaged literacy. Still more would control what others should be allowed to read. Yet writing continues to be our principal form of communication beyond the range of conversation.

Of writing's many advantages, a few stand out:

- Writing stores much of mankind's transmittable knowledge. Humans, of course, are the only animals able to store knowledge outside the body.

- Knowledge no longer needs to be limited to memory. With stored writing, our potential knowledge has no limits.

- Written information in a fixed form can travel across any distance. It can be organized thoughtfully and shared widely.

- Written information can travel from generation to generation for centuries without change. We can and do build upon what we already know.

- The literate own an immensely powerful tool—or weapon—denied to individual illiterates and to oral societies.[2]

Oral Cultures

An oral culture bases itself upon two-way, restricted information. It has a human dimension, a human limitation. Members speak of a "hammer" or a "saw," not of the more abstract "tool."[5] Oral cultures pull their member together to communicate information. Writing and reading usually are done alone, solitary and silent activities. In an oral culture, to communicate means to be in the presence of a listener, an audience. To communicate by writing, no listener is present. The listener is imagined and is separated from the writer. Writing splits thought from action, as Marshall McLuhan noted.[3] Without writing, the literate mind could not think as it does, said Walter Ong, one of the foremost authorities on oral and print cultures: "More than any other single invention, writing has transformed human consciousness."

To move comfortably in a world of abstractions is one of writing's gifts to us, but only at a cost. Did we pay for that gift with the coin of memory as Socrates predicted? Bards and other members of oral cultures have a tradition of memory that astounds those of us who learn to memorize from written text. It was said that medieval minstrels could hear an hour's recitation just once before repeating it verbatim. Yet today, having the gifts of paper and printing, indeed having computer flash memory encased in a bit of plastic, we don't seem to care.

Knowledge in an oral culture is handed down to the next generation by parents and storytellers. Wisdom is passed to the younger generation by the elders. Writing began the shift away from the wise old grandmothers and grandfathers, who could not possibly tell all that writing has stored. What we have instead is a written culture so extensive that no human being can absorb its totality. Who can, for example, recall every scrap of information in an encyclopedia or, for that matter, in a textbook for a college introductory course? No one is expected to, because the book is there. Now, after so many centuries, who will need the book if an online source is there?

Written language undergirds most of civilization, yet there have always been societies without writing. Most of the ancient world remained illiterate. And oral cultures continued to serve most people. In considering the advantages of a written culture, we should remember that the praise that always accompanies literacy comes from the literate. A degree of self-satisfaction should not be overlooked.

Oral learning continues today as part of the literate world. Learning what is written by rote recitation, such as at many Muslim madrassas for young pupils, has old roots. In places where most people are illiterate, a literate priest or teacher can read aloud. The European religious upheaval marking the Reformation spread Gutenberg's invention of printing through a largely illiterate population. According to one estimate, German-speaking regions in Martin Luther's day had as many as 90% illiterates and semi-literates.[6] However, the printed word could still reach them by being read aloud by the literate few.

The Beginnings

Symbols date back to cave paintings drawn well before foragers became farmers. The oldest known is the Chauvet Cave in southern France, with drawings of animals that are 30,000 years old. The alphabetic markings that Western cultures identify as writing are different than drawings because they give permanence to the system of *sounds* that is spoken language. They leave marks that combine into meanings understood by others. However, writing did not start that way.

Instead of marks on a surface, writing may have begun as physical tokens representing numbers and goods. The history of producing and storing information in the form of these molded clay objects began about 8000 BCE in Sumer, possibly in towns along the Euphrates River.[7] One theory, which is not accepted by all scholars, holds that over many centuries small triangles, spheres, cones and other tokens were molded to represent sheep, measures of grain, jars of oil and other possessions. These tokens kept track of goods for the purpose of pooling and redistributing a community's resources.[8]

As settled communities grew, fed by local agriculture and trade, their need for records expanded. About five thousand years ago, numbers broke away from other information. Mathematics was born. The symbols for sheep or jars of oil came to differ from the symbols for their quantity. Tokens were placed in round sealed clay envelopes, but the need to identify a envelope's contents led to scratching or pressing a representation of the tokens on the surface of the envelope. It could not have taken long to figure out that with the scratches on the outside, the tokens were no longer needed. The clay envelope itself was flattened into a tablet.

About this time the first logograms emerged, those written symbols that represented meaning. These scratches were true writing, the representation of what someone might say. Pictograms, the symbols representing objects and concepts, and ideograms, the symbols representing ideas, would in future become Egyptian hieroglyphics, Babylonian cuneiform and Chinese characters. Centuries later, independently, the Mayans developed a script. Even later, so did the Aztecs. The Incas used dyed yarns attached in specific patterns to convey messages.

The Role of Priests

Recognizing the value of marks on clay or papyrus, men would eventually control them and punish anyone who intruded into their mysteries. Writing became sacred. The priests of many religions, the keepers of the mysteries of the gods, found writing to be a natural fit for themselves. By keeping records, they could inventory food stocks in the nation's granaries, predict weather cycles and the rising of the Nile or the Yangtze. They guarded the skill, aware of how it conferred authority. All societies had their gods, with a priestly class to interpret the gods' mysterious behavior and to intercede for frail mankind. Each priesthood in societies as remote as Easter Island in the Pacific Ocean has needed ways to separate itself. Those who could write stood apart and above the illiterate mass of their fellows. As the priests were often the healers as well as the guides to the afterlife, it was to them that the common folk had to appeal, at times receiving charms to ward off illness and danger, as in ancient China and Japan. What will men and women not pay for health and salvation?

In society after society, priests chose the task of teaching selected youths. Scribal cultures developed. Priests educated boys in temple schools denied to outsiders. From the ranks of

Socrates

Unless you believe in old Egyptian gods, Socrates was the first to observe how media change us.[1] According to Plato, Socrates, who wrote nothing, opposed the teaching of writing, the first significant medium of communication beyond the body. He called writing "inhuman," for when confronted with a contrary point of view, text is mute. Socrates was right in saying that the use of letters would encourage forgetfulness, but this did not discourage the spread of literacy. Socrates did not prevail. Writing has proved more powerful and more arguably human than any media that followed.

It led to the greatest changes in human life. Just to imagine any of the sciences or medicine or law or commerce without writing is to sense this immediately. As for oral culture being more human, if Socrates was correct that some humanity is lacking in writing, consider that the oral stories that have come down to us, such as Homer's epics, have flat characters. Well-rounded, fully human characters emerged out of written culture.

students came an aristocratic class, public administrators and new priests. Literacy and education, the outpourings of mediated communication, gave them an indisputable advantage. A surviving papyrus says, "It is only the learned man who rules himself."[9]

Writing became central as trade grew more complex. As writing moved out of the Fertile Crescent, it was transmitted from one culture to another. In Egypt, hieroglyphics, that most visually beautiful of written forms, were used on monuments and tomb walls. Egyptians created hieratic (the later Greek word for "priestly"), a cursive version of hieroglyphics with about 400 signs, a mix of pictograms and consonants. It became the written language of rulers and priests, used for their documents and letters. A simplified secular version, demotic (the later Greek word for "popular"), was used for record keeping and letters, useful for merchants and craftsmen and the slaves lucky enough to become scribes. Just as it is true today for mathematicians, doctors and musicians, those who could make sense of certain symbols held the key to a specialized knowledge that set them apart, giving them something denied to others. One reason that empires held together for centuries was the capacity of a central government to write and transmit messages to governors of outlying provinces.

Alphabets

Who developed the first true alphabet, in which a written letter represented a spoken sound (a phoneme) rather than an object or concept? Linguist Amalia Gnanadesikan called the early alphabet "a dumbed-down version of writing for the illiterate."[11] Demotic had some alphabetic characters, yet was still not a full phonetic alphabet. The Akkadians in Mesopotamia also had alphabetic symbols in their writing, but not an alphabet.

The first true alphabet may have emerged about four thousand years ago from managers at copper and turquoise mines in the Sinai, a Semitic outpost of the Egyptian empire, or it may have been born in an outpost manned by Semitic mercenaries in the Egyptian army.[12] But why? Why would one of the most important advances in human history come out of a remote and relatively unlettered corner of the Near East? Why not a center of culture like Thebes? A definitive answer is not possible. One may guess that a rigid, centralized education system of the Egyptian empire or the much later Persian empire would not be inclined to change in this way. Why would those ancient priests and scribes see any need for a simplification that would spread literacy? Rather, would they not think that a series of sound symbols was an absurd substitute for a single word symbol? They would have no reason to make writing simple or to educate the illiterate masses. Quite the contrary. Mystery and complexity served them well.

However, copper mine managers or military officers who did not dream of entering the restricted doors of temple schools could learn an alphabet. Literature could hardly have interested them,

God's Word

Beneath an organized religion that was founded upon written scriptures, an oral culture breathed. Israelites in Egypt were likely to be illiterate, as were most Egyptians. Writing itself may have been unknown to them. According to the Bible, Moses brought down from Mount Sinai more than commands for righteous conduct. He brought the very words of God.

Yet they were in a form unfamiliar to the people gathered below. According to media ecologist Robert K. Logan, the manner of presentation was unique, "written with the finger of God."[10] If one believes that the sight of God's speech given as marks on tablets convinced idol worshippers to reform their ways, Logan's theory would seem to be early evidence of the potential of media to effect change.

but a more practical way to keep records and to communicate would be as welcome as a more practical way to do anything. The alphabet's ease enabled them to figure out how to use it.[13] A simple phonetic alphabet, first developed in a remote corner of the civilized world, served mercantile needs.

For traders moving among a variety of languages, a phonetic alphabet was a useful tool even if they did not remember everything just as they had learned it. Traders have seldom been linguistics scholars concerned with the exactness of orthography or the niceties of definitions. Copies of texts contained mistakes. Ears tuned to local dialects misheard pronunciations. As it traveled, the alphabet changed and so did the languages it supported. An alphabet can support any spoken language, any dialect.

The Greeks

We speak of the "Phœnician" alphabet, but Phœnicians did not invent it, just as we speak of "Arabic" numerals that actually originated in India. "The Phœnicians did not create the alphabet," said historian Will Durant. "They marketed it."[14] This Semitic seafaring people trading across the Mediterranean established colonies in Greece and at Carthage on the North African coast. It is probable that the Phœnicians gradually brought the alphabet to the Hellenic world and the dispersal of written magic charms. As the alphabet spread over the centuries, local communities changed and improved it to fit their own spoken language. The Greeks added vowels and democratized the alphabet by simplifying it. But they added much, much more, using the basic blocks of communication media to move the world in new directions.

With the alphabetic script and the availability of papyrus,[15] the Iliad and the Odyssey, the epic poems of Homer, based on tales that evidently had been repeated orally for the previous four centuries by storytellers or sung by bards, were written down, probably during the 8th century BCE. Writing enabled the tellers of tales to separate themselves from their memories. It allowed them to leave those memories and come back to them, for it also allowed them to forget.

What followed was totally new in the history of the world, an outpouring of intellectual, artistic and political ideas, an intellectual revolution conveyed by literacy. From this ferment arose the concept of the individual. According to classics scholar Eric Havelock, "This amounts to accepting the premise that there is a 'me,' a 'self,' a 'soul,' a consciousness which is self-governing… the counterpart of the rejection of the oral culture."[16] Among most Greeks, the oral tradition remained. Nevertheless, during ancient Greece's classical age (about 480 - 320 BCE), the era of Socrates, Plato and Aristotle, the Greeks developed the literate basis of modern thinking.[17] Far more than simple pictographs on walls or a tally of accounts, they created a means of surviving their own life span by leaving a legacy of their thoughts, satisfying the human desire to be remembered. Egyptian and Mesopotamian kings had done this, but not ordinary people.

Greek Accomplishments

The Greek adoption of literacy, said Havelock, accompanied "the ascent of man through education from the life of the senses towards the life of the reasoned intelligence… how did the Greeks ever wake up? The fundamental answer must lie in the changing technology of communication. Refreshment of memory through written signs enabled a reader to dispense

Aristotle

During the fourth century, Aristotle set about gathering and classifying the available body of knowledge. He could not have done so without a written language and the papyrus to hold it, giving him a permanent record on a storable medium.

Because of Aristotle, education in the Greek world would be based on reading, not simply listening to lectures. His library and other ancient storehouses of written information began the collections that would carry information from generation to generation down the ages. Oral transmission could not begin to match it.

Mathematics, medicine, astronomy, geography, and biology advanced because of ideas, conclusions, and reports of experiments written and stored on the transportable medium of papyrus.

with most of that emotional identification by which alone the acoustic record was sure of recall."[18] The Greeks separated mankind and human accomplishments from the world around them, regarding nature as a separate entity worthy of study. Greek scholars wrote of philosophy, metaphysics, history, several sciences, mathematics, medicine and politics. They wrote plays both comic and tragic. They wrote to explain the nature of truth and beauty. Their scholars had a genius for abstract thought, rational thought and for plain common sense. Writing helped the Greeks to govern themselves. It allowed the Greeks to conceive of objectivity, separating the knower from what is known. It was the gateway to the scientific method, to logic and analysis.

Scrolls carrying fresh ideas not only circulated in the cities, but also reached isolated scholars thanks to the trading ships plying the Mediterranean, truly the world's first information highway. Poetry, plays and essays traveled not only horizontally but vertically through the generations.

More than any previous civilization, the Greeks used written language to create different kinds of expertise. The Greeks became the teachers, the source of much of the Mediterranean world's

Scribes

The world's first formal educational system involved the training of scribes, those programmers of the ancient world. Slaves fortunate enough to be scribes probably considered themselves more intelligent than other slaves, an illusion of the literate that survives the centuries. Indeed, reading and writing were skills often beyond the capacity of masters who could only stare dumbly at the marks on clay or papyrus.

In ancient Egypt, a scribe might be a government bureaucrat, and exempt from heavy manual labor, taxes and military service. To a household slave, literacy was the path to a better—and longer—life than anything else available. The household scribe kept the accounts, recorded tributes to tax collectors and priests, noted what was bought, what was sold, and how much was paid. He read and wrote contracts, oversaw commercial dealings, and engaged in exchanges of diplomatic notes. In doing all this, he achieved a measure of influence rare for slaves. The clerical, scribal skills also appealed to many of the freeborn.

Yet, as it was everywhere, most people in the ancient empires remained illiterate. Except for the scribe, a literate peasant or slave would have been a stench in the nostrils of an illiterate nobleman. Not many people had ever heard of such a thing as a book. Communication was by word of mouth.

Museum of Luxor

culture, knowledge and education. Aristotle is credited with showing the Egyptians how to set up proper libraries instead of mere collections of books. The Greek-controlled port city of Alexandria became the leading center of book publishing. The Alexandrian Library was the greatest of the ancient world. Greek knowledge and ideas would travel the world in phonetic letters on papyrus and, later, the treated animal skins of parchment and vellum.

Thanks to the influence of Greek teachers and Greek thought, a growing literacy enriched the Roman Empire. The first daily news reports, the Acta Diurna, on waxed wood tablets were posted in the Roman Forum to let its citizens know what the Senate was doing. By the 4th century CE, the city of Rome itself had at least twenty-eight libraries with 20,000 or more papyrus rolls each. Throughout the empire there were city and private libraries and book collections. According to Seneca, private libraries became as common as baths.

The Middle Ages

Learning and communication suffered following the fall of the Roman Empire, except in the monasteries where knowledge was kept alive and books were patiently copied by hand. To be a scribe was no longer a mean calling fit for slaves. It was to do God's work.

Sacred Duty

With the collapse of Roman rule European civilization entered the Dark Ages. The pursuit of knowledge shrank into the pinpoints of lighted candles in remote monasteries. Monks, especially Benedictines, took up the scribe's pen to transfer the writing on the crumbling, old papyrus manuscripts onto parchment that was prepared in or near the monasteries. They huddled over their painstaking illuminations of the Bible, religious commentaries, and, in some orders, copies of works from classical Greece or Rome.

In chilly and drafty rooms, their fingers stiff and their backs aching, the monks sat hunched over their scriptorium desktops as they hand-lettered and painted magnificent copies of books for libraries and cathedrals.

These scriptoria may have been cold and grim, but they were not silent, for monks customarily mumbled or read aloud as they worked, or they listened to readings accompanying the scratching of their pens on parchment.

When universities arose in Europe starting in the 12th century, Latin was the language of scholars. Out in the towns and the countryside, people spoke a babble of vernacular languages made all the more separate because the network of Roman roads had fallen into decay, but all the scholarly books were written in Latin. Literacy during the Dark Ages meant knowledge at least of Latin, to which scholars could add Greek and Hebrew, and this knowledge set them apart from the rest of humanity.

The monopoly of the monasteries over book production and distribution had ended with the founding of universities in Western Europe, starting in Bologna in 1158. In the back shops of stationers in university towns, scriveners copied books by hand that were still too expensive for poor students to buy, but students could rent the books and perhaps copy the copies to share among themselves. Not until the printing press did education significantly change.

England in the 12th century allowed defendants who could read Psalm 51 to be tried before an ecclesiastical court where sentences were likely to be milder than in common law courts. That would encourage literacy for, as Samuel Johnson observed, the prospect of hanging concentrates the mind wonderfully.

In medieval Europe before printing, it was expected that the clergy could read and ordinary folk could not. Neither could many knights nor even lords. Except for a few who were high-born, medieval women were illiterate. As Europe entered the modern age, the ability to read at some level became a means to social advancement, despite the occasional protest that feudal distinctions should predominate.[19] Societies' elites erected and guarded the literacy barriers from commoners, convinced that only they had any need to know the intelligence contained in books and news reports.

Education was still mostly for the wealthy, but the promising son of a poor family occasionally was accepted by a teaching scholar. Lucky families eagerly and gratefully sent off their sons for such schooling, the way for him to a better life. As illiterate marauders gained power, they absorbed the culture along with the treasure of those they conquered. They opened schools or hired tutors for their own children to make sure they were taught to read and write.

A Growing Literacy

Toward the end of the 17th century, Sweden required reading literacy of its citizens, but not writing. Elsewhere, writing masters advertised their skill at teaching different levels of penmanship. At the bottom level was handwriting for business. A letter might be written in a secretary hand to show that it had been dictated, then signed in the "fine Italian hand" of its high-born author. To perversely show scorn for plebes who had learned the "mechanical" art of penmanship, some English and French aristocrats cultivated an illegible scrawl as a sign of their breeding.[20]

As societies became more complex, the need for writing grew. Far from Europe, other civilizations advanced in their own ways, with their own oral and written languages. Despite little formal contact, similar approaches developed in unconnected cultures for the role of written language. Writing everywhere emerged as a tool of the class of priests. Everywhere it marked authority and conferred power. Everywhere it was rationed.

Where reading was taught to girls, as in Colonial America, the goal was to read scripture, not to write anything and not to read handwriting.[21] When girls were taught penmanship in 19th century schools, it was a shrunken style suitable for private correspondence, not the generous "mercantile running hand" that their brothers learned.[22]

Chinese and Korean Writing

The Chinese written language consists of ideographs, the representations of images, but ideographic writing is no friend to simple literacy. You have to work at it. The complexity of its language supported a rigid imperial hierarchy, yet China developed written civil service examinations and a large, literate bureaucracy.[23]

An 18th century Chinese dictionary listed 40,545 characters, far more than any scholar could ever memorize. This is as elitist as language gets. Efforts to simplify Chinese writing can be traced back for two thousand years, but they always ran into opposition from conservative scholars. The most recent efforts came under Mao Tse Tung in 1955, with a simplified Chinese script, and in 1958, with a Latin script, Pinyin.

Scholars across East Asia used Chinese ideographs. One of the coincidences of history is that Johannes Gutenberg in Germany lived contemporaneously with the Korean king, Sejong the Great, who is credited with a major advance in literacy. In 1443, when Gutenberg was starting to print, Sejong created hangul (or "hang' ul"), a simple phonetic alphabet for commoners, with seventeen consonants and eleven vowels.[24] It may be the world's most efficient script for reproducing human speech, an alphabet based on Sanskrit. Sejong

Hangul, the simplified Korean writing system.
Courtesy Keith Enevoldsen, Thinkzone.wlonk.com.

said he wanted to further education and "to satisfy reason to reform men's evil nature."

Most Koreans remained illiterate, and only aristocrats and officials had ready access to books. Here too aristocrats argued against giving commoners access to writing. Historian Amalia Gnanadesikan noted, "Fierce objection to Sejong's work surfaced almost immediately... By lowering standards of literacy, the new alphabet would lead to rampant cultural illiteracy as people would neglect the study of Classical Chinese and of high culture."[25] Commoners were entitled to read, but as schools were for the most part restricted to the children of the aristocracy, education was limited.

However, Korea followed China in starting a national competitive civil service exam that was open to commoners. Unlike Europe's contemporaneous medieval nobles who sometimes boasted of their illiteracy, Korea's feudal aristocrats saw themselves as scholars. The degree of literacy among Koreans has long been a point of national pride. Today, Korean students are among the top scorers in annual international competitions, following one of history's better traditions.

American Literacy

By the start of the American Revolution, 90% of New Englanders were functionally literate. They read well enough for daily life. Other northern colonies were about 80% literate, but this was not the situation throughout the colonies. In some new colonial settlements, illiterates served as part-time county justices because nobody else was available. Within narrow limits girls were taught to read. Boys could go on if the money could be found. Blacks had almost no chance.

Literate when they arrived, many New Englanders brought books that their children would inherit. Reading the Bible for themselves was central to the faith of the religious dissidents who were early settlers. Pilgrims had hardly landed at Plymouth Rock when they began primary schools. Several were operating in Massachusetts by 1635. Many children were schooled at home.

Sequoyah

We deeply admire the illiterate Sequoyah, who recognized the power of the black scratches on the white men's papers, and created a written language for his people, the much abused Cherokee nation.[26]

In the presence of many communication tools, we may take writing for granted, but Sequoyah did not. He produced a syllabary, the first writing system in modern history made by an illiterate people themselves.

For the lower classes, sending a child to school—which wasn't free—or going oneself offered a path to new occupational skills and maybe even to upward social mobility. Parents considered unfit to educate their children might see them put out as apprentices to local craftsmen to learn a useful trade and to acquire the functional literacy needed to read the Bible and to participate in the rural commerce.

Not everyone was keen on education. Remote villages sometimes paid a fine to the colonial government because that was cheaper than building a school.[27] Many colonists were indifferent to literacy. Where low taxes competed with literacy, illiteracy often won out. The governor of the Virginia colony in 1671 gave thanks for the lack of free schools or printing, "for learning has brought disobedience and heresy and sects into the world, and printing has divulged them."[28] An examination of wills and other records in colonial America showed literacy among adult (white) males ranging from 44% to 93%. Generally, two out of three were literate at some level. Marriage registries and other documents in Western Europe from the 17th to the 19th centuries showed similar percentages among adult males, and a growing literacy during the advancing decades.[29]

Extending Literacy in Modern Times

By the start of the 19th century nearly all men and most women in the northeastern United States were literate. Out in the expanding west, pioneers wanted to keep in touch with events in the rest of the world, particularly in the places they had come from, and newspapers and letters were treasured.[30] By the middle of the century, nine out of ten white people throughout the expanding nation had at least a basic reading skill. When slavery was still in existence in the South, blacks were usually prevented, sometimes violently, from learning to read.

The Industrial Revolution saw significant advances in both Western Europe and North America. For all its ills, the Industrial Revolution was midwife to a rise in literacy among the middle and working classes. For the first time in history nations adopted policies of universal education. In theory, everyone, not just the sons of the wealthy, would be given at least a rudimentary education. In practice it did not quite work out that way. Many parents saw no need for educated children. Many factory owners pressed to keep all hands, large and small, at labor.[31]

We read today about American high school diplomas handed out to functional illiterates. How well can someone get by in the digital age barely reading? Could you get by only with common sense? If learning can occur with just the most meager literacy, then the labor to become fully literate has diminished value. This is painful for teachers whose efforts are challenged by the popularity of television, video games, movies and recorded music. A survey by the National Endowment for the Arts reported that fewer than half of all American adults had read any fiction in the preceding year. Fifty-seven percent had read at least one non-fiction book.[32]

At the Samangan School in Afghanistan, girls entered school eagerly. USAID-supported educational programs renovated classrooms, provided new textbooks and supplies. The girls are learning to read and write and prepare to contribute to their country's future.

Photo Credit: IOM-ATI Staff.

At national and international levels the distinctions of the "knowledge gap" and the "digital divide" have brought to our attention the disadvantages of a lack of information. The "knowledge gap" argues that each new medium of communication increases the distance between the information rich and the information poor.[33] As mass media information increases, the higher socioeconomic communities tend to acquire it faster, increasing the gap in knowledge. The "digital divide" refers to the gap between populations who have access to computers and the Internet, and those who do not.

Controlling access to literacy has always been a way to keep social order. To withhold literacy was a way to hold serfs and slaves in their place. It was a policy during the American Civil War era. Everywhere and at all times up to the present, it has been a way to control women. Even in recent days headlines have told of the destruction of schools for girls in Afghanistan and horrific reports of acid hurled into the faces of girl students. According to a CNN report, al Qaeda in Iraq sought illiterate women to serve as suicide bombers.[34]

With the first decade of the 21st century behind us, mediated communication is perversely giving us the tools for illiteracy. Spend too many hours absorbing frivolous content and you might end up functionally illiterate. Yet Stanford University professor Andrea Lunsford concluded after a five-year study that media technology is actually reviving writing and pushing it in new directions: "I think we're in the midst of a literacy revolution the likes of which we haven't seen since Greek civilization."[35] Examining thousands of college student writing samples, she did not encounter a single instance of texting speech in a paper that was handed in for a grade. Instead, students used what ancient Greek rhetoricians called kairos, which meant adapting their style to their audience.

Summing Up

Armed with the gift of writing, human beings built soaring edifices of thought. As the centuries passed, writing led to new means of education and to libraries. The human mind was no longer restricted by memory's limitations. Writing enabled its users to hold thinking and memory outside the brain, sharing their inferences and deductions with other people in other places. Literate people reflected upon the writings of others, added to them and packaged knowledge for future generations. Readers were the first people to learn from contemporaries they did not see. In culture after culture, writing contained and communicated information, along with myths, prejudices, observations and the gathered knowledge derived from all of these.

Timeline

BCE (many dates are estimates)

10000: Notches in bones found in the Near East presumed to be a lunar calendar.

8000: In Sumer, clay tokens appear; may symbolize goods like sheep jars of oil.

3500: In Sumer, tokens representing goods are placed in clay ball envelopes.

3100: Sumerians cuneiform numerals are separated from symbols of goods.

3000: Egypt develops hieroglyphic writing.

2600: In Egypt, scribes employ hieratic writing, a condensed, cursive hieroglyphic.

2200: Oldest extant writing on papyrus.

1700: The written law code of Hammurabi, in Babylonia, carved on a stone pillar.

1650: Alphabetic symbols derived from hieroglyphs found in Sinai inscriptions.

1500: In India, sacred Hindu hymns of the Rig Veda are written in Sanskrit.

1200: The Phoenician alphabet, 22 letters, all consonants, appears.

950: The oldest books of the Bible are written.

900: Phonetic alphabet spreads across the Mediterranean.

Olmecs, a pre-Mayan people, invent first writing system in Americas.

Oldest extant Hebrew text: schoolboy's clay tablet listing months of the year.

750: The Iliad and the Odyssey, 300 years after the Trojan War, ascribed to Homer.

800: Greeks improve Phoenician alphabet by adding vowels; capital letters only.

600: Mediterranean cultures agree on left-to-right writing.

First appearance of Latin.

213: China's Ch'in emperor, Shihuang, orders destruction of all books.

59: Julius Caesar orders postings of a daily gazette, the Acta Diurna.

47: Alexandrian Library survives fire set by Julius Caesar's troops; many books lost.

CE

65: Mark writes the first Gospel.

105: Chinese imperial eunuch Ts'ai Lun is officially credited with inventing paper.

391: Alexandrian Library destroyed; said to have been ordered by Archbishop of Antioch.

520: The start of Western monasticism; will keep learning alive in Christian Europe.

1002: Murasaki Shikabu's The Tale of Genji, the world's first novel.

1200: Books are copied and sold for profit by stationers, usually at universities

1333: Petrarch's discovery of classical manuscripts helps bring on the Renaissance.

2. Printing

Writing spread knowledge across ancient civilizations, but in a limited way because literacy was limited. Few people had even heard of a book. Printing changed it all. It enabled mass education. It began mass communication. Publication created a sense of "the public." Printers ran the first assembly line and started mass production.

Beginning in the late 15th century printing set the Reformation ablaze, although most of Europe remained illiterate and most people depended on the local priest to read the printed sheet. Printing also spread the Florentine Renaissance, that awakening of intellectual life based upon ancient Greek and Roman texts. It introduced humanistic thought to a widening population. It aided the commerce that would replace a millennium of feudalism. For those who were already educated, printing added to their knowledge and expanded what they believed.

Could any of this have been imagined in the Mainz goldsmith's shop where it began? The seemingly modest accomplishment of Johannes Gutenberg and the printers who followed him helped transform the political and economic structures of Europe from feudalism to mercantile capitalism and encouraged the growth of cities.. Feudalism declined, nationalism rose. A world of knights could not withstand the onslaught of the printers. Printing would later undergird the Enlightenment that substituted reason and scientific inquiry for tradition and doctrine. It would lead to declarations of human rights and to governments based on laws and constitutions.

A Chinese Invention

Printing today is so deeply embedded into our lives that some mental effort is needed to imagine the world without it. We might conclude that, by providing the means for spreading information to a broad segment of the population, printing set the basis for democracy in all the nations that now enjoy it. True, but printing also exists in dictatorships.

Wherever printing has gone it has been followed by censorship and propaganda. As far back as 1486 censorship of the printed word can be traced to Archbishop Berthold von Henneberg in the same German city of Mainz, where Gutenberg had his printing shop.[1] Gutenberg did not

The Invention of Paper

If printing was the engine for the Modern Age, another Chinese invention supplied the fuel. The papermaker's art as much as the printer's art led to our modern world. The availability of printed books, made possible by the paper mills of Europe, allowed the growth of literacy. Literacy in turn increased the demand for books, pamphlets, broadsides, and ever more paper. It should come as no surprise that dictatorships control the paper supply in their nations.

Its technology a guarded government secret, paper was used in China alone for five centuries until Buddhist priests carried it east to Korea and Japan, and west to the outposts of its empire. The Islamic conquest of the city of Samarkand in 751 turned up some Chinese papermakers, who were taken west as prisoners. Learning the art of fabricating paper, the Arabs set up paper mills in Baghdad and Damascus. The following centuries saw the height of Muslim culture, expressed by a love of learning and great libraries established from Baghdad to Córdoba.

According to one report, a crusader prisoner named Jean Mongolfier escaped from Damascus, where he had been a slave in a paper mill. Finding his way home to France, he set up the first paper mill in Christian Europe. Although more fragile than parchment, the superiority of paper in taking ink and its lower cost soon led to paper mills springing up across Europe.

The supply of rags to make paper was far greater than the supply of sheep for parchment and vellum, which continued to be used for luxury editions and for the missals and breviaries that monks were copying. The superiority of paper over parchment was evident in the printing of the Gutenberg Bible. Thirty of the 210 copies were printed on parchment, each requiring the skins of 300 sheep. By the end of the 15th century, parchment was seldom used to print books.

Starting the Modern Age

It does not take away from the significance of printing to identify other catalysts of the modern world. Change came to medieval Europe from every direction. The bubonic plague—the Black Death—first arrived a century before printing in three waves, probably by ships from India or China, and killed one European of every three. More misery came from starvation caused by the ice age. As feudal rulers huddled in their castles, bandits roamed; bands of knights were the *ronin* of Europe. Fanaticism and revolts pocked the era. The fear of the Mongols to the east and of Arabs ranging from Jerusalem to Spain added to life's unease for Europeans. Constantinople, for centuries the heart of Christendom, fell to Islam and the Ottoman Turks.

invent printing. Centuries before him, people were carving images or text into blocks of wood or clay, then smearing ink on what they had done and applying it to some sort of surface. Gutenberg did not invent the printing press either. He made use of a press that was commonly used for crushing olives or smoothing clothes. Gutenberg was not even the first person to use typography, (printing with movable type). That had been done in China and Korea, Buddhist lands where the repetitive act of making impressions was in keeping with religious practice. Yet it is the German goldsmith who is credited with one of the world's most important inventions with a superior printing system that used hard metal punches to make soft lead type of a precise height and an oil-based ink that stuck to the type. It was Gutenberg who began the process that moved the world into the modern age. Printing led Europe there, and Europe led the rest of the world. What Gutenberg invented was a remarkable, efficient *printing system*. And he did it in a time and place ready for the change it brought.

What did Europeans know of Asian printing? Did the German goldsmith and mirror maker know? Maybe not, but even if he had never heard of Cathay, did he know of the printing that had been done there for centuries? A few clues indicate that Gutenberg ought to have known something of block printing, if not of movable type. Europeans knew that paper money was printed in China and Persia because travelers, including Marco Polo, reported it.[2] Missionaries and other travelers who returned to Europe with news of the Chinese invention of paper may have reported that a great number of books were printed in China. A papal envoy to China, John of Plano Carpini, returned with a letter sealed in the Chinese style, ink printed upon paper. "Europeans could not know nothing about it," Chinese historian Pan Jixing wrote.[3]

Europe at the time was not a nation or even an idea. It was a diffusion of kingdoms and baronies. Yet decade by decade in towns and cities, no matter what else happened merchants still looked for trade and bureaucrats demanded records. Into this ferment came printing, the first efficient way to spread information and opinion beyond the range of the human voice to large numbers of people. No human endeavor had ever reached so many people in so short a time. Organized mail services began to take root. Universities, limited at first to the studies of theology and law, were established in several countries. Students sought books that came not only from monasteries but also from the shops of stationers, and on an increasing range of topics.

Early Printing in Europe

Before Gutenberg began printing in the mid-15th century, most books in Europe were written in Latin and were unavailable to an illiterate public. Newspapers and

Replica of the Gutenberg press

magazines did not exist in this oral world. Information about the world outside came from preachers or balladeers who brought rhyming news and gossip from village to village and the occasional traveling morality play. Stained glass church windows carried the only history most people ever knew or cared about. It would not be the last time that a story was told in pictures. If something written needed to be revealed, one person could read aloud to many. That person was likely to be the local priest. In monastery scriptoria, monks toiled over manuscripts while someone read aloud to them. In the thousand years from the fall of Rome to Gutenberg's press, what book production existed in Europe was copied by hand, line after line after line.

Monks gave no thought to making books available to ordinary people. The concept would have seemed absurd. Most people during the Middle Ages managed to live their lives well enough without reading, let alone writing. They knew where the butcher's shop was without reading a sign saying "Butcher," and even if they could not see the sausages hanging, a sign with a drawing of a sheep or pig informed them.

Printing and Literacy

A mark of the Modern Age, distinguishing it from the Middle Ages, is the growth of literacy.

Printing and literacy were two hands washing each other. The more printing, the more literacy. The presence of books in the vernacular language that ordinary people spoke on the street stirred a desire to understand what was written. The more literacy, the more printing. Readers wanted books.

As printers learned their craft and carried their tools to set up shop in cities throughout Europe, they published books on a variety of topics both religious and secular, including stories written to entertain as well as to inform and inculcate. Many were illustrated by wood-block engravings. The demand for books increased as schools multiplied and vernacular literacy rose. Compared with hand-written manuscripts, the easier-to-read printed texts promoted silent and quicker reading. With cheap books coming off the presses, a reading public grew. Printed books were smaller than manuscript texts, and could be carried around. Spectacles first appeared in Europe in the 13th century. The invention of the chimney, which heated private rooms, may have increased book reading among the nobility because printing encouraged silent reading, privacy, and separation from other people.

More and more, merchants and artisans learned to read for themselves. A merchant class—a genuine middle class—arose to claim its place in society. For them literacy provided a useful business tool. As historian De Lamar Jensen noted, "It was long after the invention of printing before more than a fraction of the population could read or write. Yet print technology did have an inexorable impact on people's lives from that moment on."[5] Burghers of the new middle class took their sons to school and stayed to learn themselves.

As feudalism lost its grip, noble birth mattered less and the ability to read and write mattered more to the burghers who sat in city governments where they wielded real power. They could improve lives blocked by the rigid feudal system that allocated an unchangeable fate to man from the day he was born. The nobility, who had insisted that their authority was a right bestowed by God, read the new writing on the wall. Nobles began to make sure their sons became educated.[6]

Specialized Books

Gutenberg's invention soon splintered knowledge into specialties. Having an entire shelf of books on a single subject. such as medicine, was possible. Textbooks organized what was known about a subject. As specialized books encouraged specialization, expertise, and separation from those who did not share the same esoteric knowledge, mediated communication demonstrated its force to alter society.

Some scholars who already had access to learning denounced printing as a disrespectful vulgarization.[4] Mediated communication is sometimes jealously guarded by those who would deny it to others.

Women Were Not Encouraged

Women, as usual, were not encouraged to read, for the skill was considered both unnecessary and potentially harmful. For centuries it was widely felt by literate men that reading romantic fiction was especially risky for women. Reading was regarded as pointless for the working class. Among lower class women, literacy barely existed.

The Reformation

Before Gutenberg, books were costly. Copying was weary work and often careless. Libraries were small and private. Before Gutenberg, the Church controlled nearly all education and from the beginning the printing presses were tools for promulgating faith. Inevitably, more than one religious point of view would be inked and distributed.

The pivotal religious movement was the Protestant Reformation. Beginning in the 16th century in an effort to reform the dominant Roman Catholic Church, Martin Luther made effective use of Gutenberg's invention. What followed was a campaign of posters, pamphlets and caricature drawings, first across Germany and then across the rest of Europe. Printers could hardly keep up. It was ironic that the printing trade was in the forefront of the attack on the sale of indulgences, the remission of punishment for sins. After all, who but the printers printed the indulgences that roused Luther's ire?

Martin Luther

Aided by his followers, Luther translated the New Testament into the German vernacular so that ordinary people could understand it for themselves. The Old Testament translation followed. Luther also wrote a mass in German intended for his countrymen who did not understand Latin. In the nearly seventy years between Gutenberg's printing of the Bible and the printing of Luther's translation of the New Testament, about twenty translations of the Bible in the German vernacular appeared.

Martin Luther

In Switzerland, John Calvin and Ulrich Zwingli became leaders of the Reformation, though they did not fully agree with each other on the various points of doctrine. By the end of the 16th century the separation of many Christians from the established Church had taken root. This was especially so in northern Europe. The Reformation led to new Protestant faiths throughout Europe. The Bible was translated into a number of vernacular languages.

The Renaissance

A second great movement arose at about the same time as the Reformation. Besides the art and architecture for which it is justly famous, the Renaissance introduced the classical literature of Greece and Rome to a Western Europe that had been largely unaware of the ancient books. Constantinople, the capital of the Christian Byzantine Empire, fell to the Muslim Ottoman Empire in 1453. Greek scholars fled westward with their libraries. An increasingly literate population thirsted to read the books. The copyists in the back shops of the booksellers and stationers could not have met the demand. The printers obliged. The spread of secular books and humanism led to a new division from the Church, quite different from the Reformation. Access to such books stimulated individual scholarship. Inductive reasoning, ancient literature, secular moral thinking and political awareness of classical Greece further demarcated the Modern Age from the Middle Ages.[8]

At the same time, explorers voyaged to Asia, Africa and the New World, where for good or ill, they set down roots. In this era of global exploration, printers produced engraved maps and geography texts. Written tales of the voyages of discovery stirred the kind of excitement that space exploration has generated in our lifetime. Armchair readers eagerly learned of new continents and descriptions of the peoples who inhabited them. The maps encouraged commerce and further exploration and reassured investors.

Crusaders and merchants had returned from the Near East during the Middle Ages. Some brought back a new knowledge of astronomy, geography, medicine, mathematics and philosophy acquired from a Muslim world that religious hostility had shut away. These works were eagerly translated and copied in European humanist circles. Technologies newly invented or discovered from distant lands were described: the water wheel for driving forge hammers, flour mills and mechanical saws, the crane, the wood plane, the weight-regulated clock, the rudder, the compass, gunpowder and paper.[9]

Medieval alchemy reluctantly gave way to authentic scientific inquiry. The intellectual ferment would lead in the 17th and 18th centuries to the Enlightenment, a revolution in human thought with a focus on the here, not the hereafter. Through the expansion of literacy and printing,

The Most Literate Occupations

By the end of the 16th century in Europe, certain occupations could boast of members' literacy. A survey in the French city of Lyon reported that the most literate professions were printers (of course), surgeons, and medicine dispensers. Painters, musicians, tavern owners, goldsmiths, and metal workers were also likely to be literate. Next on the scale were furriers, leatherworkers, and people in the clothing trades. Least likely to be literate were workers in construction trades, food occupations, gardeners, and unskilled day workers.[7]

ordinary Europeans would learn to think rationally and to conclude that change was both possible and desirable. The classical texts of Ptolemy, Galen and others that had been accepted as true since ancient times were newly scrutinized by scientists who questioned their authenticity and discovered their errors. Printing would make the Scientific Revolution possible.

Printing and Languages

Another change brought about by printing was a sense of nationalism. The Holy Roman Empire, an attempt to recreate the Roman Empire in a Christian world, gave way to nation states. Unlike Latin, the vernacular languages spoken in each region had not been considered fit for texts until printing codified them by making them a basis for written as well as spoken communication. Within nations a variety of languages and dialects spoken by a minority gave way to consolidation of language. If you read in English, you shared that skill with everyone else who read in English. That made you different from those who read in French or German. Medieval Latin remained a borderless international language for scholars. The English language, like the other vernaculars, identified a population that had a territory and boundaries.[11] These languages had existed before printing, but now they were fixed with distinctive structures.

Grammar and eventually spelling became boundaries of both inclusion and separation. The resident of Spain who never thought of himself as a Spaniard took pride in his new status. In the age of the divine right of kings, the kings were not slow to see the benefits of the new national spirit raised by printing and the codified national language where Latin had once ruled.

It has been argued that, since the invention of printing, communication media have been an element of all wars.[12] The savage religious wars of the 16th and 17th centuries have been laid at the door of the printing shop. And if you factor in other media, so were the vicious conflicts of the 20th century.[13]

Albert Einstein pointed out that the printing of music notation, starting around 1500, created a music revolution. A visual representation of melody became the foundation of notation.[10]

Printing and Freedom

In 1644 the poet John Milton published the *Aereopagitica,* with its famous plea for freedom of expression, "Let her (truth) and falsehood grapple; who ever knew truth put to the worse in a free and open encounter?" Milton's words made no strong impression at the time. More than a century would pass before his peculiar notion of freedom of speech would be picked up an ocean away, and would lead to the First Amendment to the U.S. Constitution.

In the new United States, among the compromises reached by Federalists and Democrats in drafting the Constitution was a Bill of Rights. The very first of its original ten amendments called for freedom of the press, along with freedom of religion, freedom of speech, the right to assemble, and the right to petition the government.

The First Amendment

"Congress shall make no law respecting an establishment of religion, or prohibiting the free exercise thereof; or abridging the freedom of speech, or of the press; or the right of the people peaceably to assemble, and to petition the Government for a redress of grievances."

The years that followed in the United States were marked by agitated newspaper attacks against opposing politicians, as the press and its news columns were used as the principal tools of persuasion in resolving the many issues that confronted the vigorous new nation. In 1798 a polarized Congress passed the Alien and Sedition Acts, threatening two years imprisonment and a then forbidding $2,000 fine for anyone who would "write, print, utter, or publish . . . any false, scandalous, and malicious writing" against the government, the president, or Congress. A partial reversal of the First Amendment, the Acts did allow truth as a defense, an echo of the John Peter Zenger trial, and did not forbid criticism of government, only false and malicious criticism. The Sedition Act stood for two years, generally supported by the Federalists and opposed by Jeffersonian Democrats before it expired.

The press continued to serve as an enthusiastic partner in the growth and political development of the nation as it spread westward across the continent. Newspapers reported, commented, opined, cheered and criticized as the country grew and divided into two bitter, warring camps, North and South. The press itself was changing as technology, literacy, and the thrust of democracy resonated across political life.

Jefferson never abandoned the principle of a free press, although in the years to come, he clearly grew sick of the "lying and calumniating" of the Federalist press that opposed him. The press continued to serve as a vigorous partner in the growth and political development of the nation as it expanded westward across the continent, built up its industry and divided into two bitter, warring camps, North and South. But the press itself was changing as technology, literacy and the thrust of democracy resonated across political life.

The Industrial Revolution

The Industrial Revolution of the 19th century saw inventions in paper production, printing, the telegraph and photography. All these helped to make the newspaper the primary tool that the public used to learn of current events and one of its primary sources of education and entertainment. Steam presses accommodated daily newspaper print runs of a million or more copies. By the end of the century the telephone, phonograph, typewriter, radio's dots and dashes, and motion pictures afforded new means of communication. To this list we may add compulsory free public education, at least at a basic level to turn out factory workers who recognized letters and numbers. Also add public libraries, mass advertising, cheap books and periodicals, and international postal agreements that encouraged communication. There were even experiments that would lead in the next century to computers, television, and tape recording.

The rotary press arrived early in the 19th century, but the flat page of lead type was unsuited to it. Because of the risk that pieces of type might burst their bonds and spill all over the floor, the make-up of a page was limited to single columns tightly bound by column rules, giving the appearance known as a "tombstone" layout because of the heavy, black, single-column headlines sitting above the type. The stereotyping method solved this problem. An impression of a flat page of lead type was made on a pliable cardboard-like mat, which was then put into a semi-circular mold, molten lead was poured into it, and the lead hardened and cooled to give the printer an image of the page that could be fitted onto the rotary press. Stereotyping also freed the pieces of type in the original page for reuse.

By the 19th century's close a typesetting machine had replaced the slow process of hand-setting the type. Named for the rows of lead it spit out, the Linotype would be the noisy centerpiece of newspaper production well past the middle of the 20th century.

The problem of how to put photographs into a newspaper was solved toward the end of the 19th century by the photoengraving process. Photoengraving converted a paper photograph into a halftone photograph on a zinc plate that held ink in the areas intended to be dark and rejected ink in the rest. On March 4, 1880, the New York Daily Graphic published the first halftone engraving in a newspaper, a photo called "A Scene in Shantytown." (See Chapter 7, Photography)

With the accumulated technology of the telegraph, paper made from trees instead of cloth, typewriters, telephones and the electric light bulb, the modern newspaper began to take form. Technology in the 20th century added offset lithography, phototypesetting and the computer.

The Typewriter

The typewriter, which produced so many words for more than a century, deserves mention. Today these machines gather dust in the antique shops of the cities of the industrialized world, but they can still be found in developing countries doing their job of generating information along the mediated communication trail leading from someone's brain to everyone's eyes. Even in the computer-rich West, a battered typewriter may still be found at the fingertips of a self-professed Luddite who will have nothing to do with digital media.

The idea of a writing machine may have originated with an English engineer, Henry Mill, who received a patent but did not construct a machine. During the 18th century, actual machines

Typewriters constructed during the 19th century.

were built in Austria, Switzerland, France and Italy. One goal for such a machine was to emboss letters on paper so that the blind could read, an enterprise perhaps motivated by the example of a French youth, Valentin Haüy, who started a school for the blind. A French youth who had gone blind, Louis Braille, attended the school, where he improved on Haüy's book embossing code. Another impetus for a writing machine came from the new telegraph industry. Skilled telegraphers could understand messages as fast as the clicks arrived, but could not write them down by hand fast enough.

Patents flew thick and fast in several countries as imaginative citizens thought up machine designs that resembled everything from a small piano to an oversized pin cushion. The fifty-second typewriter patent issued by the U.S. Patent Office went to Christopher Sholes of Milwaukee, a printer who joined friends to design a workable machine that sent keys moving up to a print point. Because the key fell back slowly, pulled just by the force of gravity, it was easy for an ascending key to block a descending key; hence the "scientific" design of the keyboard to reduce the number of jams. Incremental improvements by Sholes and his friends were speeded up when the Remington company, maker of guns and sewing machines, took on the new business. The sewing machine foot treadle was adapted as a carriage return. Of the dozens of companies that later manufactured typewriters, International Business Machines (IBM) made the most changes with its line of electric typewriters, notably the Selectric typing ball.

The computer keyboard maintains the anachronistic QWERTY keyboard designed for mechanical typewriters to minimize jamming the keys at the print point by positioning the common letters "a" and "s" under the weak fingers and the uncommon "j" under the strongest finger, an arrangement that also separated the most frequent pairs of letters so that they are struck by alternate hands. The rationale for QWERTY disappeared with the electric typewriter and certainly does us no favors in the electronic world. Yet each generation learns this keyboard arrangement only because the previous generation is accustomed to it, rather than learning a more efficient arrangement like the Dvorak system.

The concept of the typewriter, a personal writing machine that would replace a pen that cost a penny, did not catch on immediately. Before the typewriter, offices did not have machinery, but the advantages of mechanization ultimately became apparent. Typewriters were followed by dictaphones, mimeographs, adding machines, bookkeeping machines, envelope addressers, check writers and postal meters.

Newspapers

The first newspapers were published in Europe in the early 17th century. For the next two hundred years newspapers existed mostly to promote a political point of view, such as the Colonial press that stirred up rebellion in the years leading to the American revolution, or to

A small 19th century printing press

provide business information. A popular press did not exist. Gossip was exchanged in coffee houses. Then, starting in New York in 1833, the "penny press"—hawked on big city street corners—changed the dynamic by reaching out to the large segment of the population who had little interest in business or national politics, but had a thirst for gossip, sensation and local news.

Here was mass communication, something new in the world, a business of funneling information to large numbers of people from a limited number of providers. Supported heavily by mass advertising, the penny papers satisfied that thirst for sensation, competing for the working man's small coin against the apples and small cakes also hawked on city streets. The newspapers were enjoyed by Americans coming out of a public school system that taught them to read but did not necessarily equip them with a burning thirst for knowledge.

Sharing the pages with sensational stories were advertisements addressed to a mass audience. These penny press ads were an integral part of the Industrial Revolution through which its readers were living. Mass advertising created the demand for consumer goods leading to the mass consumption needed to support mass production. Newspapers grew fat with advertising.

News came to have value as a commodity instead of merely supplying the basis for political partisanship. Like a bushel of oats or a yard of silk, news packaged in a newspaper had become a product. Certain stories had more value than others. Local news had more value than distant news of a similar event. Sensational news had more value than dry reports. Readers thirsted for stories of adventure and the exotic. Reports of battles mattered, the closer the better. What also mattered was political news that might impact the reader's life. Out of an understanding of these relational values, the modern newspaper evolved, as did the radio and television newscasts of the next century.

Then as now, news reports were regarded with a special stamp of authenticity when the reporter at the scene of events told of personal observation and interviews with the important players of each drama, such as statesmen and battlefield generals. The practice of active investigation soon followed as did a rise in the circulation of newspapers willing to pursue news actively. In response—or self-defense—organizations from police to government to private business learned myriad ways to cope with an interviewer's questions. A public relations industry developed. Some organizations actually improved the ways they were behaving.

News, opinions framed in editorials and advertising were not the only products a newspaper had to offer as the decades went by, nor were they the only means to shape attitudes toward political issues. (See Chapter 14, Persuasion) Political columns, political cartoons, photographs and advice columns have all done their bit to persuade. So have comics, ranging across the political spectrum from the conservative Orphan Annie to the liberal Doonesbury. The line between information and entertainment was frequently crossed in the never-ending quest for more readership. Horoscopes, household hints and dozens of other features crowded the printed pages.

What the newspaper has done is not only to connect readers to their community but also to the world beyond the horizon. For many generations the newspaper was the primary or indeed the only medium of mass communication. That is no longer the case. For the public, particularly the young public, a loss of interest in newspapers reflects the changing times.

Historically, most news has been transmitted mouth-to-ear. Radio and television newscasts are basically extensions of such communication. Newspapers struggled for decades to compete, and now wrestle with challenges from the internet. Charging for content by erecting "paywalls" for premium access has been one answer.

Another is the tablet news app like Livestand, Zite, Editions and Flipboard. They deliver to tablets like iPad that are not only constantly updated but are also customized from many sources to the user's choice of topic. It is news-on-demand in your pocket. But newspapers have a history of change ever since the world's first newspaper appeared five hundred years ago.

Magazines

The magazine was born in England in the 18th century as a weekly periodical. The remarkable and busy Daniel Defoe, author of *Robinson Crusoe* and *Moll Flanders,* founded the *Review* and filled it with essays, some of which he wrote.[14] Defoe also wrote the first modern newspaper editorial. He is considered a founder of the English novel and, because of his interviews, the founder of modern journalism. And he was a spy.

In England, the *Tatler* and *The Spectator* followed the *Review.* In 1741 the Philadelphia printer Andrew Bradford published the first magazine in the American colonies. It lasted only three months. Three days later Benjamin Franklin launched *General Magazine.* It lasted six months. Other colonial printers tried publishing magazines. Most failed, even though newspapers and magazines accepted goods for ad space and subscriptions, such as the Massachusetts publisher willing to barter subscriptions for butter and groceries.[15]

Without advertising or the postal considerations given to newspapers, magazine survival was difficult. Lack of illustrations, except for the occasional woodcut, limited their attraction, as did their high cost plus the poor quality of paper and presses. Yet the growth of the new United States was matched by an increase in the number of weekly, monthly and quarterly periodicals, including magazines for genteel middle and upper class women. In England *The Penny Magazine* was written for literate workmen. Religious magazines and those aimed at the working class were early examples of the fragmentation that specialized magazines brought to a community.

"Do You Know Why We Publish?"

Congress extended low-cost mailing privileges to magazines in 1879. The end of the 19th century saw several dozen illustrated mass circulation national magazines supported by advertising. Cyrus Curtis published *The Saturday Evening Post* and *The Ladies Home Journal* based on the concept that large circulation magazines could profit more from advertising than subscriptions. His policies allowed him to pay top dollar for the best writing and art, but he saw editorial content as incidental to advertising.

Curtis once asked an audience of advertisers, "Do you know why we publish *The Ladies Home Journal*? The editor thinks it is for the benefit of American women. That is an illusion, but a very proper one for him to have. But I will tell you the real reason, the publisher's reason, is to give you people who advertise things that American women want and buy a chance to tell them about your products."

During World War II, homesick soldiers who received special editions without advertising complained that the ads told them more about home than the editorial content.[16]

No matter how well-heeled first adopters are, media of all kinds eventually seek a wider range of users. A few magazine publishers continued to appeal primarily to a well-educated readership, but success depended on a broader audience. In 1893, publishers Frank Munsey and S.S. McClure and *Cosmopolitan* editor John Walker engaged in a circulation war that dropped the price of their magazines below production costs. In doing so, they contributed to a societal movement for change in America. Creating the first national mass audience, their magazines built large circulations that commanded high ad rates for the mass-produced goods their magazines advertised.

Popular taste magazines reached out to all members of the family with articles on the latest trends, sentimental romance fiction, pictures and exposés, notably in *McClure's Magazine*, by investigative reporters whom Theodore Roosevelt called "muckrakers." He meant it as an insult. The writers considered it a badge of honor. The power of muckrakers, expressed through magazines or books, could be formidable. As one classic example, Upton Sinclair's *The Jungle,* an exposé of the meat packing industry, led to passage of the Pure Food and Drug Act. It also created a lot of vegetarians.

By the middle of the 20th century, thousands of trade and specialty magazines were published for targeted readerships. They fared better than the mass circulation *Life, Look, Coronet* and *The Saturday Evening Post,* magazines that lost the struggle. Mass circulation popular-taste magazines succumbed to assaults by the new medium of television, which also appealed to popular tastes. A few mass circulation magazines, notably *Reader's Digest*, continued to thrive, but for most magazines, targeted readerships and targeted advertising provided the greater profits.

News magazines like *Time* and *Newsweek*, bedeviled by the need to compete with daily television newscasts for timely reports, fought back successfully. To speed the process of getting news into readers' hands, they sent pages via communication satellite to regional printing plants from which magazines with imprinted addresses were flown or trucked to local distribution points to be mailed. National newspapers like *The Wall Street Journal* thrown on doorsteps chose similar solutions to reach their far-flung readers.

While most newspapers address a geographic community most magazines connect shared interests. It may be in politics, religion, occupation, social life, or hobbies. It is an endless list that includes city magazines (geography) too. A few general-interest magazines are sold, but millions of readers prefer magazines that address their preferences, and most of the 19,000 magazines published in the United States do that. People tend to go where they can get specifically what they want. The specialized magazines also give us a nationwide or even worldwide sense of community for each of our special interests, sending readers to find connections at a distance.

If a common theme can be found in the history of the magazine, it is that targeting a specific readership succeeds better than trying to reach the most diverse audience possible. In the world of printing, desktop publishing and e-readers are changing book and magazine publishing. Anyone who wants to imagine the future of television or any other medium of communication might do well to browse magazine racks for specialization.

Books

Before the 18th century, few books for children were published. One exception, the bestiaries, those moral fables with woodcut drawings about real or mythical animals, were available for pleasure and nightmares. As with much medieval writing, they made points about vice and virtue, of Christ and the Devil. In many homes the Bible and an almanac were the only books to be found. Both helped to advance the desire to read.[17] At home, families read Biblical passages aloud. The Bible, read aloud and children's bedtime stories have the effect of bringing family members together, unlike what happens when books are read privately and silently.

Morality is a recurring theme in books. In 19th century America, the popular *McGuffey Readers* promoted hard work, study, good behavior, kindness and honesty. They encouraged not only children but their parents to acquire the skill of figuring out the message on the printed page in front of them. They emphasized oral techniques like reading aloud passages from speeches, accompanied by pronunciation and breathing drills. More than one hundred million of William McGuffey's *Readers* were sold. Another Victorian, Horatio Alger repeatedly wrote of poor boys who succeeded by following the path of virtue. His books also sold in the millions. They served as guides for generations of youth growing up in America. Their influence lingers.

Pulp Fiction

A reaction to uplifting tales was inevitable. Public appetite for inexpensive, easy-to-read novels filled with action, adventure, and romance led in the 19th century to the dime novel. A survey showed that most readers of this cross between a book and a magazines were working class men with a grade school education.[18]

The books were nicknamed "pulp fiction" because of the rough wood-pulp paper they were printed on, and sometimes called "blood and thunders" because of their content. (English boys bought the similar "penny dreadfuls.") By the 20th century their shiny covers in bright colors often featured drawings of scantily clad women and men in violent action. Priced from a nickel to a quarter, they contained up to 130 pages of short stories that bore little connection to the garish covers. They carried advertising for physical or mental self improvement such as correspondence courses and muscle building.

Novels

The public also learned to love novels. England, France, Germany and Russia developed rich traditions of literary fiction in the 18th and 19th centuries. But the novel was still an unusual literary form in 1719 when Daniel Defoe wrote of his shipwrecked mariner Robinson Crusoe and Samuel Richardson told his readers about Pamela, whose virtue was rewarded, albeit sorely tested.

Written with middle class sensibilities for middle class readers about matters that concerned them, like social pretensions and the desire to improve one's status in a class-conscious society, the English novel set new standards for literature. Popular novels such as those by Charles Dickens were serialized in magazines. To keep the readers buying new issues, writers ended chapters on a note of suspense. This may also explain the large number of chapters. The important point is that these novels influenced behavior. They set standards of conduct. They created heroes and heroines that readers regarded as models.

Occasionally, we hear of traditional parents who oppose advanced education for a daughter or, in fewer cases, a son. The parents fear that books will take their children away from them. They may be right, but if you fear change, books are not the only media you should fear. All media change us. They inform, educate, entertain, channel and disengage us, separating us from what is near, connecting us to what is distant, different, strange.

Every type of mediated communication becomes more egalitarian with the passage of time. This has been true of books since the invention of printing, but never truer than in the run-up to the Great Depression of the 1930s and the years since. The Book-of-the-Month Club and The Literary Guild, both started in 1926, became a new way to sell books to middle class readers, or a "middle brow culture" as some would have it. By the end of the 1920s several more book clubs joined them. Buying books in bulk, printing cheap editions and peddling subscriptions, the clubs sold hundreds of thousands of novels, non-fiction titles and reference books at prices that bookstores could not match. Department stores advertised popular titles at bargain prices to woo customers into their stores.

During the Depression, when the book business was hurting, publishers dropped the price of new novels. They still could not match the price of *Little Blue Books*, a "university in print." Three hundred million of the small, stapled booklets were sold between 1919 and 1949, at prices ranging from ten cents to a dollar. Fitting into a worker's shirt pocket, the booklets aimed at getting literature and a range of ideas to as wide an audience as possible. Paperbacks followed what was by now a tradition of affordable reading. Because many titles still sold at regular prices, book buyers might get confused and angry at the cost of books. An indignant *New York Times* editorial worried that prices might rise enough to cause "abandonment of the reading habit."[19]

In the 21st century, despite the competition from other media, books still sell well, although Borders and some smaller bookstores have not survived. Book chain stores feature coffee shops and encourage browsing. Amazon.com and Barnes & Noble do a brisk book business online. The most popular books boast sales of more than a million copies each. Meanwhile, books extend their reach through non-print media, particularly audio books that entertain drivers on the daily commute and e-books everywhere.

Changing Technology

Paper and bindings are part of technology currently in flux, but they no longer determine what a book is. Consider Google's effort to place all books into a vast electronic database. Now add the emergence of Apple's iBook and e-book tablets like the iPad, Kindle and Nook, plus the popularity of audio books. They all add up to the conclusion that the book will endure for the foreseeable future no matter in what form it reaches us because it has proven to be a most desirable way to package both knowledge and entertainment.

Print-on-demand books occupy a small but growing segment of publishing. For university presses, small presses and self-publishers, printing a few copies at a time in response to a customer's order makes practical sense. No big investment is needed, the price-per-copy method is affordable and no copies are sitting in warehouses waiting to be either sold or destroyed. Inevitably, more producers and more readers emerge for a wider range of material. New machines and companies have arisen to do business here.[20] The suspect, old-line vanity presses have both more opportunity and more competition.

Hyperlocal News

Unfortunately for admirers of the printed page, although the second half of the twentieth century brought improved printing technology through computerization, newspaper readership has declined as more people turned to competing communication technologies. News could be delivered by radio and later by television.

When the 21st century began the internet allowed what may prove to be, for printed newspapers, devastating competition. Readers, especially younger people, turned away from the daily newspaper, but not from news. They liked internet news and entertainment, they liked the opinions of bloggers, and they liked it all free.

Once again, communication media affected the general society, this time in the disturbing direction of inadequately informed or grossly misinformed opinions based on the skimpy information of bloggers with a political agenda. Nothing new here. The first newspaper printers had done much the same. Yet it was not long before "hyperlocal" news blogs brought professional standards to online local news sites. For example, AOL has targeted dozens of mostly small affluent communities as "Patch" sites, where local news is gathered by trained journalists and presented along with local advertising. AOL seeks to make them online version of community newspapers without the costs of newsprint, ink, and delivery.

In the digital age, journalism is no longer limited to journalists, but trained journalists bring reporting, editing and layout skills that bloggers may lack. Taking advantage of internet and digital technology, hyperlocal blogs are easy and cheap to produce and access. And they attract advertising from the local shops and classified ads that are the bread-and-butter of the free newspaper "shoppers" that land on doorsteps. Hyperlocal news may pull in participants who are everyday neighbors, and, in fact, anyone with a digital camera. The addition of parking spaces to a local strip mall can be "front page" news.

With such competition, the days of the free shopper may be numbered, driven out of business by news blogs that compete without paper.

The real concern need not be for the survival of ink-on-paper, but rather for a news delivery structure with the virtues of professional preparation: honest, accurate, thoughtful, balanced, interesting, informative and engaging.

Each year e-book devices come closer to the reading experience of holding a book in your hands. Several dozen manufacturers like Apple and Amazon have competed at bringing devices to market. Hundreds of thousands of titles are for sale at sharply lower prices than printed books. Quite a few may be freely downloaded through Project Gutenberg.

And what can be downloaded can be uploaded, giving self-publishing authors instant access to readers through gateways like the Amazon Digital Text Platform. Magazines and newspapers are available as well. Online libraries may one day consign the bookcase to join the buggy whip.

The fragmentation and recombination of readers into narrow but national and even international interest groups also expresses itself in newsletters. Once mimeographed and stapled, modern newsletters are either slick products that draw on desktop publishing techniques or are sold for online delivery that requires no paper at all.

The ranks of newsletter publishers have risen exponentially because of the minimal costs of online publication. "Zines," published on such personal subjects as the publisher's music tastes, are a version of internet blogs.

Censorship

Along with people who want to convince you of something, some people want to prevent you from learning something else. Often, they are the same people. Those able to restrict the communication choices of others—by any method, subtle or coerced—own a jealously guarded. authority, legally acquired or not.

The pages of communication history are stuffed with efforts to censor, control, or eliminate. It is happening now in, of all places, our schools. It concerns both textbooks and curricula, arguing such questions as whether evolution should be taught without also teaching creationism.[21]

The quarrels bubble up from ideologues using government levers to limit what can be printed or shown. They want to protect children, the targets of all this concern. A fight over K-12 textbooks has been focused on test questions, because they guide what publishers put in their textbooks. The terrain is further focused on Texas and California because smaller states frequently follow the lead of these two large states that adopt books on a statewide basis. It takes only a few persistent ideologues in those two states to have an outsized influence on what is included or excluded from what millions of children are permitted to learn.

Avoided Topics

Among the many topics to be avoided in modern textbooks are abortion, unpleasant creatures like rats and cockroaches, death, disease, disrespectful or criminal behavior, evolution, magic, witchcraft, people's height and weight, politics, religion, child abuse, animal abuse, addiction, unemployment, weapons and violence.[22] Textbooks dealing with such unavoidable subjects as literature, history and biology are minefields. Self-appointed experts hold fast to their familiar staked-out positions on issue after issue. Renowned authors and famed literary works are not spared the wrath of ideologues intent on protecting children from what they deem harmful.

In this textbook battle, government does not instigate the censorship. It acquiesces. Caught in the middle, publishers who want to stay in business are desperate not to offend anyone. Children are, not unsurprisingly, bored by what their teachers assign. The kids find their natural desire for mental stimulation in video games, television, comic books and other non-school outlets.[23]

It may be cynical fun to examine ideologue complaints about Aesop's fable "The Fox and the Crow" for gender bias (the clever male fox flatters the vain female crow) or to wonder why the faces on Mount Rushmore cannot be discussed in a history class (the Lakota Indians don't want the sculptures there), or to reflect on how dinosaurs got along with humans riding on their necks like the old comic strip character Alley Oop.

But let us take a broader perspective. Take a step back from specific examples to consider that a bottom-up wish to censor, coming from ordinary citizens rather than the government, is as natural to a free-wheeling democracy as the wish to persuade. Media control is now within everyone's reach. In this case it is K-12 textbooks. It could be any medium at any level. Aware that they can exert enough force at educational pressure points to change content to suit their opinions, some people are doing just that: changing what other people may be allowed to learn.

Considering the long history of top-down censorship, bottom-up censorship is remarkable, if no less questionably motivated. However, in the world of modern communication, nothing is certain except change, a lesson the Greek philosopher Heraclitus taught. Movement away from mass communication to individualized, on-demand content had by 2011 started to take hold in textbooks also. The interactive Discovery Education Science Techbook was replacing traditional textbooks for tens of thousands of elementary and middle school children across several states.[24]

A Bomb Thrown into the Medieval World

Before the invention of printing, the Roman Catholic Church from time to time found heresy in books. When Gnostics in the 2nd century preached salvation through study and self-knowledge, their books were burned by Church authorities who demanded that only the Bible could be the source of knowledge and only the Church hierarchy were permitted access to it. However, during the thousand years of the Dark and Middle Ages, when few but Church scholars were literate or had access to books, the authorities thought little about heresy in books. What chilled them were preachers who spoke to the masses in the common language.[25] Medieval bishops actually supported civil illiteracy.[26]

One of the principal concerns of the Church had less to do with common people (most of whom were illiterate anyhow) than with priests and monks who might be won over to heresy. Before printing, the Church considered books to be the tools of scholars, who were relatively free to express themselves as long as the common people were not disturbed.

Movable type printing was a bomb thrown into that world. The rapid spread of vernacular printing undercut Church and State. The Church's response was to print for its own purposes and to censor but not totally stop what others did. Church leaders ultimately concluded they could not stop printing, nor was it necessary to do so. They could deal with it.

After Gutenberg, the Inquisition to root out heresy consigned books as well as human beings to public bonfires. In 1502, the Church issued a papal bull ordering the burning of all books that questioned ecclesiastic authority. This was followed in 1516 by a directive banning printing that lacked Church approval, followed further in 1559 by the Index of Prohibited Books. The burning of unapproved Bibles, other books and pamphlets as well as their authors limited but did not stop the printing and secret distribution of banned works.

One of the few havens for printers and writers was Holland after it won its freedom from Spain in the 17th century. Dissidents who found their way into Holland not only continued publishing but also smuggled their works back into their home countries.

The pages of the centuries are studded with such well-known book burners as Savonarola, the priest in Florence who damned the Renaissance, which was born in Florence. Censorship is by no means unique to any group. In his *Aereopagitica* the poet John Milton pleaded before a Protestant-dominated English Parliament, his political allies, for an end to censorship, to "let her (truth) and falsehood grapple." Most of the Roundheads now in power were not impressed.

Fiction has always been vulnerable to controversy. The popular colonial preacher Jonathan Edwards, known for his fiery sermons, said reading novels was an indulgence leading to a moral decline. Not untypical was this warning, couched in an epistolary novel, from another minister: "The free access which many young people have to romances, novels, and plays has poisoned the mind and corrupted the morals of many a promising youth."[27]

Anthony Comstock

In the 19th century another private individual, Anthony Comstock, took it upon himself to clean up the mails. Comstock founded the New York Society for the Suppression of Vice and convinced Congress to pass what became known as the Comstock Law, prohibiting the transportation or delivery of pornography. This included birth control information and anatomy textbooks for medical students. Wangling an appointment as an unpaid postal inspector with the right to carry a weapon, he began a one-man, anti-porn crusade. Using a New York anti-obscenity law as his weapon, Comstock cracked down on medical and sociological articles that offended his sensibility, regarding anything he disapproved of as filth. He boasted that he was responsible for three thousand arrests, the destruction of fifteen tons of books, untold numbers of printing plates and nearly four million pictures.

The urge to control all media remains vigorous both in and out of government. The last few years have seen all too many reports of journalists killed in Russia, Mexico and Colombia, of imprisonment in Egypt, Turkey and Iran, and of writers, journalists, newspaper and television executives harassed in many countries. Reporters Sans Frontieres (RSF), based in Paris, compiles an annual index of such attacks. China is a leading example of how far a government will go. Their principal target, the internet, continues to be a stubborn example of how a communication technology—overcoming opposition—expands the numbers of people who send and receive information. Messages are trickling through the most imposing dams. The battle between wanting to know and wanting to block knowing never ends.

Timeline

   550: Chinese develop xylography, printing from carved wooden blocks.

   740: A newspaper is printed in China.

   751: Paper moves west when Muslims capture Chinese workers in Samarkand.

   868: The Diamond Sutra, Chinese block-printed book; it's the oldest existing book.

1048: Pi Sheng, a Chinese commoner, fabricates movable type using clay.

1234: Koreans use movable metal type.

1276: At Fabriano, Italy, the first paper mill is built in Christian Europe.

1295: Marco Polo tells of paper money in China. Few Europeans believe such nonsense.

1423: Europeans use xylography to produce books."

1440: Possible date of Johannes Gutenberg's first printing effort.

1456: Gutenberg's 42-line Bible is illuminated and bound.

1486: In Gutenberg's town of Mainz, the first censorship of printing.

1490: Books are widely printed across Europe.

1498: In Venice, the printer Aldus Manutius publishes a book catalogue with prices.

1500: England sees the growth of middle class literacy.

1522: Martin Luther publishes a German translation of the New Testament.

1559: Pope Paul IV creates Index of Prohibited Books; bans books by humanist Erasmus.

1584: Printing is introduced to the New World in Peru.

1605: In Antwerp (now in Belgium), the first regularly published weekly newspaper.

1611: The King James Version of the Bible is published.

1650: In Leipzig, Germany, a daily newspaper is published.

1702: The first daily newspaper in the English language appears, the *Daily Courant*.

1704: Daniel Defoe publishes the first weekly periodical, the *Review*.

1783: Pennsylvania's *Evening Post*, the first daily newspaper in America, is published.

1791: Congress passes the First Amendment to the Bill of Rights.

1800: Iron presses permit printing on large sheets of paper and thicker fonts.

1819: In England David Napier's rotary printing press; two-sided impressions.

1833: The penny press, the *New York Sun*, opens a mass market.

1840: German paper makers experiment with wood pulp.

1846: Richard Hoe's cylinder press produces 8,000 sheets an hour.

1867: Christopher Sholes of Wisconsin constructs a Type-Writer.

1880: A halftone photograph, "Shantytown", appears in a newspaper.

1886: Ottmar Mergenthaler's Linotype at *New York Tribune* replaces setting type by hand.

1904: Offset lithography becomes a commercial reality.

1917: Photocomposition begins.

1985: Desktop publishing becomes familiar.

2000: People read e-books.

2004: Google begins scanning millions of books for online searches.

2012: iBook 2 displays interactive textbooks; students use them on iPad.

3. Mail

The Snail That Could

It was not so long ago that most families lived isolated lives, their principal links to the outside coming through the local post office. Compare the Postal Service with radio or television. Each has had a considerable impact on our world. Each brings information, entertainment and advertising to our homes. Each depends upon international agreements, national standards and some government supervision. Each is built upon broad communication technologies. The most obvious is the Postal Service's dependence on paper and printing. Ralph Waldo Emerson called mail delivery "a first measure of civilization."

The Postal Service and broadcasting are alike in having competition in what they do. Federal Express, United Parcel Service, DHL and the U.S. Postal Service compete heavily. The mail carrier also competes in the message delivery business with fax machines, cell phones, instant messaging, email, electronic banking, automated bill payments and even preprinted inserts in newspapers.

Because Netflix uses the Postal Service to deliver movies, the mail carrier is partly competing with the cable television provider. Of course, distinctions exist. The Postal Service provides personal, point-to-point communication. Radio and television provide the physical reality of the machine in the living room. Mail dates to the dawn of history. Both the postal service and broadcasting in most countries are fully or partly government run, though not for broadcasting in the United States. A closer analogy can be drawn by comparing the Postal Service with the telephone, the telegraph, the communication satellite and the internet.

Ancient Posts

Moving the mail was never a simple matter. Delivery has included carrier pigeons, human runners, fast ponies, slow donkeys, dog sleds, stagecoaches, all manner of boats, trains, trucks and airplanes. The days when almost the only way to send a personal message was to drop it in a mailbox are long gone.

Postal beginnings are lost in antiquity. Like language itself, messages went out in a hundred disorganized oral and written ways over the centuries.[1] Their oral delivery obviously came before writing, but it was writing that led to the organized postal services. The mail carrier followed two trails, the path of the government and the path of the private citizen and the merchant. In some places at some times the two paths were one, but only in the last few centuries, a fraction of postal history, have they merged. Because of necessity and suspicion, governments still keep separate channels.

Postal service is the handmaiden of central government, essential to retaining power. Kings knew that if they wanted to control their land, they had to control communication. The Chinese Empire had an official postal service in the 10th century BCE. By the 13th century CE, Kublai Khan had the world's best courier system. A network of 1,400 post houses and relay stations for an estimated 50,000 horses were on duty throughout his empire. Boats waited at river and lake crossings. Camels and carriages hauled ordinary mail as well as passengers. First-class mail, limited to royal and military mail, always went by pony express in relays. A rider who didn't meet his schedule faced a whipping. Marco Polo was sufficiently impressed to include a description in his reflections.[2]

Government postal services in China until recent centuries were meant only for government departments, just as they were in other countries, but merchants also used the system, and no doubt love letters sneaked in. To the east the Japanese postal system was officially limited to government use until a private courier service began in the 17th century.

The New World had no horses until European invaders introduced them, so Aztecs, Incas and Mayas employed relay stations of human runners. Certain Native American tribes notched or painted sticks to convey messages. Incas in South America stored and conveyed information on knotted colored cords that the Spanish invaders called quipu. In Peru the Chimu tribes wrote in code on lima beans delivered by runners, though such media had limited advantage aside from being easily carried. Aztec couriers also delivered freshly caught fish to inland villages, an early parcel post service.

The Old and New Testaments mention letters. King David's letter to the battlefield sealed the fate of Bathsheba's unlucky husband. Dispatches are mentioned in the Book of Esther. Job lamented, "My days are swifter than the post." Paul sent many letters to Judea and Macedonia.

The first record of a written message stamped with a seal and apparently delivered by a courier dates to King Sargon of Babylon, about 2300 BCE. The Egyptians had a relay system that helped maintain central control of their empire. An ancient Egyptian papyrus scroll carries the request, "Write to me by the letter carrier." In the 3rd century BCE, Ptolemy II introduced the camel into Egypt and organized a camel post to carry government and commercial messages to the south. Under the rulers Cyrus, Darius and Xerxes, Persians built roads and established pony express relay stations throughout the empire. To interfere with the mails was punishable by death.

Observing that messages could be sent 200 miles in a day, the Greek historian Herodotus wrote, "Nothing mortal travels so fast as these Persian messengers... And neither snow nor rain nor heat nor gloom of night stays these couriers from the swift completion of their appointed rounds."[3] The inscription is carved into the stone of the New York Post Office.

In Homer's day communication was by messenger or by signal fires from mountain top to mountain top. Ancient Greece, lacking a central government, had no known postal service, but several tales of running messengers have come down to us. The most famous Greek messenger we know of, Pheidippides, ran so hard to report the victory at Marathon that he collapsed and died uttering the message "Nike!" ('Victory"). Marathon races honor his achievement, be it fact or myth. So do running shoes.

The Romans

The large Roman postal system, the cursus publicus, stretched across the Empire from Egypt to Britain. It was so fast that no postal organization matched its speed for nearly 1,900 years.[4] One reason for those famous Roman roads was the wish to improve the mails. Like Persia, the Roman Empire established relay stations with post houses that the dwellers of nearby villages reluctantly maintained but were not allowed to use themselves. To reach its distant colonies, Rome also organized the world's first sea post. It is likely that the English word "post" is derived from the Latin word for relay station, "posita." We use it in "postal," "post office," and, of course, "postage."

In the Phillipics of 44 BCE, Cicero railed against spying on private letters, but this bureaucratic addiction has proved durable over the centuries. By the 4th century CE, the emperor Diocletian placed the Roman postal system under an imperial secret service that included officials called "curiosi." Their duties included government spying and catching mail fraud. No doubt they opened letters. More than fifteen hundred years after Cicero, Martin Luther had the same complaint as that Roman senator.

Ordinary citizens of the Roman Empire, forbidden to use the government cursus publicus, devised their own means of long distance communication, but contact remained sparse between Rome and the aristocrats who preferred to live on their country estates. Some of the best and brightest citizens did not participate in government as long as they were out of the city. No equivalent of a newspaper existed.

Over short distances, servants, usually slaves, carried letters. It was not the softest of jobs, for a slave could be killed if his master's enemies caught him, but if he failed to deliver the letters promptly, his irritated master might slay him. The phrase "to kill the messenger" recalls the ancient tendency to punish the bearer of bad tidings.

The postal system changed over time, with the distinction of backsliding during the Dark and Middle Ages. When the Roman Empire collapsed, so did the efficient Roman postal system. Illiterate peasants certainly had no need of a postal service. Hardly anyone else did either. The roads were no longer safe for post riders, nor were they as necessary during the Dark Ages that followed the fall of the Roman Empire because of illiteracy and the isolation of communities.

A mailed letter was probably less secure then than an Assyrian or Persian letter four thousand years earlier. Walled towns flourished when literacy and writing were at their lowest point. Marshall McLuhan noted that a simple alphabet written on easily transportable papyrus and parchment encouraged communication, which was later discouraged by the walled towns and city-states that rose as Rome fell.[5]

During the Dark Ages, postal service could be of little value even for nobles where illiteracy was the norm for all but a few. Independent thought had as little meaning as the notion of freedom to choose a government or a religion. You were what you were told that God intended.

Medieval Postal Service

Four centuries after the fall of Rome came Charlemagne, the first of the Holy Roman Emperors, who dreamed of reviving the glory of Rome under the mantle of Christianity. He restored a rudimentary postal system using the old, deteriorating Roman roads. Postal routes and stations were established.

By the 12th century, monasteries had established regular links with their distant brethren. Written information was borne in the rotula, a round-robin newsletter. The abbot of a monastery would report monastic events on a parchment scroll, such as who had died during the previous year. At the next monastery the abbot might add a fresh item or two about other events, plus such entries as "Common report has it that the Antichrist has been born at Babylon."[6]

Craft guilds and merchant guilds set up their own mail operations. Service by service, the illiterate feudal age of Europe was giving way to the mercantile age, to literacy and to the desire to gain knowledge.

The advent of universities, the expansion of towns and the needs of trade increased the amount of written communication. Peddlers, pilgrims, merchants and crusaders carried news and private messages across Europe and the Near East. In the 13th century at the University of Paris the foundation of a truly national postal service began in France under the umbrella of the Roman Catholic Church. It came about because university teachers and students were regarded as ecclesiastics. The messengers received the same royal guarantees and exemptions that faculty and students enjoyed, such as safe conduct when they traveled and exemption from military duty and taxes. In other words, the postal

News Balladeer

Some news arrived in disorganized ways. Gossip of distant events was borne on the lips of traveling minstrels. It was said that they that they could repeat without error a rhyming ballad of a thousand lines heard only once. The rhymes, sometimes accompanied by a lute, aided the memory.

Van Dyck portrait of a boy playing a lute

carriers had some of the same privileges as priests. As a result of this generous gesture the job of carrying messages became coveted. To put it more precisely, the franchise to employ messengers was hugely valuable. As the years passed, despite restrictions, the messengers added to their income by carrying outside mail.

Just as the absence of mail was a mark of the decline of Roman civilization into the Dark Ages, so a growth of mail marked a renewal of civilization into the Middle Ages. The spreading mercantile interests of cities and towns led to arrangements to protect their trade with the outside world, particularly against bandits and feudal lords who taxed and sometimes seized goods crossing their lands.

The few literate people who could not take advantage of an existing postal system might have sought out a guild or Church courier willing to carry an extra letter for a coin. In time, such a side business was openly incorporated into the organization and became part of the courier's duty. By 1500, letter routes were open to the public across Europe. Postal fees were based on what the public could bear and could be heavy. If a letter would cause financial damage to the receiver, the person wishing to write might have second thoughts about it.

Postal fees were based on what the public would bear. And these fees could be heavy. Where rival postal systems sprang up, overly zealous competition led to highway ambushes and royal court intrigues. During the English civil war of the 17th century, in a battle over who had the franchise for delivering the mail, the Earl of Warwick's men stopped a mail carrier on a rural road and seized his mail. They had not ridden far when another group of men seized these men.

In the 14th and 15th centuries, the Italian Della Torres family ran a private courier service that over the years spread across Europe. Rich and powerful, and operating under charters of the Holy Roman Empire, the firm built a swift and dependable postal system across central Europe. Reflecting some noble marriages, the firm took on the name Thurn and Taxis, a name that is used the world over to identify a vehicle for public use. It was then a kind of pony express, at first serving emperors and military officers. Inevitably, it served merchants as well.

In 15th century France, Louis XI revived a national postal service strictly for government use, the first national service since Charlemagne. The king ordered two hundred couriers to be stationed in towns across France to convey royal messages. The king declared that anyone who dared to inject private letters into the service was doomed to Hell. That was serious, for the Middle Ages acknowledged the divine right of kings. Louis, after all, communicated with God!

Fear of Hell did not stop all private communication when a coin or two might change hands. In 1600, the Spanish ruler of the Netherlands, the viceroy Cardinal Duke Albrecht VII, legalized what had been a crime openly practiced. He gave the Taxis service officials permission to charge for private letters. ("Taxi," a word used around the world, derives from the name.) William Shakespeare mentioned the post in several plays, sometimes in the phrase "post haste."

The Post-Boy

For centuries the "post–boy" with his mail pouch was a familiar sight in Europe, sometimes on foot, sometimes poking along on a swayback horse, if artists of the period can be believed. On his back he slung his post–horn, which he blew to announce to villagers that he had arrived with the mail. He was an easy target for highwaymen.

Actual letters, written on parchment and sealed with wax, sometimes bore this request for urgency: "Haste, Post, Haste, for Thye Lyfe, for Thye Lyfe, Haste." Maybe it helped.[7]

A postal service depended upon the king's permission for a price. A king appointed a postmaster the way a city today grants a franchise to a cable television company. The franchisee paid for an exclusive right to pursue a profitable enterprise called a "farm". The postal "farmer" paid rent to the king or the government for the privilege of managing the posts. The farmer "harvested money" from those who used the service. Starting in 1627 most of the British government's postal service and private operations merged into a single State Post, but additional private services continued as early versions of UPS and Federal Express.

Most letters were not sent inside envelopes prior to the invention of postage stamps. Instead, letters were folded to put the writing inside and show the blank side out for the address, seal and indication of payment. The widespread preference for envelopes separate from their contents began in France about 1845.

The New World

In 1639, less than 20 years after the Pilgrims landed on Plymouth Rock, a post office was set up in the tavern and home of Richard Fairbanks of Boston, following the European practice of using taverns and coffeehouses for mail drops. Arriving ship captains delivered their mail packets and picked up those bound for Europe. As the New World's first postmaster,. Fairbanks was allotted one penny per letter.

For the most part, letters were carried by friends or trusted strangers. Dependable regular delivery inland waited until postal routes were planned through the wilderness. Even then, the trails of the colonial letter carrier on foot or horseback were little more than footpaths used by local Native American tribes.

The first private post boxes consisted of a row of old boots nailed against a wall at a river steamboat landing. Each bore a settler's name. The mail sat in the boot until the settler came to town. A letter at a remote outpost might sit for six months or more before the settler picked it up. Someone might open someone else's mail just to learn the most recent news from back East.

In colonial days, the Atlantic crossing was safer, surer and cheaper than the roads. From Boston it cost only two pence to send a letter to England, but fifteen pence to the closer parts of Pennsylvania and New Jersey. From Boston to New York it cost nine pence to have a letter delivered. Going the other way cost twelve pence.

A struggling printer and newspaper publisher in Philadelphia, Benjamin Franklin was appointed postmaster of Philadelphia in 1737 when he was 31. The Crown's colonial postal service was a financial mess, yet it had advantages for a publisher. The former postmaster did not allow his post riders to carry Franklin's newspaper. Franklin had to bribe them until he became the postmaster, but he proved fair in dealing with other publishers. Many colonial newspapers were mailed postage free at the postmaster's choosing. Postal officials had the power to order newspapers to pay letter rates or pay on the basis of an agreement between postmaster and publisher. By contrast, when they were one and the same, the postmaster-publisher could reach such an agreement with himself while shaving.

In 1753, having grown wealthy, Franklin was again promoted by the Crown, this time to be deputy postmaster general for all North American colonies. He improved service and showed the first surplus in the colonial postal service budget, but Franklin believed that running the postal system only to make money was a ruinous policy. Putting service first, he felt, would ultimately produce a profit through greater use of the mails. His arguments fell on deaf ears.

During his tenure, Franklin established post roads from Canada to Florida and set up a regular schedule between the colonies and England. He organized auditing procedures and ordered land surveys that shortened several routes. Under Franklin, the Philadelphia-New York delivery time was cut in half. He also started the modern postal inspection service. Riders started hauling mail at night.

However, no angel, Franklin engaged in the nepotism common in his day. He appointed his brother John as postmaster in Boston. When John died, Franklin chose John's widow to succeed him. Mrs. John Franklin became the first woman postmaster (or postmistress) in America, the first woman to hold public office in America.[8]

Serving the Revolution

The Crown mail service added to the colonists' complaints that led to the American Revolution. The British government had never abandoned the idea of squeezing out a profit from its postal service. The colonists grew more convinced that the Crown's colonial post was just another way to tax them, and taxes on newspapers in both England and the colonies were denounced as "taxes on knowledge." The British Parliament might well have expected an uproar when it passed the Stamp Act in 1765, taxing newspapers and documents as a means of raising revenue The public outcry, "No taxation without representation," echoed across the colonies. The British Parliament rescinded it the following year. Nevertheless, the Stamp Act was one of the causes of discontent that led to the American Revolution and one of the arguments for freedom of the press in the First Amendment.

To refuse to use the royal postal service was considered not only the morally right thing to do, but it also saved money. The colonists ignored the postal laws and sent letters outside the official mails, depriving the Crown of income. By the end of 1775 so few letters were passing through the royal postal service that it was shut down. A patriot postal service, the Constitutional Post, had all the business.

At a time when few letters carried prepaid postage, post riders earned extra money by carrying postage due mail and pocketing what they collected. Stagecoach drivers employed a sly trick that allowed them to swear their coaches did not *contain* mail that they profited from. They hung a pole outside the stagecoach, from which a bag of letters dangled. Therefore, the mail was technically not *in* the coach, so the coach did not contain the mail. Franklin eliminated some of these sharp practices. By assigning postmasters to collect postage and subscription fees, Franklin in effect turned postmasters into publishers' agents. He arranged for the free exchange of newspapers among editors. His policies made the American colonial post office the most progressive in the world, well ahead of those in England.

Crown authorities censored the mail and, despite what Franklin had accomplished, they dismissed him in 1774 because of his revolutionary activities. A year later, with the colonies breaking away from Britain, the newly formed Continental Congress met to create an independent government. Close to the top of the agenda was how to deal with mail. The Second Continental Congress chose Franklin to set up a separate postal system, the best way to get word to colonists who wanted independence. Franklin was the new nation's first postmaster general. He served for 16 months.

Working with Newspapers

In combination, newspapers and the postal service were the most important means of informing the public at the birth of the United States. Vestiges of their fruitful collaboration lie in the number of newspapers today that have the word "post" in their names. Both the Federalists and their political opponents, the Jeffersonian Republicans, supported postal subsidies for newspapers in a new nation as thinly populated, as spread out and as diverse as the various regions of the United States of America. Together, newspapers and the postal service were much needed glue to bind the nation.

The Constitution authorized a national postal operation with the sentence, "The Congress shall have power… to establish Post Offices and post Roads." The new Congress set up the General Post Office, but only on an annual basis and for only five years. The postmaster general reported to the Secretary of the Treasury. He and his postal service would not be subject to control by the individual states. In the years to come, the postal service would have an integral role in supporting the provision calling for freedom of the press in the First Amendment.

At the time the Constitution was being adopted, a letter traveling along the main post road from Georgia to Maine might take three weeks to arrive. And it wasn't cheap. A one-page letter going up to 30 miles cost six cents, which was a penny more than the cost of a dozen eggs. (The cost of a first class postage stamp today roughly equals the cost of three eggs.) The same one-page letter going more than 450 miles cost twenty-five cents. To avoid paying for a second sheet, letter writers not only wrote small on both sides of the page, but filled up the margins by writing up and down. Postal receipts for the entire nation in 1789 were $25,000.

Interrupting the U.S. mail was a grave matter. As in many other countries since the Middle Ages, only one penalty existed for interfering with the mails: death. However, the United States had trial by jury and jurors hesitated to inflict such a dread sentence. At first, Congress voted flogging as punishment for a first offense, death for a second. Later, prison sentences were substituted. Until 1872, however, mail robbery could still bring the death penalty.

"There is an astonishing circulation of letters and newspapers among these savage woods," wrote the French aristocrat Alexis de Tocqueville as he traveled across the new country. He recorded his observations of the American people with a shrewd, admiring eye. To Tocqueville, that heralded better economic conditions. "I only know of one means of increasing the prosperity of a people… communication," he wrote in *Journey to America*. "In Michigan forests there is not a cabin so isolated, not a valley so wild, that it does not receive letters and newspapers at least once a week; we saw it ourselves."

Press and post grew side by side, each affecting the other. Thanks to newspapers and mail reaching the cabins scattered across the huge, new land, settlers figured out that they belonged to the national community that was taking shape. They also gradually understood that what the government decided impacted their lives.

Slaves were frequently used in the antebellum South to deliver mail. This practice made some slaveholders uneasy when they reflected that the slaves might acquire enough knowledge to be dangerous. A federal law in 1802 forbade anyone except a free white man to carry the mail, but the practice of using slaves to carry the mail continued. Slaveholders were correct to be worried. From 1835, northern abolitionists flooded the mails going to the South with abolitionist pamphlets. In parts of the South, postmasters themselves destroyed abolitionist mail.[9]

Carrying the Mail

Pioneers blazing trails through the wilderness, crossing mountains and clearing forests for farms did not ask much of the government back east. They did ask for mail service, post offices and post roads. Mail service struggled to keep up with the growing nation. By 1820, the young United States had more post offices and newspapers per capita than any nation in the world.[10]

As communication between cities increased, a better means of transporting mail was needed than a man on a horse. The stagecoach was the answer, but was not without problems. Roads, even highways, were usually unpaved, rutted and full of potholes. Streams had to be forded. When rain fell, a coach-and-four or a coach-and-six (horses) was needed to drag its heavy load through the mud. Some roads were so bad that no wheeled traffic ever used them. A guard often sat next to the driver because of the danger of highwaymen insufficiently troubled by thoughts of the noose.

As the stagecoaches bounced over the rutted roads, the heavy mailbags shifted as if fighting the passengers for seats. Postal couriers sometimes refused the added weight of newspapers, so they piled up at loading points. As for magazines, postmasters had the authority to exclude them from delivery if facilities were inadequate. Newspapers and magazines lying on the ground were likely to be pilfered by otherwise honest citizens eager to catch up on events. If they were not stolen and were eventually delivered, they might be handed over wet and dirty. When a stagecoach arrived, people gathered around as the driver called out the names for whom he had newspapers, not unlike a modern summer camp or military mail call.

Steamboats

Steamboats went into passenger service beginning when Robert Fulton steered the Clermont up the Hudson River in 1807. Six years later, steamboats were carrying mail under contract. On inland navigable waters, designated as post roads by Congress in 1823, steamboats were a familiar sight hauling mail along with passengers and freight up and down America's rivers. On tow paths alongside canals, sacks and their cargo. It was slow, but mules or draft horses pulled barges carrying mail free of the mud that stagecoaches dealt with. For the most part, it was also free of highway robbers.

The Hudson River steamboat Alida.
Courtesy: Wikimedia.

Sorting Mail on a Moving Train

The Puffing Billy – a nickname for early trains – replaced slow coaches jouncing over bad roads. Chugging at unaccustomed speed over long distances, the iron horses carried all the letters that anyone cared to write, plus all the newspapers and magazines, with no threat to throw them off at the next station to make room for passengers. Mail delivery by rail began in 1829 in Pennsylvania. The westward expansion of the railroad solved most of the problems of irregular and unsure newspaper and magazine distribution.

By 1930, more than 10,000 trains carried mail to every hamlet in the nation that rail lines served. Railroad postal service ended as a result of the Transportation Act of 1958, which favored airmail. A dozen years later, almost no first-class mail was carried by train. The last railway post office, running between New York and Washington, D.C., was shunted to a side track in 1977.

Courtesy of the Smithsonian National Postal Museum

Postage Stamps

Let us cross the Atlantic to look inside the General Post Office in London in the 1830s, the years before postal reform introduced postage stamps. A postman, who collected letters by walking through the streets ringing his bell, arrives. The room he enters is dark and windowless, so that postal clerks working in the gloom must hold each envelope up to a candle to see how many items are enclosed. If there is one enclosure besides a single sheet, double postage is charged. Two enclosures, triple postage.

Is money in the envelope? A mistake by someone too trusting. The letter is furtively slipped into a trouser pocket. The clerks keep busy weighing letters and writing information. They record each letter onto a form so that the cost of sending it can be debited against the postmaster of the town to which it will be sent.

When a letter finally is delivered to a cottage in the country, the postman will knock. Whoever answers will be asked to pay for the letter before it is handed over. That may lead to an argument

Mail by Sea

Sending mail by ship was chancy. Schedules were erratic. Sailing ships needed favorable winds, of course, but a ship owner's wish to sail with a full load could send a ship from port to port gathering cargo while letters sat in the mail packet. The solution was the small, fast packet ship that carried passengers and goods, but was foremost a ship to carry the mail and to follow a schedule for doing so.

Mail was sometimes handled in imaginative ways. Ship captains docking to take on casks of fresh water at Cape Town (then known as "Table Bay") on the southern tip of Africa knew that bags of mail waited near a freshwater stream in a hole at the foot of of Table Mountain. A stone over the hole had a painted sign, "Hereunder look for letters."

Eastbound letters were picked up by eastbound ships, which deposited westbound letters under the stone. This post office served ports as far away as Batavia, in the present Indonesia. The English and Dutch were often at each other's throats in the competition for colonies, but they forwarded each other's mail.

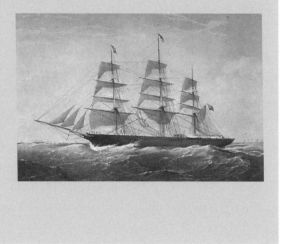

because the postage will not be cheap. Although methods vary from country to country, it is the custom for recipients to pay for receiving mail, just as the buyer of potatoes pays for the potatoes. But what if the recipient refuses? One mail carrier complained that it took him more than five minutes to deliver a single letter. Sometimes the addressee is unwilling to pay, unwilling to receive what may be bad news.

Another reason the British Post Office lost money was that members of Parliament and certain state officials had franking privileges, which meant they sent mail postage free. The word "frank" or "free" next to a seal with a unique mark was all that was needed. The officials' idea of "mail" included: *Thirty dogs sent to Rome, two laundresses sent to an ambassador, a cow that accompanied a doctor on a trip, a parcel of lace sent to a duke's regiment.*[11]

The government tried to limit the worst misuses, but the members of Parliament and the lords —often the same people—used every loophole they could to keep this privilege. The British Post Office in the 19th century, a victim of so many abuses, faced bankruptcy. It was saved by postal reformer Rowland Hill. He calculated that the cost to the Post Office of delivering a letter bore no relation to the distance it traveled within Britain. The real cost, said Hill, was in the complex handling of a letter so that the recipient would pay. He said this in one of the most famous pamphlets ever written, *Post Office Reform: Its Importance and Practicability.* Instead of raising postage rates once again, Hill recommended lowering them sharply so that even poor people could afford letters. At the time it was estimated that the postage on an ordinary letter cost half a day's wages for a factory worker or shop clerk. Obviously, working class people wrote few letters.[12]

Hill proposed a uniform rate based on the weight of a letter regardless of distance within Great Britain or the number of sheets of paper, with a one-penny minimum for a half-ounce letter irrespective of the distance the letter traveled within Britain. Increasing the weight of the letter,

Pony Express

The Pony Express advertised that it could get telegraph messages from San Francisco to New York in eight days and letters in twelve days. Riders galloped through alkali deserts, mountain passes deep in snow, and rocky ravines where a stumbling horse could mean death. "Road agents" lay in wait to snatch money sent by mail. Native American war parties lay in wait. Hungry riders sometimes resorted to eating wolf meat. It was no job for the faint of heart. "Orphans preferred," read the job ads.

The Pony Express lasted only 18 months during 1860 and 1861, unable to match the new technology of the telegraph. The Pony Express had carried a total of nearly 35,000 letters. Today it's part of American lore.

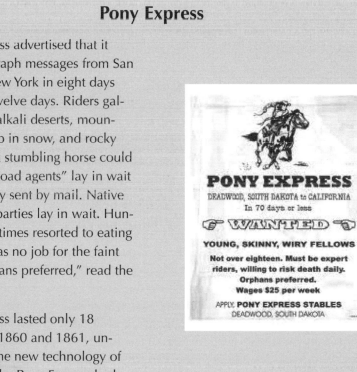

A Clever Ruse

Some Britons managed a ruse to get a mailed message without paying. A frequently told tale tells of a man walking in the Lake District one day when he saw the postman stop outside a mean cottage. An elderly woman came out, took a letter from the postman, turned it over in her hands, and then gave it back. It was from her son, she said, but she did not have the money to pay for it. The observer, moved with pity, offered to pay the fee, but the woman refused with warm thanks.

When the postman had gone, she confessed that the letter would have contained no writing. Her son regularly sent her such letters. The way he spaced and wrote the address told her essential things about how he was getting on. It seems likely that the postman knew all about the little ruse but sympathized with his poor client. Such use of codes in addressing letters grew common.[19] Had she paid, the Post Office would not have known unless the postman told them, for it was not unusual for postmen to pocket some of the postal fees.

not the number of enclosures, would increase the postage. He suggested that senders should be required to mail letters in wrappers or "little bags called envelopes" with markings showing that postage had been paid. Hill also proposed abolishing the franking privilege and charging newspapers postage. Most important, he proposed that postal charges should be collected in advance from the sender of a letter. That the letter was prepaid would be noted by "a bit of paper just large enough to bear the stamp and covered at the back with a glutinous wash."[13] And so, in 1840, after the government recovered from the shock of these radical proposals, was born the postage stamp.[14]

Merchants supported the plan to lower postal rates and use postage stamps. So did a number of newspapers and a public-spirited citizenry. Reform supporters argued that to increase revenue the Post Office should charge less so that more people would use the mails. Yet even such a slight blurring of class distinctions as postal reform had its opponents. They responded that toincrease postal revenue, it made sense to charge more. In class-conscious England, the notion that the poor would write letters if mailing costs were reduced to a penny not only failed to move the opposition to reform, it was an argument against reform. Stamps dented the wall of privilege. One opponent argued that the Post Office would be overrun with mail if this reform took effect. A few of the rich expressed snobbish displeasure that just anyone could now use the mails. Lord Lichfield, the Postmaster General called postal reform "the most extravagant of all the wild and visionary schemes" he ever heard of. "The walls of the Post Office would burst," he said.[15] Of course, that was the idea.

As Hill predicted, letter writing rose sharply and the poor benefited. Within twenty years most of the world had adopted Hill's reforms. Postcards at a halfpenny each were particularly popular. Hill received many proofs of what his work had meant to the poor and humble. On a journey in Scotland, he once gave his coat for mending to a journeyman tailor in a little village. On learning who Hill was, the man refused payment.

The Penny Black

Letter carriers must have enjoyed some easing of their stressful lives with payment now severed from delivery. The mail carrier no longer had to seek out someone at each home, no longer had to cajole someone into buying a letter, no longer had to wait or to trudge back to the station with unwanted letters. The postage stamp also aided business. The flow of information by this means of mediated communication soared. In 1838, 75 million pieces of mail went through the British Post Office. In 1841, the number jumped to 208 million and continued to climb. People who had never received a letter were now sending and receiving them even if the reading was slow and writing was difficult. Many letters still had to be written by surrogates and read aloud when they arrived, but literacy climbed. The mail carrier became the partner of the schoolteacher.

Rowland Hill died in 1879, filled with honors. His system of cheap prepaid postage had spread across the world. Nations everywhere adopted his reforms because they produced a service that was at once profitable to the government and a delight to people all over the world who were getting dependable and speedy delivery of personal letters and public information at modest cost. It was all based on a tiny bit of gummed paper stuck on the outside of an envelope dropped into any corner mailbox day or night. This was truly a revolution.[16]

In 1847, the United States followed Britain's lead in selling adhesive-backed postage stamps, followed five years later by stamped envelopes. However, for eight more years the use of prepaid postage stamps was voluntary and most mail went collect-on-delivery. Nevertheless, as in Britain, stamps and other reforms led to a huge increase in mail.

Free Delivery

The U.S. Post Office Department was not tasked with putting letters into mailboxes. It just had the responsibility of hauling mail from one post office to another. Before free home delivery, a city or town resident normally took mail to the post office. The addressee went to another post office to get it, saving the penny or two for voluntary delivery.

International Mail

By the 19th century the postal services in several nations were a mess, with their own rules, their own rate scales and their own suspicions of foreign mail, all adding up to a maze of conflicting regulations. A letter crossing several borders added charges by each country. From the U.S. to Japan, a letter could cost anywhere from a dime to sixty cents in postage, based upon five routes and five rates. Nations negotiated separate treaties with each country. Strong nations served as transit points to weaker nations not only for the postage income but to exert influence over their neighbor. Nor did possibilities for spying escape notice.

In 1863, in the midst of the Civil War, United States Postmaster General Montgomery Blair called an international conference. Delegates from fifteen nations met in Paris and agreed to use the metric system to calculate distance and weight. Eleven years later, twenty-two nations met in Berne, Switzerland, for the first International Postal Congress, which created the General Postal Union. The Treaty of Berne, signed on October 9, 1874, is now observed as World Post Day. In 1878, because membership grew so fast, the name was changed to the Universal Postal Union, the world's first truly international organization. UPU members agreed on a single rate for foreign mail, with no difference in the treatment of domestic and foreign mail. Each nation would keep the money from its sale of stamps, but it would not charge to deliver foreign mail.

The delivery of letters would no longer be part of international scheming for power. It was no longer necessary to add postage stamps of every country that a letter or package passed through. However, some payments to the receiving countries still exist. The Universal Postal Congress still meets every five years. It has added such services as money orders, registered mail, parcel post, and reply cards. Each country issues its own stamps.

In 1855, the law in the United States was altered so that the sender had no choice but to buy a stamp, but still went to the post office to mail the letter. That began to change in 1858 with the appearance on New York City streets of mailboxes. Those proved so popular that they were installed in most cities. At the other end, the addressees still paid extra to have a mail carrier deliver the mail, though they could trudge to the local post office to get their mail without paying. Some newspapers routinely listed people who had letters waiting, an early form of "You've got mail."

In 1863 Cleveland's assistant postmaster, Joseph Briggs, adopted the idea of free city home delivery because he "was appalled at the sight of anxious wives, children and relatives waiting in long lines at the local post office for letters from soldiers off fighting the Civil War."[17] By coincidence on July 1, the first day of the Battle of Gettysburg, free home delivery began in forty-nine cities. Before the century ended, post offices were offering free delivery to homes in cities throughout the nation.

Rural Free Delivery

If you lived in the country, you still went to town for your mail. Of course, you combined that trip in your buggy with shopping in the general store and visits to the doctor or the blacksmith. A trip to town could occupy most of your day. Actually, the post office was as likely as not to be set up in the general store. When a weekly trip to the village post office was the farmer's only way of receiving mail, there was little reason to subscribe to a daily newspaper. The country weeklies best served his needs.[18]

Country folks, outnumbering their city cousins by four to one, might envy city free home delivery, but it wasn't until 1890 that free delivery was offered to rural areas. Postmaster General John Wanamaker had been pushing for rural free delivery for some time. Opposition came from small-town postmasters who correctly saw that rural free delivery would shut down the smaller post offices. The small town tavern owner was especially upset. So was the owner of the country general store where the fourth-class rural post office had been situated until postal routes came along. Storekeepers knew that when the farmer and his wife came to town for mail, they often stopped to buy something. If they didn't have to come to town, they might prefer to order from the mail order catalogue sent by Aaron Montgomery Ward of Chicago, who started printing catalogues in 1872 with a one-page price list. Not only did the storekeeper lose the postmaster's salary, but also the extra business generated by people coming in for their mail.

Wanamaker's supporters for rural free delivery included the urban newspapers, who saw the possibility of getting a daily newspaper into farmers' hands. Effects on advertising rates could be substantial. Farmers wanted daily newspapers not only for the news and general reading pleasures but also in these pre-radio days for weather and crop market reports. And, very important, by

Congress voted funds for a test of rural free delivery (RFD) in 1893. Opponents in Washington called RFD a foolish expenditure, believing that sending a mail carrier out summer and winter over bad roads or no roads at all to every home in every hollow was a waste of money. That was not the opinion of people in the country. They craved mail service. In the years before radio and rural telephones, a chance to read the latest happenings in letters and newspapers eased their isolation. The new free rural delivery service was made permanent nationwide in 1902.

Rural Free Delivery helped to expand the American network of roads and bridges. The mail carrier who trundled down the road stopping at the rural mailboxes needed a better road to trundle down, or at least a road without deep ruts that would be under water in the spring and under ice in the winter. The U.S. Post Office Department rejected hundreds of applications for RFD service after inspecting the roads. It required that roads be passable all year. Heeding the frustrations of farmers, local governments raised the revenue needed to gravel roads, repair bridges and construct culverts. As the years went by, the gray, tunnel-shaped rural letterbox with its red flag popped up on fences and posts along dirt roads across the country, replacing the lard pails and soap boxes that were used at first. Circulation of daily newspapers skyrocketed.

Mail and parcel post bringing newspapers and magazines as well as goods are two means of mediated communication that have made country living less isolated and more desirable. In a curious way, the internet has joined RFD in encouraging a return to village and rural life. The internet makes it possible for many professions and businesses to function from anywhere, including deep in the countryside. Various jobs are performed via high-speed connections. Education is available through the internet and so is entertainment by means of television, DVD and the internet.

Parcel Post

Fat catalogues sent to millions of households were a principal means of shopping, thanks to RFD. Bulk mailings could be enormous. Catalogue stores were the Wal-Marts of their day. The 540-page catalogue mailed out by Montgomery Ward in 1887 listed 24,000 items for sale. Sears Roebuck in 1897 said it sold one watch and four suits every minute.

The introduction of parcel post was a political minefield, an issue that brought the federal government into competition with private express services and small town shopkeepers. Like rural free delivery it was a boon to farm families but a bane to the fellow who ran the general store in town. Unhappy local merchants put pressure on their newspapers to fight the "Mail Order Trust" by refusing their newspaper ads. Coupled with catalogues, parcel post doomed their businesses. The small town general store, which once thrived, survives mostly as American folklore. Today, online shopping, based on an even newer means of communication, the internet, has in its turn seriously hurt catalogue sales.

Early 20ᵗʰ century train mail car and truck

Modernizing

Directed by the Espionage Act passed by Congress during World War I, the Post Office suppressed newspapers, magazines and other printed matter that were considered subversive. The publications came from socialists, pacifists and labor unions, plus some whose offense was that they were written in German, the language of the enemy. Postal authorities only backed away from this kind of suppression during World War II and after.

Meanwhile, the Post Office's money problems did not go away. Postal policies changed over the years, sometimes to save money, sometimes in the cause of efficiency. During World War II, V-mail ("V" for "Victory") became the way to correspond with military personnel and others overseas. The lightweight pale blue sheets were photographed, reduced in size and weight, flown overseas, then recreated. V-mail arrived quicker and took up less space on cargo planes.

In 1950, home delivery was cut from twice daily to once. When President Dwight Eisenhower's choice for postmaster general, businessman Arthur Summerfield, began his new job in 1952, unpleasant surprises greeted him. Summerfield's inspections uncovered a massive, creaking 19th century bureaucracy. Equipment and facilities were outdated. Shopworn equipment was housed in run-down, overcrowded, poorly lighted postal buildings. Wages were low. Despite all this, the Post Office Department was bleeding the U.S. Treasury of millions of dollars a day. Summerfield began a modernization program that successive postmasters general have carried on.

Charles Lindbergh inaugurated the first flight on April 15, 1926, from Chicago to St. Louis, stopping to pick up mail in Peoria and Springfield, Illinois.

Courtesy Roy Nagl

The 1960s witnessed a steep rise in the amount of mail, especially business mail. Computers at banks, utility companies, insurance companies, credit card issuers, department stores and other firms were sending bills, receipts, notices and advertising to their millions of customers. The government mailed truckloads of Social Security checks each month. Yet at post offices thousands of clerks still sorted the mail by hand, throwing letters into bins or sacks, moving them to central locations and then unpacking and sorting them again. The Post Office Department knew its operations had to be mechanized.

In 1963, five-digit ZIP codes were added to addresses. The Zoning Improvement Plan (ZIP) code, built around eighty-five big city hubs, reduced the congestion especially on busy downtown streets. These hubs became the core of 552 sectional centers. Each center managed from 40 to 150 local post offices. For the next step, each sectional center got a code number. Beyond this, numerical codes were issued to neighborhood post offices. The result was a five-digit code that covered the entire United States. Every home and business address had its five-digit code. The

Pigeon Post

During the Dark Ages the Arabs established pigeon courier services. According to one tale, a caliph in North Africa satisfied his taste for Lebanese cherries by having pigeons fly them in. Each carried one cherry inside a silk bag, the first parcel post. Reportedly, a prize pair of carrier pigeons could fetch one thousand gold pieces.

Pigeon post was the world's fastest communication system for all the centuries of the Dark and Middle Ages and remained so until Samuel Morse's invention of the telegraph in 1844. Stockbrokers and bankers continued to rely on pigeons through much of the 19th century. In 1840 the European news agency Havas ran a London-to-Paris pigeon news service with the promised flying time of six hours. In the Franco–Prussian War of 1870-71, a gap existed in telegraph lines between France and Germany. Julius Reuter bridged it with pigeons and made the fortune that he used to found what is now Reuters, one of the world's great news agencies.

Even in modern times, pigeons have been postal couriers. In 1981, Lockheed engineers in California needed to send photographic negatives on a regular basis to a test station. The birds covered the distance in half the time and at less than one percent of the cost of a car delivery. Other means of communication have replaced the cooing messengers, but here and there they can still be found doing the useful work that made them the email of the Middle Ages. And they work for… pigeon feed.

first digit represents a region, from 0 in the Northeast to 9 in the Far West. The next two digits identify cities and sectional centers that fit the USPS transportation plan. The last two digits identify individual post offices or urban postal zones.

As it modernized, the Post Office Department automated. Pigeonhole boxes were thrown out when machines could sort the mail, including parcels. Envelope addresses were read by optical character readers. Conveyer belts moved letters along. Vending machines sold stamps, including the popular self-sticking type. Other machines canceled them. Computer scales at the postal clerks' window not only weighed but calculated costs for various classes of mail. Bar codes stamped by mass mailers of national newspapers, magazines and catalogues moved them rapidly through the system.

The newest generation of automated equipment can read an entire address optically and convert it into a bar code sprayed on the envelope that is read by an electronic sorter that processes nine envelopes a second. Even some hand-written envelopes can be moved along like this. The combination of regional printing plants and bar code addresses puts newspapers and magazines in home mailboxes often within hours of printing.

Privatization

As the national mood swung toward privatization of industry, eyes turned toward the postal service. After lengthy negotiations and a strike by postal workers, Congress passed the Postal Reorganization Act in 1970. President Richard Nixon signed it. By its provisions, a year later the Post Office Department became the U.S. Postal Service (USPS), an independent organization. The postmaster general left the president's cabinet.

The U.S. Postal Service would become a self-supporting business corporation wholly owned by the federal government, run by an independent Board of Governors appointed by the president for nine-year terms with approval by the Senate. A separate five-person Rate Commission would determine the price of postage stamps and the Postal Service would be fully independent of Congress. Even the postal emblem changed, from a post rider to the national symbol of the bald eagle standing on a block labeled U.S. Mail. In 1977, to compete with Federal Express and UPS, the Postal Service introduced Express Mail.[19]

To honor the Postal Service the National Postal Museum was opened in Washington, DC, in 1993. A Smithsonian Institution museum, it is housed in the old Post Office Building. It features the artistry that goes into the engraving of stamps. But all is not well, as the rising cost of stamps and services attest. Because the Postal Service runs deeply in the red, its future remains cloudy. It has been hurt by the advent of email and smartphones, but is unlikely to be replaced. In 2012 the USPS cut mail service sharply and that slowed delivery of first class mail and packages. The mail carrier's bag, lighter than before, is stuffed with junk mail yet continue to carry what we want. In the world of the 21st century modern communication companies like Amazon.com and Netflix still depend upon the mails.

Summary

Postal service has mattered to every society that used it and to everyone who has looked forward to getting a letter. Empires depended upon it. So did the growth of business.

The postage stamp belongs in the category of media that changed the world. The simple bit of printed and glued paper and its accompanying reforms added to the rise of both democracy and literacy. They are among a series of 19th century changes in mediated communication that left a permanent mark on society, giving us photography, phonograph records and advances in printing and paper technologies, plus the electric inventions of the telegraph, telephone, movies and radio. Because of them, we all live in a much different and more egalitarian world.

Timeline

BCE (dates are estimates)

2350: Mesopotamian king uses homing pigeons.

900: China's Zhou Dynasty sets up a pony express postal service for its government.

500: Persian government also establishes a pony express.

490: Pheidippides dies after bringing to Athens the news of victory at Marathon.

CE

14: Rome sets up network of relay runners carrying messages 50 miles in a day.

650: Muslim caliphs set up regular pigeon post, the first news service.

1200: The University of Paris is granted its charter, starts mail, messenger service.

Monasteries contact each other by their own postal systems.

1305: Europeans have a private postal service run by the Taxis family.

1464: In France, a government postal system.

1627: French government establishes registered mail as a way to send money.

1639: Boston tavern receives European mail brought by ship, starts U.S. postal service.

1653: Paris gets mailboxes.

1775: Continental Congress establishes a postal service.

1792: New U.S. government passes Postal Act.

1815: U.S. postal service expands rapidly; now 3,000 post offices.

1837: Rowland Hill's pamphlet on postal reform is published; will have global influence.

1840: England starts penny post. Stamps are cheap, so people write more letters.

1855: Americans are required to put stamps on letters.

Registered mail.

1858: Some American cities get mailboxes.

1863: Mail is delivered free to some American city homes.

Paris is host to an international postal conference.

1864: Post offices are put in trains to speed mail handling.

1869: From Austria, postcards are introduced.

1873: Penny postcards are sold in the United States.

1880: U.S. gets parcel post service.

1887: Postal mass marketing takes off with fat Montgomery Ward catalog.

1896: Rural free delivery (RFD) is inaugurated in the United States.

1911: A U.S. postal savings system offers banking service, a boon for poor people.

1912: Air mail.

1916: Postal detectives solve the last known stagecoach robbery in the U.S.

1939: Trans-Atlantic air mail service.

1942: Lightweight V-mail is created, mainly to handle wartime armed forces letters.

1963: Five-digit ZIP codes improve delivery.

1970: Troubled U.S. Postal Service becomes self-supporting.

   Express mail service set up to compete with FedEx, UPS.

1983: ZIP codes add four more digits; postal bar codes.

1992: Automatic stamp delivery machines.

1993: The National Postal Museum opens.

1998: Postage stamps downloaded from the Web, then printed, go on sale in U.S.

2007: The "forever stamp" is sold to be usable always for first-class mail.

4. Telegraph

Uniting the United States

In the decades leading up to the Civil War, most Americans were scattered in small towns and villages or on farms. Cities did not have easy contact with the countryside. Roads were bad. Railroad tracks were just being laid in the East. Boats that chugged along rivers or ran along the nation's coasts carried information in personal letters and newspapers, but news from New York might reach London by clipper ship before it arrived in a Southern port. The price of food varied from place to place more than prices do today. National politics was sectional. The United States was united mostly in name, and soon enough that would fall apart.

What the Telegraph Did

Like so many communication technologies, the telegraph was expected, at least in some quarters, to change the world by bringing understanding to all mankind of a shared humanity and world peace. It did, and it did not. It helped to connect the scattered communities of the vast American nation. However, the hope that the telegraph might lead to world peace was never realized. Instead, what followed in the United States was the Civil War.

The telegraph was the first device to use electricity for a practical purpose. It allowed people for the first time to communicate instantly with each other beyond the reach of a human voice. The telegraph sped information through society at speeds the Pony Express could not dream of. Overnight that colorful

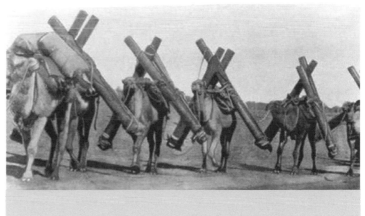

Camels carry telegraph poles in Australia in the 1870s.
Source: State Library of South Australia

enterprise went out of business. The last telegraph pole became the new information frontier. By giving businesses the ability to learn what customers wanted to buy, the telegraph encouraged mass production. It helped to reduce the prices of goods. It expanded the delivery of perishable foods. By alerting station agents, the telegraph made the railroads safer.

The telegraph connected communities and businesses, not families and ordinary individuals, so its effects on us were political and societal rather than personal and emotional. It brought about standard time zones and it altered the nation's economy by smoothing out the variation in prices among different regions. It allowed branch offices to communicate daily with head offices. It sharply reduced the time between an event and public awareness of it.

Urgency to News

It gave news urgency. The telegraph altered the look of news and, to a degree, its very nature. Before the telegraph no distant communication could exist without transportation, with the limited exceptions of semaphore flags, smoke signals or homing pigeons. Semaphore was being used for some information transmission in Europe, and from ship to ship or between ship and shore, but it never gained a foothold in the United States.

Freight trains hauled the heavy poles and the telegraph wires that ran alongside the tracks, the nerve beside the spine. Each brought business to the other. The railroad had so much need of the telegraph to dispatch trains and carry messages that the jobs of railroad station agent and telegrapher were combined. Dots and dashes alerted switchmen so they could send to a siding any trains heading in opposite directions on the same track. The engineer had less worry about whether the "9:05" was on schedule. Rail operations were more efficient, with lowered freight charges and consequently more goods.

Now it made economic sense to carry daily newspapers and the magazines that too often had been abandoned near a stagecoach stop to end up in soggy piles. Delivery of information by horse and stagecoach was quickly forgotten with the dawning of the age of the railroad and telegraph. Their paired growth stimulated another means of communication — the mail system, which required dependable transportation. U.S. stamps went on sale in 1847, three years after American telegraph companies began stringing wire.

Samuel F. B. Morse

No Single Inventor

The idea of electricity as a means of sending messages was considered well before Samuel F.B. Morse thought of it. No one person really invented the telegraph, just as there was no single inventor of the photograph, the motion picture or the computer. In 1684 scientist Robert Hooke laid out plans for a visual telegraph more than a century before electricity came out of the laboratory. A Danish scientist, Hans Christian Oersted, discovered electromagnetism in 1820. In 1830, an American scientist, Joseph Henry, rang a bell more than 1,000 feet down an iron wire circuit from an electromagnet hooked to a series of small batteries. Morse, an artist not a scientist, may not have known of most of the previous experiments with this invisible "fluid." According to a frequently told tale, Samuel Morse was a passenger on a ship taking him back to America after three years in Europe trying to make a living as an artist. A dinner conversation with other passengers about electromagnetism led him to conclude that an electric telegraph was feasible, saying, "I see no reason why intelligence might not be instantaneously transmitted by electricity to any distance."[1]

An electric telegraph functioned along the Great Western Railway in England in 1839. A renowned physicist, Charles Wheatstone, and a businessman, William Cooke, built a workable system based on an alphabetic code system that required five needles and five wires. Two years later the inventors came up with the first printing telegraph; it sent as much as fifteen words a minute. The British public and the government paid little attention until they learned its role in the capture of a murderer and a pickpocket gang. All of them had tried to escape by train but ran into police who had been alerted by telegraph messages. Such seemingly insignificant news reports helped to establish the telegraph in the minds of government officials as well as newspaper readers. And from the telegraph much of modern communication has evolved.

Assembled by Morse and his assistant Alfred Vail, an experimental telegraph wire reached Baltimore with news of the Republican political nominating convention. Morse chose as his first public message a quotation from the Book of Numbers: "What hath God wrought?" The pious artist and inventor was convinced that God had chosen him to improve communication on Earth. Not all religious leaders agreed. In Baltimore, ministers expressed the opinion that the telegraph was too much like black magic.[2] Some people assumed that the wires were hollow. Others believed they could transmit physical objects. One woman in Europe wanted to telegraph a dish of sauerkraut to her soldier son.

Private Industry

When Congress chose not to buy the patent rights to the experimental line, private news express companies rushed in. Once Morse had shown the way, the technology was simple to copy. Within a few years more than fifty telegraph companies were active. The American telegraph, unlike most of the world's telegraph systems, would be managed as a commercial venture. Soon after, private industry embarked on development of the telephone, radio and television. Most governments chose the path of government control and often ownership of all these forms of mediated communication.

The Crimean War, 1854-1856, saw the telegraph used both for military orders and reportage. During the American Civil War both armies relied on telegraph communications, but the South suffered from a lack of wire and other supplies. Wires radiating from General Grant's headquarters enabled him to coordinate troop movements across a wide front. President Lincoln was able to to keep abreast of military operations without being at the front.

By the end of the Civil War, as a result of mergers and acquisitions, only three fiercely competitive telegraph companies remained. Western Union bought out its two rivals, the U.S. Telegraph Company and the American Telegraph Company, and became the first major company of any kind in the United States to gain a business monopoly. The main use of the telegraph was for commerce, echoed today by the internet's "dot.com" enterprises. Speculators thrived on early information. The messenger who arrived first to report a rise or fall in cotton prices promised large profits for his quick-witted employer.

Europeans had entered the news service business even before the Associated Press was created in the United States. In Paris in 1833, the year the penny press began in New York, Charles Havas began a news agency using the mails and carrier pigeons. In exchange for his news reports, newspapers gave him advertising space that he could sell. The enterprising idea led two of his workers, Bernard Wolff and Paul Julius Reuter, to start their own news agencies. When the telegraph lines went up in Germany and France, Reuter observed that the lines of the two nations were unconnected. Seeing a business opportunity, he covered the gap with carrier pigeons, which he had already employed to report the latest market prices. In time, Reuter moved to England, where he founded the news agency, now known as Reuters, one of the world's largest.[3]

Transmitting News

Newspapers had begun to compete over the speed of news delivery in the late 1820s, when two New York business periodicals, the Journal of Commerce and the Courier and Enquirer turned to pony expresses and fast boats that met clipper ships from Europe to get a beat on news. Combining the telegraph with the railroads also transformed commerce. Manufacturers could bypass wholesalers, saving on commissions, by dealing directly with retailers, often undercutting the prices of competitors. With the telegraph, dealers in fesh foods could gauge market demand more accurately. Perishable food moved more easily from farm to table. Wholesalers and retailers alike could keep small inventories when they could reorder quickly. Prices could be more competitive.[4]

The frequently voiced argument that a truly dispassionate objectivity does not exist, particularly in political news, has some validity. However, at least the striving for objectivity in the American press does tend to minimize the number of people offended. Yet it was also true that American journalism lacked the pungent flavor of the European press. All in all, the new American news

The telegraph chipped at the barrier of time in transmitting news. When information could be transmitted instantly from distant places, the value of news dispatches as a commodity increased. Independent "telegraph reporters" tried to get a foothold in the new industry, but newspapers preferred their own system. Several Eastern city newspapers agreed to create something new, the news gathering cooperative. In some cases, competitive newspapers shared the services of the same reporter. The Associated Press arose out of these combines in 1848, formed by six New York dailies that otherwise competed furiously. To a great extent the telegraph changed the American newspaper from being primarily a political party organ to being primarily a purveyor of news.[5]

Newspapers and telegraph companies, in a stormy debate over costs, got into a battle of wits concerning what a word was. Because the telegraph companies charged by the word (as much as fifty cents to send ten words between New York and Boston), editors grew creative. Dispatches combined verbs and prepositions into single words that Noah Webster had not identified, never mind the occasional blunders. They also used codes such as "GM" ("good morning") and "SFD" ("stop for dinner"), just as teenagers today tweet "LOL" ("laughing out loud"). Telegraph companies retaliated by charging every five letters or even every three letters as a word.

American news writing also became more concise. The writing style known as "the inverted pyramid" replaced the opinion-filled narrative style. Within the new style the most significant elements, the 5-Ws (who? what? when? where? why?), were combined in the first sentence. As the story progressed, the writer added information in declining order of importance.

When small town newspapers could get news just as quickly, city newspapers in the American interior could compete on the same footing as the eastern press. Equal access to news encouraged the growth of dozens of new dailies.[6]

Objectivity

A new concept took hold on what news was and how it was to be delivered to the mass audiences who read the penny press newspapers that took root a few years before the telegraph was invented. The concept was objective reporting.[7]

A wire service made money according to how many newspapers it could sign up. Because newspapers did not agree on political issues, a wire service saw a greater value in impartial reports that irritated the fewest number of editors. And so, objectivity was born, defined as providing information containing only verifiable assertions and avoiding value judgments that lack clear attribution to source. As one test of objective news reporting, an informed reader should be able to determine no bias by the writer. Overt opinions were confined to the editorial page, and there they have remained.

Publishers of large city newspapers did not greet the equalizing effect of the telegraph with unalloyed joy. The manager of *The Times* of London said he wished the telegraph had never been invented.[8]

As for the telegraph's legacy of objectivity, a new standard may be emerging for the 21st century, one that admits that journalists have views no matter how they try to suppress them. It recognizes that a public awash in sources of information is willing to accept opinion so long as accuracy and honesty accompany it. Sources should be fully identified. "Transparency" is the new term.

Spreading the Technology

Telegraph wires also spread across Europe, Canada and parts of South America. However, the Europeans continued to thwart Morse's dream that the telegraph would encourage international understanding and goodwill. For example, Austria and Prussia built their German language national telegraph services with no direct connection between their political and commercial centers in Vienna and Berlin. Instead, at a shared border office a telegraph clerk from one country physically handed a message to a clerk from the other country for retransmission. This stand-off policy was no accident.

19th century telegraphy and telephone wires

In time, interconnection agreements would be signed, but the telegraph made diplomats nervous, for diplomacy required patience, not the instantaneous awareness brought by the electric wire. If a message could zip to a national capital in no time at all, troops could be ordered to the frontier just as quickly.

Laying cables underwater proved a challenge because it was difficult to find a suitable material to cover the wires. Unsheathed iron did no more than stun fish. Rubber cladding failed because it rotted in water. When the problem was solved, Brittania would rule not only the waves, but also the ocean floors where cables were laid. It was Britain's Malayan colony that grew the gutta–percha trees whose gum sheathed the cables as nothing else could.

A cable under the English Channel allowed British and French merchants to exchange news and prices in just minutes by 1851. After several failures, the first transatlantic cable was laid in 1866 between England and Canada by the Great Eastern, a vessel five times the size of any other ship afloat. Australia was connected to the telegraph network in 1902. In 1906 Shanghai became the first point of connection to China.[9]

Thomas Edison made improvements that allowed transmission of two messages at a time in each direction. He was working on further improvements to this "harmonic telegraph" when he stumbled onto a way to record sound and invented the phonograph. Another inventor trying to improve the telegraph, Alexander Graham Bell, came up with the telephone instead.

Singing Telegrams and Bad News

Decades after the telephone was invented and a national network was in place, it was still cheaper to send a telegram than to place a long distance phone call. Telegrams became more popular than ever. They reached a peak of sorts in popular culture between the two World Wars. Radio comedians joked about using the word "stop" in place of periods because punctuation cost extra but "stop" usually went free. They also joked about Western Union messengers delivering off-key versions of "Happy Birthday" singing telegrams. During World War II, families feared the sight of a Western Union messenger because the telegram might be from the Department of War reporting that a soldier had been killed.

Facsimile (fax) and email eventually overtook the telegram. By 2006, the newer technologies proved too much. Western Union got out of the telegram business. It is still used to transfer money from country to country, allowing foreign workers in Europe and the United States to send wages home. Meanwhile, the use of fax has been fading for several years under the onslaught of email. One recent failed experiment was the facsimile newspaper. The idea was to transmit news directly to homes and businesses but the costly fax machines were slow and the output was poor. However, there was a demand for the service itself that is now met by news outlets on the internet.

Today, the telephone and email have replaced the telegraph. Other inventions that grew out of the telegraph include the telex, the teletype and the teleprinter, which are combinations of printers, typewriters and telephones that were used mostly during the 20th century by newspapers, government offices and businesses; the tieline, a direct private line between a telegraph office and a business office; and the Telequote and Quotron machines, also derived from the telegraph, that provided instant reports on stock market prices. The iPhone has had many ancestors.

Timeline

1794: In Revolutionary France, Claude Chappe sets up semaphore signaling system.

1800: Allesandro Volta's battery provides the first long-term source of electricity.

1803: Semaphore code is used on ships.

1814: Under Napoleon, an optical signal system stretches from Belgium to Italy.

1819: In Germany, experiments with an electromagnetic telegraph.

1830: Scientist Joseph Henry sends a signal down a wire using an electromagnet.

1837: Samuel Morse shows pendulum telegraph, but Alfred Vail invents Morse Code.

1839: Wheatstone-Cooke electric telegraph runs along a railroad line in England.

1843: Congress gives Morse funds to build an experimental telegraph line.

   Gutta percha, a future underwater cable wrap, is found in Malaya,.

1844: Samuel Morse constructs a telegraph between Washington and Baltimore.

1846: Printing telegraph is forerunner of ticker tape.

1848: Using the telegraph for news transmission, the Associated Press is created.

1850: Submarine cable briefly connects England and France.

1851: In London, Frederick Bakewell demonstrates fax machine to send pictures.

1854: Telegraph brings out news of the Crimean War.

1859: Telegraph crosses U.S. from Atlantic to Pacific.

1861: Telegraph brings Pony Express to an abrupt end.

1861-65: Telegraph helps Union win the Civil War.

1866: Atlantic cable ties Europe and U.S. for instant communication.

1869: Edison patents stock ticker and printing telegraph.

1870: Telegraph across Europe and Asia connects London with Calcutta, 11,000 km.

1970: Mailgrams.

1974: Mailgrams are bounced off communication satellites.

2006: Western Union gets out of the telegram business.

5. Telephone

Reaching Without Touching

To succeed, an invention must find a social use. Those that fare best improve some aspect of life in the society of their time. The telephone was originally envisioned as an aid to business, such as a doctor contacting a pharmacist. That it would find so many more uses took time to evolve, but it did not take long for people to recognize the value of being able to speak directly to someone without meeting face-to-face. Before the telephone's invention, access to such emergency services as the fire or police departments was slow and often too late. By connecting people the telephone made life safer and more pleasant. It erased some of the loneliness of living remotely from other people and some of the sadness of being far from loved ones.

Before the telephone, if you were sick you turned up at the doctor's office or sent someone to fetch the doctor; you could not call ahead. If you needed a policeman in a hurry you were in even more trouble. If you needed a fire wagon in a hurry, too bad. If you lived alone how would you manage during a sudden illness or after an accident? If you were elderly, to live alone invited problems. If you lived out of town, as most people did, you took a risk to live alone no matter how old you were.

Before the telephone, speaking with someone outside your home meant traveling. When a son or daughter married or moved out of the house to enter a distant school or start a career, your tears were for more than joy, for the child's familiar voice might never again be heard in your home. Such a departure might feel as complete as a death. Before the telephone, people tended to spend their entire lives close to those they knew and loved. It was not unusual to die in the home where you were born.

Today, with phone calls, emails, messaging and personal blogs, physical separation no longer means complete separation. Thanks to camera phones and social network sites like Facebook, distant communication that includes speaking and seeing eases any decision about going away to take a job, attend school or spend the winter. The telephone has become such a part of our lives that we use it when we have no need to. We answer a ring regardless of how it intrudes into what is immediately going on around us, intimate or not. It is also such a part of our lives that we use it to push people away. Phoning Grandma is so much easier than visiting her.

At the time the telephone was invented, the height of the Industrial Revolution, business and industry moved at a slower and more cautious pace than they would in the years to come. If, say, you were a wholesaler of fruits and vegetables, how would you know what to load onto a wagon for the grocers you served? Or if you wanted to build a skyscraper, how would the workers at the top communicate with those on the ground? The answer: before the telephone (a time that also preceded the safety elevator and cheap steel), there were no skyscrapers. If you worked in a mine how would you call for help after a cave-in? Recall the rescue of the thirty-three Chilean miners in 2010. Mine safety is imperfect today, so you can imagine what it was before the telephone.

Something of a Toy?

The dream of speaking at a distance did not originate with Bell. "Lovers' telephones" consisting of two cans attached by a wire could carry a voice the length of a football gridiron. Other inventors had tried to create an electric version of a voice carrier. On the same day that Alexander Graham Bell, a professor of vocal physiology at Boston University, got his patent, the well-known inventor Elisha Gray informed the U.S. Patent Office that he had invented "the art of transmitting vocal sounds or conversations telegraphically through an electric current." Like Bell, Gray had started out to improve the telegraph with harmonic tones. He is now regarded as the father of the music synthesizer. Whether he is the true inventor of the telephone may never be settled.

The outcome of a lengthy court battle between them ended in Bell's favor, but the apparatus designed by a 29-year-old Scottish-born teacher of the deaf did not inspire universal confidence.

"My God, it talks!"

A famous moment enshrined in telephone lore occurred at the 1876 Philadelphia exposition held to commemorate the centennial of the signing of the Declaration of Independence. Bell went there to demonstrate his telephone, but he attracted little attention until the visiting emperor of Brazil, Dom Pedro II, recognized Bell, the professor who had given a lecture in Boston that Dom Pedro had attended. When Bell demonstrated his device, the emperor exclaimed, "My God, it talks!" The publicity that followed made Bell's telephone the hit of the exposition.[1]

In London, Bell's demonstration was ridiculed as something of a toy. James Clerk Maxwell, the Scottish scientist whose theory of invisible waves would underlie the invention of radio, concluded that Bell's apparatus could have been "put together by an amateur."[2] The chief engineer of the British Post Office, William Preece, reported to a committee of the House of Commons that Bell's invention might be more useful in America than in Britain, which enjoyed "a superabundance of messengers, errand boys and things of that kind."[3]

In the United States, when Cole Younger, a member of Jesse James' outlaw gang, was released from prison, he told a reporter that "it was all I could do to keep my face straight at the spectacle of a fellow jabbering into a dumbbell."

Alexander Graham Bell

Alexander Graham Bell (shown with the first telephone) and his assistant, Thomas Watson, in working with tonal frequencies to develop a harmonic, multiplexed telegraph signal, recognized that the on-and-off signaling of the telegraph would have to be replaced by a continuous current whose frequency had to be modified.

The human voice could be transmitted if a current could be varied to reflect the variations in air pressure as words are spoken, and the voice might be heard with better fidelity if an instrument received the arriving sounds the way an ear does.

That moment famously came on March 10, 1876, when Bell called out from an adjoining room, "Mr. Watson, come here. I want to see you." And the telephone was born.

Bell and his financial backers initially conceived a business model for the telephone, but were delighted when the doctors and merchants who were the first customers ordered telephones for their residences. That inspired the Bell System to rent out the phones. Its newspaper advertisements soon stressed the telephone as a social tool, offering up such slogans as "Friendship's path often follows the trail of the telephone wire," "No girl wants to be a wallflower," and "Call the folks now!"

Telephones were considered part of an integrated system that included the wires that connected them to a switching network and to the phone operators who were needed to make the connections. Improvements in equipment convinced potential users that what Bell had invented was a tool, not a toy. Within two years of the awarding of Bell's patent, some ten thousand Bell telephones were in use.

At first a single megaphone was used for both speaking and listening, with the user alternately pressing his ear to the device and turning his head to shout into it. This yielded to a separate transmitter and receiver. The transmitter took a bell shape to focus the sound of the voice. A metal disk substituted for the original skin diaphragm at the receiver. To add to conductivity, copper wire replaced telegraph iron wire.

It was evident from the start that each telephone could not be connected directly to every other telephone. A centralized arrangement was needed. Bell even envisioned a central switching system to connect distant cities so that long distance calling might be possible, even though the existing equipment was not yet up to the task of sending a clear vocal signal between cities. Subscribers who had to shout might have given up. But along came another inventor, Emile

The Boys Were Too Rowdy

The original telephone operators, teenage boys, who did well as telegraph messengers, proved too rowdy in the confined space of a telephone switchboard room. But who could take their place?

It represented a significant social change to replace boys with women because in starchy Victorian times it was unusual and a bit daring for a young woman to take employment outside the home and thereby jeopardize her marriage prospects.

Nevertheless, the chance to get out of the house and earn money of her own to spend as she pleased won over many women. Never mind that the pay packet was light and the headsets were not. Telephone engineers later discovered that the frequency range of a typical woman's voice more closely matched the early frequency transmission band than a man's voice did. Women speaking on the phone were easier to understand.

Berliner, who was also improving the phonograph, to develop a more sensitive transmitter.[4]

Western Union executives came to what proved to be a shortsighted conclusion when a Bell partner offered to sell the Bell Telephone Company to them for $100,000. Western Union turned down the offer. But in 1878 Western Union decided to compete in the telephone business itself, using a receiver designed by Gray and a transmitter designed by Thomas Edison, both superior to the Bell instruments. Western Union had the additional advantage of thousands of miles of telegraph wire already strung along poles.

The newly formed National Bell Telephone Company sued Western Union over patent infringement and won. Western Union gave up its telephone business. National Bell became American Bell and later the American Telephone and Telegraph Company, with the goal of establishing phone service around the world. By the end of the century, upon the expiration of the first Bell patent, a number of entrepreneurs went into the telephone business.

To reach all the telephones in town, subscribers frequently had to sign up for both Bell and a competing service. The Bell Company expanded to create a phone equipment manufacturing company, Western Electric, and a research unit that would become Bell Laboratories. In the future, Bell Labs would be the source of many communications ideas and inventions, including information theory, motion picture sound, transistors, laser beams, optical fibers, the communications satellite and advances in computers and television.

Headsets weighed as much as six pounds.

Telephone operators were part of the social revolution that allowed women to work outside the home. Women were hired as store clerks, typists and, thanks to stories about Florence Nightingale and Clara Barton, as nurses. Middle-class subscribers regarded phone operators—"hello girls"—as household servants. On the other hand, the Chicago Telephone Company found it necessary to instruct operators to query, "Number, please," instead of saying "Hello" or even "What do you want?"

Social Changes

All in all, compared with what they would be after the telephone became a common household fixture, the good-old-days of the late 19th century were lonely for many, uncertain for most and pinched. Although it allowed no more than a confined intimacy, for the infirm or the solitary, the telephone was a lifesaver. Despite the old saying, the Englishman's home was no longer his castle. The Victorian head of a household may have harrumphed with displeasure at the ringing telephone that interrupted the well-regulated family dinner, but the farmer's wife regarded the telephone as a godsend.[5] The telephone has been— and still is—both irritant and blessing, and it just might be the last means of communication you would willingly part with.[6]

For those you loved, the bittersweet that accompanied separation dissolved, for you could continue personal communication without being there. Daily letter writing took effort, but the telephone easily connected lovers who were physically distant. The traveling businessman, the university student and the vacationer now stayed in contact with home. Yet a phone also disconnects us by allowing each of us to erect a wall of separation from others. Today we pay extra for services like Caller ID that filter who gets through. Like most mediated communication, a degree of separation accompanies the telephone, the opposite of the no-touching "Reach Out and Touch Someone."

Good for a laugh line on TV is the mother's complaint that the child never calls. The "Reach Out and Touch Someone" contradiction of the telephone manifests itself keenly in achieving such family obligations as an adult child maintaining regular, if sometimes reluctant, contact with an elderly parent. The telephone replaces a little of the need to stop by for a chat and a cup of tea

Status Symbol

Some effort was made to restrict telephone usage to those who could afford to rent one. Just as postal reform led to the postage stamp, a division arose between haves and have-nots. The telephone was one of those communication technologies that some wealthy subscribers regarded as a status symbol not to be shared with the lower classes. A Bell advertisement of the times encouraged these middle-class sensibilities: "Telephones are rented only to persons of good

The Switchboard

In 1878, the first commercial telephone exchange was opened in New Haven, Connecticut with a switchboard of eight lines and twenty-one telephones. A year later saw the introduction of telephone numbers in place of a subscriber asking the operator to place a call based on the operator recognizing a name.

This reportedly came about during a measles epidemic when a physician in Lowell, Massachusetts, feared that if the city's four trained operators came down with the illness, inexperienced substitute operators would throw the phone system into disarray without the simpler use of numbers instead of names. Lowell telephone managers were concerned that the subscribers might bridle at being assigned numbers, but the common sense of the numbering operation prevailed.

All this happened before the automatic dial telephone invented by Almon Strowger in 1891 came into use. A Kansas City undertaker, Strowger believed that another undertaker had bribed a telephone operator to tell callers that Strowger's line was busy. To protect his business, Strowger invented the forerunners of the dial telephone and the automatic telephone exchange.

The need for several telephones in one location led to the private switchboard, called a Private Branch Exchange, or PBX. Although many are still in use, they have been replaced at large companies by a "local area network," or LAN, to link their telephone systems and computers.

breeding and refinement. A householder becomes morally responsible for its proper use by all members of his family. There is nothing to be feared from your conversation being overheard. Our subscribers are too well bred to listen to other people's business."[7]

Snobbish objection was expressed to any widening of access to the Bell system by such additions as coin-operated public telephones or telephone directories available to the general public. One Washington, D.C. hotel proprietor had to go to court to keep his phone service after he allowed guests to use the phone in the lobby. In Leicester, England, a subscriber was criticized for calling the fire brigade about a fire that was not on his property. It took a ruling from the postmaster general to establish that a telephone could be employed in the event of fires and riots.[8] In time, as telephones became as common in homes as the refrigerator, the telephone took on an egalitarian hue.

Under the leadership of Theodore Vail, a distant relative of Alfred Vail, Morse's assistant in inventing the telegraph, usage spread. The American Telephone and Telegraph Company (AT&T) grew to be a communications giant. It proceeded to try to standardize everything possible, even the shape of the black—only black—telephone in every office and home. AT&T bought up all the small telephone companies it could. Its control of the industry was absolute until government rulings during the late 20th century forced dissolution of AT&T's monopoly and led to greater diversity.

Telephone use spread rapidly. As the United States entered the 20th century, more than one million phones were being used. By 1930, that number had jumped to more than 20 million phones. A single, black, party-line phone ringing and interrupting a radio program or the family dinner became quite typical in an American home. In rural areas, where four or even eight-party lines were common, people picked up the ringing phone even though the ring pattern of shorts and longs informed them the call was not to them. The occasionally embarrassed listeners defended their behavior as making sure there was no emergency that might need their help.

Long Distance

It was a while before technology caught up with Bell's dream of a nationwide and even an international telephone service. M.I. Pupin's invention in 1900 of the loading coil, Lee de Forest's invention in 1906 of the three element vacuum tube and H.D. Arnold's vacuum tube amplifier in 1914 added clarity to phone calls and changed a local service into an operation that could comfortably replace the dots and dashes of the telegraph with the human voice. In 1915, AT&T had a transcontinental line running from New York to San Francisco. That year also saw successful testing of the wireless telephone, a boon to the U.S. Navy, which had been trying for years to improve military communication. The government took over all telephone and radio service for a brief time during World War I.

A few years later, AT&T began laying deep-sea cable and providing transoceanic radiophone service. Radiotelephony—combining wireless radio and wired telephone technology—between the New York and London financial centers started in 1927 during the boom of the Roaring Twenties, then was extended to other large European cities and to South America.[9] In 1947, the transistor, an invention out of the Bell Telephone Laboratories, replaced the vacuum tube. Microchips would follow. A transatlantic telephone cable was laid in 1956. High-speed computer data phone service followed. A fiber optic cable link between California and Japan was laid in 1989. Meanwhile, communication satellites able to carry thousands of calls simultaneously were placed in orbit. How a phone call or an email message reaches its destination is no longer of concern except to engineers. The remark, "You sound as if you are next door," can be heard halfway around the world.

Opening the Network

The 1956 Supreme Court Hush-a-Phone decision opened the telephone network to non-Bell equipment. Further changes came with the Federal Communication Commission's MCI ruling that opened up the long distance market, the Carterfone decision and an FCC ruling in 1968 that allowed customers to connect non-Western Electric devices such as their own phones and fax machines to the Bell System, and the breakup in 1983 of AT&T into seven regional operating companies. Small companies bought line capacity wholesale, then retailed their use through telephone cards and special phone numbers. The days of POTS (Plain Old Telephone Service) disappeared as the public snapped up their own telephones in colors and shapes far removed from the AT&T black, rotary dial phone.

Improvements in voice communication were joined by improvements in sending *data* anywhere in the world, from the printing telegraph to the teletypewriter to the teletype to the digital computer data stream, all used by governments, global businesses, wire news services and even by you and me. In addition to text, images were converted into digital data streams flowing along telephone pathways to be reconstructed as still and motion pictures.

Thousands of inventions have improved the telephone system, including the Touch Tone, the coaxial cable, the means to transmit computer data, the conversion from analog to digital signals to improve clarity, microwave, satellite communication and fiber optics. With Digital Subscriber Line (DSL) technology, the slender telephone line can transmit a movie. You can download *The Wizard of Oz* on a telephone line. These inventions nudge our world into what author Thomas Friedman labels a "flat Earth."[10] Telephone networks with fiber-optic "backbones" are essential elements of the flat Earth.

However, technological progress is not always positive, and certainly the telephone has not always been employed to benefit the social order. *Telemarketing* may be a case in point, with sales calls buzzing in from boiler rooms as far away as India. Adding to a general sense of social disorder is pornography in the form of "adult" phone lines. On the other hand, unlisted numbers, Caller ID, anonymous call rejection, voice messaging and the answering machine remind us that tools also exist to keep the world at bay.

Wired Broadcasting

Well before a point-to-point Morse code radio changed into a mass communication voice and music broadcasting business, there was *wired broadcasting*. Several European capitals offered a service that allowed customers, for a fee, to listen to operas, plays and concerts picked up by microphones in theaters and fed along telephone wires to headsets. In Buckingham Palace Queen Victoria could hear the opera coming from Covent Garden or the Royal Theater in Drury Lane, while in Paris the Theatrophone Company offered coin-operated headsets at holiday resorts.

Several American cities had church services similarly available. One Canadian tavern owner found a judge willing to set a microphone on his bench during a murder trial. A wire carried the testimony to customers who could listen in on one of twenty earphones sets for a fee of 25 cents an hour. The Telefon Hirmondo in Budapest distributed a printed schedule of programs that included music, a calendar of local events, a weekly children's concert and even commercials, all presented a full generation before regular programming by radio.[11] It tapped into people's newly discovered desire for information and entertainment on a regular basis, piped into their homes and public spaces.

The popular desire to be entertained would be more fully met when technology came along in the form of radio broadcasting and all the entertainment media that followed. As for wired broadcasting, it continued, notably in dictatorships. Radio service consisting of one preset station blaring from atop a pole in a village square or on a train to a captive audience, with no competitive broadcasts, is a perfect propaganda tool.

Cell Phones and Hand-held Devices

Let's look in on a familiar noisy family setting in a developing country with a traditional culture. Mother, grandmother, and the girls are busy serving dinner. Father and the boys are busy eating the main meal of the day. But in their midst is the oldest son on a cellular phone that not only behaves like a telephone, but takes pictures, plays video games and music, calculates, moves money around, and tweets. He is in his comfort zone and his new mobile marks his social status.[12] It has changed the pattern of daily life, never more so than in the developing world, leaping from as much as a ten year wait for a land-line dial tone.

Call it a "mobile" (England, Spain), a "handy" (Germany), a "sho ji" (Chinese word for "hand machine"), or "keitai" (Japanese for "portable thing"). For anyone in any country a personal cell phone matters. So does a private email account, or a Twitter or Facebook connection that is yours alone. For the young, it is a rite of passage in the new millennium. Cell phone technology has improved life for many people in all countries, particularly teenagers who expand their social world. In Haiti, where an estimated four out of five residents have cell phones, a "crisis mapping" network helped people in the aftermath of the 2010 earthquake who could text for help.

Despite complaints, it hardly seems to matter that motorists and pedestrians on cell phones are less aware of their surroundings. Bicycle riders steer with one hand or no hands as they weave through traffic, a cell phone pressed against an ear. Joggers run awkwardly because crooking an elbow throws them off their rhythm.

The cell phone has altered the telephone call. Before the cell phone and earlier mobile phones, a telephone call was directed toward an instrument at a fixed location where, the caller hoped, a specific person would be present. A daughter phoning her mother over a "landline," for example, is actually calling her mother's home in the expectation that her mother will be nearby. With an active cell phone in her handbag, her mother will always be nearby, always "home."

We telephone because we cannot "reach out and touch someone." Cell phones have made it easier to have communication with physical separation. The smartphone with Twitter texting makes it still easier. The tweets promise a kind of intimacy—the sharing among friends of momentary emotions, fragmentary thoughts without visibility or proximity, let alone touching. "Tweets" let anyone in a Twitter network know, for instance, that the sender is at the mall. The total number of tweets—messages limited to 140 characters—is well up into the billions.

Newsweek columnist Anna Quindlen noted, "The BlackBerry device alone makes it seem as though we're living in a '50s futuristic film. The paradox is that all this nominal communication has led to detachment from what is nearby, with people hunched over handhelds or staring into the screen of the computer. There is the illusion of keeping in touch, but always at arm's length. Sometimes it seems that what people want most is the one thing they no longer have: human contact."[13]

Users are likely to keep phones within reach all day and all night, as much a part of their garb as their shoes. Some people relish a constant connection, but not everyone does. For the employee whose boss wants to reach him at any time, there is no certain time off. An unwanted cell phone has been compared to a slave collar and its ringing to a dog whistle. Calls too often are received or initiated on highways, in restaurants, cinemas, bathrooms, on buses, even on skateboards. A ringing backpack in a classroom is not unusual. Concert halls and movie theaters post signs to remind patrons to turn off their communication devices.

Multitasking does not have to include a cell phone, but it usually does, offering another example of focusing on what is far away at the expense of what is around us. Being unaware of what is around you, sometimes referred to as "inattentional blindness," can kill you, as we are told but few of us hear. A study at Western Washington University reported that three out of four test subjects who were on their cells while crossing the campus failed to notice a clown on a unicycle passing by.

A Short History

The cell phone has a short, explosive history. Invented in the United States in 1938, the walkie-talkie saw extensive military use during World War II. Mobile radio systems connected to the telephone network were developed in Sweden after the war, expanded to the United States, and gradually shifted from calls placed through an operator to direct dial. Among the early users of these radiophones were police cars, fire trucks, and television news crews who raced to where the police and firemen were headed. Low-powered walkie-talkies were sold as toys.

The modern cell phone, a version of two-way radio invented in 1973 by Martin Cooper of Motorola, transfers calls from a relay station as a user travels. Portable phones found a ready market in Japan, where many people were quick to adopt innovations in personal technology. By 1979 the Japanese had the first cell phone network up and running. The FCC did not authorize full commercial cell phone service in the United States until 1982.

In the blink of an eye, modern life needed the cell phone. Not even the fear of brain cancer has dissuaded users. As phone size shrank with every new model, a rumor started that sending radio waves into and out of devices pressed against the side of the head, damaged brains because the phones were basically low-powered microwave ovens without

The walkie-talkie hand-held, two-way radio transceiver, designed for military use, saw extensive service during World

walls. The accusation was neither confirmed nor fully refuted. Sales continued to soar. Cell phone signals have also been accused of killing honeybees by sending electromagnetic signals that confuse worker bees.[14]

If you are over fifty, you may not know that texting (instant messaging—IM or "IMing," also called SMS for Short Message Service)— sends abbreviated written messages by cell phone. Because cell phone use spread rapidly in parts of the world where telephone landlines were scarce, Cell phones spread rapidly and instant messaging got an early foothold. In the United States, teens and pre-teens IM'd friends the instant the closing school bell rang. In addition, IM could connect a group as well as two people for business or personal exchanges in real time.

The Thrill smartphone
Courtesy of LG Electronics

New Products

New products continue to tumble out. The telephone, the camera and wireless technology came together in the camera phone, a pocket digital cellular phone that could take and email pictures or post them on a website. In 2007 the iPhone created excitement with a cell phone that combined with an iPod music player, email, Web access and clever touch-screen that featured hundreds of independently created applications—"apps". The handy little units expanded into smartphones that offered a telephone, a camera, email, text messaging, games, 3D viewing of stills and video, music and image storage, access to the internet and other computer functions. Smartphones and other cell phones became the coolest, must-have accessory for teens and the fashion conscious. Manufacturers, quick to seize upon trends, turned them out in a variety of styles. A Samsung model for women featured rich colors, a ring of synthetic diamonds, a biorhythm calculator, a calorie counter and a calendar to track menstrual cycles.

In Minnesota a shopper surfs the internet from a supermarket to pull down a recipe that includes a shopping list. In a McDonald's in Japan, customers point their cell phones at the wrapping around their cheeseburgers to get nutrition data. They point their phones at a magazine to get insurance quotes. If, on the way to the airport, they pass a billboard advertising a movie, pointing their cell phone downloads a trailer. At the airport, pointing their cell phone substitutes for a ticket. In our century, microchips inform microchips. The wristwatch radio-telephone fantasy of the Dick Tracy comic strip decades ago, was almost at hand.

Posting Pictures

The little devices have created millions of citizen photojournalists around the world who have the rare opportunity to record history and some encouragement from established media willing to buy newsworthy photographs or videos. This has been more than a nuisance to celebrities. If no one wants to pay, the video-sharing network YouTube still beckons. The cell phone has made life easier for organizers of political demonstrations. They use the cells, the BlackBerries and the internet to gather a crowd in short order. When President Obama took office, a national dialogue began over whether it was safe for him to use his trusty BlackBerry. He insisted.

But not everything about the camera phone is positive. In the hands of a sexual predator, it can create a dangerous invasion of privacy. That problem has yet to be solved.   Women have also used them to take pictures of strangers who harassed them, then posted the pictures on websites. School administrators have raised concerns that camera cells could help students cheat on tests.

Despite its smartphone contributions, the United States has not always been in the wireless forefront. Americans have been slower than others to "cut the cord." Look to Europe and East Asia for that. In many of their cities young people quickly abandoned fixed-lines for mobility in phone calls, chat lines, messaging and email. Europe and Asia jumped far ahead of the United States for two reasons. First, most cell phone systems were begun by a government-owned and subsidized telephone monopoly that could set standards and run matters as they wished. That could save years of regulatory hearings and competitive wrangling. Second, developing countries had a relatively small—even meager—telephone infrastructure in place, coupled with a huge backlog of requests for telephones. The market for an alternative to landlines was ready and waiting. In poverty-stricken Cambodia in 2003, nine of ten phones reportedly were cell phones.[15] The low cost of wireless technology was a dream come true. It spread like a fire.

Helping Societies Everywhere

Where roads are bad, travel is dangerous, postal service is slow or corrupted, telephone lines do not exist, and computers are scarce, cell phone messages get through. Even in impoverished Africa, two people in five have a mobile phone. In developing countries a micro-finance program has allowed "telephone ladies" to go into business by purchasing solar-powered cell phones for villages without electricity and sell phone time to other villagers.[16] A researcher in India estimated that a single new phone line in a developing country adds an average of $3,700 to its national wealth.

Cell phones can be used by election monitors in places even where vote counting ranges from shaky to shady. In another example of how mediated communication can enable democracy, *The Economist* reported that a Pakistani bureaucrat required land transfer clerks to send him a list of the cell phone numbers of the people who came to them for document approval. He planned to inquire about bribe demands. Buyers and sellers reported an immediate improvement in honest service.[17]

Using a prepaid billing system is easy in a traditional cash economy. Across the world, in shops along unpaved roads where people hand over cash to "top-up" the value of their phone cards, banking services are conducted without banks. No need to waste a day to travel to a bank. No need to risk keeping cash or gold at home. You can deposit money to your account, withdraw it, or send it to someone else by phoning a shopkeeper in your village and reading the code on the card. The shopkeeper ends a transaction by handing money to your family, less a commission.

In Kenya, half of the population have mobile phones, and close to half of them use a mobile banking service. Studies of agricultural marketing in India and Niger concluded that access to mobile phones make markets more efficient by reducing price variations from one market to another, bringing down consumer prices, and raising the income of food producers.[18] Governments that now offer agricultural advice by coaxing farmers to gather at regional locations reach more of them more cheaply by cell phone. News for health workers, weather reports, and information for teachers and local government staffs also flow more easily.

Costs Drop

The fast drop in cost of mobile handsets has naturally made a difference in usage. In the 1990s, even a basic handset cost $250, a luxury item in much of the world. By 2009 a basic model sold for $20 and a Chinese manufacturer was ready to supply them for $13 apiece.[19] Approximately seven billion people now live on Earth. In 2011 about five billion mobile phones were in use. By 2013, an estimated one billion will be smartphones.[20]

Technology has developed that chop voice traffic into digital bits and ship it around the world via the internet the way that email travels. Cheap internet telephony known as VOIP (Voice Over Internet Protocol) is already available with reasonable voice quality from Skype and competitors like Google Talk and iChat. Inventive users from non-English speaking countries like China are using the VOIP service to contact VOIP users in English-speaking countries at random just to practice their English skills, a kind of audio version of finding a pen pal.

It was only a matter of time after broadband replaced narrow bandwidths that the capacity to make phone calls would bypass local phone companies. One difficulty of internet phone calls lies in the difference between an email transmission that lasts fractions of a second and the voice transmission of a phone call that lasts as long as the call itself. Early efforts resulted in poor transmission, but the quality has improved and the cost is hard to beat. Calls by a Skype user to any other Skype user anywhere in the world would have been astonishing just a few years ago.

As it has often done with other kinds of telecommunication in recent decades, Japan has led in using the internet for voice calling. But cell phones and their smartphone descendants now do more. Italy's Telecom Italia rebuilt its network around internet equipment. In Finland, a long-time leader in cell phone technology and manufacturing, the national telephone company, TeliaSonera, ran radio and newspaper ads in 2002 urging customers to give up their wired telephones for the mobile cell phone. What will happen to the 3.2 million copper lines that are the "last mile" to Finland's homes and businesses? They will do the "Negroponte flip" and be used for broadband. TeliaSonera operates DSL connections to the internet, which can make better use of those copper wires.

In country after country, new companies are offering a variety of communication services. Established companies are not accepting these changes quietly but are adapting new technologies themselves. It is much cheaper to set up a cell phone network than to erect telephone poles. More than half of all telephones in the world today are cell phones and that percentage is rising rapidly.

When full mobile satellite service is realized, a portable phone call could be placed between any two spots on Earth. The ultimate goal is to allow any two people anywhere with cell phones to talk to one another with the clarity that attends digital communication. With the camera phone rapidly being diffused into society, those conversations across continents will undoubtedly someday be routinely accompanied by letting the people who are speaking look at each other, and also see what the other is seeing, another step in the ongoing effort to shrink the globe.

Timeline

1876: "Mr. Watson, come here. I want you." Bell invents the telephone.

Elisha Gray files phone patent application the same day Bell does.

1877: Edwin Holmes builds a telephone switchboard.

Emile Berliner invents the microphone. So does David Hughes.

1878: Thomas Edison invents a better microphone.

A telephone central exchange. Telephone directories are issued.

Emma Nutt is the first woman hired as a telephone operator.

1879: Starting in Lowell, Massachusetts, telephone numbers replace names.

1888: To make a phone call, drop a coin in a public telephone.

1891: A mortician, Almon Strowger, develops dial phone, switching exchange.

1900: Michael Pupin's loading coil extends the range of long distance calling.

1904: The telephone answering machine.

1907: U.S. Cavalry tests mobile phone; horse's flank provides the ground.

1913: AT&T pledges universal phone service, expands to rural areas.

1915: Americans average 40 phone calls a year.

Long distance phone lines connect New York and California.

1919: Automatic switching systems reduce need for phone operators.

1920: Multiplexing allows phone line to carry several simultaneous calls.

1921: Detroit police use mobile radios in their squad cars.

1927: Two-way AT&T radiophone service, U.S. to London, $75 for 5 minutes.

1929: Ship telephones can contact telephones ashore.

1935: First telephone call made around the world.

1937: Pulse Code Modulation, a precursor of digital dialing.

1941: Push button phone, Touch Tone dialing, microwave transmission.

1945: St. Louis gets a mobile radio-telephone service, but it's hard to hear.

1946: Area codes join phone numbers.

1947: From Bell Labs comes the transistor, replacing vacuum tubes.

1948: Claude Shannon's information theory; will aid phone communication.

1949: FCC approves radio channels linking mobile and land line phones.

Model 500 phone combines a ringer and a handset.

1951: Direct (no operator) long distance calling begins.

1956: U.S. follows Sweden in using car phones that are not car radios.

First trans-Atlantic telephone cable (Scotland to Nova Scotia).

1962: Telstar 1 launched; carries phone, data, television signals.

In Illinois, digital transmission replaces the analog system.

1963: Touch-tone phone; 10 push buttons replace rotary dial.

1964: Picturephone tested: Disneyland to N.Y. World's Fair.

Transpacific submarine telephone cable service begins.

Drivers can dial car phones without need for operators.

1965: 9 of 10 U.S. telephones can use direct distance dialing.

1968: 911 calls for emergencies, a nationwide service.

1973: Martin Cooper of Motorola invents the personal mobile phone.

1974: Telephone "hot line" set up between the White House and the Kremlin.

International digital voice transmission.

1975: Fiber optics improve communication; starts with U.S. Navy.

1977: In Chicago, AT&T transmits telephone calls by fiber optics.

1982: Caller ID.

1984: 25,000 cell phone subscribers in U.S.

1985: Drivers start making (dangerous) calls on cell phones.

1991: TDMA cell phone technology is made available to the public.

1993: Nokia sends text messages between mobile phones.

Rumors fly that cell phones cause brain cancer; sales continue to soar.

1994: Phone calls over the internet: VoIP.

2000: From Japan, the camera-phone.

Nokia cell phone eliminates external antenna.

100 million cell phone subscribers in U.S.

2001: Cell phone popularity drives Bell South out of pay phone business.

3G high-speed data network.

2004: Survey identifies the cell phone as the chief American love/hate object.

2007: iPhone surfs, emails, plays videos and tunes, makes calls, takes pictures.

2010: Portable phones get smarter, add apps.

Google introduces Nexus One smartphone.

6. Recording

Beyoncé Sings Better Than Our Sister

Every tribe on Earth responds to music. Melodies from voices and instruments lie at the heart of every culture. Yet, mediated communication has changed the centuries-old custom of listening to the expressions of our own culture, music we create ourselves, indifferent to a throat's rasp or a finger's slip. Instead, we prefer the refined and packaged expressions of many cultures. Professional audio fidelity is at our touch in endless quantity. And, after all, the Jonas Brothers and the Dixie Chicks do it much better than sister Susie or neighbor Joe.

Hold an iPod in your hand, and any of your thousands of stored music selections comes flooding into your ears. All of this is improbably stored in a shiny device the size of a pocket comb. Whether anyone needs thousands of songs at the push of a button is not the point. Technology makes them available.

The old-fashioned pleasures can still be found, if we make the effort, in karaoke, the beat-up piano or impromptu guitar when friends gather. But recordings by professionals set our standards. The clever marketing and immense popularity of the iPod, its competitors and the iTunes library of music have tapped into a deep root in the human spirit. Listeners today may know more *types* of music than our great grandparents knew *tunes*. Do you like classical symphonies? You have them, along with new age music, rock, jazz, reggae, Latin, Christian music, country music, hip-hop, movie soundtracks, Broadway show tunes, grand opera, melodies of any nation, or whatever else suits your fancy. Just turn the dial or push the button.

What Is Lost

Few things come into our lives without a price. Beyond the ninety-nine cents we pay to download a song we give up listening to Susie warble or Joe bang on the piano. It is the price of a loss of self-expression and family closeness. The air guitar and the audio mix do not quite compensate for it. In earlier times families might gather in the evening to listen to Mother or Father read aloud or sing. Except for bedtime stories that practice has gone the way of high-button shoes. Instead, by choosing recorded music over the enthusiastic music we make ourselves, we extend our choices well beyond those of our own culture. The music of other cultures that we hear is of our own choosing.

Until the phonograph was invented, unless you were rich there were no means other than books and magazines to bring mediated professional entertainment into the home. The phonograph led the way, to be followed by radio, television, cable, audiotape, VCRs and DVDs. Certainly more will come. As the communication theorist Marshall McLuhan put it, the phonograph broke down the walls of the music hall.[1] Other technology would break down the walls of sports arenas, auditoriums and cinemas. The Walkman family and their i-descendants have drilled further, burrowing into the walls of our homes, our cars and our pockets and purses..

Recalling the Phonograph

Recording began when age-old dreams of capturing the human voice were realized during the last quarter of the nineteenth century. As a result, music has broken old cultural boundaries and has moved in new directions. Recording brought jazz out of the confines of the African-American milieu, just as it carried Irish folk songs beyond their Irish roots, and we have learned to appreciate gypsy tunes, Latin tunes, Arab music, Indian music, Chinese music and dozens of others.

The first device to deliver recorded sound, Thomas Edison's phonograph was invented about the time of its sister invention, the telephone, extending—for the first time since humans began to speak—the sound of the voice beyond the distance someone could shout. By capturing the voice, recording caught some of the unique personality of the individual.

Both the phonograph and the telephone were unintended results of research into improving the telegraph, with the difference that the telephone was an intended invention. The phonograph came out of an accidental discovery, so unusual that the U.S. Patent Office, looking for connections to other inventions, could find nothing like it. The first invention remotely like the phonograph was Thomas Young's device, built in England in 1807, to trace the amplitude

of sound vibrations by means of a stylus on a cylinder blackened with smoke. In France, a half century later, Leon Scott's "phonautograph" used a similar stylus to record the sound of a voice, but could not replicate an actual voice. Again in France, twenty years later, the impoverished poet Charles Cros, in a sealed letter left at the Académie des Sciences in Paris, described a device that reproduced the voice so that the deaf could hear what was said. This was the country where in 1829 Louis Braille had published his reading system as an aid

Young Thomas Edison and phonograph

to the blind. In the same year that Cros left his note, 1877, Edison designed a voice recording device, one year after Alexander Graham Bell and Elisha Gray had invented competing voice transmitting devices.

"Whooooo"

Trying to adjust the rate of telegraph transmission, Edison heard a musical note at a certain speed. Curious, he pursued the sound by putting a new piece of paper in the revolving disc he was working with and, as he described it, shouted "Whooooo". Sending the paper back through the machine, he heard his voice faintly. He tried it again with some words from a nursery rhyme: "Mary had a little lamb. Its fleece was white as snow." He listened with amazement as the first words ever recorded came back to him.

Ever the businessman, Edison thought of recording as a business tool. He made several improvements, but the quality of the tinfoil phonograph he constructed gave no promise of commercial success, so he put it aside to concentrate on the electric light bulb.[2] However, other inventors took up the talking machine, leading Edison a decade later to rethink his dismissal of its commercial possibilities. Increasingly deaf, he did not at first focus on music, but instead considered the potential for dictation, books for the blind, talking dolls and even a record of someone's dying words that relatives might want to preserve. Edison took out patents for an improved microphone, a phonograph that played cylinders and a battery-operated motor. For its potential as a court recording device, two Supreme Court stenographers were franchised to sell the equipment in Washington, D.C. and Maryland. The product did not sell as a business tool, but their company, the Columbia Phonograph Company, would one day become CBS, the Columbia Broadcasting System. Edison took several of his inventions to an exposition in Paris, where he set up listening booths for the phonograph.

When his phonograph cylinders were improved enough to provide entertainment that could return income, Edison placed his "automatic phonograph parlors" in stores all over the nation. For a penny or a nickel listeners could put a sound tube against their ears to listen to singers, whistlers, instrumental soloists and humorists, or that most popular choice of all, marching band music. Listeners sat with rapt expressions or burst out laughing at the new entertainment.[3] The well-lit phonograph parlors, with rugs and potted plants providing a homey touch, attracted families, couples who shared listening tubes and young women whose entertainment choices were limited by Victorian propriety. There were also home versions of the machines on which their owners could record. Columbia's advertising slogan was, "That Baby's Voice in a Columbia Record." Attractive as this feature might be, buyers really wanted the phonograph to play records by professional singers and musicians.

Further improvements came from Emile Berliner, who had invented a microphone and improved

Bell's telephone, For his Gramophone, Berliner used records with lateral grooves instead of the up-and-down "hill and dale" tracks, a coating of fat as its wax, and most important of all, a flat disc instead of a cylinder. The disc was part of a master system that stamped out records, an efficient and cheap way to produce them. A customer brought his hand-cranked Gramophone to the New Jersey machine shop of Eldridge Johnson, who became so intrigued with the notion of recorded music that he went into the business himself, worked for six years to improve the sound, and joined Berliner to found the successful Victor Talking Machine Company.[4]

Victrola

Victor Red Seal records recorded operatic music, a far cry from the turkey-in-the-straw tunes that Edison preferred.[5] This was also the period when Scott Joplin produced some of his best music, such as *The Maple Leaf Rag* (1899), which combined the syncopation of African-American folk music with European romanticism. Then came jazz. Increases in sheet music sales reflected a public enthusiasm for playing the music. The recording industry was still quite young when the public indicated their preference for packaged music over home-made. Wrote an observer in 1893, "The home wears a vanishing aspect. Public amusements increase in splendor and frequency, but private joys grow rare and difficult, and even the capacity for them seems to be withering."[6]

The phonograph player, augmented by a large horn, went into lecture halls. A smaller version was sold for the home, where the device joined two other machines in the family parlor that produced sound, the piano and the telephone. Each machine in turn would find a central place in the home, although some of these mechanical assemblies would have to be disguised as a kind of furniture to civilize them. When the Victor Company encased its machine in a wooden cabinet and replaced the large external horn with an internal horn, its "Victrola" looked like furniture and truly belonged in the family parlor. Millions would be sold.

Machines that delivered sound and then pictures created at a distance would multiply in different rooms of the home and spread to the family car. In miniature form they would even find a place on the body during walks and bicycle rides. Family meals would be eaten within earshot of the machines. Conversation would stop. Visitors vied for attention with the radio or television. The food industry produced TV dinners to serve the new mode of living. The notion that people could take them or leave them alone now seems quaint.

The excitement fueled by recorded music sparked a strong interest in new dances like the one-step, the turkey trot and the tango around the time of World War I. To an older generation accustomed to decades of Victorian mores, the American dance craze and the rising popularity of jazz were part of a disturbing pattern of accelerating change.

Under pressure from the musicians union, the radio networks before World War II banned recorded music, but following the war and the arrival of television, radio needed a new format to survive. Recordings and the disc jockeys who played them would dominate the radio industry. Radio needed records for programming; records needed radio as sales promotion.[7] One public change that emerged from this was that life became noisier. Once heard only when people actively listened to it, music was now also background to accompany other activities.

When the public was first introduced to high fidelity, the prevailing wisdom in the boardrooms of the radio and recording industries was that the public would not pay for hi-fi. That was challenged by a number of audio engineers whose speakers for the home market set new standards. They included such names as James Lansing, Henry Kloss, Paul Klipsch and Rudolph Bozak. Sapphire-tipped needles instead of steel needles, condenser microphones instead of ribbon mikes and turntables without rumble made a difference, but the scratchy clay-and-shellac 78 rpm (revolutions per minute) recordings limited to five minutes of playing time were still a barrier to listening purists. Peter Goldmark of CBS alleviated the problem in 1948 with the better sound and longer wear of the LP ("long playing") record made of plastic, thinner, lighter material that was played at a slower 33 1/3 rpm and provided twenty-three minutes of music on each side. RCA responded with the small, cheap 45 rpm disk in a variety of colors, just right for an exciting and controversial new kind of music, one song per side. Teenagers loved it.

Nipper

The most famous advertising painting ever done was of a dog named Nipper listening with his head cocked to a phonograph record. It was called *His Late Master's Voice*.

Named because he nipped at visitors' legs, Nipper lived in England and died in 1895. Artist Francis Barraud, who acquired the terrier after his brother died, recalled how puzzled he was to hear a voice from a cylinder recording. Three years after Nipper died, Barraud painted the scene from memory.

He sold the painting to the Gramophone Company on condition that he replace the cylinder machine with a flat disk Gramophone machine. The final painting over the years became the logo for a number of audio recording companies.

Music Choices

Choice of music was traditionally influenced by economic class and ethnicity. People listened to what their community knew. At the start of the age of recording most people preferred the lively melodies that reflected their own roots. Wealthy patrons of the arts, who shared a European heritage, supported classical music in the grand European tradition, the staid music of drawing rooms, symphony halls and opera houses.

Discovering new types of music and entertainment in recordings, people bought what they liked and later tuned into what they liked. Recorded music offered new and enriching choices to multitudes of listeners. All were accommodated by the expanding recording industry.

In Cleveland, disc jockey Alan Freed discovered that white teenagers in large numbers were dancing to the African-American music known as "rhythm and blues." He helped to bring it into the mainstream, called it "rock 'n' roll" (a phrase from a 1923 song by Trixie Smith) and rejected accusations that he was corrupting a generation. It took white performers, notably Elvis Presley, to broaden the appeal of rock, leading in time to a general acceptance of African-American performers.[8] The white teenagers of the 1950s and '60s who fervently embraced the new music over the objection of their parents would themselves get heartburn a generation later when their own children used a different recorded music genre to identify and separate themselves.

Recordings can lead to action. If you remember the scene in *Casablanca* when French and German nightclub patrons competed in singing patriotic songs, you will recall how they stirred emotions. Tin Pan Alley churned out many recorded songs during World War II, such as "The White Cliffs of Dover" and "Coming in on a Wing and a Prayer." German soldiers had "Lili Marlene" to rake up memories of home. Emotions were also stirred decades later by "We Are the World," which helped to raise $50 million to buy food and medicine for drought-stricken regions of East Africa. Different emotions were touched by rap rhythmic talk, which became a source of identity but was also accused in its early years of demeaning women and spreading hate. There were arguments that some recordings should be labeled "dangerous," like cigarettes.

Phonographs with coin box attachments, invented in 1890, foreshadowed the jukebox. Gaudy, neon-lit jukeboxes made by Wurlitzer and other manufacturers later were featured attractions in bars and restaurants. A nickel offered a popular song from a menu of up to several dozen choices. The patron watched as a mechanical arm plucked the desired record from its berth, then returned it at the end of play. Still later, smaller versions were installed at tables and along the bar. Patrons danced to the music, listened or talked over it, but seldom were able to ignore it totally.

The Wurlitzer Jukebox Music recorded electrically went on sale in 1925 during the "flapper" era.

It was the start of high fidelity and of public interest in the technology of "hi-fi." Engineers improved every audio element between the microphone and the speaker. They replaced mechanical systems with electronics and added pre-amps and amplifiers. Vacuum tubes would remain in wide use until transistors replaced them after World War II. Bell Labs created stereophonic sound. The public was introduced to "stereo" in Walt Disney's animation film *Fantasia*. First adopters could now listen to music of concert hall quality in their living rooms.[9]

Another example of recorded music was actually intended to be ignored by the conscious mind while it worked to soothe the mood of shoppers. The Muzak company hired arrangers who reworked passages of popular tunes to create melodies that were heard as background music, a pastel environment meant to relax shoppers. Critics derided Muzak and called it "elevator music," but its omnipresence indicated that it did its job. There were even reports of its success in the farmer's barn to soothe cows and chickens as a means of producing more milk and eggs.

Audiotape

In an 1888 experiment, Oberlin Smith noted that iron filings on a piece of paper rearranged themselves into arcs when a magnet was passed under them. He theorized that permanent magnetic impulses could record sound. Danish inventor Valdemar Poulsen proved it in an experiment with steel wire wound on a drum. Poulsen demonstrated his "Telegraphone" in 1900, expecting that it could become a telephone answering machine or a music recorder and playback device. However, he lacked the funding to accomplish this. Success came to another inventor in 1928 in Germany, when Fritz Pfleumer built a prototype of a tape recorder, and the I.G. Farben chemical firm began its long history of manufacturing audiotape.

Magnetophon audiotape recorders that delivered better sound quality than phonograph records were one of the best-kept German secrets of World War II. Allied shortwave listeners who heard music with excellent fidelity from the Berlin Philharmonic in the middle of the night finally realized that the Germans had moved far ahead in sound recording.[10] The Allies had nothing better than steel bands and steel wire as magnetic recording media. American radio journalists using portable wire recorders not only had to endure poor audio quality, but a break in the taut hair-thin steel wire could cause a snarl worse than a fishing line tangle.

As World War II ground to an end, U.S. Army Signal Corps engineer John Mullin discovered audiotape recorder/players at a German radio station. "Liberating" two of them, he brought them to the United States. Mullin was hired by singer Bing Crosby, who did not like live

Valdemar Poulsen's Telegraphone

broadcasts, to tape his radio shows for later playback. Mullin would in a few years help to invent videotape.[11]

Radio news changed in fundamental ways because listeners could hear interviews and ambient sound, everything from artillery to crying babies. Reporters could edit tape with a snip of the scissors and a bit of adhesive tape. The superior sound of audiotape also replaced phonograph turntables, first in radio studios, then in the home. The early tape players were reel-to-reel. These gave way to the endless loop cartridge player, first four-channel, later eight-channel. They in turn were replaced by the simpler cassette, introduced in 1963.

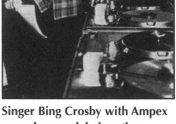

Singer Bing Crosby with Ampex recorders modeled on the German Magnetophon, 1948
Courtesy: Ampex Corporation

New Ways to Listen

The Sony Walkman, the personal audio cassette player with earphones introduced in 1979, was the first of an enormously popular line of listening devices that changed how people listened to music. For the first time people could take their favorite music, a part of their environment, with them. The Walkman line was expanded to include radio, compact discs and even television. The unpleasant news that earphones from the Walkman to the iPod could lead to hearing loss did not seem to deter sales. The portable cocooning that earphones offered, a bubble of privacy amid the urban hubbub, trumped hearing worries.

Videotape

Videotape has yielded to digital recording and storage, so it is easy to forget its impact. The explosive growth of television in the 1950s sharpened a demand for recorded programs. In 1951, seeking an electronic solution, engineers at Bing Crosby Enterprises demonstrated a black-and-white videotape recorder that used one-inch tape running at 100 inches a second. Crosby was driven not only by its business possibilities, but by his wish to play golf without being tied down to live performances. Two years later, RCA engineers fabricated their own recorder, which turned out not only black-and-white, but color pictures. However, this tape ran past the heads at 360 inches a second, which is more than twenty miles per hour. It was just not possible to produce a stable picture at such a high tape speed.

In 1956 a California firm, Ampex, built a machine on a different principle. Instead of sending the tape racing past a stationary recording head, its engineers spun the recording head. The quality was a tremendous improvement over fuzzy kinescope images. Engineers who saw the first demonstration actually jumped to their feet to applaud. Programs could now be recorded for playback at any time. Stations on the West Coast could delay live East Coast network news and entertainment broadcasts to be aired during evening prime time, when most viewers were home after work and had eaten dinner. A few years later, sports fans could watch instant replay. By 1958, video was broadcast in color. One of the engineers on the tape project, Ray M. Dolby, began work on audiotape just after he left high school and later grew famous for his tape noise reduction process.

When VTR went portable, news film cameras became obsolescent. Videotape was reusable and was more suited to the television medium than film. Videotape needed no developing time. Photographers used portable machines in the field to cover news stories that were microwaved back to the station. As the technology improved further, television news editors stopped cutting tape with razor blades and began editing electronically marking the start of ENG—electronic news gathering. For the audience, this meant more pictures at the scene of news events, more coverage of late breaking news and live reports combining commentary by a reporter at the scene with videotape of earlier activities.

With broadcasting, educational, and industrial markets in hand, Japanese video companies turned their attention to the vast home market. Sony president Akio Morita asked, "People do not have to read a book when it's delivered. Why should they have to see a TV program when it's delivered?"[18] Sony introduced its half-inch Betamax machine in 1975. A year later, rival Japanese companies led by JVC brought out VHS (Video Home System) machines, a format incompatible with Betamax. Sony lost the competition as VHS gradually captured the home market.

After DVD players pushed them aside, it was easy to forget that videocassette recorders had been the fastest-selling domestic appliance in history. DVD players would sell even faster. A *Wall Street Journal* poll reported, not surprisingly, that people most desired those inventions that gave them convenience and control.[12]

number of audiophiles who wanted to be early adopters sharply increased, spurred by clever marketing.

Not every innovation was snapped up. Quadraphonic sound systems and recordings did not catch on. The compact disc (CD) player, introduced in 1982, was not an immediate hit because of competing, non-compatible formats. Other formats popular in the 1990s included the digital compact cassette (DCC) and the MiniDisc (MD), but they were not compatible with anything else or with each other.[13] Ultimately the CD won out over other technologies. Its optical pickup head did not make physical contact with the disc, a huge advantage, but it suffered the disadvantage that the home user at first was not able to record.

Digital audiotape (DAT) and tapeless recording angered and frightened the music industry because they could copy music without any degradation of audio quality. In a precursor to the Napster court battles, music industry spokesmen lobbied for federal legislation to force Japanese manufacturers of DAT players to modify these machines to prevent illegal copying. To no one's surprise, the manufacturers resisted. The ability to copy was, after all, one reason why people bought such machines.

At the end of the 20th century, the MP3 software format for compressing and transmitting files was welcomed because of the ease of downloading music from the internet. The music-downloading Napster was born, but soon silenced by court order because of its advocacy of illegal downloads. It was reborn selling downloads legally. In 2001, Apple's iPod MP3 player, which legally downloaded songs for 99 cents each from its iTunes online music store, was immediately and extraordinarily successful. It met the desire for choice, advertised as putting "1,000 songs in your pocket." By 2010 it had sold more than 300 million music downloads. Meanwhile, the video iPod was being used to view movies and television programs downloaded on computer hard drives, then easily transferred. It was one more process to worry entertainment moguls.

At the same time, owners of CD collections were transferring them to iPods. In less than a lifetime, the technology had gone from standard 78s to LPs and 45s to reel tape to cartridges to cassettes to CDs to digital storage. Where the original Walkman tape player was based on an analog audio format, the iPod was a digital player that could hold several thousand songs. The shuffle feature of random play added to the pleasure of iPod listeners. Attics groaned with the weight of still shiny but already outdated audio devices and recordings.

While music has been the dominant product of these digital audio technologies for the home market. The public also bought audiotapes and compact discs of spoken content. Audio renditions of novels were sold at bookstores, grocery stores, gas stations and stop-and-shops. The growing popularity of audio books met the public's wish for listening choices beyond music. The visually impaired have also been appreciative users. For many people, audio books provided an opportunity to listen to a self-help book, a good novel, or a language lesson during a long, humdrum daily commute. They made being stuck in traffic an educational opportunity.

Boombox and Walkman

Music stored on a medium that traveled became more than personal entertainment. It developed into both an irritant that reached into the private space of others and a shield that blocked the outside world from intruding into the user's own private space. Both were uses that their inventors had not considered. Walkman and boombox owners may have been trying to control some acoustical space, but they have affected human interaction in two important yet contradictory ways. First, music pouring out of car radios and hand-carried boombox players at volumes louder than needed for hearing is an expansion of personal space, a challenge to anyone in the listening vicinity. At the same time it is an invitation for a friendly response from those who share those musical tastes. In short, recorded music is a social instrument, even a weapon and the boombox owner may be making a statement.[14]

A portable music source, the boombox.

Courtesy: Ron Thompson Sr.

The opposite effect surrounds an iPod unheard by anyone but the earphoned listener who tunes out the surrounding sound environment. It helps to make an unbearable job bearable and a monotonous job less so. And like so many other means of mediated communication, the incoming sound tunes out silence and the thoughts that inevitably accompany silence.

Akio Morita and Masaru Ibuka attached headphones to a small audiotape recorder to create the Walkman in 1979.

Sony founder Akio Morita originally thought the Walkman would offer a way to share music, a mistake he later admitted. "I originally thought it would be considered rude for one person to be listening to his music in isolation... We found that everybody seemed to want his or her own." Media writer Steven Levy added, "The Walkman was not about sharing, it was about not sharing. It was a *me* machine, an object of empowerment and liberation."[15] The now familiar vacant stare into mid-space continues as people listen on MP3 players, iPods and iPhones as they walk, run or ride a bicycle. Add drivers with cell phones and you have a community of isolated people occasionally bumping with consequences. A Washington *Post* critic wrote about "the look and sound of the Walkman dead: the head cocked at a slight angle, the mouth gently lolling. The eyes flicker with consciousness with consciousness but they don't see. They're somewhere else." Author Richard S. Hollander added, "Look at the faces. They are blank. With earphones on, the individual closes out all outside stimuli. He is his own captive audience."[16]

Downloading

If music delivered by an MP3 player with earphones isolates the listener, shared music does the opposite, at least at a distance through communication media. Exalted status comes from cool music libraries.[17] Some owners of music collections offered them at no cost to their friends or to anyone who wanted to be a friend. Why not?, they argued. They had bought the music. Why not share it with everyone everywhere? The distinction between inviting a friend to their home to listen to a song and sending the song to strangers via download was no big deal, they argued. Having come into their possession, the music and videos were theirs to do with as they wished. Their opinion, not shared by the courts, was reminiscent of the argument that cable signals that crossed your yard should be free for the taking.

Legal action proved difficult because the global nature of communication limits governments from taking prompt action across frontiers, further evidence of a weakening of nation-states in confrontation with a global community hooked on media, no matter how transitory that community may be. After Napster began downloading on a massive scale, Time Warner CEO Richard Parsons protested, "This isn't about a bunch of kids stealing music. It's about an assault on everything that constitutes the cultural expression of our society. Worst case scenario: The country will end up in sort of a cultural Dark Ages."[18]

The courts put a stop to Napster's free sharing but the desire to use downloading technology to acquire music remained. Along came iTunes offering songs for 99 cents. Rdio, MOG, Earbits, Rhapsody and other services followed with downloads and streaming available free or by subscription depending on the level of service. In 2011 Spotify combined with Facebook to make music sharing a mediated communication social event. Of course, music has been a social event for all the centuries since humankind first began humming.

With Spotify Facebook "friends" can acquire their friends' playlists and listen to what their friends are hearing halfway around the world. If the friend lives down the block it is not necessary to get together to share an evening of music listening. Like the telephone, we can reach out without touching. And we can listen on the go with Smartphones as well as computers.

Timeline

1821: In England, Charles Wheatstone reproduces sound.

In France, Léon Scott's phonautograph is a forerunner of Edison's phonograph.

1869: John Hyatt's celluloid, the first plastic, will lead to phonograph records, telephones.

1877: In France, Charles Cros invents the phonograph. Doesn't matter.

In America, Edison invents the phonograph. Adds to his fame.

1886: Sapphire stylus improves recorded sound.

1887: Emile Berliner's flat "gramophone" disk.

1888: Edison's cylinder phonograph is manufactured for the general public.

Engineer Oberlin Smith conceives of magnetic recording, does not build unit.

1889: Coin-operated phonographs are placed in bars, arcades, the first jukeboxes.

1895: Artist Francis Barraud paints *His Late Master's Voice*, with Nipper listening.

1898: Magnetic sound is recorded on a wire by Valdemar Poulsen of Denmark.

1900: Eldridge Johnson produces double-sided phonograph records.

1905: Phonograph records may be 6 2/3", 7", 8", 10", 11" 12", 13 3 /4", or 14" wide.

1906: The phonograph is housed in a wooden cabinet, like furniture: the Victrola.

1907: Lee De Forest broadcasts music from phonograph records.

1913: *Billboard* magazine publishes its first list of most popular songs.

1919: Americans spend more on records than on books, musical instruments.

1922: Muzak, developed by George Squier.

1925: Music recorded electrically starts high-fidelity popularity.

1928: In Germany, Fritz Pfleumer creates audiotape: magnetic powder on paper, film.

1935: Martin Block's *Make Believe Ballroom* introduces disk jockeys.

1939: The wire recorder is invented in the U.S.

1945: Capt. John Mullin "liberates" two German tape recorders; starts U.S. industry.

1948: LP ("long playing") record: 25 minutes per side; replaces 4-minute records.

1949: RCA challenges the LP record with the one-song 45 rpm record.

1951: Disk jockey Alan Freed introduces the term *rock 'n' roll*.

Videotape experiments supported by Bing Crosby.

1956: Ampex invents a breakthrough videotape machine for networks, TV stations.

1958: Color videotape.

1959: The Grammy Awards, starting with the music of 1958, are presented.

1963: Phillips of Holland invents audiocassettes; from Sony: home videotape recorders

1979: The Sony Walkman tape player, a new way to listen.

1980: Sony introduces the consumer camcorder.

1983: CDs (compact discs, not certificates of deposit) go on sale.

1984: CD-ROM disk holds equivalent of 270,000 typewritten pages.

1986: International standards are set for audio, video, digital recording.

1991: VCRs are the fastest selling domestic appliance ever; 4 billion tape rentals.

1997: DVD players and DVD movies are on the fast track to success.

1999: Napster is created to allow free music downloading.

2001: The iPod holds 1,000 tunes, but fits into a shirt pocket.

Court ruling ends Napster's free sharing.

2011: Facebook and Spotify make music downloading a social networking tool.

7. Photography

Personal and So Much More

Not many centuries ago some of our ancestors believed they lived on a flat Earth patrolled at its edges by dragons and gryphons. If they wanted to know about the world, they could see graphic representations in a church where stained glass windows told Biblical stories in pictures. Then came photography. By the mid-19th century ordinary people could see with their own eyes who or what actually lived beyond the horizon. Photography made the world less strange and more interesting.

Photography was invented before the telephone and the phonograph. Each impressed itself upon us through one of our five senses. Each has had effects beyond calculating. Yet more than education or entertainment or political calls to action, the greatest effects of photography are personal. Our individual actions attest to the emotional impact of photographs. We put snapshots on our walls and display them on our furniture. They preserve the memories of what matters to us, capturing time and affirming our personal past. Fleeing a burning house, we may leave everything but a photo album that tells the family story. Our wallets hold the thumb worn images of loved ones. Our computers may hold them by the hundreds. We treasure photographs of distant relatives we never met and search their faces for connections.

Significant occasions in life seem to need a camera to record them. A wedding is incomplete without photographs; a memorial service means more with old photographs on display. Today, by the push of a few buttons of her camera phone, a young mother takes pictures of her children and transmits them instantly to her soldier husband on the other side of the world.

Many Effects

Yet we know that photography has impacted our lives in so many other ways. The Holocaust photos told the world "never again," even though too much of the world has learned to forget and find excuses. The eyes of starving African children with flies hovering at their faces launched cargo planes filled with medicines, blankets, food and doctors. The pained eyes of brutalized women in Somalia, Rwanda, Bosnia, Congo and Darfur have shaken the world. Degrading photos of Abu Ghraib prisoners have outraged a nation that prided itself as being above such acts.

The noted photographer Gordon Parks said such pictures change those who see them: "One should not grow tired of witnessing these things—corpses stacked, awaiting the fire of a Holocaust oven; two young black lynch victims, dead before a cheerful white mob; a Viet Cong guerrilla, his eyes tightly shut, grimacing as a policeman fires a bullet into his head—for that is the photographer's charge to us, that we never forget... The cameras keep watch as mankind goes on filling the universe with its behavior, and they change us."[1]

There is much, much more. The eyes of baby harp seals just before the fur hunter's club crashed down led to a limit on the slaughter, just one of many examples of how photographs of animals being killed or abused has generated anger, humiliation and change.

Hubble Telescope

Photography has served every branch of science from electron microscope photos of the invisible world around and within us to the Mars pictures taken by the Spirit and Opportunity rovers and the Hubble Telescope's probes for the origin of the universe. What is there that has not been captured through a lens? Photography today is a tool of every occupation, every kind of business, every hobby. As a tool of medicine, photography has helped to improve our health. As a tool of journalists, photography has generated both pride and feelings of humiliation.

Documentary and travel photography have enriched our culture and our awareness of other cultures. Through pictures posted on internet sites like YouTube and Facebook, the digital age has enhanced our awareness of ourselves and the people around us. Photography is, in short, an essential part of our lives.

Ancient Roots

Still photography is less than two centuries old and motion photography a little more than a century old, but the technology has ancient roots. Imagine a sunny street in an old city, a house with a dark room and a tiny hole in the wall facing the street. If you sit inside the room and look at the wall opposite the hole, you might see an image of people walking by upside down. Because the world is full of dark rooms with holes in the walls, this phenomenon has been known for centuries. Aristotle mentioned it in the 4th century BCE. The Arab scholar Alhazen described it at some length in the 11th century. Later, so did Leonardo da Vinci.

During the 16th century in Italy a room called a *camera obscura* that reflected images aided drafting and painting. The term comes from the Latin "camera" ("room") and "obscura" ("dark"). To sharpen the image, artists placed a lens over the pinhole. To preserve the image, they traced it onto a sheet of paper. By the 17th century portable rooms were built, usually a kind of tent. When the users realized that they did not actually have to stand inside the room to capture their

A 1544 engraving of the early *camera obscura* as a "dark room."

The *camera lucida*

image, the *camera obscura* shrank to a box carried under the arm, a herald of our own cameras.[2] Each had a peephole, a lens and sometimes a mirror, plus a pane of glass on which a thin sheet of paper could rest for tracing an image. An even smaller portable device, the *camera lucida*, invented in 1807, consisted of a glass prism suspended by a brass rod over a piece of paper. Looking through the prism, the artist traced an image. No other way existed to save an exact image, but photography was only a few years off.

Chemical discoveries in the 18th century provided the way. For thousands of years it has been known that colors change outdoors, such as colored cloth that fades in the sunshine. It was also known that certain salts of silver darken in the open air, although it was not known if this was due to the air itself or the heat of the sun. In 1727 German scientist Johann Schulze observed that a bottle filled with a silver compound turned violet black on the side that was accidentally exposed to sunshine. Experiments confirmed that *light* was responsible.

Thomas Wedgewood, of the family famed for fine china, produced photographic contact prints by placing a tree leaf against chemically treated paper which he then exposed to light. In order to show his photographs to visitors, he had to display them for moments by dim candlelight before they blackened.

Niépce and Daguerre

In 1827, precisely one century after Schulze's publication of his discovery and following a decade of experimentation, French inventor Joseph Niépce used a *camera obscura* to produce what until recently was considered the world's first true photograph, an image of the courtyard outside his window. In 2002, the French National Library paid about $500,000 for a photograph believed taken a year earlier than Niépce's courtyard view, a photo of a Dutch engraving showing a man leading a horse. The photographer is unknown.

Niépce became partners with Louis Daguerre, a painter and theatrical producer, who was also trying to capture a camera image. After Niépce's death, Daguerre improved the process. In 1837 he produced a photograph of surprising quality on a copper plate coated with silver and exposed

A street in Paris photographed (circa 1838) by Daguerre.

to iodine fumes. Daguerre named his result a daguerreotype. The exposed plate was the final picture; there was no negative.

In 1839 Daguerre delivered a significant paper to France's Royal Society describing his process. It remains a mystery why a century elapsed between Schulze's discovery and the breakthrough experiments of Niépce and Daguerre.[3]

While Daguerre was experimenting in France, amateur English scientist William Fox Talbot, frustrated by the difficulties of drawing with the *camera lucida*, achieved some success in taking contact photographs by laying such objects as a leaf, a feather and a piece of lace directly on sheets of translucent paper that had been treated with silver chloride. This method created a negative image, the dark and light areas reversed. The translucent paper allowed Fox Talbot to make any number of contact positives, something that Daguerre could not do.

The problem of the darkening image was solved in 1839 with sodium thiosulfate (still used today as a photo fixative, commonly called "hypo") followed by washing with water. Its discoverer, Sir John Herschel, an English scientist and a friend of Fox Talbot, also suggested the terms "photography" to replace Fox Talbot's phrase "photogenic drawing," and "positive" and "negative" to replace the terms "reversed copy" and "re–reversed copy."

Fox Talbot was soon taking pictures of buildings, rooftops and chimneys. His choice of subject was dictated by their immobility and the need for a great deal of light. Only after years of chemical and optical improvements in photography was Fox Talbot able to take pictures of people, whom he posed stiffly with instructions not to move during the long exposure time his pictures required.

Both Daguerre, the French artist, and Fox Talbot, the wealthy English botanist, had been working independently and unaware of each other, yet they were producing similar pictures with similar chemicals and equipment. While Daguerre's results were far superior, Fox Talbot could make multiple copies of images.

Hobby and Business

Photography as a hobby spread across Europe and into North America as the technology improved. The daguerreotype process received an enthusiastic welcome in the United States even though the nation was entering an economic depression just as photography was being introduced in Paris in 1839.

Connecting two cameras and displaying the results side by side, the 19th century viewer saw stills in three dimensions. Stereography was first described by Charles Wheatstone, the British physicist who is also credited with devising the first working telegraph.

Smaller cameras reduced the size of photographic plates, reducing the time that a subject would have to sit without moving. With the aid of a portrait lens the time needed to pose dropped to a manageable fifteen to thirty seconds. One reason subjects in early photos look grim is that it was hard to freeze a smile for so long, resulting in the stiff expressions on the faces staring at us in old photographs. Yet the subjects eagerly posed, sometimes aided by iron supporting stands that stiffened the spine and held the head in place.

Photographs were taken not only outdoors in the sunlight but also in the new portrait studios by photographers known as daguerreotypists. Their brisk trade took business away from portrait painters such as the artist Samuel Morse, who was one of the earliest American experimenters in daguerreotype photography before he became famous for a different means of communication.

By the 1850s in the United States the cost of a photograph had dropped enough to make them available to most Americans. Miniature portrait paintings were available only to the wealthy, but miniature photographs were affordable to middle class families by the mid-19th century.

Family pictures became popular, especially pictures of children, partly because of the high mortality rate. Many children died in infancy or while barely toddlers. Epidemics were common. Photographers in the mid-19th century advertised their readiness to take pictures of the dead in their coffins or, for a child, in a mother's lap. They appear to be sleeping. One advertising line for postmortem photographs based on an old saying was: "Secure the shadow 'ere the substance fade." A photograph of the deceased would also be mounted in a headstone. Such images were called "memento mori" (reminder of mortality).

Wet-Plate Photography

Until the mid 1880s the two known methods of taking photographs had severe limitations. *Daguerreotypes* were one-of-a-kind positives, usually on copper plates. They were fragile and had to be kept under glass. They were expensive, hard to copy and required a number of chemicals, including the dangerous mercury. The term "mad as a hatter," familiar to readers of *Alice in Wonderland*, could have been matched with "mad as a photographer," because mercury fumes used by both hat makers and photographers affected the brain. The daguerreotype produced a sharper image and was better

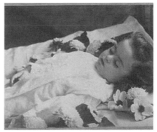

Post-mortem photo of child.

suited to portraiture than the *calotype*, which was Fox Talbot's improvement on his original grainy and blotchy paper prints. Unfortunately, the calotype prints faded in the light over time. Daguerreotypes, which produced positive prints, could be used as the source for engraving.

In 1851, Frederick Archer introduced wet-plate photography. Within a decade, daguerreotype and calotype methods were obsolete. Wet-plate provided greater sensitivity and a shorter exposure time and made multiple prints possible from one glass plate, although the process was complicated and untidy. Because photographs had to be developed immediately or the emulsion would dry, chemicals had to be applied in fairly rapid succession in darkness.

Using the wet-plate method, a photographer on the road brought along a darkroom. For a negative, a glass plate was coated with collodion, a clear, thick, sticky liquid that was also used as a surgical dressing. A layer of light sensitive silver iodide was applied before the plate was inserted into the camera. After exposure, the still wet glass plate was developed, fixed and washed on the spot before the negatives could be printed on paper. Photographers needed wagons to haul around hundreds of pounds of bottled chemicals, plus the glass plates, dishes, measures, funnels and a water pail, to say nothing of the heavy camera, lenses and tripod.[4]

One version of wet-plate photography was the ambrotype, offered by photo studios. Ambrotypes lacked the brilliance of daguerreotypes but they were cheap, easy to produce and, best of all, would be prepared while you wait. Tintypes printed on iron sheets instead of paper were sturdy enough to be mailed or carried in a shirt pocket, yet thin enough to cut with scissors to fit a brooch or locket. During the Civil War, soldiers mailed them to the families they left behind and received tintypes in return of mothers, brothers, sisters, wives and children. (Tintypes were shown in the film *Cold Mountain*.) Besides the familiar stiff portraits, photographers also took pictures of groups in a variety of activities and settings. Many survive today.

Capturing the World

The Western public had read and talked of the pyramids or of how different Asians must appear in their strange clothing. Now, realizing that they had in their hands a new way to record life, travelers using the new wet-plate system could hardly wait to haul their heavy cameras and darkroom equipment to distant corners of the world. When they returned home their photographs were projected on a screen or wall as lantern-slide shows, a popular form of entertainment.

In 1854, an album of photographs of ancient Egyptian monuments was published. Actual prints of photos were sewn into books,. For the first time people could not only see but even own such images. However, the *printing* of photos on regular book pages along with text would have to wait until the art of *photoengraving* advanced sufficiently toward the end of the 19th century. After that, newspapers and magazines blossomed with photographs.

Artist Roger Fenton traveled in 1855 with fellow Englishman James Robertson and a darkroom

Crimean War and American Civil War photographers traveled to battlefields in wagons filled with the chemicals they needed for their the wet-plate technology.

in a covered wagon to the Crimean War. What Fenton saw appalled him, but he took no pictures of the horrors of war. In part because he had been commissioned to shoot only portraits of officers and scenes of the Crimea and because he was suffering from cholera and several broken ribs as a result of an accident, Fenton spent little film on the misery of war. His task was made more difficult because collodion was a tricky chemical in the Crimea's summer heat.

Felice Beato, an Italian, and Robertson recorded the aftermath of an uprising against the British in India. For the first time in history people safe at home saw a little of what went on in a war. Beato also went to China to take pictures of the Opium Wars, then on to fascinating Japan, newly opened to the outside world.

Civil War Photos and More

The public would soon see the aftermath of American Civil War battles. A well-known New York portrait photographer, Mathew Brady, hired other photographers to join him at some risk. They traveled to the battlefields with their clumsy, clattering wet-plate wagons. Before the Civil War ended, hundreds of photographers had followed Brady's lead to record the scars of battle. They took more than seven thousand pictures of battlefields, encampments, soldiers living and dead, officers and men, weapons and equipment. They revealed war stripped of glory—a brutal, wearying misery. Brady himself nearly died at Bull Run. When Brady displayed photos at a New York gallery of the dead of Antietam, the *New York Times* commented: *If he has not brought bodies and laid them in our dooryards and among our streets, he has done something very like it.*

Photography as an aid to science and medicine began. Studying pictures of how people walk, a physician designed artificial legs for maimed soldiers.

After the war, photographers headed West to continue what, in a few years, had evolved into a tradition of visual documentary. Piling 300 to 400 pounds of wet-plate equipment and chemicals on the backs of mules, they left to posterity a permanent record of the Native Americans, of great vistas without a trace of human habitation, of the coming of the railroads, of the miners, the settlers and the cowboys. William Henry Jackson's photographs helped in the political effort to establish Yellowstone as the first national park. This may have been the first time in the United States that photography influenced political change. It would not be the last.

Photography already had some influence in England. Photographers traveling to distant countries captured images of ordinary life to give visual support to what later would be called *ethnography*.

The English traveler John Thomson recorded the life of the people he encountered in Asia. On returning to London he published a four-volume illustrated anthropological study. While in London he continued his documentation by photographing the daily life of the London poor, publishing the results along with written text in 1877 as *Victorian London Street Life*. In doing so, Thomson opened a new door for photography: social documentary. To a comfortable Londoner, scenes of poverty in far-off China were a quaint curiosity. Displaying poverty at one's doorstep was something else again, especially if you were in a position to do something about it. Thomson usually photographed reasonably pleasant views in working class neighborhoods, but not always. One subject for criticism was the failure to deal with annual floods that made life so miserable.[5] Eventually an embankment was built to prevent the Thames from periodically spilling over into the slums of London.

The Muckrakers

Journalists recognized photography as a means not only to present information but to stir emotion. Jacob Riis, a Danish immigrant hired as a New York City police reporter, was determined to reveal the humanity of the poor that the better-off ignored. One of the first journalists to recognize that photographs could help to bring about social change, Riis used both words and pictures to expose conditions in the New York slums. He went about his personal mission even when he panicked a roomful of people sleeping or actually set fire to himself and to a house by using flash powder, a recent invention that for the first time enabled photography in darkness. (The flashbulb would not be invented until 1925.)

Riis' books, *How the Other Half Lives* and *Children of the Poor*, became an important part of *muckraking*, dredging up awful conditions for the public gaze. Theodore Roosevelt coined the term "muckrakers," an insult that the objects of his derision wore as a badge of pride. The polite term today is "investigative journalist."

Sociologist Lewis Hine recorded the miserable lives of many immigrants who were pouring out of Europe into Ellis Island. From there they often went to fetid homes and sweatshops where they eked out a threadbare existence. Hine followed with camera and notebook. In 1908 the National Child Labor Committee hired Hine as an investigator. He drew public attention to the plight of child workers. For the generations that followed, Hine built a searing record of documentary photography. "I wanted to show the things that had to be corrected," he said. He focused especially on children sent to work in food processing plants, factories and mines. He found them at every turn, but had to disguise his picture taking and fact gathering missions to avoid beatings, or worse. He sometimes pretended to be a fire inspector to avoid detection.

Hine showed his photos in public presentations as he carried his message about the need for child labor laws. He considered himself a social photographer. "Perhaps you are weary of child labor pictures," Hine wrote. "Well, so are the rest of us, but we propose to make you and the whole country so sick and tired of the whole business that when the time for action comes, child

Child Labor

Images of children working all day in a textile factory fueled public outrage and eventually helped to promote child labor laws and free compulsory education. This photo was taken in stealth by 19th century sociologist Lewis Hine, who frequently risked his life to document child labor.

labor pictures will be records of the past."[6] Publication of his photos in magazines, books, slide shows and traveling exhibits stirred efforts against heavy opposition to pass child labor laws that took children out of the mines and factories and into schools.[7]

During the Depression of the 1930s, the Resettlement Administration was created as part of the New Deal to help small farmers who were driven to bankruptcy because of years of drought in the central and southern states. Crop failures were all too common. Topsoil disappeared down rivers. To help argue its case, the RA turned to social documentary photography. Both still and motion pictures were used to show how bad the rural economy was and how government aid could make a difference. Dorothea Lange, Walker Evans, Carl Mydans, Horace Bristol and Ben Shahn were among those whose photographs have endured through the decades.

From the wellspring of feeling for the downtrodden and anger at social injustice sprang the social documentary motion picture. This was especially so in Great Britain and the United States. The tradition continues today and has spread internationally in both still and motion pictures. We are now accustomed to seeing images of misery on the streets of Baghdad, in the desert of Darfur in the Sudan and in other pain-racked corners of the world.

Photoengraving

Some documentary photographs found their way into photo magazines. The most outstanding, *Life*, was first published in 1936. But the picture press itself had started much earlier. In fact, it is just about as old as photography itself. The weekly *Illustrated London News* began to publish in 1842 with engravings, usually carved from daguerreotype photographs or artists' sketches into wooden blocks.

At first, engravers laid tissue paper over a photograph to trace the image, which they transferred to a wooden block. Just before the Civil War, the engravers learned how to coat the surface of a wood block with light-sensitive silver nitrate. Placed in a camera pointed at a photograph, the wood block captured an image good enough to guide the engraver's knife.

Actual publication of photographs would not be possible without a technology that could convert an ordinary photograph into a picture that could hold ink and be printed on the same page as type. The first printed newspaper photograph was of New York's Steinway Hall in 1873, but the first fully captured image was of a New York slum, "A Scene in Shanty-Town." It appeared in the *New York Daily Graphic* in 1880. *Photoengraving* started in England, but results were poor until 1881, when Frederick Ives at Cornell University created a *halftone* process that broke a photograph into tiny dots that could pick up ink, giving the appearance of a continuous tone from light to dark. The *halftone* set pictures next to words, leading to one of the great advances in the history of mediated communication: *photojournalism.*

Although they could be seen in the pages of weekly journals and magazines, photographs would not become common in newspapers until the quality of newsprint—the paper itself—improved toward the end of the 19th century, when photographs on the printed page were commonplace.

More Technical Improvements

Based on 19th century inventions, *offset lithography* became the basis of most photo publication in the 20th century. In the 21st century, the process of putting photos in newspapers has become entirely digital as it moves from the photographer's camera to a page plate containing photographs and printed matter is mounted on a press.

From the beginning photographers felt frustrated by the time it took to expose a picture. Because the early cameras lacked shutters, the photographer simply took the lens cap off for several seconds to expose the plate. As film improved, inventors formulated ideas for exposing the film for shorter and shorter time periods. Demand for stop-action pictures pushed the

Photos in Newspapers

"A Scene in Shanty-Town," the first fully realized halftone photograph printed in a newspaper, the New York Daily Graphic, March 4, 1880. The original was photographed through a fine mesh of cross-hatched lines. Thanks to halftone, photos could appear in newspapers and magazines more quickly and more realistically than was possible by the engraving method.

inventors of optical and mechanical equipment and photochemistry to bring new products to the marketplace. By the end of the 19th century, focal plane shutters, located between the lens and the film, could limit exposures to 1/1000th of a second.

The wet-plate process gave way to a gelatin silver bromide dry-plate process that provided even greater sensitivity and shorter exposure. It also freed the photographer from carrying a darkroom wherever he went. Yet as long as glass plates served as the recording medium base, cameras would remain bulky. Glass plates, limited by weight and fragility, required special chemicals and special handling.

These difficulties led to a search for a substitute material, something lightweight but flexible enough to be rolled around a spool, yet tough, transparent and impervious to photographic chemicals. Inventors turned to nitrocellulose, the source of collodion, an important chemical in glass plate photography. Simply put, they threw away the glass and kept a version of the sticky stuff that stuck to the glass. At first, flexible film on a roll holder was fitted to the back of a folding-bellows camera. Later, cameras small enough to hold in the hand plus fast shutters removed the requirement of a tripod.

During the 19th century it was common to color prints with paint. Retouching by hand was a common feature of studio work. Delicate daguerreotypes needed special care by colorists. By the turn of the 20th century, color film and color filters had become the basis of attractive color photographs.

Photography also became art. Alfred Stieglitz and Edward Steichen built reputations rivaling painters who used brush and palette. Henri Cartier-Bresson, Ansel Adams and Edward Weston followed them. Stieglitz led a movement devoted to the idea of photographic art as a means of personal expression. He pioneered the one-man show for photographers and founded *Camera Work*, a magazine for fine photographic art.

Taking Your Own Pictures

Having your picture taken is not the same as having your own camera. Changing technology and lower costs have consistently enabled people all over the world to own cameras and participate in the making and acquiring of photographs of better and better quality. In the 20th century some fifty different camera models were manufactured.

A self-taught inventor in upstate New York, George Eastman was instrumental in making photography affordable and simple. Determined to make the camera "as convenient as the pencil," Eastman in 1888 introduced the Kodak with roll film, a fixed focus, fixed aperture and one speed. It reduced the somewhat complex process of taking a picture to the three steps of pulling a cord, turning a key and pressing a button. The first Kodak was a wooden box encased in leather; it sold for twenty–five dollars.

Once they snapped their photos, owners returned the camera to the company, where the film

The Kodak Box Camera

was unloaded, processed by transferring negatives to glass plates for printing and returned to the owner with paper prints and a fresh roll installed. Eastman's slogan was, "You Press the Button, We Do the Rest." His ten-dollar charge for this service wasn't cheap, but if you could afford the hobby of photography it was certainly convenient.

Almost overnight, just about anyone who could afford to wanted to take pictures. The photographer did not need to understand chemistry when, for the first time, if you could press a button you could take a picture. As prices came down, millions of people soon carried cameras to outings and events. Camera clubs sprouted up everywhere. Eastman said his cameras brought photography "within the reach of every human being who desires to preserve a record of what he sees."

When Eastman's Brownie camera in 1900 sold for a dollar with a six–exposure roll of film that cost fifteen cents, photography was truly available for "the man in the street." Eastman had designed the Brownie for children, but adults used it, too. Eastman's slogan was, "Plant the Brownie acorn and the Kodak oak will grow." He also sold a developing and printing kit for seventy–five cents. Pictures that could be taken so easily came to be known by the same term as that used for firing a gun at a fast moving target: a snapshot.

Postwar Years

The years following the end of World War II saw Americans flush with cash, soldiers returning to civilian life and ready to buy homes, cars, television sets, appliances and whatever else they could afford. Into this happy situation came new models of the 35 mm camera from Germany and Japan. The 35 mm camera was just the thing to take along on that long delayed vacation. Some models were single-lens reflex. Some had rangefinders. The German Leica and Rolliflex returned to the American marketplace along with Japanese newcomers such as Nikon, Canon, Minolta, Ricoh and Pentax.

In 1947, Edwin Land's Polaroid camera process allowed film development and printing inside the camera. The back of the camera carried separate negative and positive film rolls. The act of tugging the film out of the camera pulled it between two rollers that broke small pods of developing fluid, spreading them evenly across the film surface. One minute later the positive print was ready to peel away. This "instant print" process was available in color by 1963. It combined the negative and positive materials in a single unit, thanks to fourteen separate coatings.

Canadian military photographer with an Anniversary Speed Graphic, 1944

Canada. Dept. of National Defence / Library and Archives Canada

Obtaining quality pictures required training, practice and skill. But help for everyone came from Japan with the point-and-shoot, automatic everything camera with coated lenses and synchronized internal flash. The focus adjusted instantly to whatever stood in front of the lens. Like so many inventions, the camera itself grew more complicated in order to make its operation simpler. Cameras now are crammed with microcircuitry and intricate mechanical and optical parts, yet the instrument responds to the press of a button by a child. Eastman's old advertising slogan, "You Press the Button, We Do the Rest," could hardly be truer for the automated single-lens reflex camera controlled by computer chips and infrared sensors.

The filmless camera arrived from Japan in 1981 with Sony's Mavica, but only as a prototype. It did not go into full production because of its poor images. Five years later another Japanese firm, Canon, marketed a better camera. The SVC (still-video camera) recorded images onto a small magnetic disk. Without chemical processing and after transmission over ordinary telephone lines or by satellite, stills were immediately available for viewing on television screens around the world. And it could be posted on websites when they came along.

One of the social effects of the digital revolution has been to enable average people to do what only professionals using expensive equipment were able to do in the past.[8] Great numbers of people—tens of millions—throughout the world express themselves through photographs. Call it "crowdsourcing." Facebook, YouTube, MySpace and Flickr display images that anybody clicks on, needing no particular skill. If you can be energized for a political cause by looking at videos, YouTube will provide them by the dozens, even by the hundreds. As *Time* put it, "People have had cameras for decades and Web access for years. It's the combination of two simple things—easy, cheap recording and easy, free distribution—that makes YouTube so potent and its impact so complex. It's not just a new medium; it's several in one... It's a Surveillance System... a spotlight...a microscope... a soapbox… This is just one sign of how much YouTube—and similar video-sharing sites—has changed the flow of information."[9]

Pictures That Lie

Truth and photography have been separated almost from the start. Manipulation dates back at least to the early 1860s, when the head of Abraham Lincoln was placed atop the body of Senator John C. Calhoun, the result placed on the original five-dollar bill.[10] Photographs became an instrument

A composograph of the 1925 marriage annulment trial of Alice Rhinelander, a domestic servant who married a socialite. She stood accused of "passing" herself as white. Obviously the "photograph" is fabricated, but it sold newspapers.

of propaganda by the French government against the uprising of the Paris Commune in 1871 in opposition to the Franco-Prussian War. After soldiers killed an estimated 40,000 of the alleged Communards who supported the rebellion, photographers were summoned to take pictures of the dead in the streets and the revolutionaries who were executed. One photographer did not stop there. He produced fakes to display what seemed to be atrocities committed by the Communards.

The notion that pictures never lie had been suspect from the start. In the 1920s a few newspaper editors combined pictures into "composographs," which brought images of people from different photographs together in close proximity. Publishers justified using them because they sold newspapers. Such distortions also had political value. Enough voters were deceived during the McCarthy "Red Scare" era of the 1950s to defeat liberal Senator Millard Tydings in his bid for re-election after he was shown standing beside Communist leader Earl Browder, an event that never happened.

For decades newspapers routinely used darkroom techniques to alter photographs. After 1989, photos could be digitally manipulated on a home computer. Now the tampering could be almost impossible to detect. Digital imaging converted images into dots—pixels—that could be moved or removed, but retouching can lead to public embarrassment. Computer software for digital retouching shifted the pyramids at Giza for a *National Geographic* cover in 1982. That improved the framing, but chipped away at the magazine's reputation for authenticity. A *Newsweek* cover in 2005 placed Martha Stewart's head on a slimmer body to show that she had lost weight upon being released from prison.[11]

Off-the-Shelf Software

To enhance old photographs that had seen better days, customers came to the shops of experts who cleaned up the damaged areas with such software as Photoshop. Actually, it is no longer necessary to turn to the experts for much of this. With off-the-shelf software like Photoshop or Smart Erase, images can be altered or replaced by whatever color and pattern is in the background. Another feature allows the combining of images from more than one photograph into a seamless whole. Changes have included taking unidentified people out of a photograph, removing a divorced spouse from a family scene, adding missing relatives to a family reunion, bringing grandmother, mother and daughter together for a three-generation portrait, closing gaps in a photograph of relatives to make the scene cozier and eliminating braces from teeth before the orthodontist does.

During the 2004 election campaign a fake photograph circulated on the internet showing John Kerry on a podium with Jane Fonda in a demonstration against the Vietnam War. The two never shared a podium, but the toxic effect of this digital imagery may have affected a presidential election. A character in the film *Flags of Our Fathers*, recalling U.S. propaganda efforts during World War II, remarked, "A picture can win or lose a war."[12]

Cartoons

Photography is not the only way to communicate messages by images. Sketches that originated with political cartoons and the sharp drawings of the 18th century English artist William Hogarth gave birth to a worldwide phenomenon of comic books, newspaper comic strips, magazine cartoons, internet drawings and, of course, the ever popular political cartoons. (See chapter 14, Persuasion: The Push Never Stops.)

In 1896, a few years after photographs started to appear in newspapers, the technology supporting color in newspapers improved enough for William Randolph Hearst to bring out a comic strip supplement in the *New York American*. Yellow ink was added to an outlandish skirt worn by a little boy in one strip, "Hogan's Alley." Renamed the Yellow Kid, it was a hit with readers and opened the way for a major industry with dozens upon dozens of comic strips.

Some comics were intended to be comical. Others were intended to be serious, but in the United States the term "comics" has stuck to them all. Italians call them "fumetti," meaning "smoke." In Portuguese they are "história em quadradinhos" (a story in little squares). The French prefer the no-nonsense "bande dessiné" (drawn strip). Whatever they are called, they are a staple of the modern newspaper, frequently the first place a reader turns. "Manga" is the Japanese word for "comics". Its style has spread worldwide to both children and adults, a billion dollar industry.

For many newspaper readers, the comic strips are the one part of the newspaper they would never do without. Reading Dilbert or Doonesbury is as much a part of their morning routine as a cup of coffee. The effects on society of single cartoon panels, comic strips and comic books have been debated, but little doubt remains that cartoons stir something in many readers. Psychologist Fredric Wertham's accusatory book, Seduction of the Innocent, argued that comic books corrupted youngsters with pornographic images and excessive violence. Untold numbers of adults have complained that comics rot the brains of youngsters. The youngsters themselves just keep on scanning these durable media.

Some comics have a stronger appeal to adults than to children. Art Spiegelman's Maus won a Pulitzer Prize in 1992 as it set off an increasingly popular genre with adults—the graphic novel—combining text and drawings in stories that are more complex and frequently darker than traditional comic book tales. V for Vendetta and Sin City became films not only drawn from graphic novels, but produced to look like them. Purists may scoff at the notion that what appears in comic books can be considered art, but when a museum hangs a Roy Lichtenstein painting of a single comic book panel, admiring visitors gather.

Timeline

1038: Arab scholar Alhazen describes a room-size camera obscura.

1727: Johann Schulze sees silver nitrate darken, begins science of photochemistry.

1802: Thomas Wedgewood produces silhouettes with silver nitrate, but they darken.

1816: Joseph Nicéphore Niépce captures a negative image on paper, but it darkens.

1825: Copy of a Dutch print. It is now thought to be the first true photograph.

1827: Using a camera obscura, Niépce makes a true photograph on a pewter plate.

1835: In England, W. H. Fox Talbot produces his first photographs, the first negatives.

1837: In France, Louis Daguerre creates daguerreotype photographs.

1839: John Herschel's hypo fixative stops darkening of photographs.

Daguerre's paper to Royal Society begins photography craze.

1849: Photographs of Egyptian pyramids begin travel photography.

Twin-lens camera can take pictures for stereoscopic viewing.

1851: Frederick Scott Archer invents wet-plate photography.

1861: Mathew Brady and others begin to photograph the American Civil War.

1880: A halftone photograph, "Shantytown," appears in a newspaper.

1881: The first photographic roll film is available.

1888: The inexpensive "Kodak" box camera. And the "snapshot" is born.

1896: X-ray photography appears.

1900: Kodak's $1 Brownie puts photography within almost everyone's reach.

1902: Alfred Stieglitz publishes *Camera Work* to promote photography as art.

1937: An American, Chester Carlson, invents the photocopier, Xerography process.

1947: Dennis Gabor, Hungarian engineer in England, invents holography.

Edwin Land's one-minute Polaroid method prints pictures in the camera.

1978: From Japan, an automatic focusing, point-and-shoot camera goes on sale.

1982: Japanese filmless cameras store pictures electronically.

1991: An x-ray photograph is taken of the brain recalling a word.

2004: 2-D and 3-D photos taken by Rover vehicles are beamed back from Mars.

2007: Camera phones are everywhere.

8. Movies

The first moving pictures were brief slices of real life. So are the newest, as homemade videos on YouTube go viral to the world. If something is strange or funny or if you are upset enough about an injustice you can do more than blog about it. Film it and upload your video. The digital revolution makes it easy and cheap. If you can make a persuasive documentary, Netflix and Sundance are open to you. Camcorders and phone cameras are everywhere, more common than the Kodak Brownie once was.

Like so much of mediated communication, videotape and its successor digital technologies have been egalitarian, empowering ordinary users. Recall that the Rodney King beating by four police officers in 1991, taped by an amateur from an apartment window, reverberated nationwide and has affected the way police behave during arrests. It played again and again on television, fueling the African-American anger behind the Los Angeles riots. Now think of all the camera phones that are being pointed at police during recent demonstrations, then going viral.

Production and distribution of moving images are decentralized as never before. People of a great variety of beliefs and agendas use the powerful medium of movies to try to persuade us. And, of course, the established motion picture industry continues to exert its influence.

More Than a Diversions

It would be easier to find someone who never read a newspaper, a magazine or a book than to to find an adult who has never seen a movie.[1] From our childhood, movies have been part of our lives. To watch a movie with enough understanding to have an emotional response, literacy is not necessary. Steven Spielberg called films "the most powerful weapon in the world."[2] For most of us a world deprived of film would be grayer, less pleasant. Watching movies has also substituted for other activities and for direct contact with other people. The movies have encouraged us to sit back and let the people who make them entertain us so that we do not entertain ourselves.

The movies are more than occasional diversions. Beyond the plots, the action, the actors and the computer graphics, both fiction and non-fiction movies carry messages. And the messages get through despite cultural differences.[3] Only some messages are intentional, but films that do not set out to send a message still do so in subtle ways: the condition of the streets and buildings, the cars, the food, what the actors wear and their attitudes, the behavior of police and politicians can tell an audience that this is how things are in other places. If life is different where you live, maybe you will want changes where you live. Sukarno, the first prime minister of Indonesia, once said that Hollywood, in effect, preached revolution because it showed a society in which ordinary people had houses with several rooms and possessed automobiles.[4]

Movies have knocked down barriers among races, religions and nationalities. Movies can help to turn our focus from local and parochial matters to broader perspectives. Sometimes they firm flabby sympathies into the sinews of active commitment. And they have also encouraged ridicule. Even when no hostility was intended, the movies, especially in their early years, got cheap laughs out of stereotypes. Historian David Nasaw recalled, "Most of the early comedies borrowed their characters, if not their plots, from vaudeville skits. As in vaudeville, ethnic and racial parodies were prevalent, with dim-witted Irish servants blowing themselves up trying to light the stove or taking off their clothes when asked to serve the salad without dressing, unscrupulous Jewish merchants in full beards and long black coats cheating their customers and blacks behaving like children—cakewalking, grinning, shooting craps, stealing chickens and eating watermelon."[5]

Considering the diversity of those who contribute their skills and where the product goes, the motion picture industry is among the most international of enterprises. All leading nations of the world and many of the smaller nations have their own film industries, a point of pride like a national airline. Some have had notable histories, such as the film industries of the Soviet Union, Britain, France, Germany and Japan.

The Roots

Motion picture technology has three roots that go back for centuries. The *chemistry* of film has its roots in still photography. The other two roots are *projection*, which had its origin in the magic lantern, and *stills-in-motion*, which began as toys that depended on *persistence of vision*. Because it takes the eye and the brain a fraction of a second to lose an image, a series of still pictures presented in quick succession will appear as a single moving image. An examination of the flickering images of the persistence-of-vision devices built throughout the 19th century may lead to the conclusion that the invention of the motion picture was inevitable.

From the Thaumatrope, invented in the early 19th century, to devices with complex names like the Phenakistoscope, the Praxinoscope, the Zoetrope and the Zoopraxiscope, inventors strove to fool the eye. The Thaumatrope is a disk attached to a string. On each side of the disk is a different image such as a cage and a canary.

The zoopraxiscope, invented by Eadweard Muybridge, projected moving images on a wall. It may have inspired the Kinetoscope built by W.K.L. Dickson for Thomas Edison.

Eadweard Muybridge's images of a trotting horse.

Spinning the disk gives the illusion that the canary is inside the cage. The inventor was possibly influenced by a scientific paper on persistence of vision by the remarkable physician Peter Roget, creator of Roget's *Thesaurus* of English synonyms and the inventor of the logarithmic slide rule.

Railroad baron Leland Stanford, ex-governor of California and founder of Stanford University, wanted to settle a bet on whether a trotting horse lifted all four hooves off the ground at the same time. In 1878 he hired professional photographer Eadweard Muybridge, who, after several trials, set a row of twenty-four cameras along a racetrack. Strings that stretched across the track tripped the camera shutters as the horse trotted by. That resulted in a series of stills. Flipped in rapid succession, they displayed the horse in motion. (Stanford won his bet; all four feet lifted off the ground.)

Muybridge continued his experiments by photographing the movements of a variety of animals. Exhibiting his work in Paris, he met physician Etienne Jules Marey, who was doing research in such animal locomotion as the flapping of a bird's wings. That meeting led Marey to take an inventive step forward. Adapting a "photographic revolver" designed by astronomer Pierre Janssen to record the transit of Venus across the sun, Marey built a single camera that rapidly shot a series of images on a single plate. It did not require strings, which would have interfered with the fluttering wings. Inventors in several countries solved other mechanical difficulties. Among them were William Friese-Greene in England and the brothers Louis and Auguste Lumière in France.

Edison and the Lumière Brothers

Thomas Edison, who originally thought of motion pictures to accompany the sound in his phonograph parlors, assigned assistant W.K.L. Dickson to build a motion picture system, based on the French photographic revolver. Working in Edison's New Jersey laboratory with strips of celluloid film manufactured by George Eastman for his Kodaks, Dickson in 1894 invented the Kinetograph camera and the motor-driven "peep show" Kinetoscope, running 50 feet of film in 30 seconds. Sprockets guided the film's perforated edges past the lens with a controlled, intermittent movement like the ticking second-hand of a watch.

To produce something to display, Dickson erected a studio building that could be turned to take advantage of sunlight. Workers referred to the studio building as the "Black Maria," because with its tarpaper covering it vaguely bore the shape of a police wagon with that nickname. Trained animal acts, circus entertainers and the like performed there.

Kinetoscopes for viewing the films went into parlors modeled after Edison's successful phonograph parlors, with the difference that admission was not free; customers paid one quarter for tickets allowing them to peep into five machines. Start the electric motor, gaze into the

A Kinetoscope parlor

peephole, and there was magic! The viewer stared into a box to see the frames of film flicker by. The inventive Dickson later built the Mutoscope peephole machine, with a series of cards that were flipped by a handle; Dickson made the Mutoscope different enough from his early Kinetoscope to get around Edison's patent. (Mutoscopes can still occasionally be found in old-fashioned penny arcades.)

Yet it was not *projection*, which appeared first in France. The Lumière brothers, Louis and Auguste, owners of a photo products manufacturing business, set about to improve a Kinetoscope they saw on display in Paris. This they did with their Cinematographe, a combined camera, film printer and projector. Substituting a hand crank for Edison's electric motor, the Lumières reduced the machine's weight so that it could be carried to any location. Edison's bulky, fixed Kinetograph required performers to appear before it in the studio. Where Edison's films gave the view of a stage, Lumière films were like looking through a window. In addition, the Lumières projected their films onto a screen where a number of viewers saw them at the same time. Only one viewer at a time peered into the Kinetoscope.

The Lumières' first film, of workers leaving their factory, was shot in March 1895, and shown at a special exhibit for photographers. On December 28, 1895, in the basement of a Paris cafe, they showed the first motion pictures projected to a paying audience. For one franc apiece the audience saw a twenty-minute program consisting of ten films, accompanied by a piano, commentary by the Lumière's father and their own gasps of amazement.[6] In no time at all long lines formed outside the cafe to see the show. The movies were born.[7]

Two months later, projected films were shown in London. Two months after that, New York. Audiences were soon drawn not only from the wealthy or the middle class, but from the working class who previously had no opportunity to dress up for a night at the theater, the concert hall or the music hall. The wealthy had the opera, the symphony and private amusements to occupy their leisure and had little use for social mixing. The middle class enjoyed music hall vaudeville. A strong sense of "middle class morality" based on Victorian scruples kept many Americans out of any theaters.

The Nickelodeon

A few entrepreneurs foresaw that customers who so eagerly parted with their hard earned coin to look at moving pictures in a Kinetoscope box might be even more willing to spend it on pictures projected against a screen. One way or another budding entrepreneurs acquired projectors, buying them or building their own. In the cities they converted stores, restaurants and dance halls to look like vaudeville houses, or they cordoned off a section of a parlor or penny arcade and placed wooden chairs in front of a screen, even if it was no more than a white wall or a bed sheet. At county fairs a tent would do. Lecturers who illustrated their talks with slides adopted the new medium when they recognized how moving pictures would improve their presentations.

The idea of the nickelodeon—a nickel admission—started in Pittsburgh in 1905. Within a year 2,500 were in business. Here was something entirely different: sitting in the dark among strangers to share the laughter and tears and thrills of an unfolding story that was easy to understand. Reading a magazine or book was mediated communication, but it was a solitary pursuit. Attending a lecture, a circus or a concert was a direct experience, not mediated and these events took place in lighted halls or outdoors.

At the nickelodeon a nickel (five cents) was the admission price.

The entrepreneurs themselves arose from the masses of the poor. Some of the more successful were immigrants, mostly Jews born into the poverty and the anti-Semitism of Russia and Eastern Europe, not fully comfortable with the English language or the dominant Protestant culture of their new country. Yet they were totally at home with the Protestant work ethic that has infused the lives of so many immigrants: work hard and success will follow. They had an instinctive sense of the simple narratives that would appeal to the poor, working class families who crowded into nickelodeons. Marcus Loew, who started as a furrier, would one day see his name identifying a large national chain of cinemas. Louis B. Mayer started out as a scrap dealer who switched over to nickelodeons. Samuel Goldwyn and Mayer started MGM. William Fox gave his name to 20th Century Fox; his name now identifies the Fox media empire. Adolph Zukor began Paramount. Out of a clothing store in Oshkosh, Wisconsin, Carl Laemmle came to run Universal. The four Warner brothers began in Manhattan by borrowing chairs from a nearby funeral parlor; when the chairs were needed for a funeral, movie patrons stood.

Albert E. Smith and a partner bought a projector and a supply of movies from Edison, who sold projectors but refused to sell cameras in an effort to control movie production. It dawned on Smith that he could make more money producing films and that a camera was a kind of backwards projector. Converting one into the other, he and two partners created the Vitagraph Company in 1899 and went into competition with the powerful Biograph Company, which had begun four years earlier as the nation's first motion picture production company.

Battles over patent infringements were fought in the courts as a trust of bankers and businessmen sought to acquire enough patents to monopolize the motion picture industry despite anti-trust laws. Established companies fought the newcomers fiercely. The trust, the Motion Picture Patents Company, charged cinema owners fees for a projector, a projectionist and films. They could not show unauthorized "outlaw" movies. Eastman at first sold raw film stock only to members of the trust. The trust did not care that their heavy-handed methods choked efforts to produce more imaginative pictures, especially the fictional stories that audiences by this time wanted to see. Business was business. The legal warfare lasted for seven years until a federal court outlawed the trust.

Hollywood

D.W. Griffith and actors from the Biograph Company, including Lillian Gish, Mary Pickford and Lionel Barrymore, went to Southern California in 1910, moving as far away from the heart of film making in the New York-New Jersey area as they could manage. In Los Angeles they could escape the subpoenas and the heavy hand of the trust's Pinkerton detectives and at the same time find cheap labor and adequate sunshine for their filming. Nearby ocean, mountains, lakes, desert, woodlands, pasture, Spanish architecture and town settings offered a variety of outdoor locations.

In a friendly village called Hollywood, the relocated filmmakers began cranking their cameras. Soon, the motion picture companies started by Laemmle, Jesse Lasky and a few others joined them. They rented barns and hammered stages together. The first movie studio occupied a converted saloon. In the United States, New York would remain the distribution center for films, but Hollywood would become the production center. These breakaway moviemakers would become the Hollywood studio establishment. One day the studios themselves would battle television and independent movie makers just as hard as the trust once battled them.

Lloyd Morris, popular historian of the early 20th century, described the urban audiences, "In the slums of the great Eastern and Middle Western cities there were herded vast immigrant populations. Largely unfamiliar with the English language, they could not read the newspapers, magazines or books. But the living pictures communicated their meanings directly and eloquently. To enjoy them, no command of a new language was essential. They made illiteracy and ignorance of American customs seem less shameful; they broke down a painful sense of isolation and ostracism. At the movies dwellers in tenements, workers in sweatshops, could escape the drabness of their environment for a little while at a price within their means."[8] The poor of the day had little money to spend on entertainment, but a young man or young woman who earned a dollar a day might be willing on a Saturday night to spend a nickel or two amid blazing lights and cheerful crowds. A nickel could seat you in a room with your friends and neighbors to share the experience of watching a program of motion pictures projected against a wall. Language was no barrier.

Attracted by their gaudy lights, phonograph music piped outside and shouting barkers, the public poured in by the hundreds of thousands daily. To keep up with demand for new movies, exhibitors changed the bill daily or even twice a day. Customers packed in from morning to night, one show after another, seven days a week. They streamed out of one nickelodeon into another, beguiled by the barkers, the flashing lights and the colorful posters outside until endurance and pockets were drained. Between shows the nickelodeon owners sent their relatives up and down the aisle selling snacks and soda pop. In some theaters the attendants squirted the air with a solution to mask the fetid air, but did nothing about the pestilential germs that worried city inspectors.

The nickelodeons, the storefronts, the backs of the arcades and the circus tents were joined as movie venues by cinemas built specifically for watching films. The architecture became gaudier and grander with the construction of movie "palaces" in the downtown sections of large cities. These new motion picture palaces featured orchestra pits, pipe organs and plaster Byzantine architecture. Some advertised "Air Conditioning" in marquee letters as big as the names of the stars. The palaces were designed to attract those middle-class patrons who wanted to see motion pictures but did not want to sit in dingy, crowded nickelodeons. The largest movie palaces could seat several thousand patrons, with uniformed ushers to guide them down the aisles.

For women, who had limited options for entertainment, the nickelodeon and the movie palace were safe, affordable and interesting.[9] Historian Miriam Hansen wrote, "More than any other entertainment form, the cinema opened up a space—a social space as well as a perceptual experiential horizon—in women's lives. Married women would drop into a movie theater on their way home from a shopping trip, a pleasure indulged in just as much by women of the more affluent classes. Schoolgirls filled the theaters during much of the afternoon, before returning to the folds of familial discipline. And young working women would find in the cinema an hour of diversion after work, as well as an opportunity to meet men."[10]

The appeal of the movies expanded to middle-class Americans in the early years of the new century. An unexpected mingling of social classes followed into other commercial amusements in the American melting pot.[11] But this was likely to be a whites-only audience. At many nickelodeons African-Americans were barred. When the nickelodeons were replaced by large, permanent cinemas, African-Americans were often directed by ushers to the balcony or along the sides. The entertainment bill of fare changed, too. Instead of a series of one- or two-reelers, the cinemas showed the longer feature films the public had already come to love. Film exchanges, instead of *selling* films to exhibitors, *rented* them. In time, as the industry matured, distribution centers and chain owners would dominate the mom-and-pop beginnings of film exhibition. Movie theater chains with hundreds of outlets either contracted with studios or had the same corporate ownership, guaranteeing both a steady supply of product and dependable distribution. Warner Bros. films opened in a Warner Bros. theater, Paramount films at a Paramount, MGM films at a Loew's theater.

Escapism

The sight of ocean waves coming toward the camera elicited squeals from the early patrons, who half-expected to be soaked. The earliest Lumière and Edison films were scenes from real life: people in a park, workers leaving a factory, a man playing a fiddle, a baby being fed, a parade. In time, audiences tired of such banal fare.

For audiences that loved stories, French magician George Méliès produced the first openly fictional films. Even today, audiences enjoy his *A Trip to the Moon* (1902), which is still shown as a whimsical introduction to the history of space flight. Méliès was among the first to stretch the film from less than one minute to an entire reel of ten to fifteen minutes.

Méliès' humorous moon fantasy was innocent, unlike a number of serious efforts that were patently fraudulent and intended to deceive the naïve public. The run-up to the Spanish-American War purported to show Spanish atrocities in Cuba. The scenes were filmed in New Jersey. The famous charge up San Juan Hill was filmed at another hill considerably later. The Boer War was filmed on a golf course. Mount Vesuvius erupted far from that mountain. A safari into the heart of Africa featured two elderly zoo lions who politely allowed themselves to be shot on camera.

People Want Fiction

Motion pictures might have ended as just another novelty. What made the difference was *fiction*. In 1903, director-photographer Edwin Porter made *The Great Train Robbery*, the first memorable story film and the first to utilize film editing to establish relationships. In eight minutes, bandits hold up a mail train, a posse is formed to chase after the bandits, a shoot-out follows and the bandits are wiped out. For the first time, too, the camera moved with the action, indoors and out. Excited audiences lined up to get in.

A distinct preference emerged for the scripted fiction narrative film. Realistic films led to newsreels and documentaries, but the movie-going public by their ticket purchases made their choice clear. They had enough troubles at home. Reality in the form of actuality film was not why they entered the darkened theater. The documentary would come to be respected more than enjoyed. Movie makers knew that, like everything else for sale, money—in the form of box office receipts—would identify the type of movies that they should produce. Hollywood production was measured by that yardstick, not critical judgment or classical theatrical artistry. Little wonder that Hollywood became "the dream factory." In time the public would also express its preference for sound and color. These added even more escapist pleasure to an evening of going out to the movies.

Although actors in the early films were not identified, it was soon apparent that the public was developing an affinity for certain featured players and a curiosity about the actors' lives. An early survey of audience preferences for film plots received instead questions about the actors and actresses. What was he like? Was she married? The fiction film itself was only a few years old when *Photoplay* was published in 1911 to discuss film plots and characters, the first movie fan magazine. As the familiar faces loomed over them in close-ups on the big screen, patrons could sometimes feel a closer identity with the stars than with members of their own families. The mediated pleasure sprouting from this connection has continued to displace flesh-and-blood connections from generation to generation. It has spawned its own world of press agents, fan magazines, Hollywood reporters intent on the smallest private details, paparazzi, bodyguards and millions of viewers watching the Academy Awards and other events honoring these luminaries.

Fred Ott's Sneeze (1893), an early Edison film for the Kinetoscopes, began a long tradition of film comedy. Under the guiding hand of Mack Sennett, slapstick grew from its limited roots in burlesque to an art form. The Keystone Kops' nonsensical appearance and incompetence invited people to laugh at a social institution that was anything but funny. For immigrants from repressive police states, regarding the policeman as a figure of ridicule must have been a strange and liberating experience.

Melodrama

Trains were a vehicle for action on the silent screen. The heroine might be tied to the railroad tracks or the hero might be in a car that crosses the tracks an instant ahead of the locomotive. Moviegoers could be sure of a happy ending

Movie-goers wanted formula films that did not vary much from one comedy to the next, one cowboy western to the next. Most of all, they wanted happy endings. The hero dashed up at the last minute to save the tied-down heroine from the oncoming train, then turned to thrash the villain. Film cuts and dissolves kept the pacing and mood. Fades that marked a change of time and location replaced the theatrical practice of raising and lowering a stage curtain. Real locomotives and spinning circular lumber saws heightened the sense of danger more than the cardboard imitations used as stage props. Melodrama and outdoor filming were made for each other.

The popular melodrama easily made the transition from stage to screen. The melodrama evolved into the romantic drama with *The Birth of a Nation* (1915), a feature film nearly three hours long. Director D.W. Griffith's manipulation of long, medium and close-up shots, pacing, cross-cutting and optical effects, plus his choice of locations and his attention to actors' movements set new standards for the motion picture. He insisted on close-ups of actors despite protests from studio executives that audiences wanted to see the actors from head to toe and would not accept "half an actor."

Starting with *The Birth of a Nation*, movies would create a visual language that the public understood, a language to which it responded. Although a silent film, *The Birth of a Nation* had the accompaniment of live music, anything from a seventy-piece symphony orchestra to a single pianist playing a musical score specifically written for the film. After seeing it, President Woodrow Wilson is said to have remarked, "It is like writing history with lightning."[12]

Griffith has been lauded as the single most important individual in the development of the motion picture as an art form, but *The Birth of a Nation* was also a racially biased movie that fostered lingering stereotypes of African-Americans as vicious and inferior subhumans. The Ku Klux Klan was portrayed as noble, galloping up on horses to save the heroine. Griffith was a Southerner, the son of a Confederate veteran, raised amid the post-Civil War resentments of a conquered people. He had not finished high school.

Making Amends

This is a set from the 1916 D.W. Griffith film *Intolerance*. Stung by the negative reaction to *The Birth of a Nation*, the director showed the effects of bigotry during four periods of history. It has been called a masterpiece of the silent screen but it failed at the box office.

For all its artistry, *The Birth of a Nation* evoked protest marches. The NAACP tried unsuccessfully to have the film banned or at least to have certain scenes removed. Griffith tried to make amends with an even more ambitious film that ran for three and a half hours, *Intolerance*, which identified bigotry during the Babylonian, Judean, Renaissance and contemporary American periods.

The Stars

Realism was exaggerated to absurdity by fast-motion film, ridiculous props, split-second timing and incongruous film cutting. When the screen comic hero's automobile missed the oncoming locomotive by inches, the audience suspended belief and laughed. Director Mack Sennett's pie-in-the-face slapstick competed with silent film actors who took the comic art to yet greater heights. Harold Lloyd, Buster Keaton and, above the rest, Charlie Chaplin blended slapstick with pathos. His meld of mirth, romance and sadness created one of the classic characters of any age and culture, the little tramp, in such films as *The Kid*, *The Gold Rush* and *City Lights*.

People willingly plunked down their nickels for visual comedy and stories, especially when they featured actors they had learned to adore. The first screen actors were people who appeared in front of the camera only because they were not busy working behind it. Wives, friends and visitors took a turn. When trained stage actors rode the trains west heading to the new movie studios to look for work, they were given acting jobs but not the publicity they expected. Studio owners were afraid this would lead to demands for better pay. This situation changed after theater owners reported to producers that audiences looked forward to seeing familiar faces. Word raced through every town that the actor or actress who had appeared in such-and-such a role could be seen again at the Bijou in a new motion picture. That resulted in ticket sales and the start of the movie star system. In 1914 Charlie Chaplin was being paid $125 a week. By 1915 he was getting $10,000 a week plus $150,000 for signing the contract. Mary Pickford was paid $10,000 a week plus half the profits of her pictures.

The star system reached its zenith when the big studios peaked in the 1930s, '40s and '50s. Politicians counted themselves fortunate when a movie star agreed to a joint appearance at a rally. Actor George Murphy was elected to the United States Senate. Arnold Schwarzenegger was twice elected governor of California. Ronald Reagan was not only elected governor of California but was twice elected president and is an iconic figure in American history. Today George Clooney and Angelina Jolie are among many actors who use their celebrity to make positive changes throughout the world.

Not So Silent

Silent movie theaters were anything but silent, for the audience kept up a cheerful racket. Slides carrying the message "Please Do Not Stamp. The Floor May Cave In." may have seemed to young patrons like an invitation to stamp. Some movie palaces boasted orchestras, organs, or sound effects machines like the Noiseograph, the Dramagraph, and the Soundograph, whose keyboards imitated crashing glass and galloping horses. Professional actors working in the movie houses interpreted the dialogue behind the screen.

In Japan, a unique occupation arose from the Japanese oral tradition. A benshi, a kind of storyteller, narrated the films, altering his voice to speak for each of the characters. More popular than movie stars, benshi could order directors to alter scenes so they could extend their own performances. When sound films finally arrived in Japan, the benshi were able to delay their widespread distribution for several years.

Sound

Sound heightened the entertainment and informational value of films. But the "talkies" did much more. They gave the movies a cultural value akin to books and plays. The sound motion picture in the United States, along with the radio, helped to standardize American speech. By bringing forth a shared cultural experience, the movies and the radio tightened the bonds that held a large and diverse country together. Like the telegraph and the telephone before them and the radio and television to follow, the talkies helped to unite the United States.

Efforts to produce sound to go with film began with the invention of movies. In 1895 Edison invented the Kinetophone, a cylinder phonograph for his Kinetoscope viewers. Later, phonograph records were synchronized mechanically to the projectors. This system worked passably well when the film and the record were new. Unfortunately, the record started to wear out after about twenty plays and after a projectionist spliced a few film breaks, removing a few frames here and there, the soundtrack was totally out of sync with the picture.[13]

In Hollywood, interest in sound films was propelled by Warner Bros., which was desperate and nearly bankrupt by the late 1920s. Using Vitaphone, a system that paired a phonograph with a projector, In 1926 Warner Bros. presented some sound shorts and a silent film, *Don Juan*, to which the studio added a music score plus the clash of swords during a duel, but made no effort to lip-sync words. A year later the troubled studio tried again with a silent feature film that had musical accompaniment and four singing or talking sequences. *The Jazz Singer* starred Al Jolson, who belted out "Mammy" and, in the second reel, uttered those prophetic words, "Wait a minute! Wait a minute, I tell ya! You ain't heard nothin' yet."

Most Hollywood executives wanted to leave well enough alone and stay with silent film.[14] They saw no reason to pay for sound-proofing studios or noisy cameras or figuring ways to position microphones so they would not show up on camera. Efforts to hide mikes can be seen in films of the early 1930s when actors huddled over a prop, like a vase of flowers, to deliver their lines. Unfortunately, some of the best known actors had thick foreign accents or squeaky voices in sharp contrast to their all-American, matinee idol looks. Changes were inevitable.

Most studios and stars, notably Chaplin, preferred the silent screen with the dialogue printed on cards that appeared after the words were spoken. Ticket purchases forced the switch to sound. The public again determined the direction that films would take. Lines at the box offices swept aside the argument that talkies were for lowbrows while the more sensitive, intelligent audiences wanted silent films. Hollywood executives should have known better because talkies followed right behind broadcasting, which was spreading as fast as people could afford to buy radio sets. Ticket sales rose sharply for the talkies that soon poured out of the Hollywood studios. Two years after *The Jazz Singer*, the Academy Award for best picture went to *Broadway Melody*, a splashy musical.

Color

The first patent for a color process was issued in 1897, shortly after movies began. At first, a few films were hand painted frame by frame, clearly an impractical solution. In another process, scenes were tinted; segments of black-and-white film were simply dipped into dye so that scenes showing a lot of sky might be blue while scenes of a burning building might be tinted red. These attempts were meant to heighten the mood of the film rather than to add realism. Several optical color processes used colored filters or dyes with less than spectacular results. Only Technicolor, invented by Herbert Kalmus, was successful, emerging in 1922 as a two-tone process. It was later replaced by a much better three-tone process. This complicated method involved not only printing images on film containing layers of emulsion, but shooting with camera lenses that split the light beam, sending the split images through different colored filters.

Most of the Hollywood establishment did not seem to care about color one way or the other. The public did care and, as usual, prevailed. Long lines for *Gone With the Wind* in 1939 should have convinced any doubters that the public loved romantic stories in lush Technicolor. During the 1980s, when old black-and-white films were colorized for television, the establishment did come out firmly, this time against adding color, arguing that computer-generated colors ruined the directors' original visions.

The Studios

The major studios that dominated Hollywood during its Golden Age, starting about 1930, developed genres and kept stars identified with a particular genre under contract. For MGM, it was the musical and the light comedy. 20th Century Fox specialized in musicals and biographies. Columbia became known for romantic comedies and for the populist films of director Frank Capra. Paramount had European sophistication. Warner Bros. had cowboys, gangsters and swashbucklers. Republic had westerns and cliffhanger serials. Universal did well with horror films.[15]

The musicals made from the 1930s onward were Hollywood at its brightest. If audiences loved fantasies mixed with music and glitter, the "dream factories" were only too happy to turn them out on the production lines. That the plots were absurd and always predictable only added to their charm. The audiences wanted to escape into a singing, dancing, Technicolor fantasy. The studios gave them what they wanted.

Westerns could be turned out cheaply and quickly, with familiar plots, pedestrian dialogue, heroes in white hats, villains in black hats and Indians who said little more than "How!" and were shot off their horses on cue, perpetuating the stereotype. Generations of small boys, dreaming of growing up to be cowboys, attacked little brothers assigned to be the Indians.

Movies with Messages

During the Depression years of the 1930s viewers sought light-hearted or escapist fare. By 1939 an average of 85 million movie tickets were sold each week. The quarter that paid for an average cinema admission could have bought a pound of beef, a gallon and a half of gasoline or enough postage stamps to mail eight letters with a penny left over for a postcard. Few moviegoers wanted to see sad or serious films, so the Hollywood studios shied away from making them. Although a few films like *The Grapes of Wrath* and *Mission to Moscow* were produced, the studios avoided message films that could provoke trouble. Producer Samuel Goldwyn is supposed to have said, "If you've got a message, send it by Western Union."

The preference for escapist fare changed sharply with American entry into World War II. Besides patriotic, war-themed films, Hollywood began to turn out films of home front patriotism, documentaries like the *March of Time* series, weekly newsreels and a variety of training films. All the countries on both sides of the conflict, especially Nazi Germany, recognized the power of motion pictures in their own productions.

After the war a few Hollywood producers summoned up their courage to tackle such social issues as racism and anti-Semitism with *Home of the Brave* (1949), *Pinky* (1949) and *Gentleman's Agreement* (1947). *The Lost Weekend* (1945) dealt with alcoholism, *Brute Force* (1947) with prison brutality, *The Snake Pit* (1948) with horrid conditions in mental asylums, *The Man with the Golden Arm* (1955) with drug addiction and *Blackboard Jungle* (1955) with juvenile delinquency.

Animation

In the early years of the motion picture, a few movie-makers, in a throwback to 19th century pre-motion picture devices, drew a series of pictures, each a little different from the last. The first animated cartoon short may have been *Gertie the Dinosaur* (1914), using 10,000 drawings. But audience enthusiasm really began with Walt Disney's *Steamboat Willie* (1928), one of the first animated cartoons with synchronized audio. The first color cartoon reached cinemas in 1932.

During the Depression, audiences expected that a night out at the movies would include—in addition to one or two feature films—a newsreel, previews of coming attractions, and a color cartoon. Mickey Mouse was more famous around the world than any actor. Tom and Jerry from MGM and Bugs Bunny from Warner Bros. offered him competition.

The popularity of the shorts led Disney to risk a feature-length animated film based on a popular fairy tale. *Snow White and the Seven Dwarfs* (1937) combined the story with song. The public, old and young, was enchanted. A long string of feature-length animated films followed, notably *Fantasia* (1940), which introduced stereophonic music to the public, and *Beauty and the Beast* (1991), which earned an Academy Award nomination as the best picture of the year. The cost of frame-by-frame cel animation prompted shortcuts, starting in the 1960s by the Hollywood company Hanna-Barbera and in the 1970s by Japanese animators, at the expense of quality.

In the 1990s, computer-based animation restored and lifted animation standards. In the decade of the 2000s, advanced digital animation from Pixar, Dreamworks, and other studios pulled in audiences with stories and dialogue that allowed both adults and children to enjoy films like *Shrek* and *Ratatouille* at different levels of understanding.

In 2001, a computer-generated feature film, *Final Fantasy*, tried to make its characters look and move like real people. From England, ignoring computers, the "Wallace and Gromit" films, patiently animated with clay figures, built a loyal fan base.

Computers enhanced movies in still other ways. In live action movies, morphing or shape shifting, starting with *Terminator 2* (1991), could smoothly change one character into another before our eyes. *Jurassic Park* shocked us with hungry dinosaurs (1993). *Titanic* (1997) brought us a realistic ship crashing into an iceberg and sinking. *Troy* (2004) was one of several historical epics that used computers to transform a relatively small number of extras into vast armies. And, of course, the computer has revolutionized feature-length animated films.

Gertie the Dinosaur

The Cold War, which closely followed World War II, brought with it the "Red Scare." A deep political division tore Hollywood apart. Actors, writers and directors suspected of Communist leanings were blacklisted and denied work. They could not be nominated for Oscars. Following hearings by the House of Representatives Committee on Un-American Activities, a few went to prison. Frightened studios put a temporary end to films that advocated social change. Escapism was more popular and less worrisome.

It took years, but over time this pain dissipated, though its scars persist to this day. Social problems reappeared in movies, which became increasingly frank as they attracted the interest of Main Street as well as the critics. Hostile race relations, homosexuality, police brutality and political corruption became film topics. Spike Lee won critical applause and lines at the box office with *Do the Right Thing* (1988), which examined the raw reality of black-white race relations. The theme was further explored in the controversial *Malcolm X* (1992). The best picture Oscar for *Midnight Cowboy* (1969) and the nomination of *Brokeback Mountain* (2005) for an Academy Award confronted the subject of homosexuality. Today few controversial social issues lie beyond the boundaries of what mainstream moviemakers will examine.

National Traditions

All large nations and many small nations developed a movie industry even if a limited national language base held small promise of financial success. Like a national airline, a film industry seemed essential to national prestige. While American motion picture production was shifting to Hollywood at the dawn of the last century, other nations constructed their own film industries. Germany and Denmark each claimed to have built the first motion picture studio.

World War I gave a boost to Hollywood because almost all the European studios shut down. Among the wartime shortages was cellulose, the film base, needed to make explosives. Lacking their own films, Europeans began to import American product. After the war, their national production resumed, but European audiences had developed a taste for American films, especially westerns. What followed in subsequent decades has been a melding of influences, ideas and talents into what has truly become an international industry.

France, the early leader, fell behind in building a strong film industry after World War I, but led experiments into unusual forms of expression, notably the avant-garde movement in film as well as in poetry, painting and music, which looked at the world in new, symbolic ways. Expressions of art that had a shock value were prized, "decadent" or not. After World War II a new tradition

Newsreels and Documentaries

The history of motion pictures began at the end of the 19th century with scenes from real life, both true and faked. Fiction films soon dominated the public's interest, but reality did not disappear from the screen. Broadly, it took two forms, the newsreel and the documentary.

Cinemas showed newsreels shot by independent companies and studios: Pathé, Fox Movietone, Paramount, Universal, MGM, Telenews, and Gaumont, plus the newsreel-like March of Time. Because governments were quick to recognize their propaganda value, a number of countries had their own government-sanctioned newsreels, such as Nazi Germany's Deutsche Wochenschau and Japan's Yomiuri. Networks of film photographers and processing laboratories churned out thousands of feet of film each week, despite technical limitations.

The same 35 mm film equipment that studios used for features slowed photographers in reaching a news scene and getting the film to a processing lab, with further delays in sending prints to thousands of cinemas. Hand-held 16 mm silent cameras shot many stories, with narration and music added in postproduction, but this process was also slow.

As a result, a typical cinema newsreel began with a hard news story a week or two old, followed by several light features whose timeliness barely mattered. Because New York City was a major processing and distributing point, socialites leaving aboard an ocean liner or a New York dog show, were newsreel staples. Newsreels often deserved the reputation of being frivolous, even if audiences enjoyed them or did not seem to mind when they were pointless.

When commercial television began in the late 1940s and early 1950s, two kinds of news were available: newsreels and non-visual newscasts transferred from radio. In time, the two melded into the timely and visual newscasts we see today.

The word "documentary" takes in a great deal of territory, from Michael Moore's filmed political tracts to nature movies. "Documentary" should not be equated with "truth," but may be defined as the creative interpretation of reality, with variations in the degree of creativity.

The first well-known documentary was Robert Flaherty's Nanook of the North (1922), a look at the life of an Inuit hunter, his family, and his village. In truth, Flaherty portrayed the more primitive life that Nanook's grandfather had lived.

As with newsreels, governments realized the value of the documentary as a political tool. All nations with film industries made some documentaries under government supervision.

swept the revived French motion picture industry. "New Wave" films rebelled against accepted moral standards and normal codes of behavior. With it grew the *auteur* tradition, which evaluated movies as the product of a single mind, that of the director, rather than as a collaboration of the talents of writers, actors and dozens of others. That tradition continues to influence movie making around the world.

In Russia after the Bolshevik revolution of 1917, the emerging Soviet film industry and the world's first film school fostered Marxist-Leninist ideology. Recognizing the political power of mass communication, Lenin said, "The cinema for us is the most important of the arts." To build support, "agitprop" (agitation and propaganda) trains fanned out across the countryside to promote Communist ideals for an illiterate proletariat. Meanwhile, radio sent the message across the vast reaches of the new Soviet Union. In rural areas where few radios existed, loudspeakers went up on poles in village squares. The Soviet film industry was led by such brilliant directors as Sergei Eisenstein, whose theory of montage—the relationship of one scene to another—influenced later

Famous scene from *Battleship Potemkin* **(1925). An unattended baby in a carriage rolls down the Odessa Steps.**

film makers. His *Battleship Potemkin* (1925) has been called the most important film ever made because it showed the broad possibilities of film editing based on rhythm and the connecting of visual images.

In Germany a sturdy film industry grew in the fifteen years following World War I, with films that explored more psychological themes than the lightweight American product. German filmmakers reached for darker visions of the soul, reflecting the despair of a once proud nation bitter and defeated, plagued by astronomical inflation, when a barrel of money bought one loaf of bread. It was said that Germany's low point as a nation was the high point of its silent film. Here the techniques of the moving camera expanded. When the Nazis took power in Germany during the 1930s, directors, actors and technicians fled to Hollywood. The Nazi takeover transformed German cinema into a propaganda arm of the state. In *Triumph of the Will* (1934) and *Olympia* (1938), Nazi Germany's most brilliant director, Leni Riefenstahl, demonstrated the sheer political power of film even in a hateful cause. After World War II a revived German film industry emphasized strong and unusual dramatic themes.

In Britain a social documentary tradition grew during the Depression and World War II that identified national problems and suggested governmental solutions. One of Britain's leading filmmakers, John Grierson, called it "the drama of the doorstep." The British were also able to enjoy a good laugh at themselves. A string of postwar British films like *Passport to Pimlico* (1949) and *Whisky Galore* (1949), released as *Tight Little Island* in the U.S. tapped a vein of gentle self-mocking humor. They drew appreciative audiences in the United States and the British Commonwealth. Monty Python's humor evolved from earlier examples of dry British wit.

Censorship

The impact of movies on society is too great to be evaluated only on their artistic quality, no matter what the critics may say. No cultural force of such power settles in without opposition and censorship has consistently been film's companion. Almost from its onset the motion picture had its enemies. Middle class reformers who attacked working class drinking went after the nickelodeon.[16]

Nickelodeons troubled those who thought the movies were presenting revolutionary ideas. Starting in the early years of the 20th century, there were calls for regulating, censoring, or suppressing films, limitations cheered by saloon owners who saw business dwindling. In 1909, the National Board of Censorship of Motion Pictures was created, independent of Hollywood. In that year the New York Society for the Prevention of Cruelty to Children stated in its annual report, "God alone knows how many (girls) are leading dissolute lives begun at the 'moving pictures'."

The motion picture industry responded by various means of self-censorship to ward off tougher government standards. Hollywood in 1922 created the Hays Office, named for its first president, Will Hays, to protect audiences from indecency and violence. A code of acceptable behavior was adopted in 1934 and a Production Code Administration enforced it. Guidelines have been softened over the years as moviemakers challenged the limits.

Church leaders argued that Hollywood's self-censorship code was too weak. Their attack went on for decades. The focus on sex and violence was soon expanded by self-appointed critics to include political topics. Disputes between labor and management were frowned on, as were stories featuring government or police corruption and official injustice. Films that failed to meet strict standards were blacklisted and boycotted.

A number of states and cities set up their own censorship boards, but the standards varied from one board to another, a difficult situation for a national industry. The Kansas board, for example, banned scenes of smoking or dri,nking, limited kissing scenes to a few seconds and even cut a scene showing diaper changing. A series of United States Supreme Court decisions from the late 1940s to the 1970s overturned state obscenity laws and resulted in more leeway for moviemakers.

Foreign films and television influenced an easing of restrictions. Generally more open in regard to sex content, European nations could be stricter about political ideas. *All Quiet on the Western Front* (1930), denounced for its pacifism, was banned by a number of European governments. Pressured from all sides, the motion picture industry in the United States decided on new national standards based on age. In 1968, modeled on a British system, a self-censorship code was adopted that we know by the G, PG, R, and NC-17 (formerly X) designations.

Italy after World War II originated a school of neorealism, the opposite of Hollywood glitter. Films like *Open City* (1945), *Shoeshine* (1946) and *The Bicycle Thief* (1948) had the gritty feel and look of the documentary as they chronicled the bleak lives of the urban poor.

Japan's film industry after World War II sparkled because of its great directors. Akira Kurosawa, the director best known to Western audiences, made *Rashomon* (1950), a costume drama set in Japan's long feudal era. This classic film is often mentioned in ordinary conversation to argue that people who share the same experience have different memories and recollections of the event. Critics list *Rashomon* among the great films of all time.

India and China have also developed notable film industries. India's Bollywood produces more films than Hollywood and in the *masala* films that mix genre fills them with melodrama, music and dance. From China in recent years have come award winning dramas and fantasy films that have captivated audiences with their ethereal action. Iran is among smaller nations that have recognized the influence and goodwill that can follow the distribution of strong film stories of ordinary people dealing with ordinary problems. International films reveal a shared humanity that all mankind can recognize existing beyond cultures, languages and frontiers.

Enter Television

The Supreme Court, in a 1948 anti-trust decision, *U.S. v. Paramount*, ordered the studios to divest themselves of ownership of theater chains. It took Hollywood several years to recover from the triple blows of divestiture, an influx of foreign films from postwar European film studios and competition from the newly emerging television industry. Box office receipts plummeted.

With fear and hostility Hollywood at first tried to ignore television as just a fad, denying the new medium access to its actors, directors, scripts, studio back lots and film libraries. Little by little, television chipped away at each of these barriers. None stand today. With their heavy overhead and expensive talent on contract, the big studios were losing millions of dollars. To protect themselves they cut their staffs, ended contracts with their stars and other high priced talent and began renting out their studio facilities to television production companies.

Resultant weakening of the Hollywood studios allowed independent producers to step in to make smaller films, take artistic chances with new approaches to subject matter and distribute their films to theaters no longer in the tight grip of the major studios. Some independent films tested the limits that censors would allow. A fresh breeze was blowing through studios whose practices had become stiff and stale. Efforts to compete by expanding the screen with new projection systems like 3-D, Cinerama and CinemaScope had mixed success, but greater use by the studios of color and stereo, especially in musicals, showed favorably in comparison with the monaural, black-and-white of the television screen. The 1950s also saw movie stars break away to make independent deals instead of being tied to studio contracts, starting with James Stewart in 1952. The era of the big studios was coming to an end, but audiences still wanted movies.

The Drive-ins

Downtown movie palaces and single neighborhood theaters shut down as television reached across the land after the close of World War II and middle and working class families migrated outward to the suburbs. However, one kind of movie theater thrived during the 1950s and 1960s. In the postwar era of outdoor living, of gardening, boating and barbecuing, the drive-in theater was an easy fit and reflected the return of automobile production as well as the suburban population shift. By 1958 nearly one theater in three was a drive-in, nearly 5,000 across the nation. They were so popular that they remained viable businesses even though the weather closed them for months in the northern states. More families had automobiles, gas was cheap and so was an evening at the drive-in, with free admission for kids and no problem about bringing your own sandwiches, even a whole dinner.

An evening at the drive-in was family time, an evening with friends or a date and no strangers to shush you if you talked. You could even bring infants. It was not unlike an evening with the television, except that the movies were more fun than most of the available live television fare, and the screen was much bigger. The drive-in theatre was a harbinger of improved television and later of video rentals. It fit marketing consultant Faith Popcorn's phrase to "cocoon," which means insulating oneself or hiding from the normal social environment, which may be perceived as distracting, unfriendly, dangerous or otherwise unwelcome.[17] Technology has made cocooning easier than ever before. The telephone and the internet are inventions that invite a kind of socialized cocooning in which one can live in physical isolation while maintaining contact with others.

Rising real estate values along with the improving quality of television eventually shut down the "ozoner" (so-called because of the car exhaust odor). The adoption of Daylight Savings Time also hurt drive-ins because it pushed show starting times too close to bedtime. Teenagers found their escape from the family at the new shopping center's air-conditioned multiplex. The rest of the family would do their eating, talking and baby minding in front of the tube, maybe with a tape or DVD.

The drive-in has not totally disappeared. In fact, it has seen a slight resurgence with some new drive-ins using DVD players, digital projectors, iPods and FM transmitters to show films on large outdoor screens.[18] Some cities have had outdoor rooftop showings. Families in summertime are enjoying movies under the stars, catching up to what poor people in tropical countries have been doing for decades.

Watching Movies at Home

The public left indoor movie theaters for drive-ins partly for the convenience and cheaper cost. Later they left theaters and drive-ins to sit in front of television screens to watch sitcoms and movies, again partly because of convenience and cost. Today we can watch what we download or what arrives in the mail at home without any worry about what friends will say or neighbors

Renting or Owning

The neighborhood video store once impressed us with its wide variety of movie tapes. Today Netflix and Blockbuster do the same with DVDs by mail and download. In addition to the new releases, far more choices are available than are found in all the theaters in town. Centuries ago a book was a precious possession that only the rich could own. Now anyone can own a book and it is almost as easy to own a movie. It is by no means unusual for a home library to contain more movies than books. Home entertainment is often scheduled around a DVD that was ordered online or picked up on a shopping trip. The reason is obvious: choice, convenience, and control.

Business-man Andre Blay made a deal in 1977 to buy cassette production rights to fifty 20th Century Fox movies, but Blay discovered that few customers wanted to buy his tapes, although everyone wanted to rent them at a lower price. Video rental shops soon sprouted like corner groceries. In fact, sometimes the corner grocery itself devoted a shelf to videotapes, making it simple to stop by after work to pick up the fixings for the evening's dinner and entertainment, maybe to be consumed together.

In time, these video shops would be joined by video supermarkets that displayed tens of thousands of titles stored on both videotape and DVD discs in sections labeled *new releases, comedy, adventure, horror, science fiction, romance, children, family, inspirational, exercise, travel, concert, foreign, classics, documentary*, and, in a separate room, *adults only*. Music videos and games got their own sections as did "how-to's" on everything from losing weight to cooking. Candy bars, ice cream, and bags of popcorn for microwaving at home mimicked the cinema. Immigrants from non-English countries kept a shelf of films in their native language.

The cinema is a fixture at the shopping mall. For couples, it is the place to go on a date. For youths, it is a place to meet friends, to hang out, to escape the family for an evening. For kids, it is a Saturday afternoon treat. It continues, but the studio system has largely collapsed with the growth of cable subscribers and cable channels.

will think. There is no need to dress up or get dressed at all, pay parking fees, hire a babysitter, be quiet or even sit up. We can phone a friend, leaf through a magazine, eat a seven-course dinner, stop the DVD to go to the kitchen, the bathroom or the baby's crib, watch a scene over or set the machine to record a TV program while we are away. We won't miss a syllable. Did Cecil B. DeMille have it any better than this? We time-shift programs, so prime time is any time. Fast-forwarding through taped commercials gave advertising agencies heartburn before TiVo did.

As a result of the appeal of this easygoing lifestyle, we as a society are less social. Like all mediated communication, motion pictures substitute for direct contact with other people. Our pattern of life has been marked by less reading of books, a drop-off in church attendance and fewer visits to lectures, concerts, friends and family. A pattern has developed of staying home to watch movies instead of going to dances, sports events, club meetings or bowling alleys, activities that television and stored media have to some extent displaced.[19] Watching a film with someone provides a limited degree of human contact. When adult friends or relatives drop by for an evening, it does not promise an evening of conversation as it once did, but perhaps a little conversation and a lot of movie watching. When a child's friends visit, look for a video game accompanied by a minimum of conversation.

There is one other thing that home viewing is not. It is not an *event*. Going out and surrounded in a darkened theater by strangers who are sharing the moment is more so. Seeing the action on a big screen and hearing the sound all around adds to a sense of escapism.[20] Although that sense, along with the heavily advertised first run movies, can pull patrons to the box office line, it is not enough on a blustery evening to coax large numbers of people out of their homes. We "go" to the movies in other ways, using new hardware for the software we love to watch.

Despite fears about the new medium, television certainly did not kill the motion picture. Nor did it kill the motion picture theater. Economic realities did force changes. Gone are most of the ornate downtown picture palaces, the mom-and-pop single neighborhood theaters and the suburban drive-ins. In their place has come the more efficient, unadorned multiplexes in shopping malls, where they share parking spaces with supermarkets. Multiplexes started in 1963 in Kansas City with two cinemas side by side. The landscape would in time be dotted by mega-multiplexes with fifteen to twenty screens sharing a lobby redolent of popcorn in an effort to make going out to the movies an event more enjoyable than just watching the same movie at home. Facing economic pressures on all sides, cinemas derive most of their income from the snack bar.

We "Go" to the Movies

It is a mistake to think of motion pictures as an industry that begins with production and ends in a movie theater. Considered that way, the old medium certainly suffered with the advance of the new medium, television, just as the television industry later suffered with the popularity of newer media. Videotape suffered in turn with the arrival of DVD, which at this writing is competing with downloading from the internet. Seen purely from the production standpoint, however, the motion picture medium has expanded. Around the world more movies are being made on a variety of media than ever before and they are distributed through an increasing number of outlets to an increasing number of viewers.

We may travel no further than our comfortable living room sofa, fortifying ourselves with a bowlful of freshly microwaved popcorn before we tune in or pop in a promising movie. Replacing physical film or tape with digital files, the delivery media are different, yet movies are still movies.

In the changing software distribution pattern, a feature film usually starts life in first-run mall theaters in the United States and large cities in other countries. The more popular films next go to cheaper second-run discount theaters, others straight to DVD. While the public still remembers the ads and reviews, films reach cable pay-per-view, video shops for sales and rental, the red envelopes of Netflix and the Red Box at the supermarket and streaming or downloading for computers. HBO, Cinemax, other premium cable channels and any channels willing to pay a fee for early release line up. Next, network television. Several years after they are first issued, the films are syndicated to stations and free cable channel "superstations." Along the way are strands of an extensive network of foreign distribution and such specialty outlets as airlines.

Home Movies

"Home movies" have been around at least since 1923, when the Cine-Kodak film camera and the Kodascope projector went on sale. They, too, form part of the story of motion pictures. Today, in homes far from Hollywood, more movies are being made than ever before as a result of the availability of inexpensive, easy-to-use desktop video hardware and software. After the video camera-recorder—camcorder—was introduced, millions were sold each year, the digital camcorder gradually supplanting the analog version, followed by tapeless cameras (*See chapter 11: Computers*). That more people than ever before are shooting video clips or even producing entire movies is due in part to digital technology. Making a film that looks relatively professional has become affordable for many people. It was not possible during the golden age of the studios. The phrase *desktop video* has found its way into the language next to *desktop publishing*. Desktop video films can't match the Hollywood product, but they are gaining in popularity and sophistication.[21]

The term "film" itself is an anachronism both as a noun and as a verb. Filming was done on a photographic film base, on videotape and then by digital memory units such as discs, but it has left its language behind. "Filmmakers" still "film," no matter what they record on. And despite all the changes, movies are still movies. They are different because of all of us. We are different because of them.

Timeline

1646: In Germany, Athanasius Kircher invents a magic lantern to throw images.

1791: In London, the opening of the first Panorama.

1825: Thaumatrope, a disk with image on each side, demonstrates persistence of vision.

1878: Eadweard Muybridge photographs a trotting horse, forerunner of movies.

1882: Etienne Jules Marey designs a rifle-like camera that shoots 12 photos per second.

1890: From England, the kinematograph, a combination camera and projector.

1894: Thomas Edison and W.K.L. Dickson construct the peep-show Kinetoscope.

1895: France's Lumière brothers' portable movie camera can also print, project films.

In a Paris cellar, a paying audience sees Lumière's motion pictures projected.

1896: Edison's Vitascope, designed by Thomas Armat, brings film projection to U.S.

1900: Much of Europe and Japan begin to make movies.

1903: *The Great Train Robbery* introduces editing, creates demand for fiction movies.

1905: Pittsburgh's Nickelodeon cinema creates template of showing movies for the masses.

1910: D.W. Griffith sets up shop in California at a place called Hollywood.

1912: Movie cameras abandon cranks for motors that smooth motion.

1913: *Gertie the Dinosaur*, the first animated cartoon, requires 10,000 drawings.

1914: Grand cinema houses start to replace nickelodeons.

1915: Hollywood begins star system. Charlie Chaplin goes from $125 to $10,000 weekly.

   The Birth of a Nation is praised for its film art. Its racism leads to riots.

1922: Robert Flaherty's *Nanook of the North* is the first feature film documentary.

1927: Al Jolson's *The Jazz Singer* establishes the idea of movie sound.

   The Academy of Motion Picture Arts and Sciences is founded.

1929: 24 frames/second established as sound motion picture camera standard.

1933: Camden, New Jersey, introduces the drive-in movie theater.

1937: A full-length animated film, Disney's *Snow White and the Seven Dwarfs*.

1939: Blockbusters draw audiences: *The Wizard of Oz, Gone with the Wind, Stagecoach*.

1952: 3-D movies make audiences duck.

   The Supreme Court gives movies First Amendment free speech protection.

1955: Movie studios open their vaults for television rentals, sales.

1956: Foreign language films get an Oscar category. This year: Italy's *La Strada*.

1963: In Kansas City, the first multiplex opens: two cinemas side by side.

1968: Hollywood adopts an age-based rating system; at first: G, M, R, X.

1993: IMAX 3D digital sound system goes into a New York cinema.

2001: From Harry Potter to *Crouching Tiger*, CGI special effects rock audiences.

2002: Desktop video: making movies becomes more affordable.

   DVD burners download movies; film piracy becomes an international problem.

2010: A woman, Kathryn Bigelow, wins the Oscar for best director (*The Hurt Locker*).

9. Radio

Helping Us Through the Rough Years

Radio was never just one thing, one isolated invention. It did not have just one effect on us. People involved with radio at its beginning did not consider broadcasting. They were not concerned with connecting with the public. As point-to-point *wireless* Morse code communication, radio extended the telegraph where wires could not run. Radio's dots and dashes were primarily for ship-to-shore, point-to-point communication. As a point-to-point *voice carrier*, it extended the range of the telephone. When its potential as a point to multiple point service was recognized, when technology opened a path and when advertising provided an economic underpinning, radio found a new social use. As *broadcasting*, radio gave uniformity to a diverse population, contact to the lonely and comfort to scattered listeners. And as it did so, it created a landscape that depended on unseen others for information and entertainment. Ironically, out of radio broadcasting and its effort to reach the broadest possible audience, *narrowcasting* evolved, reaching a closely defined audience.

Radio broadcasting changed the way that people chose to be amused and informed at home. Many people alive today grew up in homes where reading aloud was a common activity in the evening. Radio added a new dimension to family entertainment as listeners gathered around a machine instead of a parent. Reading aloud in a family setting requires active participation. As she reads, a mother looks at her children for their silent responses or questions. Even sitting passively in a theater or concert hall requires dressing up or at least dressing before venturing out to share the event with others in an auditorium, making such a trip a social experience. Listening to the radio requires none of this. The listener can sit quietly at home and let the newscasters, deejays and music do all the work. Once agreement about a program choice is reached, listening is passive. The speakers and musicians do not need your nods of encouragement.

"Golden Age"

During radio's "golden age"—the Depression years, World War II and the early postwar years—announcers chosen for their lack of regional accent spoke to all Americans. Illiteracy did not matter. The medium proved quite a leveler, especially ideal for a poor society with millions of immigrants eager to learn the language of their new country and to fit in.[1]

Radio's golden age saw families everywhere gathered in the evening to listen to dramas, comedies, music, quizzes, variety shows and, of course, commercials. A culture was transmitted and absorbed. The broadcast schedule made the radio in the parlor the place for the family to gather. It brought entertainment, information and hope to an American population in need of all three. Comedians became household names. After school and on Saturday mornings children's adventure serials delivered the same tune-in-tomorrow message. (but Britain's BBC after-school "children's hour" meant silence.) The dinner hour brought news and commentary. Comedies and drama were broadcast in prime time. Sunday offered church services, classical music and sports. In the midst of the misery of Depression and then war, the American public welcomed the free entertainment and did not regard listening to commercials as a cost.

From the White House, FDR's mastery of intimate conversation in his "fireside chats" circumvented the newspaper barons arrayed against him. This was not the local, democratic politics of shaking hands and delivering food baskets on election day, but it was certainly democratic in the sense that FDR was reaching out for support to everyone within earshot.

In the morning, soap operas captured the housewives. The real message, from day to day, through plots that never resolved was: stay tuned.[2] The soap operas gave listeners a sense of participation in the lives of people they would never meet. The fictional characters became such a part of listeners' lives that when a soap opera character had a baby, they sent gifts. Letters would be addressed to fictional characters warning them that other characters were up to no good. Here was still more evidence of the power of mass communication to transcend physical space and forge distant connections.

More than any other medium in history up to that time, the radio gave people a sense of sharing what the day held for them. If you already owned a radio set—and the price of sets dropped significantly in the Depression years[3]—it delivered all this and more at no cost to you except a minute or two of your time every so often to listen to a commercial, and some of these were just as much fun as the programs.

Here was *broadcasting*, a word that previously had been used only to describe what a farmer did when he sowed his field with seed. The U.S. Navy appropriated the word during World War I to describe messages sent to a number of ships at once. The wireless industry derived its word from this. Based on the idea that rays of electromagnetic waves radiated from a transmitter, the word *radio* itself came into general use in the United States only after the vacuum tube sent voices into the air. The term much used in Britain was *wireless*.

Scientific Roots

During the 19th century, scientists puzzled over the nature of electricity and what it might be capable of doing, sharing their discoveries in papers and lectures. Michael Faraday in England and Joseph Henry in the United States published papers on electromagnetism. Scottish physicist James Clerk Maxwell added to what was known with his theory of the existence of invisible waves. It was widely believed that light waves and electro–magnetic waves could not simply travel through "nothing." Scientists imagined a substance like a thin, colorless, odorless jelly in the air that they named "ether" (not to be confused with the gas used as an anesthetic). That theory has long since vanished, but the word stuck around to refer to radio transmission.[4]

Heinrich Hertz, a German physicist, supported Maxwell's theory by experiments that sent electrical current through the air. French scientist Édouard Branly put iron filings in a glass tube. When he sent an electric current through the air, the filings packed together—or *cohered*—around metal rods at the ends of the tube. This action in his coherer completed a circuit so that electricity passed through the tube. English physicist Oliver Lodge went a step further by tuning the transmitter and the receiver of the current to the same frequency. He wanted to send a Morse Code message through the air, but his coherer could do no more than identify brief bursts of electric energy.[5] In Moscow, Alexander Popov in 1895 demonstrated to fellow scientists a practical application of radio waves, but he did not seek a patent.

Marconi

These researchers were scientists, not businessmen, but entrepreneurs perceived that practical commercial and military potential existed for the new technology. Guglielmo Marconi, the teenage son of a well-to-do Italian landowner, who was fascinated by reports of the research, began his own experiments at home in the hope of creating a business with wireless telegraphy. He received some guidance from a physics professor, Auguste Righi, who was a neighbor.[6] In 1894, young Marconi sent a current through a coherer to sound a buzzer ten yards away. Soon he was able to send Morse Code dots and dashes for miles across the hills around his home. Marconi's mother, Anne Jameson Marconi, a member of an Irish family famed for its whiskey, foresaw the possibilities for ships at sea to signal and to receive messages from coastal stations. According to Marconi family lore, a short-sighted official in the Italian Ministry of Posts and Telegraphs turned the invention down as having no value.

Anne Marconi and her son took their wireless equipment to England, the nation with the world's greatest navy. Anne's well-connected relatives arranged meetings with telegraph officials of the British Post Office, including William Preece, who once dismissed Alexander Graham Bell's telephone invention because England had plenty of messenger boys. Successful demonstrations of Marconi's wireless led to financial offers as well as to claims that others had already sent such signals. Marconi held firm. His family arranged to sell equipment to the British army and navy and to train the wireless operators. They also provided equipment for commercial shipping companies, along with operators on ships and at shore stations. With this, wireless communication emerged from the laboratory and strode into the world of commerce.

Guglielmo Marconi

Extending the signal's reach, in 1901 Marconi transmitted the three dots of the Morse Code letter "S" faintly across the Atlantic from Cornwall to Newfoundland. He formed an American subsidiary, the Marconi Wireless Telegraph Company of America that would eventually become RCA, the Radio Corporation of America.

Competition and new inventions came from several quarters. Marconi's transmission was not too complex to imitate. His efforts to monopolize the wireless business by refusing communication with non-Marconi operators except in emergencies raised a storm of protest. The German government was furious. Its navy was operating its own system, originally based on Marconi's experiments. A rising militant nationalism among the great powers of Europe that led to World War I hardly softened mutual suspicions. A 1906 Berlin conference resulted in the world's first international radio agreement, mandating that international coastal stations must handle all messages, and that the letters "SOS" should be used for distress. Marconi operators generally ignored the decision and continued to use "CQD" ("seek you, distress").

Other scientists and inventors also saw the business possibilities. They included Oliver Lodge in England and Reginald Fessenden, Lee de Forest, John Stone, and E. Howard Armstrong in the United States. The quarrels that resulted among them would end years later in lengthy court battles fought by corporations.

Commercial shipping added wireless equipment, nudged by new laws. In 1909 off the coast of Nantucket the merchant ship *Republic* collided in the fog with the Italian liner *Florida* packed with Italian immigrants. The repeated distress call "CQD" led to the rescue of all aboard both vessels. The next year Congress required most passenger ships to carry wireless equipment but did not

Radio Goes to War

Radio first went into combat in the Russo-Japanese war of 1904. Both the Russian and Japanese fleets had installed the signaling devices, but the Russian admiral chose wireless silence in hopes of eluding the waiting Japanese fleet. Meanwhile, warned by shore radio at lookout points of the impending arrival of the Russian "great white fleet" into Asian waters, the Japanese navy set a trap that sank most of the imperial Russian ships at the battle of Tsushima Strait.[4] The Japanese fleet suffered almost no losses, achieving the most one-sided naval victory in history. Russia sued for peace. Now radio had played a small but vital part in affecting the course of history.

News of the Japanese victory in the Russo-Japanese War was hailed all across Asia and Africa. At last, a non–European country had defeated a European imperialist. Japan was firmly entrenched on the Asian mainland, remaining there and expanding its territory until the turn of fortunes in World War II. Radio's military possibilities took to the skies in 1911 with the first air-to-ground transmission; World War I airplanes served as artillery spotters using Morse code.

require operators to be on duty around the clock, an oversight it regretted two years later after the *Titanic* hit an iceberg and went down with 1,522 passengers and crew on its maiden voyage. The *Titanic* was on a well-traveled sea lane. The *Californian* reportedly was only nineteen miles away, but its wireless operator had gone to bed. The ship sailed on, though ships further away responded. Bad as it was, the death toll would have been higher had wireless communication not existed. Like travel by ship, air travel would also find safety in the reach of radio communication. Radio has made travel safer.

Congress followed with the Radio Act of 1912, requiring that a federal license was needed for transmission. Unlike the right of publishing guaranteed by the First Amendment, broadcasting would be a privilege the government could grant or take away. Getting a license was as simple at first as sending a postcard to the Department of Commerce. At the time, no sense emerged of the chaos that would arrive a decade later with the arrival of commercial broadcasting. If one purpose of the Radio Act of 1912 was to limit the number of amateur broadcasters, it failed. Most licenses went to hobbyists who used spark transmitters to send Morse code. By 1917 there were 13,581 of them, plus uncounted thousands of other hobbyists who broadcast without a license. Alone among the large industrialized nations, the United States would allow all three forms of mediated point to point communication—telegraph, telephone, radio—to remain predominantly in private hands.

Other Inventors

At the start of World War I, radio meant wireless dots and dashes for military and commercial purposes. The main business of radio was the manufacturing of wireless equipment for ships, shore stations and military communication. The other part of the business was the sale or lease of communication services to the shipping industry and the government. That would change because inventors who were improving telephone service wanted to apply the results to radio. John Ambrose Fleming built a two-element vacuum tube, or "diode." It sent electrons flowing from a wire filament to a plate. This was the first electronic device and it carried speech on radio waves to earphones.

In 1906, while tinkering, American inventor Lee de Forest added a third element between the filament and the plate, a piece of wire bent into a zigzag grid. His "audion" tube regulated and amplified the flow of electrons. Now the wireless telegraph could carry a voice. This was truly radio. De Forest was not sure what he had accomplished, but a more competent inventor, E. Howard Armstrong, figured out how to use the audion tube as an oscillator that *transmitted* radio waves as well as receiving them. Reginald Fessenden, a Canadian who had once worked in the Edison laboratory, and Swedish immigrant E.F.W. Alexanderson, a General Electric engineer, designed a high frequency alternator that could send a radio signal thousands of miles.

Lee de Forest

Fessenden was the first inventor to send a human voice by wireless. He did so on Christmas Eve, 1906 from his laboratory at Brant Rock, Massachusetts, to an audience of some amazed Marconi operators on duty at their posts on ships and at coastal stations listening for dots and dashes. He also reached some New England fishermen, a few naval officers and some reporters whom Fessenden had notified a few days earlier. He read from the Bible, sang, played the violin, broadcast phonograph music and gave a short speech.[7]

Two years later de Forest went to the top of the Eiffel Tower in Paris to broadcast opera music that could be faintly heard 550 miles away. De Forest saw the possibility of bringing music and voices into people's homes on a schedule, telling a *New York Times* reporter, "I look forward to the day when opera may be brought into every home. Someday the news and even advertising will be sent out over the wireless telephone."[6] By 1909, Charles "Doc" Herrold, who operated an engineering college in San Jose, California, broadcast news and music on a regular schedule. In 1915, de Forest manufactured equipment that was tuned to his occasional music and news broadcasts plus the commercials he aired to advertise his equipment. He had stumbled onto the vacuum tube by chance, but his vision of the potential of broadcasting was clear long before broadcasting became a reality. Also in 1915, from a transmitter in Virginia, AT&T sent an audio signal that was picked up in both Paris and Pearl Harbor.

Listening by Catwhisker

Because a single vacuum tube easily cost a week's wages, listening to distant radio signals might have been out of the range of most purses. However, the "crystal and catwhisker" detector, easy to fashion and cheap, was the poor hobbyist's answer. A quartz crystal or a galena rock, by admitting electricity in only one direction, can detect radio waves if the crystal is touched at a certain spot with a fine wire, dubbed a "catwhisker." This discovery opened radio to thousands of hobbyists, some of whom became the cadre of the broadcasting industry. They wrapped a copper wire around a round, sturdy Quaker Oats cardboard box, the kind you still find in grocery stores. The catwhisker radio could detect a wireless signal and feed it into earphones, although it could not amplify the signal.

At the end of World War I, the business of radio was still largely vested in the manufacture of ship-to-ship and ship-to-shore radiotelegraph (Morse code) and radiotelephone (voice) communication equipment, the transmission of messages and the manufacture of spark transmitters bought by hobbyists. The idea that a vast market existed for radio was hardly credible, but in the years immediately after the war there were hints of its future.

The hobbyist's pleasure came from picking up call letters from a distant city. The hobbyists, many of them teenaged boys and young men, formed clubs that met by wireless. Their enthusiasm kept them at it day and night. This proved to be a problem for U.S. Navy and commercial operators transmitting on the same frequency. The Navy complained that children hogged the ether and would not give way. Adding a second wavelength helped somewhat, but the rancor continued. Preachers and educators who wanted to use the airwaves joined the fray.

The sound was faint until E. Howard Armstrong, still a graduate student, did more than convert de Forest's audion tube into an oscillator. He reworked it so sound came booming out of earphones. When radio sets with these redesigned vacuum tubes went on sale, it was the start of the technology necessary to change from a hobby in basements and garages to an instrument of family entertainment fit for the parlor.

It would take more than this, however, to make radio a household appliance. Radio receivers manufactured after World War I were large, clunky, temperamental metal boxes with expensive tubes, lots of knobs tricky to adjust wandering signals, a mess of wires and a large, smelly battery filled with acid, not unlike the storage battery in an automobile. A radio was hardly a fit thing to put on a good parlor rug or a polished mahogany table.

The batteries and the maze of wires that accompanied them would be replaced a few years later by plugs that went into sockets for 110-volt alternating current available in the wall; the earphones later were replaced by a loudspeaker so that the entire family could listen at the same time. The radio set was ready for its new social use as broadcast entertainment. Housed inside a wooden cabinet to match the furniture, the radio would take its place in the family parlor beside two other sound producing devices that delivered entertainment, the piano and the phonograph.

The Start of Broadcasting

Hobbyists by the thousands had become radio operators for the Army and Navy. With the war over, some of these operators wanted to start new stations to broadcast voice and music. Frank Conrad, a Westinghouse Corporation engineer who worked on manufacturing portable equipment for the Signal Corps, was among the visionaries. Setting up a transmitter in the garage of his home in Pittsburgh after returning from the war, he was an amateur who broadcast to other amateurs for the pleasure of doing it. He broadcast music by placing his microphone next to a Victrola, requesting postcards from listeners so that he could determine the range of his signals. So many listeners replied to ask for their favorite song that Conrad started transmitting the broadcasts according to a schedule, adding sports scores and some singing and instrument playing by his children. A Pittsburgh newspaper printed a feature story about it.

To meet requests for music that Conrad did not possess, the owner of a phonograph record shop agreed to lend him records in return for identifying the store on the air. The records Conrad played increased the sales of those titles. All this interest led a local department store to offer assembled wireless sets for sale. That led Conrad's employer, Westinghouse, to manufacture radio receivers for voice and music. Conrad's garage broadcasting equipment was brought onto the Westinghouse lot, a transmitter went up and broadcasting began on November 2, 1920, with the call letters KDKA. The date was chosen so that the first broadcast would be of the Harding-Cox presidential election. Following Conrad's idea, Westinghouse offered a regular program schedule. A few thousand people tuned in.

Aimee Semple McPherson

Evangelists set up stations to attract worshippers. In the 1920s Aimee Semple McPherson grew rich and famous as she built a large, devoted national following. McPherson sensed that the "wireless telephone" in the home carried a degree of intimacy and connection to the lonely. She employed it effectively to bring listeners together to share moments of silent prayer, an oddly brilliant use of the talking medium. McPherson lost her license because she would not stick to her assigned frequency, arguing that she needed to operate on "God's frequency."

Photo courtesy of University of Southern California, on behalf of the USC Specialized Libraries and Archival Collections.

The business of broadcasting became the sale of equipment to transmit or receive broadcasts, not the broadcasts themselves. Eager high school students formed radio clubs. Universities erected transmitters through which professors lectured.

Newspapers also set up transmitters to attract subscribers.[8] Some department stores set up low-powered broadcast operations in a corner of the store to attract curious shoppers, but they did not advertise their goods. At first nothing was advertised on radio. Few businesses spent much money on radio broadcasting or expected much money back. The quality of the sound was poor; scratchy phonograph records did not help. Even so, groups got together to listen in stores, hotel lobbies or speakeasies.

Commercials

Both before and after the introduction of commercials, the purpose of programming was to attract listeners to buy something, radio sets at first, then advertised products. The AT&T radio station in New York, WEAF, opened the floodgates to commercial broadcasting when it rented time to a real estate company to talk about its new apartments on Long Island. For its $300 investment in a soft-sell sales pitch repeated during one evening and four afternoons, the real estate company sold $127,000 worth of apartments.[8] AT&T, normally in the business of renting its equipment by the minute to telephone callers, had managed its station like a telephone company, initiating what it called "toll broadcasting."

AT&T considered itself to be the sole proprietor of this idea, but other transmitting stations saw the possibility to make money. It took four more years of almost no "toll broadcasts," many arguments among corporations and a final agreement between the Telephone Group headed by AT&T and the Radio Group headed by RCA. But broadcasting in the United States now was constructing a strong financial base and a new social use, even if not everyone warmed to the idea.

A number of listeners were offended that commercials were broadcast over a radio station that depended on a government license. Secretary of Commerce Herbert Hoover told broadcasters, "I believe that the quickest way to kill broadcasting would be to use it for direct advertising. The reader of the newspaper has an option whether he will read an ad or not, but if a speech by the president is to be used as the meat in a sandwich of two patent medicine advertisements, there will be no radio left."[9] The advertising industry itself, with a nervous eye on the print media, chimed in with editorial comment in *Printers' Ink*: "Any attempt to make the radio an advertising medium... would, we think, prove positively offensive to great numbers of people. The family circle is not a public place, and advertising has no business intruding there unless it is invited."[10] The National Association of Broadcasters used similar language in its first Radio Code in 1929, but soon changed its mind.

Broadcasting stayed in private hands, but the United States government was not totally divorced from it because radio stations needed licenses to transmit. To avoid giving ammunition to opponents, radio stations were cautious about what they advertised. They worried at first, for example, that toothpaste might be too intimate a product to advertise. But the potential of the new medium was just too great to do nothing. Toothpaste found its way into messages.

De Forest, who insisted on calling himself the "father of radio," attacked broadcasting for presenting commercial "spots," which he called "stains," and he lamented to the industry, "What have you done with my child?"

None of the corporations who had taken over the patents from individual owners had total control of the medium. Bitter court battles lasted for years and sometimes ended with compromises in the form of cross-licensing agreements to use each other's patents. Initially, RCA, General Electric and Westinghouse, the "radio group," concentrated on the receivers of messages, the audience. They regarded broadcast programs as a service to create public demand for their radio sets. AT&T and Western Electric were known as the "telephone group." Their concern was with the senders of messages, later called "sponsors." Today broadcasting, of course, combines programming and commercials.

National Choices

Other nations chose a different direction. Governments in most nations controlled all aspects of broadcasting. They would have no commercials for decades. The British Broadcasting Corporation, solidly pro–establishment in its programming policy, followed the principle of presenting what those in charge believed listeners should hear for their own good, not the American policy of broadcasting what listeners wanted to hear. Funds to support the BBC came from annual user license fees on radio sets. Years later, it would be licenses on television sets. In the mid–1950s, as television replaced radio, the British government finally licensed an independent commercial service, ITV, to operate. Most other industrialized nations preferred a version of the BBC model, often with direct government operation, although Canada and Mexico were among countries that permitted a mix of government and privately owned radio stations.

Totalitarian governments funded radio stations the way they funded all their departments, with annual taxpayer-supported budgets, a sure way to manage broadcasters like government employees and to keep them firmly under the thumb. Radio programming and the television programs that would follow had as their mission solidifying citizen loyalty, promoting national policies, supporting the government and security forces and opposing enemies, domestic and foreign.

The United States after World War I provided only one frequency for all radio transmission, with a second frequency added later for crop and weather reports. Still later a third frequency for music was added, based on the maritime communication model, where sender and receiver exchange brief messages, then go silent. But the broadcast stations were not silent. In fact, the broadcast stations were trying to be heard by boosting their transmission power to outshout each other and were drowning each other out. Government efforts to alleviate the clamor by opening up more frequencies were overwhelmed by new stations coming in to take advantage of commercial possibilities. Shortwave, previously used only by amateurs, was taken over for commercial and government purposes.

Communication Acts

Congress preferred not to upset anyone, yet some regulation was clearly needed. Four conferences called by the government in the 1920s had groups at each other's throats. Owners of large stations wanted stronger regulations to control who could broadcast. Small station owners wanted to be under the broadcasting tent. So did hobbyists.

Under the concept that the airwaves belong to the public, all the laws were based on the government's right to regulate broadcasting and determine who can hold a license. Stations pledged to operate "in the public interest, convenience, or necessity," but neither Congress nor the regulatory agencies ever specified what this means.

By these laws, the government is not permitted to determine what is broadcast, although it can fine stations heavily for broadcasts it considers indecent. The government's power to issue or retrieve the extremely valuable licenses is great but it is almost never enforced. The history of broadcast regulation in the United States has been one of competing influences, intense lobbying, power structures and the advantage that comes with owning stations that can help or hurt political candidates.[11]

Universities involved themselves from the start of broadcasting. Engineering departments established stations. Weather and farm conditions were reported. Professors in other departments who liked the platform were joined by union leaders and artists in several fields

A father and son listen to the radio over headsets in 1924.
Courtesy: Schenectady Museum Archives

who saw the cultural promise of the new medium. However, educators found themselves squeezed out by commercial broadcasters. Hesitant government intervention led to the Radio Act of 1927, which was expanded by the Communication Act of 1934, but not substantially changed again until the Communication Act of 1996 and the creation of the Corporation for Public Broadcasting to organize not only financial support, but also network structure and programming for non commercial radio and television.

Technology Improves

Not everyone waited for the AC power that began to replace radio batteries in 1926. In that year, one house in six already had a radio, many equipped with loudspeakers, so that listening took on the pleasure of dinner conversations. Nearly half the population lived in the countryside, far from telephones, daily newspapers or even electricity. Battery-operated radio became their connection to the world. They may have bought the radio primarily for entertainment, but it also delivered information. A rural public that might have been uninterested and uninformed about the economic and social turmoil in the nation and the world was now learning to care.

Listeners wrote warm letters to radio stations. Magazine articles described the joys of sitting at home alone or with family members to listen to their radios.[12] People *went out* to the movies, but *stayed in* to listen to the radio, as they would later with television. Radios also went into automobiles. In 1930, a battery eliminator that provided DC voltage to power radios from the car engine was a marked improvement. Cars and radios have gone together ever since like ham and eggs.[13]

Surveys and Networks

Audience surveys to determine who was listening would not come into existence until 1929. They would be started by Archibald Crossley and increase in size and sophistication as audience growth and network quests for higher advertising rates led agencies to insist on better information about who was tuned to which programs. Surveys revealed that even low income homes had at least one radio. The average home had a radio turned on more than five hours a day. In fact, low-income families listened to the free entertainment even more than middle-income families, just as low-income homes today watch more free television. During the Depression, when Americans cut back on going to the movies and buying subscriptions to newspapers, they spent even more time with free radio. Advertisers paid attention.

NBC and CBS by contracting with local stations had built nationwide networks. A nation without an authentic national newspaper now had the means to entertain and inform the entire American public. The tying together of stations, first as temporary "hookups" in a "chain" and later as permanent networks, solved a problem for broadcasters: how to pay for better programs. When stations in different cities broadcast the same program, its cost could be shared. Better programs also drew listeners away from competing stations. National advertisers who ignored individual stations were interested when a network audience could be measured in the millions.

RCA in 1926 assembled stations into two permanent networks, the "Red" (now NBC) and the "Blue" (now ABC). One year later the competitive CBS (Columbia Broadcasting System) network was formed. A fourth national network, the Mutual Broadcasting System, was put together in 1934. In New England, the Midwest and the Far West, regional networks formed. By 1940 more families had radios than cars, telephones, electricity or plumbing. A new means of communication had taken root. People accommodated their lives to it.

When broadcasting began, the broadcasters programmed what they themselves liked or what

The Commentators

If comedies and dramas during the golden age of radio brought people together to share the laughs and shivers, the news explainers pulled them into like-minded groupings. Unlike radio news today but similar to talk radio, the best-known newscasts were delivered by commentators who used a news item of the day as a hook to deliver a partisan monologue, liberal or conservative.

Listeners generally tuned to the commentator whose views made the most sense, meaning the commentator they agreed with.

During the decades, 1930-49, listeners could find answers to the miseries of the Depression and war in the voices of commentators Lowell Thomas, H.V. Kaltenborn, Gabriel Heatter, Fulton Lewis Jr., Walter Winchell and a dozen others. Listening to a politician or a commentator whose viewpoint matched your own made you feel that your opinion mattered.

In the early 21st century, radio commentary was dominated by conservative talk show speakers like Rush Limbaugh, who frequently referred with pride to their large audiences, yet insisted that they themselves were not part of media and not journalists. They identified themselves as "antidotes" to "the media."

their friends suggested. Vaudeville was popular, so some ideas came from there. It has been said that movies killed vaudeville. Radio wielded a knife, too.

In the 1920s, the networks were less likely to do their own programming than to sell blocks of time to advertisers to create the programs. Many were named for the advertised products, such as "The Eveready Hour" advertising batteries, "The Gold Dust Twins" advertising a household cleanser and "The A&P Gypsies" advertising the grocery chain. Because newspapers included program logs as an unpaid public service, the newspapers were really giving free publicity to a competing medium. As the newspapers themselves were carrying advertising for what the radio programs advertised, free publishing of program logs did not sit well at publishers conferences. During the Depression radio profits grew while newspaper profits stagnated.

News

To add insult to injury, for the two or three cents it cost to buy a daily newspaper, those radio stations that presented newscasts had access to all the news that a newspaper had labored to assemble. The stations could present the news over the air long before a delivery boy threw a copy of the newspaper onto the front porch. Newspapers struck back weakly. Some newspapers eliminated the free listings of daily radio programs, or they identified a program only as "Music" instead of "A&P Gypsies." That did not last long. Irate letters from readers and canceled subscriptions forced newspapers to abandon such tactics. Newspapers continued to list radio programs and then television programs free.

Radio coverage of the 1932 election that swept Franklin Delano Roosevelt into office and the intense coverage of the Lindbergh baby kidnapping opened the eyes of newspaper publishers to the competition. All this led to the "Press-Radio War" of 1933-35, when members of the powerful newspaper industry demanded that all newspapers stop including free daily radio logs. They pressured the wire services to deny their feeds to radio stations, except for a restricted feed by the new Press Radio Bureau that was available only for non-sponsored newscasts. Radio stations rebelled and started their own news gathering units.

Newspapers that owned radio stations joined independent radio stations and networks to oppose control. To some extent the "Press-Radio War" was a "Newspaper-Newspaper War."[14] In a short time, newspapers that tried to limit radio news gave up. As war clouds gathered in Europe, listeners sought more news from both newspapers and radio. Today, wire services are all too happy to sell their feeds, including a special broadcast wire, to radio and television stations.

Radio news reported World War II at home and abroad, delivering more news to more citizens than any other medium.[15] In a nation too large for a national press that was limited by available technology, radio commentators provided national voices, mixing their commentary with nuggets of the latest news.

Today, with exceptions such as America's Radio News Network, news on commercial radio has shrunk for the most part to little more than headlines or has disappeared entirely from local stations. However, that is not true of public radio. Both National Public Radio and individual public radio stations feature extended news reports that include field reports and interviews.

Influencing American Culture

Broadcasting has helped to both push its listeners together and to pull them apart. The most popular comedies, dramas and variety programs brought listeners of different backgrounds together in a shared experience. If you listened to Jack Benny or Fred Allen last night you could talk about them today at the factory lunch break, at the office water cooler or on the telephone. Radio broadcasting disseminated national culture and informed its listeners, and it sometimes influenced government leadership.

Listeners were also brought together by hearing a common language spoken with a standard national accent. They were pulled apart as choices increased. Compared with the few choices available during radio's golden age, broadcasting audiences today are inundated with multiple choices on the AM and FM dials plus those on cable radio.

Radio executives had not set out to alter human behavior or to educate. While evidence aplenty of cultural improvement can be found in American radio programing's long history, that was never the prime purpose of the men who created the radio industry. Nor did they consider themselves catalysts for bringing Americans together as a nation in order to continue at a deeper level what the telegraph and the telephone had done.

With announcers chosen for their neutral, non-regional speech pattern, and with strong Southern, New England and Brooklyn accents used for humor along with exaggerated foreign and ethnic accents, it was apparent for commercial reasons that the best accent was a non-accented middle-American way of speaking. The foreign, ethnic and regional characters were never presented as evil. They were intended to be funny.

However, they conformed to negative public images, notably Amos 'n' Andy, whose white actors portrayed the African-American characters as lazy, irresponsible, not very bright schemers.[16] Because of segregated housing and schools, many whites knew of blacks only through these caricatures.

Yet radio did its part to heat the "melting pot" of the American immigrant experience. The Ku Klux Klan, popular in the South and Midwest during the 1920s, did not take hold on American networks. In the 1930s Father Charles Coughlin, the firebrand anti-British, anti-Semitic and increasingly pro-Nazi priest, developed a huge radio following for a time. According to some estimates, on any given Sunday one-third of the nation was tuned into "the radio priest." A plea from him could pile 100,000 telegrams on senators' desks. But, as his attacks intensified, stations unplugged from his hookup. Under pressure from Roman Catholic Church leaders and the government, Coughlin finally left the airwaves in 1939.

FM

Armstrong's invention of FM (frequency modulation) in 1933 held the promise not only of a clearer audio signal than AM (amplitude modulation), but also a bandwidth that could accommodate many new stations. That FM was not diffused until after World War II, more than a dozen years later, was due to the machinations of David Sarnoff, head of RCA and founder of NBC. Sarnoff understood FM's potential all too well but considered it a hindrance to television, which RCA was spending a fortune to develop. Armstrong's frustration over years of legal battles led to his suicide.

After the war, new FM stations did arrive, slowly at first, most of them devoted to music to take advantage of the FM clarity. Also arriving in the postwar years were stereophonic transmission, high fidelity audiotape, LP (long playing) records and tape cassettes, all promising better sound. America shifted from being a nation of radio listeners to a nation of audio appreciators.

Even without FM, the quality of radio sound improved year by year as audio engineers, replacing vacuum tubes with transistors, labored over every part of the sound's path from the microphone in the studio to the speaker in the home radio set. In 1971, AM–FM radios were being installed by car manufacturers. Tuners, turntables, pre–amps, amplifiers and their connections were improved for the amateur audiophiles who were willing to pay for perfect tones.

Radio Survives TV

Postwar radio seemed headed for trouble. Television gobbled up radio's best programs, staff, talent, funding and energy. In the postwar boom years families moved their radio consoles out of their new tract homes to make room for the even larger television console with a 7-inch or 12-inch round screen.

Yet radio did not die. Rather, it was reinvented. Today more radio stations are on the air than ever, and 99% of all U.S. homes have at least one radio set.[17] As television took over evening prime time, radio shifted its attention to drive time, the morning and afternoon work commute. Radios went to the beach and next to the kitchen sink and the factory work bench. Clock radios woke us up and helped put us to sleep, the car radio eased the twice-daily commute, background radio accompanied a meal and music pouring through Walkman earphones accompanied a jog. Radio broadcasting would be different, but it was far from finished.

One difference between radio during its golden age and today is that we no longer look at our radios. When the radio sat in the parlor, the family that gathered around for their favorite programs watched the radio, which, after all, was talking to them. Radio now is an accompaniment to driving, working, or starting the morning. Listeners are too occupied to stare at their radios.

Radio stations today try to reach an interest group niche market, an identifiable segment of the radio market, such as listeners 18 to 35, or an audience that responds to country and western music. Some stations shifted focus to attract ethnic minorities. To the best of the ability of the fourteen thousand radio stations in the United States, listeners are channeled.

Musical tastes are the stations' most effective targeting tool. A playlist stays within an identity like rock 'n' roll, jazz, easy listening, country and western, mariachi, rhythm and blues, classical, big band, hip hop and so on. Record companies participate because it increases music sales. Combined with all the other choices people now have for mediated communication, less commonality exists at the office water cooler. Instead, those who share our tastes connect electronically from a distance. Emailing and blogging our opinions, we live in a virtual water cooler world.

Looking Ahead

The future promises to continue to segment the audience. The first decade of the twenty-first century brought rapid growth in several types of radio programdistribution. Satellite radio services like Sirius and XM carry music with CD-quality sound, plus news and talk, all without commercials. Because the signal arrives from a satellite, it remains constant as a car crosses the nation, unlike local stations with limited range.

Distance no longer implies static. Nor, as we travel, does it imply listening to the same stations that locals hear. The audio quality of satellite stations may be superior, but we miss local flavor. Other changes include AM stereo radio[18] and the conversion of analog radio to non-satellite digital transmission known as HD (hybrid digital) radio with CD (compact disk)-quality sound and without the subscription fees of satellite radio. Like standard AM and FM radio, HD radio is supported by commercials. By 2007, more than 700 U.S. radio stations had converted to HD.

In developing nations where illiteracy rates remain stubbornly high, radio stations are providing low-cost adult education via dramatic programs meant to improve behavior. A radio drama in Papua, New Guinea has a marine scientist warning a widowed father that dynamite fishing may be initially profitable but his children's future will be better if he practices sustainable fishing. An Ethiopian soap opera led to an increased demand for contraceptives and HIV/AIDS testing.[19]

Thousands of internet radio stations have come online. Some are offshoots of large commercial stations, but an internet station can specialize in, say, Albanian folk music, reaching an international audience of a few dozen if someone is willing to program for them. Established stations also stream news, weather, sports and traffic reports to the World Wide Web, to iPhones and to PDAs (personal digital assistants). It all adds up to a huge increase in choices. That, of course, extends both our connections to media sources and our mediated separation from others.

Point-to-Point Radio

Aside from broadcasting, radio has continued to serve point-to-point functions. Guardians of the public welfare such as police officers, sheriff's deputies, fire dispatchers, forest service personnel, air controllers, and the Coast Guard all have their own radio frequencies. Radio astronomy has fought for its bandwidth. Citizen's band radio, a continuation of the old pre-broadcasting hobbyists' radio exchanges, at one time counted participants in the millions, most famously the long haul truck drivers who warned each other of the "smokies," the highway patrol officers who lay in wait behind highway billboards. Cell phones have replaced most transmitting rigs, but CB (citizen band) radios, still conveying a sense of what radio was like before broadcasting, refuse to disappear.

Timeline

1873: James Clerk Maxwell's electromagnetic theory leads to radio wave discovery.

1887: Heinrich Hertz creates radio waves, discovers photoelectric effect.

1890: In France, Édouard Branly's coherer receives early radio signals.

1895: In Italy, teenager Guglielmo Marconi sends a radio signal more than a mile.

1896: Nikola Tesla invents a spark radio transmitter.

Turned down by Italy, Guglielmo Marconi takes radio gear to England.

1897: In England the Marconi Company is set up for wireless telegraphy business.

1898: The loudspeaker is invented.

1899: Marconi radio gear signals across the English Channel.

1901: In Newfoundland, Marconi receives a radio signal—the letter "s"—from England.

In Germany, Karl Braun discovers that a crystal can detect radio waves.

1904: E.F. Alexanderson's huge alternator adds distance to radio signals.

1906: International agreement on radio is reached in Berlin.

Lee De Forest's three-element vacuum tube, the audion, puts voices on the air.

Reginald Fessenden's voice surprises wireless operators at sea.

1909: Radio signals bring rescuers after ship collision; 1,700 lives saved.

First broadcast talk; the subject: women's suffrage.

1912: Titanic sinking leads to U.S. government controls on radio transmission.

1915: Radio-telephone carries voice from Virginia to the Eiffel Tower.

1916: Radio tuners.

1920: XWA, Montreal, begins first regularly scheduled North American broadcasts.

     Pittsburgh store sells ready-made radio sets, KDKA begins broadcasting.

1921: Baseball's World Series is reported by radio.

1922: In one year in U.S., from 80 radio broadcasting licenses to 569.

     100,000 radios built.

     A commercial begins "toll broadcasting."

1924: Radio hook-ups broadcast Democratic, Republican conventions.

1926: Replacing temporary hookups, U.S. gets a permanent radio network, NBC.

1928: Home radios use ordinary electric current instead of batteries.

1930: Lowell Thomas begins first regular U.S. network newscast.

     A practical, affordable car radio goes on sale.

1933: FDR begins radio Fireside Chats, bypasses hostile newspapers.

1938: Orson Welles' radio drama, The War of the Worlds, panics thousands.

     Radio begins real journalism competition with CBS World News Roundup.

1940: Regular FM radio broadcasting begins in a small way.

1970: FM stations target population segments, introducing "narrowcasting."

1994: Most popular American radio format is country music.

2001: Satellite radio appears; XM begins broadcasting.

     13,012 radio stations in the United States.

     99% of homes have a radio set; average home has six.

10. Television

It has been called a fatal attraction, a cultural death wish, blamed for social ills ranging from illiteracy to obesity to childhood hyperactivity to crime. Yet the public adopted the new medium of television with a speed unmatched in history. Even today, with all the competition from other media, television continues to be watched and watched and watched. The average American home is now likely to have more television sets than residents.[1]

Television's influence reaches every facet of life, including judgments about careers, life styles, what and how much to buy, ethical standards, relationships, conversations, daily behavior and how we should spend our free time. Dismissing television viewing as something we can take or let alone ignores its addictive nature, as study after study has shown. This is not just an American phenomenon. Research reported that the Japanese are even more addicted.[2] In every nation, in every culture where television sets are turned on, you will find that stare into the middle distance.

Scientific Roots

Television, meaning "seeing at a distance," came to mean "seeing by electricity." Its roots go back to 1818, a time of excitement about the properties of electricity, when Sweden's Jöns Berzelius shone light on selenium, a sulfur-like byproduct of copper refining. He noticed variations in how well it conducted electric current. In 1830, England's Michael Faraday sent electricity through a vacuum in a glass bottle. Scotland's Alexander Bain, in 1842 sent a current that caused a metal brush to duplicate alphabet letters onto paper. In 1847, the Abbé Caselli, an Italian researcher in France, sent drawings between two cities electrically. In 1873, Irish telegraph operator Joseph May, by varying the amount of light on selenium, sent a signal across the ocean on the Atlantic telegraph cable. American engineer Philip Carey, envisioned an array of selenium cells wired to a light bulb in a matching array in a receiver. English, Italian, German, French, Russian and American inventors added their efforts during the 19th century, leading in time to wirephotos, facsimile and the flashing lights in Times Square.

Sir William Crookes followed Faraday's path in 1875 by shooting electrons from the cathode terminal to the anode terminal of an evacuated tube. Sir J.J. Thomson added to Crookes' work with a magnet that moved the stream of electrons across the tube face. Germany's Karl Ferdinand

Braun, in 1897 coated the inner face of a tube with fluorescence so that it glowed when struck by the cathode rays. All these experiments led to the television tube.

What was missing was an image on the face of the tube. In 1884, German student Paul Nipkow introduced this by using two disks with matching patterns of holes that scanned and reproduced a scene fast enough to reach the human eye's persistence of vision. England's John Logie Baird experimented with Nipkow disks into the 1930s, but this mechanical system proved to be a dead end, even though Baird managed to send a murky image across the Atlantic Ocean in 1928. The future lay with an electronic system.

Sending a Moving Image

Russia's Boris Rosing had a workable system by 1907, partly electronic and partly mechanical, using a cathode ray tube. Others continued electronic experiments. Improbably, one was an Idaho high school student, Philo Farnsworth, who had read about such experiments in a popular science magazine. While still a teenager, Farnsworth acquired a patent for what he called an "image dissector."

Another was Rosing's assistant, Vladimir Zworykin, an immigrant to the United States who in 1923 sent a still image from a camera tube that he called an "iconoscope" to the face of a cathode ray display tube that he called a "kinescope." True television is dated from this 1923 demonstration. Zworykin's fellow Russian immigrant, RCA executive David Sarnoff, assembled a team from Westinghouse, General Electric and RCA under Zworykin to develop electronic television.

In 1925, American inventor Charles Francis Jenkins sent the first transmission of moving objects, windmills, to a receiver five miles away. In 1926, a Bell Telephone Labs team under Herbert Ives transmitted a moving picture. AT&T used a mechanical scanning system to send a black-and-white still photo from Washington to New York in 1927 and color photos in 1929. The quality was poor, an experiment of no apparent commercial use. But from AT&T also came co-axial cables and microwave transmission. Everything that anyone did was quickly followed by patent applications. Because no one held all the patents, cross-licensing agreements would be necessary for commercial development, just as radio required them.

This is an image, about 1928, from the Baird Televisor, a receiver for a mechanical system that depended on a scanning disc. About one thousand were sold in Britain during the early 1930s. The actual image is half the size of a business card, but on the screen it is crisper than it appears here.

In 1928, an experimental General Electric station in Schenectady, New York,

Vladimir Zworykin

Philo Farnsworth in 1935 with his TV set.
Reprinted with permission, San Francisco History Center, SF Public Library.

transmitted programs three times a week, mostly to its own engineers. RCA had its own NBC experimental television station in New York that would become WNBC-TV in 1941. CBS set up WCBS-TV in New York. As the Depression years leading to World War II went by and the world's attention focused on life-and-death political and economic issues, teams of dogged engineers, scientists and communication executives in the United States, Britain, Germany, Russia and Japan pursued the experiments that would lead to television. In England, the BBC started the world's first regular television service in 1936, testing both mechanical and electronic methods until it became clear that the better system was electronic. Germany began its own electronic television service in Berlin in 1935, broadcasting for an hour and a half three times a week.

The Federal Communications Commission gave CBS and NBC television broadcasting licenses in 1941, but the technology was not ready for commercialization. And World War II loomed. Even the small percentage of people in the New York area who could afford the bulky sets with tiny screens that sold for the price of a new car had almost nothing to see. A prewar home market for television did not exist. Some sets were sold to taverns that bought them for the occasional telecasts of sports events. World War I had blocked the development of commercial radio. Now World War II was blocking commercial television. Electronic research was required for such military needs as radar, sonar and navigation systems. The government froze development. Of the ten experimental stations in existence, six fed occasional programs to an estimated 10,000 sets, some of them belonging to station executives and engineers. The DuMont station alone tried to provide service throughout the war.

Where to Show It?

Where to present television was a matter of dispute. The cinema was a likely venue because movies on a celluloid film base already appeared there, and television might be considered another technology for distributing the moving image. Instead, DuMont Laboratories decided to go after the in-home market, and sold its first electronic sets to wealthy individuals starting in 1938 during the depths of the Depression.

Much of the public was introduced to television in 1939 through magazine and newspaper articles, and also at the RCA Pavilion in the New York World's Fair, whose theme was "The World of Tomorrow."

As World War II ground to an end, "Television Past" was only experimental and "Television Present" was dormant. But "Television Future" bustled with energy and promise as people permitted themselves to dream of a postwar future of reunited families and newly married couples moving into single family homes with one of those new-fangled radios with pictures sitting in their parlor.

By war's end, a huge market for television was ready and waiting, savings in hand because very little had been for sale during the war years marked by rationing and self-denial. The public demand was more than matched by manufacturers ready to produce sets, radio broadcasters and newspaper publishers eager for television licenses and a potential army of workers and entertainers waiting for an industry to come into being. Sets in use jumped from 5,000 in 1946 to about one million in 1948 to almost 10 million in 1950.

Technical Agreements

At first, the pictures were black-and-white, because RCA and CBS could not agree on a color system. As applicants quarreled over who would get the potentially valuable licenses, another battle shaped up over expanding the VHF (very-high frequency) spectrum to allow for more television stations, something that RCA resisted, not wanting more competition. With the additional concern that the narrow space between VHF frequencies was causing signal interference, the Federal Communication Commission (FCC) ordered a freeze on new stations that lasted from 1948 to 1952. This was to the advantage of CBS and NBC because most local stations had already affiliated with one or the other, rather than with ABC or DuMont. The technology continued to improve despite the FCC freeze. By 1951, network programs reached from coast to coast. As sales of new television sets soared and pictures became clearer on larger screens, prices of sets plummeted.

By extending the VHF frequency spectrum, channels 2 to 13, to a new UHF (ultra-high frequency) band, channels 14 to 69 and later expanding it still further, the FCC dealt with the limited number of channels, assigning local channel licenses in more than 1,200 communities. But many UHF stations failed. Their signals did not transmit as far or with as clean a picture as VHF stations. Early sets were sold without any UHF dials, or lacked click dials. Hunting for signals, inexact tuning, ghost images and interference reduced audiences. Without audiences, the stations could not attract advertising to pay for network programs, thus further reducing the audiences. But for VHF stations, "A license to broadcast is a license to print money," the Canadian media mogul Lord Thomson said.

The battle over color standards ended in 1953 in favor of RCA. Its proposal for an all-electronic system, won out over a partly mechanical system proposed by CBS. Another FCC decision approved a National Television Systems Committee (NTSC) picture made up of 525 lines which are "refreshed" 60 times a second, interlacing the even-numbered lines and the odd-numbered lines that are transmitted alternately. Europeans delayed for a time, then adopted two slightly better systems, the French SECAM and the British-German PAL. Based on colonial, cultural and trade ties, other nations chose one or another of the three. Because the systems were not compatible, the choice determined what programming these nations received.

HDTV ("high definition television") emerged in the 1990s, offering a sharper and brighter digital image in place of the standard analog pictures. It also offered a cinema screen-like 16x9 width-to-height ratio instead of the standard television 4x3 ratio, with more than twice the number of scanning lines of NTSC pictures and, therefore, at least twice the sharpness. HDTV offered ten times as much color information as the NTSC system as well as CD-quality sound.

The possibility that had been raised in the 1930s for cinema distribution of television programs arose again with HDTV; that is, distribution to movie theaters. Most movies still arrived in cinemas as cans of film. A proposal imagined a scrambled HDTV signal sent by satellite at a specific time to cinemas where audiences were waiting. This would not only reduce the cost of distribution but would also allow for films of limited appeal to find their potential audiences. As to the question of abandoning cinemas entirely and simply making all films available as DVDs for home viewing, the answer might well be that going out to a movie is a social event, but sitting at home is not, except for the market of teenagers and young lovers who simply want to get out of the house at any cost. In 2006 another battle over standards saw the Blu-Ray optical disc format win over DVD competitors for recording and playback. Its blue laser technology could store far more information than the red lasers others used.

The Remote

A less impressive television technology has taken its place as an artifact of modern civilization. Like the telephone answering machine, the remote control is a small, humble gadget attached to a more important device. We use the remote but pay little attention to its influence on our behavior. Family members frequently fight over its possession. It confers status on the holder. In more traditional families, the husband and father may regard the remote as his by right.

Remotes predate commercial television. During World War I Germany used them for motorboats. After World War II, remote-controlled automatic garage door openers helped sell new houses. Requiring a wire connection, Zenith in 1950 introduced "Lazy Bone," the first television remote control; unfortunately, people tripped over it. Five years later Zenith came out with the "Flash-matic," a wireless version; unfortunately again, because this remote depended on photocells, television sets might change channels by themselves on sunny days. The following year, Zenith did it better with the "Space Command," a remote control based on ultrasonics. However, their need for extra vacuum tubes raised the price and the size of a television set. The arrival of transistors reduced both. In the early 1980s, the technology changed once again when infrared remote control units replaced ultrasound.

Public Broadcasting

Not all U.S. broadcasting was for profit. A few educational radio stations had hung on during the early years of commercial television despite poor funding that translated into weak programming. Educators had learned some hard lessons in competing for radio licenses with take-no-prisoners commercial broadcasters.

The educators did much better in securing non-profit television licenses from the FCC, thanks in part to help from major organizations, especially the Ford Foundation. Federal grants also helped, leading over the decades of the last half century to a national public television network, the Public Broadcasting System (PBS). Other public radio networks and distributors emerged, such as National Public Radio, American Public Media and Public Radio International. As funding arrived, programming improved.

Of the various ways to support the television industry everywhere and pay for programs, commercials won the greatest favor as being the least painful and the least subject to government involvement. Television commercials were also the principal means of political campaigning, notably in the United States. Political managers remained convinced of the efficacy of spending tens or even hundreds of thousands of dollars for a few seconds of commercial time. The money that a candidate raised became one of the better ways to predict an election outcome.

International Changes

While television in the U.S. continued down the private path begun by the telegraph, most of the rest of the world saw government controls retained in the expansion from radio to television. The British Broadcasting Corporation's (BBC) dependence upon annual license fees on television sets to fund public broadcasting was copied by several countries, but all of them had stations that broadcast commercials as well. Even American public television gradually shifted from total rejection of commercials to sponsorship announcements that identified and even promoted a company or product. Totalitarian governments still preferred direct government subsidies because of the direct control it provided, but nevertheless allowed some commercials.

Audiences for the entire television industry declined in the competition with new forms of media. European public television networks, complacent and overstaffed, suffered far worse than ABC, CBS and NBC. Wracked by commercial competition that was permitted in the later decades of the 20th century, plus the growth of cable channels, the use of satellites and the expansion of videotape rentals, Italy's RAI, Spain's RTVE and Germany's ARD and ZDF faced financial ruin.[3] State-run Asian television networks were also hurting as viewer choices increased. In France, Russia, the nations of Eastern Europe and Mexico among others, state owned stations were sold to private interests. To keep viewers in the huge and tumultuous Indian market, the government service Doordarshan reduced its educational fare and added more commercial programs. As the 21st century unfolded, the television industry everywhere was undergoing significant change.

Programs

When radio broadcasting was new in the late 1920s, it was not uncommon, at those times when a popular show such as *Amos 'n' Andy* was on, for neighbors to seek out neighbors who owned a radio set. The first television programs had the same effect. Programs were broadcast to viewers who crowded into the homes of neighbors who owned sets, or who gathered in front of stores that sold sets. Radio store owners put a television in the window and piped the sound outside.

Marshall McLuhan observed that a new medium chooses for its content the medium it displaces. Television displaced, among other entertainments, novels and movies, both of which became television content. The radio variety show, born out of stage vaudeville, was reborn to be presented to national audiences as the television variety show. The crowds outside the stores were largest for such popular fare as the variety shows hosted by Milton Berle and Ed Sullivan. Also popular were "B" movie westerns owned by their cowboy stars. Quiz shows, such as radio's *$64 Question*, became television's *$64,000 Question*. When it was discovered that some quiz shows had been rigged to favor certain contestants to whom the audience had taken a liking, congressional inquiries followed. The public, at least as the headlines told it, felt betrayed. Fearing government sanctions, the networks embarked on a period of documentary production. Documentaries did not draw the large audiences beloved of networks but their purity of purpose was laudable.

Did television hurt the movies? It was not films themselves, but the cinemas that were partially displaced when people began to prefer to view movies in the comforts of home. The success of drive-in theaters should have served as a wake-up call. The inevitable close alliance between the television industry and the motion picture industry was delayed due to the concern of Hollywood

Quiz Show Scandal

Quiz shows were among the most popular television programs of the 1950s. History professor Charles Van Doren was a favorite contestant for the millions of weekly viewers of the show *Twenty-One*. The producers fed him and a few other contestants the correct answers, while instructing the less favored to lose. Contestants were coached to bite their nails and delay their answers to the last moment as they stood in "isolation booths" with the air conditioning off to make them sweat. Another quiz show, *Dotto*, was also revealed to be a fraud.

When the truth came out, Congress investigated and made television quiz show fixing a federal crime. The embarrassed networks adopted stringent guidelines for future quiz shows. No one went to jail, but reputations were ruined. Van Doren, the son of a famous family of educators, was fired by Columbia University.

executives who thought that television would erode their profitable business. Their fears were justified insofar as the Hollywood studios were linked financially to theater chains. The 1948 U.S. Supreme Court decision, U.S. v. Paramount, had ordered those links severed. In time a revived, restructured and thriving motion picture industry came to see television as a valuable distribution channel. The studios had the talent both in front of and behind the camera and the equipment, the sound stages and the back lots where scenes could be shot. The television networks had the audiences and cash. It was a natural fit. The live dramas that marked television in the 1950s were replaced by filmed dramas and comedies that could be filmed, edited and kept on a shelf until aired and aired again.

Cultural Effects and Criticism

As an audio-visual representation of a written culture, television programs, like radio programs before them, are positioned to take the best of both oral and written cultures. As an audio-visual medium, television reaches audiences who receive entertainment and information without the effort of reading. Literacy is no problem, although television calls upon the breadth of written culture with its infinite resources. With programs available to view on TV sets, computers, mobile phones and iPods, arriving wired, wireless, downloaded, mailed, stored on tape or disc, bought or rented, watched for hours daily, in all its manifestations television is, in a word, *us*.

Television has drawn families together but not necessarily to communicate with each other. A visitor to a home with the television on might feel like an intruder. Often as not the arrival of a guest does not result in the television set being turned off or the sound lowered. The visitor is welcome to share the sofa and the snacks and join the watching. The sofa is often where meals are eaten.

As the home audience stared at their television sets, the television industry stared back with even more intensity. With advertising rates spiking, the advertisers and the ad agencies wanted better information about just who was watching what. What ages, gender, income and other factors were involved? Demographic data would later be augmented by focus groups and by psychographic data that considered social class, lifestyle and the personality characteristics of the audience. In time, marketing decisions would do their part in converting television broadcasting into narrowcasting, removing certain groups from some marketing considerations, notably the elderly, who became almost a shadow audience for programs aimed at a younger demographic.

Critics of the commercial-based system had limited followings. Millions of viewers liked television they didn't have to pay for. They even liked looking at a favorite commercial, no matter how often they saw it. Children sometimes enjoyed commercials more than programs. In point of fact, far more thought and expense frequently go into a thirty-second commercial than into an entire half-hour program. Edmund Carpenter wrote, "The child is right in not regarding commercials as interruptions. For the only time anyone smiles on TV is in commercials. The rest of life, in news broadcasts and soap operas, is presented as so horrible that the only way to get through life is to buy this product: then you'll smile. Aesop never wrote a clearer fable."[4]

It has been said that viewers do not watch programs; they watch television, flipping the dial until they find something that might not bore them. The term "moderate liking" seems to fit, producing a compromise when several people are watching. If this theory, once prevalent in television network circles, still affects programming decisions, it would lead to bland, copycat programs not likely to offend viewers. In fact, the "L.O.P" theory (Least Objectionable Program) once guided programmers and may still influence them.[5]

Because television broadcasting not delivered by cable or satellite has traditionally been free and because most programs require little if any education on the part of viewers, broadcast television has been called a consolation prize for the powerless.[6] In the age of the internet, broadcast television remains the medium of choice for the poor, the uneducated, children and the elderly. A couple of generations earlier, a study of radio broadcasting found that our level of income influenced our listening choices.[7]

"A Vast Wasteland"

In 1961 the chairman of the FCC, Newton Minow, challenged television executives to watch a single day of their own station's programs from start to finish. "I can assure you that you will see a vast wasteland," he said.[8]

So what to do about the vast wasteland? To the industry's standard answer that the unhappy viewer should hit the "off" button comes the complainer's equally standard answer that the family did not buy a television set to turn it off. To the industry's argument that the critics

The Soaps

Soap operas moved seamlessly from radio to television and from daytime to prime time. Their appeal spread from mostly housewives to the workplace, retirement homes and campuses. Viewers spend hours each day with "their" soaps. For some, the anticipation of the coming day's episode salvages a dull or difficult life.

According to writer George Wiley, "The listener's sense of security was enhanced by emphasis placed in the serials upon such matters of special interest as marriage ties, the problems encountered by career women (a role the listener had avoided), the importance attached to the role of the wife and homemaker, and, in all things, the triumph of good over evil… The punctuality and dependability of the daily visits doubtlessly lent a sense or order to many a pointless day."[13]

On September 23, 2011, the day that *All My Children* went off the air after 41 years, some college classes were cancelled so students had the chance to watch along with everyone else. Something real and important had gone out of their lives. "I watched *All My Children* more than I watched my own children," said one woman.

Promoting Tolerance

If the United States is a more tolerant nation than it once was, give some credit to television. Starting with *All in the Family* and its comically racist Archie Bunker, some prime time television programs have been on the cutting edge of social change. This is especially true for African-Americans, who were almost invisible at the start of television in the 1940s and 1950s or in films except in minor or demeaning roles.

In television entertainment, the color bar that kept out most racial minorities, especially African-Americans, was broken by the 1970s. The civil rights movement for African-Americans and women no doubt would have progressed more slowly without the films, television programs and broadcast coverage of recent decades.[14]

want to impose their personal tastes and morality upon everyone, comes the argument that the airwaves belong to the public and the industry is giving back next to nothing in return for the public's gift of valuable licenses. To the industry's argument that television is a business, not an educational institution, comes the argument that, like it or not, television *is* an important educational institution. So go the arguments around and around without resolution.

Before TV, people did not go to the movies for hours each day. What neither side in the endless quarrel talks about much is the amount of time spent daily watching television. The set is on about 8 ½ hours a day in the average American home.[9] Neither side is campaigning to reduce the substantial amount of discretionary time spent each day staring at phosphor dots. For the industry it is a bread-and-butter issue. For those who complain, a campaign to limit viewing would be hopeless. Television is not something you and I can just take or leave alone. In one of several studies of families asked to do without TV for a specific length of time, a family in Minneapolis reflected the sentiment that doing without TV is like "a death in the family."[10]

The V-Chip

Almost no topic is off limits to television today. Think about the growth of reality shows and the placing of contestants in seemingly dangerous and more often humiliating situations, or focusing on nasty quarrels between couples until they break apart. Again, the public gets what it wants, however shameful. As for hour-long police or medical dramas and the half-hour sitcoms, the social message has changed in two important ways. First, like all mediated entertainment, and most notably movies and popular music, the content has been coarsened by violence, crude behavior and sexual activity that would not have been tolerated at the start of televised entertainment.

A Sisyphus quality attends both the criticism and the industry response. Those who want change push the rock of reform up the hill, only to be met by resistance and indifference that will lead to new efforts, over and over. Congressional committees have held hearings into the role of television in encouraging juvenile delinquency. Some changes were put in place by the Telecommunication Reform Act of 1996. A "V-Chip" was mandated for each new television set so that parents could block violent and sexually explicit programs. Networks and cable channels accepted an industry rating system. The comic book industry also created rating standards and Hollywood modified its rating system as well.

In 2007 the Federal Communications Commission asked Congress for legislation that would allow the FCC to regulate violence on TV. For decades the FCC has fined stations for stepping over the line regarding sexual material or language, but has lacked the muscle to do much about violence. In defending itself against attacks that sex and violence encourage promiscuous and violent behavior among younger viewers, the industry argues that normal viewers are not influenced. This is a position that flies in the face of the billions of dollars, euros and yen spent on television advertising, which is based on the opposite conviction that what appears on television does indeed influence behavior.

In 1975 a Family Viewing Hour, the first hour of prime time, was established, only to be overturned by a court decision. Plans for voluntary compliance gradually dissolved into standard evening fare. However, good children's fare could be found on PBS, notably the award winning *Sesame Street,* and frequently on cable channels that were striving for a young audience. The overall total number of children's programs has increased over the years, despite the arguable absence of concern by the networks and the local stations over what viewers see. Actually, *Sesame Street* itself has been accused of affecting children by conditioning them to have a short attention span. A few schools have tried on an experimental basis to provide children with silence, arguing that media have robbed us of silence and hamper child development.[11]

There were reports of changes caused by television viewing in family life-styles, sleeping habits, children's entertainment and activity preferences. It was much easier just to tune to *Dora the Explorer* than to go outside and actually explore. A nationwide study as early as 1960 funded by CBS concluded that television had replaced other means of socialization for everyone except people of high education and income. Of all household items, television was the one non-essential item in the home that nearly everyone regarded as essential.[12]

Watching News and Politics

The power to move the nation showed itself in both the rise and the fall of Sen. Joseph McCarthy. His unsupported announcements that he had lists of communists in government generated headlines and television coverage and led to the "Red Scare" that traumatized the nation during the 1950s. It was also on television that Edward R. Murrow's devastating attack on McCarthy and the coverage of the Army-McCarthy hearings brought him down.

The televised presidential debates between John Kennedy and Richard Nixon further changed the political landscape of the nation, shifting away from locally based ward politics and party loyalties. Kennedy dominated the televised debates, especially the first debate, which showed a

Senator Joseph
McCarthy

Vice President
Spiro Agnew

pale and sweating vice president facing a tanned and confident young senator. Curiously, radio teners believed Nixon had won, but those listeners were not enough when the votes were counted. Political campaigns were forever changed. The focus in future would be on television.

Television news came of age in its four days of coverage of President Kennedy's assassination and the subsequent events in November 1963. In some nations, street riots might have followed the assassination of a popular leader. In the United States viewers were glued to their television sets. At one point, nine out of ten Americans were watching.

Amid the changes of the turbulent 1960s was a growing awareness of television's reach. With its coverage of snarling police dogs, high-pressure water hoses and little girls marching off in their Sunday best to be arrested, television news shone a glaring spotlight on the South's response to the civil rights movement. As the years went by, with comedy shows about African-American families and with actors regularly appearing in dramas and variety shows, television moved to the forefront of efforts to improve racial relations.[15]

Space exploration, also covered intensely by television, fascinated the entire world, culminating in live pictures of Neil Armstrong setting foot on the moon. This historic event provided one of those rare occasions when the whole world looked at the same thing together. Marshall McLuhan's image of a "global village" was realized, however briefly.

Television newscasts added a human dimension to the daily reports of events. Network news anchors, particularly Walter Cronkite at CBS and the team of Chet Huntley and David Brinkley at NBC, were welcomed each evening into millions of homes almost like members of the family. One survey voted Cronkite the most trusted man in America.[16]

Newscasts went to color and expanded, with major cities alloting news blocks of two hours or more. Morning programs would not be complete without news. Interview programs were matched in popularity by prime-time magazine programs like the iconic *60 Minutes*.

News editors won the authority to break into entertainment programs to report momentous events, and could take over broadcasts completely, as they did to report the Kennedy assassination and the World Trade Center attacks of September 11, 2001. Less important but significant breaking news was reported as crawls of text along the bottom of the television screen.

"The Living Room War"

The Vietnam War was filmed in color, with images reaching television screens only one or two days after battlefield film was shot. It has been called the first "television war" and "the living room war." Daily reports brought the reality of bloodshed, pain and frustration home and created an intimate contact with warfare never before experienced by a whole nation. The war coverage did much to spark the student demonstrations that led the anti-war movement. War planning would change in the future to take into account home front reaction to instant battle coverage. The movements of reporters and television photographers would be more closely monitored by the military during the Gulf War of 1991 and the Iraq War of the 2000s. Journalists would be "embedded" with designated military units.

Other protests against the policies of many governments, from Tiananmen Square to Abu Ghraib, the 2009 Iranian elections and the 2011 uprisings across the Middle East have demonstrated television's power to bring world attention to unpopular government actions. The television channels of dictatorships may be blocked, but when the pictures reach the rest of the world, it is primarily television that distributes them.

Like the Asian proverb that the nail that sticks up gets hammered, the new visibility of television news had its price. Vice President Spiro Agnew attacked network news in a speech denouncing network news "liberal bias" by a "small, unelected elite." Tens of thousands of angry letters, phone calls and telegrams to the networks quickly reinforced the message. Stung by the threats to station licenses, television news started out slowly and nervously in covering the Watergate story. Newspapers did the heavy lifting, but no newspaper could match television's ability to reach a mass audience, to convey the tension and the immediacy of the Senate hearings on impeachment in 1974 and the presidential speeches that showed viewers a tired and troubled Richard Nixon losing his grip on power.

First videotape and later the digital revolution expanded what television news could offer viewers. Videotape and accompanying signaling led to electronic news gathering (ENG). The time it took to process film disappeared. Being reusable, videotape did not force photographers to ration the amount of footage they shot, as film did. With the addition of electronic transmission from a photographer's truck to a television station and the bounced signals of SNG (satellite news gathering), television reporting and photography expanded so that the Iraq War could be covered live by reporters embedded with front line troops. Television news also adopted computerized non-linear video editing. The result was quicker, more precise and more complex editing at lower cost.

Cable

Let us back up more than a half century. The story of cable television is as American as a Horatio Alger tale. Unlike cultural changes that begin in major cities and find their way to rural villages and towns, cable was the country boy who went to the big city. Born in humble circumstances in rural Pennsylvania to help folks living out in the countryside to enjoy something that only city folks had, cable TV eventually migrated to cities, where it challenged a major industry and succeeded beyond all expectations in affecting our way of life.

When cable began in 1948 as community antennas, it was just a means to bring television signals to towns too far from a large city station for good reception. The broadcast industry, if it thought about the matter at all, welcomed community antennas because they added viewers at no cost to the stations. That would change when signals began to compete with what the stations were broadcasting. Complaints from broadcasters grew louder when the CATV (community antenna TV) owners added programming of their own such as a locally produced variety show and coverage of city hall meetings and local high school sports. It began in 1951 in the town of Pottsville, Pennsylvania, when a CATV owner used a small, personal television camera to pull together a 30-minute variety show with Pottsville residents as entertainers. Neighbors were delighted with its local origination.

With the addition of locally produced content, CATV evolved into cable television. All this was taking place in the midst of the FCC freeze on new television licenses, when only 108 stations were on the air. Some broadcasters observing this fast growing business invested in it themselves. In time, media conglomerates would own cable systems as well as television stations as part of their communication empires.

HBO and Ted Turner

Cable underwent an important change in 1975 with a test in Wilkes-Barre, Pennsylvania, to deliver programming that had been unavailable anywhere until then. It was called Home Box Office, a pay channel that for three years had been feeding videotape recordings of recent movies and some sports coverage to nearby cable systems. More and more cable systems wanted to add the popular channel to their service. So many inquiries came that HBO decided to take the financial risk to sell the service across the nation by bouncing a signal off RCA's

domestic communications satellite, SATCOM. To attract a large audience, HBO chose as its first offering a boxing match in the Philippines between Muhammed Ali and Joe Frazier. What Ali dubbed the "thrilla from Manila" went to cable systems that had installed a satellite receiving dish 10 meters in diameter at a cost of $150,000.

Atlanta UHF station owner Ted Turner decided to provide a similar service via the same SATCOM satellite, but with a different financing method. Instead of charging individual subscribers, Turner offered an extra channel of movies and sports that the cable systems themselves would pay for on the basis of a few cents per subscriber. Each cable system

The "Thrilla from Manila."
Joe Frazier vs. Mohammed Ali

would be using the same dish it had installed for HBO. The extra channel gave viewers still more choices, so it was attractive to cable systems in their efforts to win customers. Turner's WTCG-TV (later WTBS) became the first "superstation."[18] His ownership of a UHF station on which he showed the ball games of two teams that he owned—baseball's Atlanta Braves and basketball's Atlanta Hawks—not only gave Turner additional programming, but also a national audience that he parlayed into much higher fees for commercials. Chicago's WGN, New York's WOR and several other new superstations followed. HBO was followed by pay channels Cinemax, Showtime and The Movie Channel. Several dozen cable channels have since been created on the way to what futurists predicted would become "a 500-channel universe," actually meaning a universe of channels limited only by audience demand.

As the programming choices increased, the technology of cable television itself was given competition by DBS (Direct Broadcast Satellite), also known as DTH (Direct-to-Home). In some communities a non-satellite wireless service that uses microwave also competed with cable. DBS suffered in competition with cable until a 1999 law allowed it to retransmit local signals back to the local community. In the first decade of the new century, more than two-thirds of all the households in the United States received a cable or DBS service. Said one cable executive, cable television was like air conditioning, "You don't need it, but once you live with it you can't live without it."[19]

Among the channels created for cable systems were those specifically devoted to shopping at home and those channels that were given over at night to infomercials (program-length commercials). These added a kind of choice that competed with the catalogues sent by Sears and Montgomery Ward: the opportunity to shop without leaving home. As watching television and shopping were two of the favorite activities of millions of people, "electronic retailing" seemed a sure bet for success. Selling goods this way started displacing the mailed catalogues, just as those catalogues had once invaded the business of the small town general store. Communication technology was again forcing change.

Still more choice was available to those willing to pay for it. Known variously as PPV (Pay-per-View), STV (Subscription Television), or pay-TV, it delivered recent first-run movies, plus original entertainment and sports events to homes and hotel rooms.

New Ways to Watch

The new century has seen popular television programs sold as video-on-demand (VOD) for downloading without commercials. For fans who missed a favorite episode, such a piecemeal purchase—quickly available—was a desirable alternative to waiting for reruns or acquiring a DVD of an entire season. Viewing would happen when it was more convenient for the viewer, and over other media than the TV set, including laptops, tiny iPods and cell phone screens. A program could be watched anywhere that a cell phone could be carried. A couple lying side by side in bed at night, instead of each reading a book, could each separately be watching and hearing a favorite program.

In retrospect, it seems inevitable that the advances of digital storage media would lead to the personal video recorder (PVR) such as TiVo that allows a viewer to pause or rewind live programs and skip over commercials. Even more than videotape, TiVo is convenient. As with any recorder, TiVo could be paused for a baby's cry, a ringing phone, or a bathroom break. Because of its widespread adoption, the television industry and the advertising industry have searched for new ways to reach those "eyeballs," such as product placement. Firms that do television viewer research are being compelled by fast-changing communication technology to rethink the basic broadcasting model, which is that viewers are given free entertainment in return for minutes of their time to watch commercials.

The new century also saw the growing popularity of alternatives to the cathode ray tube home television and the rear projection set. The liquid crystal display (LCD) and the plasma tube offer large screens and panels that may be thin and flat enough to hang on a wall. Among the experimental technologies that are likely to bring a new type of choice is optical transmission based on digital light pulses rather than electrical signals. A single hair-thin optical fiber is able to transmit 167 television channels, while a bundle of six strands can feed out more than 1,000 video signals. This broadband opens the possibility of interactive cable television. In 2007, Sony tested a TV screen as thin and flexible as paper.

Choices in the 21ˢᵗ Century

Critics have argued that a sameness exists in television, and that offering more channels does not really offer more choices. The majority of the public does not appear to agree. And we viewers always prefer choice. With so many choices, it was inevitable that the industry would fracture into narrowcasting, with some programmers shifting away from trying to reach a general audience. On occasion the audiences coalesce around a single program or event, such as the coverage of the Olympic Games, but for the most part, viewers go their separate ways.

The 21ˢᵗ century is seeing popular television programs sold or given away for downloading through websites like Hulu as video-on-demand and through distribution systems like Blockbuster and Netflix mailing, where programs can be viewed in sequence and without commercials. In 1938, when it began to attract public notice for its future potential, television drew the attention of a leading American essayist, E.B. White: "I believe television is going to be the test of the modern world and that in this new opportunity to see beyond the range of our vision, we shall discover either a new and unbearable disturbance of the general peace, or a saving radiance in the sky. We shall stand or fall by television, of that I am quite sure."[21]

Marshall McLuhan gave short shrift to television's detractors: "Literate man is not only numb and vague in the presence of film or photo, but he intensifies his ineptness by a defensive arrogance and condescension to 'pop kulch' and 'mass entertainment.' It was in this spirit of bulldog opacity that the scholastic philosophers failed to meet the challenge of the printed book in the 16ᵗʰ century."[22]

So, at the end of the television viewing day, is the television set a positive or a negative? Certainly a little of each. Its supporters say it educates and entertains. Its detractors say it corrupts. Everyone can agree on two things. First, television continues to influence our society. Second, it is not going away any time soon.[23]

Internet Competition

The arrival of the internet as a news venue, the growing popularity of blogs for news and opinions, and the 24-hour news cycle of CNN and other cable channels sharply cut into network audiences, just as newscasts had cut into newspapers readership.

Both network news audiences and newspaper readership were skewing toward the elderly, with young people going elsewhere for news, or going nowhere. Credit—or blame—for this includes a significant national shift toward increased choices, especially among the segment most desired by advertisers and networks, the better educated younger viewers who prefer to get their news at the time of their choosing and know how to surf online for the topics that interest them; impatient, they no longer need to wait.

News organizations of every medium created their own websites, offering video reports sometimes in greater depth than newscasts and print stories permit, and sometimes before they are presented on the evening newscasts. Like entertainment programs, newscasts could be downloaded for viewing anytime on a variety of devices.

Mass audiences tune in for major news stories, but drift away at quiet times. Viewing spiked at news reports of the 9/11 attack, the Iraq invasion, hurricane Katrina, Michael Jackson's funeral, and the Haiti earthquake.

On most days, Americans tune in and out of television news, radio news, and the internet news services. When we awake, tuck into dinner or go to bed, we may check to see if the world has altered.

Satisfied when it has not, we go about our lives or use the media for diversion or for learning facts that we can act upon. That is why weather reports occupy so much of local newscasts each day; we can grab an umbrella or stuff a child into a heavier jacket.

News is also diversion, which explains much of what else we see on newscasts. Many viewers prefer local newscasts and their reactive response to crimes, accidents, fires, and other nearby events, plus lighthearted features, all delivered by attractive anchors who adjust their expressions to suit the story.[20]

Timeline

1817: Swedish chemist Jöns Berzelius discovers that light changes selenium's electric flow.

1873: In Ireland, Joseph May uses selenium to send a signal through the Atlantic cable.

1875: In England, William Crookes builds a forerunner to the TV cathode ray tube.

1884: In Germany, student Paul Nipkow builds a scanning disc, early version of television.

1890: In Germany, Karl Ferdinand Braun invents the cathode ray tube.

1907: In Russia, Boris Rosing builds a working electronic/mechanical system in the lab.

1922: 15-year-old Philo Farnsworth designs a television "image dissector."

1923: Vladimir Zworykin patents an electronic camera tube, the iconoscope.

1925: A moving image is telecast in a lab experiment.

1936: BBC starts world's first regular television service, three hours a day.

　　　In Germany television cameras transmit the Berlin Olympics.

1939: NBC starts the first regular daily electronic TV broadcasts in the U.S.

1940: Peter Goldmark at CBS demonstrates television in color.

1947: *Meet the Press* shifts from radio to TV; will be longest running TV program.

1948: CBS and NBC begin nightly 15-minute television newscasts.

　　　Before cable there was Community Antenna Television, CATV.

1951: Color television sets go on sale.

1952: FCC ends 4-year freeze, sets VHF, opens UHF, reserves education channels.

1953: TV Guide; initial press run is 1.5 million copies.

1954: U.S. is shaken by Edward Murrow documentary on U.S. Sen. Joseph McCarthy.

1955: Research shows TV viewing correlates inversely with education, income.

1958: Videotape delivers color.

1960: Kennedy-Nixon debates draw huge numbers of viewers.

1963: JFK assassination sends millions to around-the-clock newscasts.

　　　Communications satellite Syncom II goes into geo-synchronous orbit.

1965: Vietnam War becomes first war to be televised: "the living room war."

1975: HBO bounces signal off satellite to reach cable systems.

1980: CNN begins round-the-clock reports from Atlanta to 172 cable systems.

1995: Direct Broadcast Satellites (DBS) beam digital programs to home dishes.

1999: TiVo offers personal television control: storing and skipping programs, ads.

2006: Television signals available digitally.

2010: 3D television arrives

11. Computers

Beyond Calculation

A four-year-old child of the early 21st century playing a game has more computer power at her fingertips than all the scientists during World War II.

Pick up a current computer magazine. Its articles and ads will describe devices that have nothing at all to do with what computers were invented to do. They were not invented to process words or do anything with language. They were not invented to communicate. They certainly were not invented to play games or entertain in any way. Computers were invented solely to calculate, to compute, but that is no longer their principle use. Our people skills are exercised more than our math skills.[1]

The need for a device to calculate started with counting boards on which pebbles were moved around ("calculus" is Latin for "pebble"). The oldest surviving counting board is the Salamis tablet used by Babylonians about 300 BCE. That led to the invention of the Roman hand-abacus about 2,000 years ago. The more familiar stringed and beaded abacus dates back at least to the Chinese suan-pan used since 1200 BCE. Partitioned to match the fingers on one hand, the abacus aided merchants and tax collectors across the ancient world to add, subtract, multiply and divide. Here and there, even in our current age of cheap, hand-held calculators, the abacus is still in use.[2]

Calculating all day long is tiresome work. The abacus and counting tables of the Middle Ages helped ease the tedium, but there was an impetus to build a better device. Leonardo da Vinci

Roman abacus

Working model of Leonardo da Vinci's sketch of a calculator

designed one. In the 17th century German professor Wilhelm Schickard constructed a "calculating clock." In France, at age nineteen, the future philosopher Blaise Pascal built a shoebox-size device to help his father, a tax collector.

In Germany, while still in his twenties, the philosopher Gottfried Leibniz designed a decimal calculator, "for it is unworthy of excellent men to lose hours like slaves."[3] Leibniz also conceived of binary calculation, but found no practical use for it. Efforts in England and Scotland brought forth the slide rule and logarithms. The first widely marketed mechanical calculator, the "Arithmometer," was built in France in 1720.

Charles Babbage

The foundations for a true computer were laid in the 19th century by a 20-year-old math student at Cambridge University. Charles Babbage grew frustrated at reading newspaper accounts of English ships foundering on rocks because published navigation tables had been calculated in error. He began to build an "engine" to figure the tables accurately. He imagined that the machine could also help in banking, surveying, mathematics and the sciences.

Part way through the construction of his "difference engine," and after being appointed as a professor of mathematics at Cambridge, Babbage had a better idea. He imagined an "analytical engine" that could solve any arithmetic problem. It would grind out the answers in a "mill" and place them in a "store." Punch cards would feed the problems into the machine. A new problem required a new set of cards. When a certain point was reached, for example at a tally of 200, a different sequence of steps would begin.

Building on these ideas, Babbage invented programming and the computer. Babbage's idea for using cards came from Joseph-Marie Jacquard, owner of a French weaving factory, who used thousands of wooden cards in series with holes punched to guide threads into complex patterns on a loom.

Charles Babbage

**Ada Byron,
Lady Lovelace**

Babbage did not complete his analytical engine, but he explained his ideas to family friend Ada, Lady Lovelace, the 17-year-old daughter of the poet Byron. She published them in a series of *Notes*, writing that the engine would weave algebraic patterns the way the punch card loom weaves flowers and leaves. She saw a use for his machine in composing music and making graphics. It has even been suggested that it was she, not he, who was the brains behind both the difference engine and the analytical engine.[4] Whatever the truth, in 1979 the programming language Ada was named to honor her contribution.

The Hollerith punch card reader. Each dial was linked to one punch location.

Cards were at the heart of a different effort in 1890 when a U.S. Patent Office employee, Herman Hollerith, set out to cross-tabulate census data such as determining the number of Minnesota bachelor farmers born in Norway. This was data processing. The holes in each card allowed for electrical contacts so that counting registers for each variable could advance one digit. This would be the basis of future computer binary calculation. Hollerith left the Census Bureau to start a company that would one day become International Business Machines, or IBM.

World War II

World War II and the postwar years saw considerable advances in both computer theory and construction. A British computing effort joined by Alan Turing, one of the geniuses in the history of computing, cracked Germany's secret Enigma military code and helped to win the war. Nazi Germany could have been aided by a genius in their own country, Konrad Zuse, who built the first computer guided by software, but he received little support from German authorities.

In the United States, ENIAC, a digital computer built at the University of Pennsylvania, was completed too late for its objective of calculating the trajectory of artillery shells, but it managed to examine a postwar plan to build the hydrogen bomb.

Ideas from mathematicians Norbert Weiner and John von Neumann charted the path taken by postwar computers. Meanwhile, Bell engineers Claude Shannon and Warren Weaver raised communication theory from a kind of guesswork to science. Universities constructed research computers with acronym names: ENIAC, EDSAC, ILLIAC, JOHNNIAC, SWAC, BINAC, MANIAC. The Air Force's Whirlwind, designed at M.I.T. was also groundbreaking in using video displays and operating in real time. Each of these advanced our knowledge of what computers could do.

The K-Model

Boolean logic (with symbols for AND, OR, and NOT) and binary arithmetic (base-2, composed of 0's and 1's, not the base-10 decimal system) set researchers on the digital path used today.

In 1937 Bell Labs engineer George Stibitz had a flash of insight about using Boolean logic and binary arithmetic in an electrical device.

One evening he took home two telephone relays, two flashlight bulbs, a dry cell battery, and some wire that he hooked up to a strip of metal he cut from a tobacco tin. He sat at his kitchen table and wired together what his wife dubbed "the K-Model" ("K" for "kitchen table"). He had created the world's first digital calculator.

The K-Model led to calculators to solve telephone engineering problems. Stibitz realized that a full-size calculator could perform a sequence of calculations under the direction of relay circuits and could store the results. The calculator that was built went through several versions during World War II that solved problems with the aiming of anti-aircraft guns.

Stibitz was unaware of similar research being done in Berlin by another engineer, Konrad Zuse, who built four increasingly sophisticated versions before and during World War II. Daily Allied bombing of Berlin forced him to flee the city. He hid his semi-finished latest version in a barn. Despite Zuse's ingenious solutions to several problems, his device was never used to help Nazi Germany.

In 1940 Stibitz went further. He hooked two modified typewriters into a telephone circuit between New York and New Hampshire to expand the world of telecommunications.

In 1952 the UNIVAC introduced the public to computers when CBS used it to help forecast the presidential election results. Instead of the close results the experts expected, it forecast an Eisenhower landslide (odds of 100 to 1). According to one version of what happened next, CBS executives nervously ordered the results adjusted so that UNIVAC would agree with the political experts. According to another version, someone accidentally dropped a zero resulting in 8 to 7 odds. The final electoral vote was 442 to 89, a landslide for Eisenhower. Univac had been off by less than 1%. Newspaper columnists later had fun writing about how unfair CBS had been to the computer.

Microchips

In 1957 millions of movie-goers heard the word "computer" for the first time when a computer figured in the Spencer Tracy - Katherine Hepburn comedy *Desk Set*. The romantic story centered on a secret effort to computerize the research department of a television network. In 1959 British scientist Charles Percy Snow told an MIT audience, "We happen to be living at a time of a major scientific revolution, probably more important in its consequences than the first Industrial Revolution, a revolution which we shall see in full force in the very near future."[5]

As long as computers depended on vacuum tubes they would remain limited devices, a handful scattered around the world in universities, military installations and a few big government agencies and business firms. Change arrived in 1948 with the invention of the transistor to replace the vacuum tube, also useful for all electronic communication equipment. That led in 1959 to the integrated circuit in a microchip and in 1970 to the microprocessor.

The history of the computer has been, in part, a history of information *storage*, from vacuum tubes and punch cards to terabytes of crystal-based optical memory. The ancient Greeks had learned that if we can store information, we can reflect upon the past in considerable detail and build upon the information. We can share it systematically. Transistors are unsuited to computer memory because when the electricity is turned off a transistor loses its on/off state. The first solution beyond punch cards was magnetic core memory, a wire mesh strung with tiny ferrite ceramic doughnuts. In 1968 computers got random access memory (RAM) microchips, which can be erased and reused, and the permanent read-only memory (ROM) microchips.

Personal Computers

The end of the decade of the 1950s saw the end of hand-built, one-of-a-kind computers. Commercial firms assembled new computers on assembly lines. The first were the large mainframe computers. Then came the mini-computers, and in the 1970s came the microcomputer.

The computer was meant to be a serious tool for scientific, government and business use. Did anyone imagine that children would use computers? The notion that a computer would ever be a common household device like a washing machine would have been considered ridiculous as recently as 1974, when the Altair 8800, a kit for hobbyists to assemble, started the move to the personal microcomputer. The hobbyists had to write their own binary code and flip a switch on the front panel for each binary digit.

Three years later the already assembled Apple II, Commodore Pet and TRS-80 opened the floodgates. The Apple II was the first personal computer with color, high-resolution graphics, sound and a way to control games. The Atari video games were in arcades and the first Osborne portable would soon be at the fingertips of reporters on assignment. When ordinary people realized how a computer could extend life's choices, they could hardly wait to get one. *Time* named the computer as "Man of the Year" for 1982.

The hand-held personal digital assistant, or PDA, to a limited extent recognized handwriting and acted like a memo pad that connected to a computer. Apple introduced the first of these, the Newton, in 1993. Like most electronic devices, it was soon superseded by more advanced devices. Succeeding the Newton was the smaller, cheaper, easier-to-use, feature-filled Palm Pilot. PDAs were pulled from briefcases, purses and even pockets, used everywhere from business meetings to supermarkets just as smartphones have been in the 21ˢᵗ century.

Engineers have added more features to hand-held computing devices, including voice recognition software. Other engineers combined features of the PDA and the cell phone into such units as the BlackBerry, which is also a handheld emailer and Web access device, the camera phone and the smartphone. Owners use them to blog, send instant messages and pay bills at any convenient opportunity, including sitting in a car while waiting for a red light to change.

Word Processing

The history of the computer is also the history of input devices like the card reader, tape drives, disk drives, the mouse, the joystick and the scanner. It is also the story of such output devices as printers, synthesizers, modems and routers, plus wireless technology like Bluetooth to connect them. Of particular application to communication, the laser printer arrived in the mid-1970s with a price tag of around $500,000. Today they can be found for less than $100.

And it is the story of software, from the 1's and 0's of the era of vacuum tubes to assembly languages, compilers, programming languages and eventually application programs available off the shelf to do hundreds of tasks.

Word processing programs gave the computer a communication capability deserving the overused word "revolutionary." The first word processors were faster than typewriters, could edit and move text around and could store text. However, as single-minded computers that could do nothing else they were bypassed when word processing software was written for general-purpose computers. Page layout, graphics, photo and video editing programs have followed to aid communication tasks. Automatic language translation proved more stubborn because languages themselves are so idiosyncratic, but considerable progress has been accomplished even here. And voice recognition software has made strides.

The computer made other forms of communication easier. Medium and large newspapers, magazines, radio and television stations, plus thousands of small ones now have computer-based online versions of their output. Computers assist the newspaper publishing process at each step from the reporter's laptop to the delivery trucks.

Computers have transmitted news since 1970, when the Associated Press switched over from teletypes. Some large magazine publishers use computers to sort subscribers by targeting advertising to specific groups. Book publishers require authors to submit their work in electronic form.

For research the information age has added electronic archives. LexisNexis is among the better known of more than four thousand databases available for retrieving information. Archive.org has archived billions of pages of text and audio that appeared on the Web.

Desktop Publishing

For surprisingly small sums of money compared with what was once required, someone working out of a garage can publish a newspaper, magazine, or book. Inexpensive microcomputers and easy-to-learn desktop publishing software today enable output of a quality that once only a skilled printer could produce with bulky machinery. Today a printing-on-demand machine runs a copy of a book off on standard 20 lb. office paper, trims it to book size, and binds and covers it with a perfect binding. Or new companies like Smashwords let you download a book for a dollar or two to any reading device a reader prefers, skipping printers entirely.

Desktop publishing began with word processing, and that began with a wish to duplicate what was typed.[6] Early attempts to do this consisted of attachments to an electric typewriter. The M. Schultz machine used rolls of paper much like player piano rolls to record typing. Form letters could be turned out one after the other with only the address and salutation changed. Paper rolls were succeeded by the paper tape of the Flexowriter, which allowed for correcting mistakes and the physical cutting and pasting of text, a precursor to what word processing would do electronically. An IBM Selectric typewriter with a magnetic tape drive began true word processing at a basic level in 1964.

The term "word processing" came from IBM and encompassed writing, editing, printing and storing text. Text could be punched on standard 80-column punch cards. In 1969, IBM's MagCards increased what could be stored on a single card from 80 characters to a page of characters. Three years later came video screens for display and tape cassettes for storage. In the early '70s, floppy disks permitted the storage of one hundred pages of text on each disk.

New Moon is one of the companies that produces a variety of printed desktop publishing products such as magazines, newsletters, brochures, posters, postcards, calendars, business cards, mailers, and advertising.

Courtesy: Mark Steele

A Chinese immigrant to the United States, Dr. An Wang, designed his Wang 1200 automatic typewriter with limited editing functions in 1971. Next came word processing software that could run on general purpose microcomputers. The Electric Pencil program in 1976 was followed by WordStar and WordPerfect. Microsoft Word has dominated the field of word processing for a number of years.

Xerox Corporation researchers conceived of a graphics-based computer that not only could be controlled by a mouse, but also displayed typefaces on a screen and sent the displayed output to a laser printer. This would be the foundation of what would become known as WYSIWYG: "What you see is what you get."

Although Xerox did not take advantage of the ideas flowing from its research division, Steve Jobs of Apple did with the introduction in 1984 of the Macintosh. In addition, the PostScript page description program and the Hewlett-Packard low-cost laser printer brought to the public the reality of "desktop publishing," a term coined in 1985 by Paul Brainerd, developer of PageMaker, which became the leading page layout program.

By themselves, computers and laser printers, the principal equipment in desktop publishing, have not created the first opportunity for people of moderate means to publish. After all, typewriters and mimeograph machines had been around for decades. What computers and printers provide is much more egalitarian, the means to offer an attractive and professional looking product at low cost.

Tens of thousands of people now do what relatively few people could do in the past. They package their writing without having to turn to printers for help. Businesses, schools, government offices, clubs and organizations of every sort turn out innumerable newspapers, newsletters, magazines and flyers. Restaurants print menus and theaters print programs. Students hand in slick looking term papers.

In a historical sense desktop publishing is as old as the start of printing in Europe. Gutenberg and those who followed him a half millennium ago were printer-publishers. So was Benjamin Franklin. Things changed with the introduction of big and costly machinery two centuries ago as part of the Industrial Revolution. Desktop publishing has, in the sense of personal empowerment, turned the clock back. Going a step further, with the internet, even the computer printer is no longer needed to publish.

A late 19th century copying machine, an early version of desktop publishing.

Email and word processing did not bring the "paperless office," a promise that always seems a decade away, but never arrives. The world continues to convert forests into sheets of paper. One change seems to be a shift from the practice of first printing, then distributing, to first distributing (electronically), then printing.[7]

Desktop Video

Desktop video is also expanding the producer base for motion pictures as well as distribution through film festivals and online venues like YouTube. In professional hands, computers are involved in every stage of major film production just as they are involved at every step in getting a newspaper or a magazine into a reader's hands.

Technology that supported motion picture production during the decades of the golden age of Hollywood required enormous sums of money. Although this helped to concentrate in just a few hands the ability to make feature films (and still does in the rarefied world of high budget film making), more recent technology has pushed in the opposite direction—outward to many hands. Production and distribution of motion pictures are broader than ever. While big budget movies are still being turned out, so are shoestring movies of quite good quality. *Desktop video* found its way into the language next to *desktop publishing*.

Computer-based technology brings within reach of the average family non-linear editing processes (providing random access) with such effects as morphing that only recently were limited to machines costing hundreds of thousands of dollars, if they were available at all. Production facilities to shoot and edit digital motion pictures, and off-the-shelf software for inexpensive digital animation, are used in schools, offices, and businesses that once would not

The Blair Witch Project

In 1999, two college students in Florida, Dan Myrick and Eduardo Sanchez, made a feature film, *The Blair Witch Project*, for $31,000, with early marketing done mostly on the internet. It reportedly brought in about $150 million, although the two young filmmakers sold their interests long before that stratospheric sum was realized.

The Blair Witch Project, admittedly a remarkable example, showed that low cost video production could produce a motion picture of technically acceptable quality at a price that would have seemed ludicrous just a few years before. In 2003 the technology market research firm IDC estimated that as many as one million camera owners have been making movies intended for a wider audience than family and friends. Amateur filmmakers post their movies on such websites as AtomFilms.com and Undergroundfilm.com; the website imdb.com listed films. Some filmmakers rent theaters and advertise, and numerous film festivals exist for these hopefuls who dream of finding a willing distributor.

have considered making a movie. In addition to editing software like Final Cut Pro and Premiere, even simpler online editing programs such as Jumpcut and Eyespot string video clips together and add soundtracks, titles and effects.

The most spectacular use of computers is in CGI (computer generated imagery) special effects, which can create a Greek fleet of a thousand ships for the invasion of Troy or a race of large blue humanoids. Animated films using computers have improved to the level of Oscar competition. *Toy Story* (1995), created by Pixar Animation Studios and Walt Disney Pictures, was the first feature-length CGI (computer generated imagery) animated film. Computers based on AI (artificial intelligence) have emerged as central characters with feelings, starting with HAL in *2001: A Space Odyssey*. The computers are usually villains.

Telecommuting

Peter Leyden, director of the New Politics Institute, observed, "When transportation meant ships, people built Venice. When it meant trains, they built Chicago. When it meant cars, they built Los Angeles. Cities have always been fundamentally shaped by the dominant transportation of their time. It's one of the givens of urban planning. But today planners are beginning to see that society is on the verge of building a new kind of city in an era driven not by transportation but by *telecommunications*."[8]

One young mother used to drop her two sons off at a day care facility at 6 a.m., drive about 50 miles to work as an insurance claims adjustor, and then hope to be home again around 5 p.m. Now 6 a.m. has her making a "two-second commute" to her basement office and taking a break at about 7:30 to get the boys off to the school bus. Then it's back to work until about 4:30 p.m., when the bus brings her boys back home. In this and so many other ways for so many people, communication replaces transportation with all its obvious and hidden costs.

Not all mediated communication change is positive. The middle management employee who is issued a cell phone to carry when he is off duty has no certain escape time in his work week. That week now contains seven days, not five. It's morning, noon and night. On the positive side, many white-collar workers are now able to spend at least part of each week telecommuting. Among the work-at-home occupations are accountants, architects, bankers, bookkeepers, clerical workers, computer operators, programmers, systems analysts, counselors, data entry clerks, engineers, journalists, lawyers, real estate agents, secretaries, brokers, travel agents and, of course, writers.[9] A broadcast journalist who must file a story or update one in a hurry can do so from a mini-studio at home. Some doctors even e-visit patients and medical insurers are covering the activity.

Interactive video for judicial proceedings cuts legal costs. Defense attorneys, prosecutors, witnesses, judges, victims and parole officers have all used the technology. The arraignment in New Jersey federal court of Theodore J. Kaczynski, the Unabomber, was held in Sacramento, California. Estimated cost of transporting Kaczynski was $30,000. Using "TeleJustice" the court conducted the arraignment on murder charges for about $45.[10]

Telecommuting holds advantages and disadvantages for both employer and employee. Employers may need less office space, saving on rent, furniture and utility bills at the expense of close connections to their staffs. In many cases the employers have eliminated full-time staff positions, substituting part-time contract workers or consultants, saving not only on health care and other costs but changing the employer-employee dynamic in favor of the employer. For the employee who manages to hang onto a job, the time, expense and frustration of the daily commute are eliminated. Concern about caring for small children may determine whether the employee is even able to hold a job outside the home. The isolation of being apart from other adults during the workday is offset for parents by the benefit of spending time with their children, other family members and neighbors. In fact, with social media, the telephone and email, colleagues are not really isolated from each other. Futurist writer Alvin Toffler used the metaphor of "the electronic cottage" to describe the increasing shift of work from office and factory to the home.[11] "The communication toolshed" would also be an apt metaphor.[12]

Some observers predict that if telecommunications succeed in pulling people out of cities, the exodus will be primarily of the middle and upper income groups, those who most easily travel the electronic pathways, leaving the poor and the elderly behind. Such a movement often erodes a city tax base, with potentially dire consequences.[13]

For at-home workers who miss the fellowship of an office but dislike a long commute, the concept of "co-working" has led to chains of offices dedicated to meet their needs and to the renting of desks by businesses that have unused capacity. By 2012 an estimated 760 co-working facilities were operating in the United States.[14]

Telecommuting has also led to outsourcing as white-collar jobs follow factory jobs to low wage countries, a change of decidedly mixed blessing that mediated communication makes possible. While it has resulted in white-collar layoffs in developed nations, outsourcing has made life better in developing countries for quite a few skilled workers, especially in English-speaking nations like India and the Philippines. In Bangalore and other Indian cities with a cadre of educated, English-speaking workers, entire industries have sprung up to do computer programming, telemarketing, banking, online product support, plus a variety of different jobs that can be handled through global communications at lower costs.

Mediated communication allows some self-employed workers to settle wherever their work takes them. The home, filled with communication and computation equipment, may be a van or a boat. A home address may be a website and an email address. As for anyone whose work requires neither a daily commute nor relocating, the choices of where to live are limitless.

Timeline

1801: Joseph-Marie Jacquard loom uses punch cards.

1823: Charles Babbage starts building a calculating machine, a "difference engine."

1834: Babbage plans an analytical engine, a computer device.

1843: Byron's daughter, Ada Lovelace, explains concept of computer programming.

1854: George Boole's *An Investigation into the Laws of Thought* logic system.

1873: Lord Kelvin calculates the tides with a machine.

1890: Herman Hollerith use punch cards as data storage for U.S. census.

1928: IBM punch cards.

1931: In Berlin, lone genius Konrad Zuse invents a computer but is ignored.

1936: Alan Turing develops the theory of a general purpose computer.

1937: George Stibitz invents the "K-model," an electrical digital calculator.

1939: In Iowa, Atanasoff and Berry build electronic computer; it is lost during WW II.

1940: Teletypewriter, calculator tied by phone line to demonstrate remote computing.

1943: British machine Colossus cracks Germany's Enigma code.

1946: Universiy of Pennsylvania's ENIAC, the first modern electronic computer.

1948: From Claude Shannon and Warren Weaver of Bell Labs: information theory.

1951: Grace Hopper discovers the first computer bug, a real moth.

1952: Claude Shannon uses electric mouse and maze to prove computers can learn.

1953: Magnetic core memory is installed in a computer, the Whirlwind.

1956: A transistorized computer and the first hard disk random access drive.

1957: A leap forward in software: FORTRAN.

1958: The microchip is invented. It will enable the computer revolution.

1964: IBM's OS/360 is first mass-produced computer operating system.

1967: The light pen and the floppy disk.

1968: Douglas Englelbart links keyboard, keypad, mouse, windows and more.

1971: The microprocessor.

1975: Microcomputers are sold in kits to hobbyists.

1981: From Tandy: the laptop.

1982: The computer is *Time*'s "Man of the Year."

1994: Almost one-third of American homes have a computer.

2009: "Cloud computing" moves to central data storage, away from PCs.

12. The Internet

The World at Our Fingertips

The more educated you are, the greater the probable effect on you of the digital communication revolution, especially the internet. But educated or not, the internet touches us all. What is happening today is sometimes compared with what Gutenberg began in the 15th century. It can also be compared with ancient Greece, when thoughts on many subjects could be stored in the form of writing for future generations and knowledge could build upon knowledge (e.g., an astronomer sending his observations to another astronomer in a distant place). Writing overcame barriers of time and space. The internet works in much the same way but for more people and at a faster pace. This creation of computer networks has produced a change in human communication. Its World Wide Web and email touch almost all of us, even non-users.

Social Networks

We keep surprising ourselves. Few imagined that what was initially a means of communicating with research colleagues would lead to a massive, global-wide sharing of personal information. Around the turn of the millennium a handful of visionary entrepreneurs like Mark Zuckerberg created the social networks of Facebook, YouTube, MySpace and the other virtual venues that make up Web 2.0. In 2009, Yahoo had nearly eight million groups dealing with every imaginable subject. Distinctions between life online and life offline have blurred.

Zuckerberg, *Time's* Person of the Year for 2010, began a social network at age 19 that by the end of 2010 had connected seven out of ten Americans and an astonishing total of more than a half billion people worldwide. They speak to each other on Facebook in 75 languages. The award was made "for changing how we live our lives," said *Time* in explanation. Facebook "started out as a lark, a diversion, but it has turned into something real, something that has changed the way human beings relate to one another on a species-wide scale. We are now running our social lives through a for-profit network that, on paper at least, has made Zuckerberg a billionaire six times over. Facebook has merged with the social fabric of American life, and not just American but human life… Relationships on Facebook have a seductive, addictive quality that can erode and even replace real-world relationships."[1] Personal privacy has taken a back seat, a point raised by Facebook critics.

The internet began when researchers working at mainframe computers wanted to communicate with each other. What once was a strictly professional connection quickly evolved into friendly chat and interest groups. It was the start of computer-based social networking. Their path led to chat rooms that filled an apparent need for a remote version of social interaction. The path has continued to Facebook and Twitter and goes on from there.

We are social beings who will make use of the available tools of online social media to connect with each other. We can connect with those who remain dear, even if no longer near. Distance is no longer the barrier it once was. In fact, there are advantages to distant connections with people we may never meet. Like strangers on a train we unburden ourselves with little inhibition about what we say.

Second Life

Millions of players from all over the world today are living the vicarious existences of *Second Life*, a 3-D virtual world.[2] *Second Life* may be as close to heaven as you can get on Earth. It is less a video game than a social network set in a fantasy realm created by the players themselves, a parallel dreamland that by 2009 had registered sixteen million players from all over the world. It might be described as an internet activity without rules or an objective or game play, just as in real life. "Residents" find a plot of land, build a house, start a business, socialize with other residents and generally live a "second life," just as the title promises. That avatar life can be a person of a different age, race, gender, or physical attributes. People move about in a life that "might-have-been" if only their lives had worked out differently.

You can be anyone you want to be in *Second Life*.

Courtesy: Linden Lab

In this fantasy thousands of residents "attend" church; different faiths and denominations are a click away. Real auto manufacturers including Toyota, Nissan and Pontiac, have opened virtual dealerships to offer virtual cars for sale for "linden dollars" to residents who want to express their tastes but don't need a car for transportation in a world where they can teletransport their avatar from place to place.

Researchers in several dozen schools and educational organizations, including the Harvard Law School, can be found there. A number of them are studying how *Second Life* can be used to advance education. The news agency Reuters has a correspondent there. You can watch full-length feature films on the Sundance Channel inside *Second Life*. Linden Labs, the company that runs *Second Life*, added a *Teen Second Life* world. Quarrels over imaginary real estate have led to real life lawsuits. In Japan, a wife who was unexpectedly divorced, logged onto the similar fantasy *Maple Story* and murdered her husband's avatar. She was arrested and jailed.

What better example can there be of how mediated communication distances its users? Isolating themselves totally from the reality of their lives, players enjoy a fantasy world of their own creation. Their connections are with people far away who have also separated themselves from their own lives. This is *playing house* for grownups.

A Variety of Interactions

Online gamblers provide an interesting example of figuring out a social interaction at a distance. Among the many internet groups are online poker players. They bet against each other with real money but for the most part never meet. In addition to playing cards, they chat with each other using their own conversational conventions. Traditionally, poker is a game full of both spoken and silent social interaction, which is limited to the chat function that the online poker site provides. In the online game, very few player "tells" (movements that might identify the quality of the cards in a hand) are involved. In live poker, studying your opponents' physical movements is an enjoyable form of interaction. Online up to ten people can be "seated" around a poker table. Typically their only form of communication is via the "chat window." On one poker site, players design their own persona by specifying visual characteristics such as facial features, haircut and clothing. At the poker table, they can modify their facial expressions and body positions, and they can even talk to each other in various accents, using "emoticons".

Politicians have used the internet as a cheap way to get their messages to voters. So have the extreme fringes. It has not been possible to stop hate; websites link angry, suspicious and even mentally ill internet users on all manner of issues. At the same time, support groups use newsgroups to deal with problems relating to physical disabilities, eating disorders, drug use, AIDS, cancer, diabetes and mental illness. It is decidedly less embarrassing to type in: "Hello, my name is Susan, and I'm an alcoholic" than to face others at a meeting.

Challenges

Internet addiction is a worldwide problem. The South Korean, Vietnamese and Thai governments tried to limit the hours that teens spend online, such as kicking them off network games after five hours. China went further, treating heavy internet use as a mental disorder and locking teens up in rehabilitation clinics. In the United States, the equivalent of Alcoholics Anonymous groups for cyber addiction have been formed online (despite the irony of the venue). It has been called Internet Addiction (IA), Internet Addiction Disorder (IAD) and Pathological Internet Use (PIU), accompanied by estimates that as many as one internet user in ten has an addiction potentially as destructive as alcoholism and compulsive gambling.

Seductive, the internet coaxes otherwise busy people to waste productive hours, detoured by websites that catch their attention. Lost hours and lost sleep can lead to dysfunctional behavior that destroys marriages and careers. More than a few users admit to being online for eighteen hours a day or more, racking up hundreds of dollars in monthly phone bills, addicted to chat lines, porn sites, or game sites. Internet addictions have joined addiction to other forms of mediated communication, particularly television and telephone use.

According to a study covering sixteen nations, online time seems to be taken mainly from television viewing rather than from time with family and friends. A study of heavy internet usage reported unsuccessful attempts to cut down on time spent online. Addicts experience anxiety when not online and significant relationship discord. Some respondents admit to pre–existing psychiatric problems such as bipolar disorder, depression, or alcohol abuse.[3] Internet addiction has also been dismissed as a fad that is easily corrected, and not an addiction at all.[4]

Allowing anyone to collect and distribute information from an unimaginably vast trove adds to, the internet's equalizing capacity and disturbing effects. The internet empowers the thieving, the sadistic and the ghoulish who unfortunately reside among us. The potential for individuals to challenge governments and even dictatorships to an extent far beyond anything ever known has importance for society. Anything is possible in this information revolution including real, bloody revolutions. "Power to the people" holds both positive and negative elements; positive, for example, in opposition to tyrannical governments; negative in enabling child pornographers and sexual predators, con men and drug dealers to elude justice. Cyber stalkers target victims, and police either cannot track them down or express disinterest in doing so across international borders. Nor can we forget the hackers who disrupt communication for the sake of gain or malicious pleasure or for no fathomable reason at all. Dealing with them has not been easy.

How the Internet Began

Like the phonograph, the telephone and the computer, the internet was conceived for purposes other than its main uses today. Along with so many communication media technologies, the internet has become more of what its users wanted and less of what its inventors intended. Its inventors could not have contemplated its use for myriad private purposes by the folks who live down the street. They certainly did not envision the internet as a global means of entertainment.

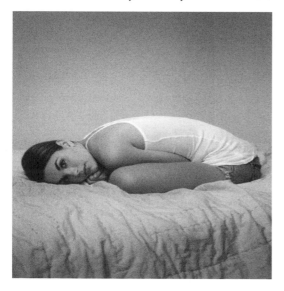

Lonelygirl15

Lonelygirl15, the widely watched and believed series on YouTube, was an example of the yearning by people all over the world for intimate communication with a stranger.[5]

An actress pretended to be a 16-year-old video blogger whose ordinary life grew increasingly bizarre. Online fans flocked in from every direction. *Lonelygirl15* proved harmless. Others are not. Social network scams have been stubborn.

The internet began quietly when some science researchers at universities and in industry wanted a better way to contact each other through their mainframe computers that were connected by telephone lines. In 1969, they sought a grant from the Advanced Research Projects Agency of the Department of Defense, which had been organized in 1958 as a government think tank in response to the Soviet launching of Sputnik.

With the grant the scientists set up the ARPANET, the Advanced Research Projects Agency Network. ARPANET was to be a test area for computer networks, a link-up of time-sharing systems. Because of the heavy cost of constructing and operating mainframe computers, sharing made sense. A principal goal of the ARPANET was to share data and programs in the days when data existed on punch cards and programs were not sold at the computer store (there were none), but had to be written by individual researchers for their own projects. Computers then were employed mostly as mathematics tools, although by the '60s some non-mathematical research was done, such as language analysis (including one study by the author of this book).

The ARPANET was seen as something more than a *research* tool. It was also a *communication* tool, an important distinction. No one had ever used a computer for ordinary communication the way people made a telephone call or sent a telegram. The ARPANET was not intended to connect computers but rather to connect the researchers who used the computers, another important distinction.

To accomplish that goal, it was necessary to establish protocols—agreed-upon ways of communicating—such as a file transfer protocol (FTP) and a remote login (Telnet). These signals would open up channels to allow data to pass through and then close the channels. J.C.R. Licklider, first head of ARPA's Information Processing Techniques Office, envisioned a network that could spread everywhere, an "intergalactic network," as he put it. The idea caught on. Licklider also moved ARPANET thinking away from a military focus to exchanging information about basic computer research.

Who Should Use the Network?

One question that arose early was access. Who should be allowed to use the network? If access were to be limited to certain universities, certain industries and certain government and military offices, it would not be "intergalactic." To be that, to be so universal that the network's potential benefit could reach all of mankind, access could not be limited, nor could control of the network.

It was decided early that the network would not have a single central command and control point. Each node—each point of connection—would be able to connect with any other node. In the event of an atomic bomb attack, the network would not be brought down by the destruction of a headquarters site. That concept grew out of a 1962 Rand Corporation study, "On Distributed Communications Networks," by Paul Baran.[6] He called for what amounted to a new kind of public utility. In describing

J.C.R. Licklider
Courtesy: Freebase

Paul Baran
Courtesy: Rand Corp.

such a utility, Baran created the concept of packet switching and store-and-forward technology that now lie at the heart of email data transmission.

By the end of 1969 ARPANET had connected computer nodes at four universities: UCLA, Stanford, the University of California at Santa Barbara and the University of Utah. Four years later forty nodes existed, including a satellite link to Hawaii and low speed links to England and Norway. Ten years later there were four thousand nodes, but the project was no longer the original ARPANET.

In 1975, as messages flew from node to node, ARPANET was declassified as a research project. Responsibility for it was given to the Defense Communications Agency. That same year the Xerox Corporation started an experimental internet. The ARPANET was eventually split in two, into a civilian internet and the military network, MILNET.

Usenet

Because humans are social animals, the researchers were also using their new pathways to create interest groups. Are there other lovers of homemade beer out there? How about science fiction fans? How about gardeners? Such personal communication lay outside the formal research-purposed structure of ARPANET, but those using the connected computers enjoyed the extra social benefit. Few complained.

In 1979, two Duke University students, Tom Truscott and Jim Ellis, created a separate online network, a kind of computerized bulletin board that they called Usenet. [7] Anyone could offer news or information articles in the form of files. The network began at two sites, Duke and the University of North Carolina. Other universities soon signed on. The University of California at Berkeley provided a gateway between the mailing lists of ARPANET and the more open Usenet.

Whereas ARPANET tried—not too successfully—to limit its discussions to research issues, any topic was fair game for Usenet bulletin boards: find a few like-minded souls and set up a newsgroup. The question of distasteful postings came up. It was decided that peer pressure via emails should nip offensive postings. Repeat offenders would be removed from the Usenet.

By 1983 Usenet had leaped the Atlantic as European sites connected to the growing network. It wasn't cheap. With the standard 300-baud modems, the transfer of data was slow enough to run up considerable phone charges, especially burdensome for impoverished college students. The arrival of the 1200-baud modem helped somewhat. So did an organized network of *backbones*—main trunk lines—in different countries to connect UNIX user groups.

Eventually Usenet spread across the world. Thousands of newsgroups discussed everything from philosophy to recipes and movies. Anyone could post. Everyone could read. The free, even anarchic nature of the internet was never clearer.

Teletext and Videotex

In many homes entire sections of a newspaper delivered each day at the front door go straight to the recycle bin. The use of natural resources in the printing and delivery of newspapers and magazines that are unread has led to several proposals for electronic substitutes to replace the printed page. Prior to internet news and advertising, there were teletext and videotex. Teletext was a one-way broadcast transmission via a television signal's unused scanning lines, or vertical blanking interval (the visible horizontal bar on a television screen when the set isn't tuned perfectly). Videotex, using telephone lines, had an interactive feature. The user requested information from a computer data bank, the precursor of current online news retrieval. Neither service succeeded, but they pointed the way to technologies that did. Today, tablets like the iPad make acquiring the daily news even simpler.

The internet—and especially the Web—brings together newspaper, magazine, book, postal service, telephone, radio and television.[0] Each originally found public acceptance for a reason. When we deplore the decline of the traditional newspaper we are really mourning the technology that once put a fat package of inked paper in our hands at the breakfast table, not the reasons we read the newspaper. That the newspaper-reading public may be diminishing is a sad reality, not an affront to human nature. This applies to all the other media that cannot do their jobs as well as the internet can. We no longer need to read a newspaper to learn how the local team did or whether to pack an umbrella. We do not need a phone to call a banker or broker to buy a bond or sell a stock. We no longer need to lick a stamp to pay a bill.

The World Wide Web

In 1990, British engineer Tim Berners-Lee wrote the first browser program, a software program that guides a user to read hypertext (non-sequential) files. He called it WorldWideWeb (written as one word). With it he created the first web server and the first website, put online in 1991. It would link directly from any website to any other and also enable the user to edit files with point-and-click ease. [9] The address of the first website was Info.cern.ch, referring to the European Organization for Nuclear Research, where Berners-Lee worked.

At a time when incompatible computers ran on idiosyncratic operating systems, Berners-Lee's browser became a means to scan networks of computers to see what was out there and to summarize their contents. It started as a tool to enable researchers to browse for other research. Later the browser was distinguished from the virtual space filled with websites. The virtual space itself retained the name: the *World Wide Web*. Over the years the World Wide Web, or " the Web," has become synonymous with the internet, but it is not. Famously, the internet is "a network of networks," a broader designation that includes email, Usenet and other systems and networks. Each quickly swelled to enormous size. The Web's virtually uncountable number of sites would be of little use if not for browsers to organize and read them, and search engines to locate what the "net citizen" (the "netizen") is looking for. A browser enables us to read the documents at websites. A search engine finds what we are looking for.

At first, college students wrote most of the browsers and search engines in their spare time. The name "Archie" for a Web navigator was intended to conjure up "archive," not the comic book character (an association that its designers detested). An improved search engine called "Gopher" took the user from directory to directory. That was followed by a new search engine called "Veronica," named just to tease the "Archie" team. Among other browsers were Erwise, Viola, Lynx, Arena, Amaya and Midas.

In 1993, college students Marc Andreesen and Eric Bina designed Mosaic, the most efficient browser at the time. To overcome its weaknesses, two years later they wrote Netscape. Unlike Mosaic, it worked almost identically with the Windows, Macintosh and UNIX platforms. It was modem friendly, enabling the user to act on the quickly available text and hyperlinks while it more slowly downloaded graphics.

In addition, service providers like AOL and CompuServe came along to improve and extend access. AOL tried to look hip for a young, with-it clientele. The Dow Jones News Retrieval began as a business information service before reaching out to the general public. Prodigy hired women to help design and market its product. Its goal was a family-oriented service, but it captured only a small fraction of the market. At this writing the most popular browsers include Explorer, Safari, Firefox and Chrome.

Google

A variety of search engines followed including AltaVista, Dogpile, Hotbot, Lycos and Yahoo plus hundreds more that specialized in specific information areas. The dominant search engine, Google, almost instantly replies to any topic request by identifying websites that relate to the topic. According to a 2005 survey, Google handled requests for information from 380 million separate users each month in ninety languages. Google offers several searches. The best known is for text websites. Others are for images, videos, Google maps and shopping items. There are also a news search and a finance search that keep up with current events across a broad range of topics. News editions are available for many different countries and in a number of languages.

The U.S. Department of Defense had originally provided the money to set up the internet in order to improve communications with the private sector. The National Science Foundation, which ran the internet backbone, soon realized that the internet had grown into much more than an accompaniment to research. In 1995 the Foundation allowed commercial invasion of a nonprofit online network, and it was the year of the Netscape browser using hypertext and the hyperlinks of the World Wide Web, changing everything again. Netscape allowed almost anyone to find almost anything, learn almost anything, write anything and buy or sell anything.

It opened a world that was, in William James' phrase of another era, "a blooming, buzzing, confusion" that now holds more than 100 million websites with domain names and content. The total number of Web pages is, of course, much larger. It is a world dominated for the most part by ordinary people, not by governments that try with marginal success to control what goes on within their own borders and not by large corporations.[10]

Using the Internet

What do we do with the internet? A 2009 Pew survey of internet use reported that the World Wide Web continues to skew toward the young. More than half the adult internet population is between the ages of 18 and 44. Internet access is available in virtually every school and library in the United States and in most homes with children. Nevertheless, more and more older adults are also going online and they are doing more, especially emailing.[11] Women above 55 have been joining Facebook at a fast clip according to an informal 2009 survey.[12] Older generations use the internet less for socializing and entertainment and more as a tool for information searches, emailing and buying products. Researching health information is their third most popular online activity, after email and online search. Generation X (internet users ages 33-44) continues to lead other age groups in online shopping.

Compared with women, men are more likely to use the internet for weather, political and financial news, sports and do-it-yourself information. Men are more likely to do job related research, download software, listen to music, use a webcam, participate in interest groups or take a class. Women are more likely to email, get maps and directions, look for medical information, religious information or support for personal problems. More women said the internet helped them find people they needed to reach. Women are also more likely than men to value the positive effects of email for improving relationships. And they are more likely to forward jokes and funny stories.[13]

The Web has shaken the traditional merchant-customer relationship. As always, when something is gained, what it replaces is diminished or is lost. The handshake and smile that concluded a sale is gone, exchanged for a global outreach for goods and customers accompanied by an impersonal, standardized acknowledgment. Thousands of websites provide online shopping that is—to paraphrase Marshall McLuhan—knocking down the walls of the store on the corner. Electronic merchandise such as books may be downloaded so the entire buying process never departs from a computer screen.

Pierre Omidyar
Courtesy: Wikipedia

Thousands of sellers make money on eBay, the electronic sales floor created in Pierre Omidyar's San Jose, California living room in 1995. Tens of millions of buyers make purchases. It has all become a significant change to an important part of life.

Email·

Of all aspects of the internet, the most powerful and transformative for many people has been email. The potential to connect distant family and friends is the feature that changes most former non-users of computers into daily users. Hundreds of millions of people use email daily. Like all communication technologies, the internet reduces our face-to-face contact with other human beings while expanding our contacts with people beyond our reach. Humorist Dave Barry wryly commented, "I prefer email because it's such an effective way of getting information to somebody without running the risk of becoming involved in human conversation."

Small talk isn't needed nor is suitable clothing. At the same time it takes just a click to receive an article or a joke from anyone anywhere, another click to add it to our personal hoard and another click to send it on to a hundred others wherever in the world they live. Some companies find email too time consuming for their staff and have declared email-free days. To communicate, those employees actually have to talk to each other. Of course, if looking at someone's face is too intense there is that older communication tool, the telephone.

Emails seem to have revived letter writing, but without the gracefulness of pen and ink. Sloppy writing is less of a problem.[14] Words are less likely to be weighed if a message disappears at the tap of a finger and sentences can so easily be changed, added to, eliminated and moved around. Beyond email we now have Twitter, limited to 140 characters at a time. This has led to new protocols of abbreviation. LMAO says in four letters what otherwise consumes nineteen spaces: Laughing my ass off.

How Email Began

How did email begin? Around 1965, users who shared a computer could put messages in one another's file directory so they would be seen when the user logged on. The users were at "dumb terminals" that connected to the same mainframe computer.

In 1971, after distant computers began talking to each other over phone lines, Ray Tomlinson, an ARPANET contractor, invented email so that messages could be sent over connected networks. He chose the @ sign as a standard between the name of the sender (or recipient) and the computer location.

Ray Tomlinson
Courtesy: Raytheon BBN
Technologies Corp.

Email grew rapidly because it met fundamental communication needs. Within two years three of every four ARPANET messages were email. In a wisp of time the messages expanded from the military and scientific to the commercial and to the personal.

This amount of communication might have been prohibitive in countries where telephone calls are expensive, but costs were kept down by the asynchronous practice of delivering a text message quickly to a computer location that a message receiver could access at any time. Protocols and mail programs were developed to set standards for message transfers. Photos, videos and sound soon joined text messages.

Younger Internet Users

If more older users are emailing, a smaller percentage of the young choose email, with telephone texting, social networking and blogging at their fingertips. Internet users ages 12-32 are the most likely to use the internet for all kinds of communicating and for such entertainment as downloaded music, online videos, games and virtual worlds. They are more likely than older users to read other people's blogs and to write their own, happily blogging and tweeting throughout the day.[15] By a large margin, the favorite online activity of the younger generation is game playing. More than three out of four teens play games online.[16] Half of Generation Y (born between 1979 and 1999) do so. The numbers drop as age rises but, as we shall see, they do not vanish.

Computer users in high schools not too many years ago were dismissed as "geeks" and "nerds." No longer true. Something else is going on. Nerds created Silicon Valley; today some are billionaires. They have set up communication enterprises like Facebook and YouTube into which everyone is welcome to provide content, an activity that can be traced back to the first letters-to-the-editor column in a newspaper. As eager, unpaid content providers, millions of us are naturally curious to learn if anyone is paying attention. Someone who displays photos on Flickr, a poem on MySpace or a political opinion in a blog wants to know how many passersby clicked on the personal page. Tracking hits can be as obsessive as stopping to look each time you pass the hallway mirror. Again, this is an example of mediated communication intersecting with our lives.

With the internet at hand, if students read fewer books and newspapers than their grandparents did, it does not mean they are learning less. (Whether what they are learning is useful is another matter.) Students now have many more choices in their sources. They do their research via *SparkNotes* and the Google search engine, bypassing original texts. Parents who once used *CliffsNotes* for their Shakespeare assignments and grandparents who got their literature from *Reader's Digest* Condensed Books can hardly complain. Once again, choice through mediated communication is transforming education.

Distance Education

The internet has augmented traditional bricks-and-mortar education and what once were called "open universities" and "correspondence courses" that depended on the mail to move lessons and teacher evaluations. The non-profit Khan Academy, to cite one prominent website, offers a library of more than two thousand simple videos, each a lesson in math or another school subject. Combined with traditional in-class teaching, the lessons enable teachers to zero in on topics each student has difficulty understanding. Excellent progress has been reported.

With email, instant messaging, newsgroups and video teleconferencing, the correspondence course has come a long way from its roots. Distance education allows high schools, trade schools and universities to offer study courses to earn credentials from a GED to a PhD. Lectures, assignments, questions and answers flow at electric speed. Books and journal articles are downloaded. Students do not have to scribble notes as the teacher speaks. With a click, students who want to understand a poem are hyperlinked to a literary review along with an author biography. Study sessions with other students may be separated by continents, but can be just as intense as late night cram sessions in a dorm.

Decades before the internet, universities used mediated communication in such areas as agricultural extension services. Nursing is another field where keeping up to date is essential, but nurses in distant locations may not be able to spare the time to return to a university for that information. Now they don't have to. To cite another example of how the internet has changed education, students must leave their classrooms if they join a military service, but not their education. Recognizing that outside education as well as military training can produce a better soldier, the Department of Defense has established a tuition assistance program. Online educators help by making allowances for military time constraints.

Web 2.0

Web 2.0, comprising the newest additions to the Web, has in the blink of an eye brought about a second revolution. Web 1.0 consists mostly of pages provided by those with something to sell or tell. Web 2.0 is provided by the rest of us for the rest of us. *Time*'s "Person of the Year" ("You") for 2006 celebrated this personal shift. The *Digital Futures Report* said, "while the internet may be subjected to criticism on a variety of fronts, it is unlikely that going online will ever suffer from the same type of scorn that television has received over the years ('the idiot box,' 'the boob tube,' 'the vast wasteland')."[17] Why not? Why does the internet receive far more respect than television? Look for the answer in the comment by Apple's Steve Jobs about users who lean forward in active engagement and viewers who lean back passively receiving whatever comes out of the tube.

Also, consider that a few television executives decide the content that millions watch. A few newspaper executives and journalists in any given community control the news output available to people in that community. This is the industrial model of *mass* communication. The internet, especially the old Usenet and the new Web 2.0, is supposed to travel a different path.[18] However, increasingly some of the most frequented web addresses are being accused of tailoring responses to each individual in ways that are not always helpful.

Concern has arisen that some organizations—Facebook and Google have been mentioned—are filtering out variety that users might want. Blame may go to the automated gatekeepers—not human editors. User A and User B might make the same request of Google for a list of websites on a certain topic, but might be given different sets of websites. This personalizing and tailoring of information are based on such collected data as what people click on most often and where they live.

Web 2.0 is packed with communal activity, but remember that these are uses that governments neither originate nor control. Yet Web 2.0 is not anarchy. It can be as businesslike as banking. At prosper.com users who want to borrow or lend money directly from or to one another provide the content. At wetpaint.com, twine.com, stumbleupon.com, hypemachine.com and the like, users share observations about stories, music, movies, ads, or websites they run across. Alone, none of the founders of these sites could possibly supply the enormous amount of content or choices that users happily contribute. Each site is actually a worldwide community, fulfilling Marshall McLuhan's prediction of a global village.

Wiki

As part of sharing information, the village collaborates. Consider Wikipedia, the communal encyclopedia, or the Apache Software Foundation, dedicated to open source programming, or the Linux operating system (or systems), the alternative to proprietary systems.

The village breeds its own vocabulary. "Wiki" refers to any collaborative website. Anyone can edit it. Amazingly, it works. At Wikipedia, millions of writers have contributed articles. A curious and controversial version of Wikipedia is located at wikileaks.org to deposit government documents. Where governments control access to newspapers and broadcast outlets, here is an outlet for whistle blowers. The site relies on volunteers to vet the information. Potential for WikiLeaks abuse is great. A storm of protest followed the release of sensitive U.S. government text files in 2010.

Not many experts thought Wikipedia would work because they believed that revolutionaries, propagandists and assorted crazies could strangle it. Instead, it would be hard to find a better example of Web 2.0's by-the-people, for-the-people promise. The vandals are there, but so are Wikipedia's protectors. The result is a quick, usually dependable source that even serious scholars use, although they may feel too shamefaced about it to footnote what they find.

More than a century ago work began on the great *Oxford English Dictionary*. It, too, depended on the contributions of volunteers.

Blogging

The internet offers a wealth of source material on almost every topic and almost anyone can contribute. With an inexpensive digital camera and an MP3 recorder-player, a self-appointed journalist can set up a news website and, at least in theory, attract an international readership to daily news and opinions. With this equipment, photo interviews can be conducted. Bloggers have broken significant stories. The writing and questions may lack polish and the video may be out of focus or shaky, but the stories have an air of immediacy. Topics ignored by journalists or dropped after a day or two were kept alive and pushed to the point that politicians felt forced to respond. For example, blogs riveted on a CBS News error regarding President George W. Bush's military service led to the resignation of veteran news anchor Dan Rather.

Websites have been helpful to the public in innumerable ways. For example, they have provided nearly instant information about the effects of a disaster, especially the identities of victims for those who search for relatives. On the internet there is no waiting for a scheduled newscast or the next printed edition. The sequential structure of broadcast news does not exist. The online reader looks at headlines and chooses stories asynchronously from a menu of online news agencies, newspapers, radio stations, television stations and news channels all over the world, often at no cost to the reader. For readers who prefer news heavily seasoned with opinion, informed or not, even laden with invective, thousands of blogs and special interest websites are just a few clicks away. News websites like *Salon.com*, *The Drudge Report* and *The Huffington Post* bring news laced with opinions to hundreds of thousands of viewers daily.

Keeping Track in China

No medium of communication with such power can exist without challenges from those who wish to change it to something that it presently is not. Nations that do not allow journalists to speak freely do not give bloggers a free pass. By 2009, China had about 350 million internet users plus twice as many cell phone subscribers. Astonishingly, half the internet users reportedly blogged. Even in rural areas, where cell phones have become common and the internet is a click away, unrest among Chinese peasants has grown.[19] Blogs by young Chinese test the limit of what authorities will allow. Thanks to Chinese character words, bloggers bundle more information into each message.

With all the new sites coming on line, authorities are hard pressed to keep track of content. They attempt to do so indirectly by holding internet service providers responsible for policing the blogs to make sure pornography and political messages hostile to the government do not appear. The ISPs were given lists of forbidden words. Filtering software either replaced the words with asterisks or blocked the message altogether. Authorities cracked down on Twitter, providing a microblogging substitute, or *weibo*. Chinese bloggers find creative ways around forbidden words such as using Chinese characters that sound like banned words when spoken aloud.

Government censors in some nations may not fully know what is being sent and, even if they did, could scarcely halt the exchange of information across their borders short of seizing all computer modems or tracking down all international phone calls. Meanwhile, Iranian college students used blogs to accuse their government of a fraudulent election. An Egyptian court sent one blogger to jail for four years for expressing his opinions. Will the internet replace newspapers and newscasts? For some people, especially educated people living in dictatorships where news is controlled, it already has.

As this book went to press, Congress was debating the Online Piracy Act aimed mainly at websites based overseas that profit from online content like movies that they do not pay for. Ranged in support of the bill are content providers led by movie and music providers. Opposition includes internet sites such as Wikipedia, Facebook and Google, which fear that the legislation could lead to government censorship of the internet.

The Dark Side

For some users it doesn't matter that the more public mediated communication we have, the less privacy. For others, the lack of privacy does indeed matter. Even when we think we are communicating privately, we are not. Digital age author Steven Levy concluded, "We think we're whispering, but we're really broadcasting."[20] And some clever people are listening. From scam to spam, they prowl and phish (attempt to gather personal data with phony email). If email eased communication for millions of people, it also eased the way for the unscrupulous.

Nastiness does not stop there. Malicious hackers spread viruses, worms, Trojan horses, spyware. Motives for writing and spreading destructive programs vary, but none is pleasant. Con artists send email to the gullible, promising fortunes in exchange for bank account information. Pedophiles locate the email addresses of children to whom they send pornographic letters and pictures, or arrange meetings. Sending a youngster a webcam to attach to a computer in the child's room as a "gift" is a favored trick. Stopping pedophiles has not proved easy.

A call for Muslims to kill all Jews as a preparation for Judgment Day registered 350,000 "likes" on Facebook before the page was taken down.[21] Like the rain, the internet is sent on the just and on the unjust.[22]

Timeline

1945: Vannevar Bush conceives idea of hyperlinks, hypermedia.

1958: Defense Department creates ARPANET, precursor of the internet.

1960: Joseph Licklider conceives the internet.

   Americans, Britons simultaneously develop packet switching transmission.

1965: Non-sequential hypertext is created. It will one day build the internet's links.

1969: UCLA computer sends data to Stanford computer, foreshadowing the internet.

1971: ARPANET, internet forerunner, has 22 university, government connections.

   Early version of email.

1973: Xerox sets up a LAN (local area network) called Ethernet.

1979: USENET begins.

1980: Internet users send and receive at 300 baud.

1982: From Carnegie Mellon U. professor Scott Fahlman: emoticons. :-)

1983: Internet domains get names instead of hard-to-remember numbers.

   TCP/IP becomes standard protocol for internet connections.

1986: Congress passes Electronic Communications Privacy Act.

1988: "Hacker" and "worm" enter the internet lexicon. First data crime reported.

1989: Researchers try to index the exploding internet; they can't keep up.

1990: World Wide Web originates at CERN in Europe. Tim Berners-Lee writes program.

1991: Internet available for commercial uses.

      Hypertext Markup Language (HTML) written; helps create the World Wide Web.

      The Web gets servers.

1992: Text-based browser opens the World Wide Web for general usage.

1996: Email use surpasses postal mail.

1997: Nearly 8 of 10 U.S. public schools have internet access.

      Streaming audio and video are available on the Web.

1998: Weblogs, or "blogs" for short, and PayPal are created.

2000: Seven new Web domain names approved, including .info, .pro, .biz.

2001: Internet has thousands of online radio stations.

2002: Google News, an automated service without human editors.

2003: Flash mobs, organized on the Net, start in New York, spread worldwide.

      An estimated five trillion unwanted messages are sent on the internet.

2004: Facebook makes friends.

      95% of U.S. public libraries offer internet access.

2008: Internet plays an important part in U.S. presidential election victory.

2009: Applications taken for internationalized domain names.

2010: 4G wireless network extends high speed internet to cell phones.

13. Video Games

Leaning Forward

In the film *The Princess Bride*, the video game *Hardball III* is seen in the opening being played by a boy whose grandfather arrives to read him a story. The grandfather takes for granted the superiority of a fairy tale in a book over an interactive game, with the grandfather, not the child, doing the reading. The audience is expected to agree that the imagination stirred by listening to a story is superior to what a game stirs. Or at least in this instance, passive listening is more fun.

It isn't. And the public knows it and says so with its money. The 2011 release of *Call of Duty: Modern Warfare 3* grossed a billion dollars in sixteen days. No motion picture release has matched that. Video games grossed $56 billion globally in 2010, more than radio, recorded music or magazine revenues.[1] Today it is not academic research or business that drives microcomputer development to be bigger and faster. It is games.

From their early days, video games sold computers. Until they heard about games, a lot of people saw no need to buy a computer. A small calculator was enough for budgets and taxes, and a typewriter for letters. Only when they saw how much fun video games were did they decide to splurge on a computer. Video game speed of play, their graphics and the amount of data needed for the different paths a story line can take is what pushes the demand for better computers. Prof. James Paul Gee of Stanford calls the games "a new form of art. They will not replace books, they will sit beside them, interact with them, and change them and their role in society in various ways, as, indeed, they are already doing strongly with movies." He added, "When people learn to play video games, they are learning a new literacy"[2] and unless they overdo it they are not wasting time.

It would seem reasonable to wonder why a discussion of video games belongs in a book about communication. Several reasons brought it here:

1. Tens of millions of players from all over the world, most of them young, use computers and other communication devices to play these games. Many of the games are played online.

2. Some "games," like *Second Life*, are not games at all, but are a fantasy social network, a means to communicate with others far away.

3. Other video games like *FarmVille* and *CityVille* are a part of social networks like Facebook and can be played with friends.. They are means of communication.

4. Many games have an educational function. Unfortunately, some games teach violence.

5.Recognizing the hold that games have on so many younger people, educators are turning to them as a way to communicate information and skills. The University of Minnesota School of Journalism and Mass Communication is just one of the institutions where research in this field is conducted. The U.S. Army has even used video games for training.

Games Are Universal

Every society on earth plays games of one kind or another. It is doubtful that a school or community exists anywhere without them. Did cave dwellers play games to sharpen their skills at bringing down hoofed food? Did quieter games in every century help pass the evening hours and long stormy days? Bet on it.

We also enjoy *watching* games of every sort, and we engage in all manner of personal competition from cards and chess to running and wrestling, just as we like team competition ranging from debates to football. The list is endless. Or we play by ourselves against a machine or against our previous "personal best".

Inserted into this world of games is modern mediated communication in the form of video games. They are all about choice. The *Oregon Trail* blazer must choose the longer river path or the shorter but more dangerous mountain path. Ms. Pac-Man must instantly go left or right to evade the gobbling monsters. The making of decisions never ends until the game does. The challenge is addicting, and doubly so against human opponents who face the same choices. We play video games against family members or friends or classmates. We carry on conversations with strangers in faraway lands as we try to "kill" them or partner with them without knowing who they are except what they tell us, and that may be as true as what we tell them. Video games are played in arcades, on game consoles, on cell phones, on television sets and in places you might not expect to find electronic games.

Leaning Forward or Back?

Steve Jobs offered this prediction: "We don't think that televisions and personal computers are going to merge. We think basically you watch television to turn your brain off, and you work on your computer when you want to turn your brain on."[3] His comments created the concepts of *leaning forward* and *leaning back*. Video games are not just child's play. Nearly three-quarters of all American households played video games. The average age of players in 2011 was 37. Nearly half were women. Games are played on office computers by employees who should be working, on home computers by "screenagers" who should be studying and by their parents. They are played quietly using software sold in stores or downloaded from the internet, or noisily in clubs and tournaments. Many games are played online against unseen opponents.

Maybe other games draw in competitors whose enthusiasm for Scrabble or Monopoly has evolved into addiction, but nothing that came before matches the mass hypnosis of video games. "I don't believe anyone ever expected video games to have such a fundamental impact on our society in so many areas," said Dr. Christopher Geist, chair of the department of Popular Culture at Bowling Green University and a member of the Videotopia Advisory Panel.[4] "[They] have become an integral part of the fabric of American life, changing the way we think, the way we learn and the way we see the future."

How Video Games Began

Video games were born in academia. A game was played a few years after the first computers were built, assembled by hand in the engineering department of a university. In 1952, the room-sized EDSAC at Harvard, depending on thousands of vacuum tubes, was programmed to play tic-tac-toe. A.S. Douglas wrote the program as part of his doctoral dissertation, just to show that it was possible. Douglas and his professors may have been the only players. In 1958, when computers still filled entire rooms, William Higinbotham, at the Brookhaven National Laboratory in New York, a nuclear research lab, created "Tennis for Two" using an analog computer and two hand-held control boxes. The screen was a 5-inch oscilloscope. Higinbotham wrote the game program to entertain visitors to the National Laboratory. Lab staffers waited for hours to play, but Higinbotham did not think enough of his little invention, the first interactive video game, to bother getting a patent.

Empire was the popular game at Cal Tech. To get around a no-nonsense systems operator, one student changed the name of his game to "Test." No one objected to a student running a test program. With millions of government dollars being spent on equipment and research time, IBM tried to ban games from their buildings, but so many employees complained that IBM executives backed off.

The first electronic game, tic-tac-toe, was played on this computer, the EDSAC.

The first commercial games went into arcades. An important difference between arcade games and handheld or console games is based on how their manufacturers make money. Arcade games make money when people plunk in quarters, so the most commercially successful games have no endings. The aliens keep coming as long as you have quarters. Console game manufacturers make money when buyers finish a game and head to the store for another. So the popular games played at home have stories that end. You can win.

During the 1950s computers were far too expensive to be used for video games, but change came with the PDP-1, a minicomputer made by the Digital Equipment Corporation. Here, around 1962, Dan Edwards and Peter Samson are playing the first interactive game played on a digital computer, Steve Russell's Spacewar!

Photo: Gift of Hewlett-Packard Company

The years went by and the games rolled out. Everything improved: the graphics, the sound, the color and the game play. Video games became an even bigger business through media convergence, as movies expanded into games and games were remade as movies. When Disney released *Tron* in 1982, the studio also created a *Tron* arcade game that more or less followed the film's plot. The game was just difficult enough to keep teenagers dropping in the quarters. As it turned out, the game brought Disney more money than the movie. The 3-D movie *Tron:Legacy* was released in 2011 as a sequel to the earlier Tron film along with a video game, *Tron: Evolution*. Modern video games have plots. The best tell a good story, but only as the player uncovers it. When the player doesn't know which way to turn and gets killed, that is not the end of the story. Like cops-and-robbers at the playground, death is never final in a video game. Even if you have run out of lives, you just reload the game and start over again, smarter. Now you know how to avoid the swamp, the ax, the ogre.

Some towns once banned game arcades altogether. That gave Nolan Bushnell, who created the *Spacewar, Pong* and Atari arcade electronic games an idea to create a place where parents and kids could visit together and the kids could play video games. His solution was a pizza parlor in San Jose, California, that included video games. He called it Chuck E. Cheese's. More than 500 outlets all over the United States have joined his pioneering venture.

Game Addiction

Many families tend to be ambivalent about video games. Parents may worry that kids spend too much time and too much money on the games. They may also worry about violent content, but recognize that many games have positive learning aspects, that the games are task-oriented and help develop dexterity and hand-eye coordination. A game may teach strategic thinking and how to deal with frustration. Parents may be pleased that their children are so fascinated by a game. Actually, "fascinated" may be too gentle a word. Playing video games often becomes obsessive for both adults and children.

A goal of every game maker is to keep the player at it. Psychologist B.F. Skinner famously devised the "Skinner box" to show how rats can be conditioned to keep at a task for the reward of a crunchy food pellet. The smart rat learned to keep pressing the lever. A nice reinforcement, but it did not go on like this forever. After a while it no longer handed out a pellet with each press, only an occasional pellet. This "partial reinforcement" kept the rats at it. Now consider the game player who is rewarded by higher and higher scores for hitting a button. The player discovers that the game grows harder with time and success, awarding fewer points. This partial reinforcement makes the activity even more addictive. The player has to try harder to build up a score. The goal—the pellet equivalent—is the higher score. The computer makes it easy to program a game to be addictive.

Excessive playing of video games is not unusual, with players logging on for twenty-four hours or longer at a session. For some online game players it becomes the most important activity in their lives. It is the most important social pursuit some teenagers and adults have, and when they are alone at the computer, exchanging messages with other players is their only social interaction. It has led to both marriage and suicide. South Korea sends teenagers to rehab boot camps to rid them of internet and game obsession.

Describing *Sim City*, Communications Professor Ted Friedman wrote, "It's easy to slide into a routine with absolutely no down

The arcade game *Tron*

time, no interruptions from complete communion with the computer. The game can grow so absorbing; in fact, your subjective sense of time is distorted. You look up, and all of a sudden it's morning. It's very hard to describe what it feels like when you're 'lost' inside a computer game, precisely because at that moment your sense of self has been fundamentally transformed."[5]

What Can We Learn?

Parents and teachers have complained that game players are so much into their games that they move with little awareness of what is immediately around them. That raises a useful question: what can society learn from an activity that is so attractive? That question was asked years ago about television programs. Now it is video games. What can teachers learn from game designers? For example, adults are nervous when they go into surgery, but a youngster can be terrified. Anesthesiologist Anu Patel noticed that a friend's seven-year-old son was so busy playing his Game Boy that he wouldn't eat or talk to anyone. Dr. Patel did an experiment with seventy-two children, ages four to twelve. She found that children who were given a Game Boy to play before anesthesia showed the least anxiety and often no anxiety at all. They did much better than children who were given tranquilizers or children whose only comfort was their parents.[6]

Video games can encourage fantasy lives, where we can do dangerous or illegal things that no reasonable person would actually do. In a fantasy game, these reservations do not matter and playing well raises self-esteem. Get a high score, surpass your personal best, or reach a goal and you feel good about what you have accomplished. Gaming can also be a conduit for social activity. Particularly in Asia, teenagers like to play video games in crowded rooms while carrying

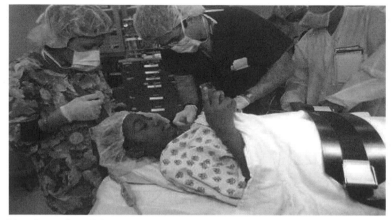

Dr. Anu Patel, left, and surgeon John Kakauberi prep patient Nykia Crawford, 10, who is occupied with a Game Boy.

Permission: AP,
photographer Mike Derer

on conversations with old friends and striking up new acquaintances. Some youths develop such dexterity that they earn big prizes in competition. Las Vegas sponsors an annual world championship. "E-sports events are played in several American cities. In South Korea, the best video gamers are treated like rock stars.

Physical Activity

Obviously, excessive game play limits physical movement. While the monsters run and jump, the players do not. They sit still, except for busy fingers making repetitive movements. Staring at screens doesn't help their bodies either, nor do sudden spurts of game-infused adrenaline. Physical problems have been blamed on heavy video game play. Joints, skin, thumbs and muscles have suffered from repeatedly hitting buttons. Players have complained of neck stiffness, wrist pain, finger numbness, blisters, calluses, sore tendons (that some doctors have jokingly called "Nintendinitis") and sore elbows (sometimes called "Pac-Man's elbow"). In rare cases, epileptic seizures were reported among players who were photosensitive. In terms of health, some critics think the best thing that can be said about video games is that they are a step up from staring at TV.

Nintendo's Wii wand gets players up and moving. The motion control gaming system has been a runaway best seller, attracting seniors as well as the youth market. Depending on the game, the player swings a virtual baseball bat, a tennis racquet, a golf club, a bowling ball, a fishing pole, a sword, or a fist. Despite their value as a spur to exercise, the games have caused some injuries and property damage in the hands of overzealous players.

In PlayStation Eye games for PlayStation3, a camera and microphone (accompanied by voice recognition software in 20 languages) pointed at the player converts body movements into movements onscreen. Crouch and your character starts to move. Lean to the right and your character moves right. Roll your arms in circles and your character does a back flip. If you want to stop, hold your arms out to the side. And so on. Your body moves. After doing this for a while, the player has acquired a day's ration of exercise but can still get sore or may even dislocate something. On a positive note, Dr. James Rosser, director of the Advanced Medical Technologies Institute at Beth Israel Medical Center in New York, headed a study showing that surgeons who played video games three hours weekly had thirty-seven percent fewer errors and accomplish tasks twenty-seven percent faster in doing laparoscopic surgery, where the surgeon's movements are guided by watching a television screen.[7] (However, it won't help your chances of getting into medical school.)

Gender Differences

A 2007 study by the Entertainment Software Association reported that 30% of all video game players were adult women compared with 23% of players who were boys under 18. Women prefer to solve puzzles, test their dexterity (Wii is popular), help their comrades put dragons in their place and heal their fallen friends. They play *Angry Birds* on smartphones; in three years an estimated 500 million copies of *Angry Birds* were downloaded. As noted in the previous chapter, the online social network *Second Life* is a favorite. If disturbances to the daily pattern of real life are too upsetting, *Second Life* lets players live out perfect dream lives.

Console manufacturers and game makers put a lot of thought into how to hang on to customers as they grow older. Teenage boys remain the most important market for many games, especially the first-person shooters known also as "twitch" games. But teenagers are a shifting market. Today's teenager is tomorrow's adult. Boys who grow up to discover that girls are not so annoying after all become less concerned about blasting monsters, so the market adjusted for changing interests. Video game makers discovered that girls wanted to play too, so welcome the Nancy Drew mysteries. Game makers took that difference into consideration. Girls' heart rates increased more than boys' rates. That was true for both playing and just watching.[8]

Women and younger girls particularly like non-violent games that require sharp eye-hand coordination, sometimes called "muscle memory." You need quick reflexes to play *Angry Birds,*

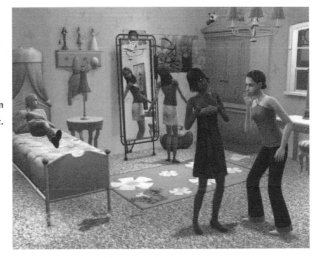

A screenshot from a Sims 2 game.

Used with permission of Electronic Arts, Inc.

Pac-Man, Donkey Kong, Frogger and *Prince of Persia*. Researchers also noted that women prefer to play in short segments, rather than to sit for hours at a game.

Another favorite of women, *The Sims* series, deals with ordinary people living ordinary lives. The player controls the characters and navigates them through human situations. Said writer John Seabrook, "As my fourteen-year-old niece exclaimed recently, when I asked her what she liked about playing *The Sims*, 'You've got one Sim who you've got to get to school and another who needs to get to his job and their kid has been up all night and is in a bad mood and the house is dirty—I guess there's a ton of things to do!'"

Looking at the blockbuster game of *Tetris*, the author of *Joystick Nation*, J.C. Herz observed, "*Tetris*… is more popular with women than any other game and notoriously addictive among female professionals… It's about detritus raining down on your head, trash falling into messy piles and piling up until it finally suffocates you. The psychological payoff for the player is a state of rapturous relief. 'Yes,' she thinks. 'Yes! The mess is vanishing! I can make the mess disappear.'"[9] The game is, of course, popular with men also. An Oxford University study concluded that *Tetris* helps block the mind from storing painful memories.[10]

Testosterone continues to get the game designers' attention. In 1996, from Britain came *Lara Croft, Tomb Raider*. Despite being a female hero, her busty, leggy appearance was designed to appeal to young males. The original script called for the main character to be a man, but the designers feared that the game looked like an Indiana Jones ripoff. Instead, Lara was born. By *Tomb Raider III*, the player who reached a higher level sent Lara into a new virtual reality in some exotic corner of the world. What seemed just a game combined a geography lesson with a male fantasy.

Electronic games have a way of getting under the skin of some players. A study of how players referred to games reported that most people referred to a game as the impersonal pronoun "it," as in "It hates me." Next most common was the personal pronoun "he," as in, "He's trying to get me." Also common was "you" ("You dumb machine!") and "they" ("They think they're so smart; I'll show them"). No one referred to a game as "she."[11]

Types of Games

Games are divided into types, but some games fit into more than one category. Here is one of several lists:

Adventure: reach a goal by solving puzzles.

God games (also called "simulation"): manage a community, an empire, or a war.

Scroll: run and jump and avoid the nasties.

Sports: play tennis, golf, hockey, football, race cars.

First-person shooters: kill the enemy.

One-on-one: hit, kick, do whatever it takes to put an opponent down.

Brain and finger busters: match your skills against the machine.

Learning: solve math, language and other school subject problems.

Role-playing: adopt an identity, wander through other worlds.

In the role-playing god game *Black & White* (2000) the player is considered a god and can decide the kind of god to be: either cruel or gentle. As a god you will be worshipped, you can uproot trees with your bare hands and you can raise fierce animals to enforce your will and expand the empire you control. What you get is up to you. If you pet an animal each time it eats a villager, guess what kind of animal you will have.

Violent Games

The effect of violent video games may be greater than that of other media because they are interactive and more involving. In some games the player identifies with the aggressor, participates in crime, learns by repeating violent acts and is rewarded for doing so. The Columbine High School killings in Colorado in 1999 were committed by two students obsessed with ultra-violent *Doom* and *Duke Nukem*. News reports came of high school shootings in Pearl, Mississippi; Paducah, Kentucky; Jonesboro, Arkansas; Springfield, Oregon; and Tabart in the Canadian province of Alberta. Studies have shown that angry boys are particularly stimulated by violent video games.

A study of brain activity among players of the shooter game *Medal of Honor: Frontline* compared with players of a non-violent game showed greater activation in the amygdala, the portion of the brain involved in emotional arousal and less activity in the prefrontal portions of the brain involved with control, focus and concentration.[12]

The industry response to complaints about violence has been disingenuous, but that is scarcely unexpected. It is not difficult to find in most industries the argument that customers should

Criticism and Praise

Doom and *Grand Theft Auto* have been denounced again and again for glorifying acts that in real life earn long prison sentences. The protests have had negligible effects. In 2004, adding to more than 30 million copies in the series already sold, *Grand Theft Auto: San Andreas* sold more than two million copies in its first week. Criticized as lacking morals and being "ethically reprehensible," the games won praise for the quality of their graphics and game play. Such praise is reminiscent of the uproar that greeted the films *Birth of a Nation* and *Triumph of the Will*, movies that were also praised for their artistry and condemned for their content.

Doom® © 1993 id Software LLC, a ZeniMax Media company. All Rights Reserved.

get what they want, not what is best for them or for society as a whole.

As usual in the world of mediated communication, the users determine its direction. Among the best-selling games are those that appeal to the worst of human impulses.

Despite a rating system, it is easy for a ten-year-old to buy a game in which scantily dressed prostitutes, begging the player to kill them, are murdered by chain saws. Filthy language spews from cartoon mouths. Cannibalism is treated casually.

Nor is it difficult for kids to get *Grand Theft Auto*, which presents drive-by shootings and drug dealing as cool, and awards points for killing innocent people and for having sex with prostitutes.

In *Clocktower 3* a little girl has her head smashed with a sledgehammer and a screaming old woman is lowered into a vat of acid.

In *Carmageddon* and *Twisted Metal* the player scores points for running over pedestrians. Similar brutality runs through other games as game designers vie for viciousness. *Quake* lets the player digitally superimpose images of people and places they know to customize the game. As video games become the storytellers for the younger generation, the cry for government regulation grows louder.

Some games are damned as sexist and racist. In one game points are awarded for killing anyone who isn't white or is Jewish. Another game awards points for killing pregnant Mexican women. We are confronted with more than the familiar question of whether fictional violence leads to real violence. Do such blatantly racist video games serve to undo the efforts of schools and governments to foster a more tolerant society? And what can be done about it in a democracy that prizes freedom of expression?

Critics pointed out that physical assault cases increased sharply not only in the United States but across Europe, Canada, Australia and New Zealand, where violent video games are popular. Many parents are unaware of what is in their children's electronic games. One survey found that while 80% of junior high students said they were familiar with *Duke Nukem*, rated "mature," a survey of more than 500 parents found that fewer than 5% had ever heard of it.[13]

Rating Games

Complaints against offensive games led eventually to a self-protective, industry-designed rating system. Hollywood had taken the same step with its G, PG, R and X ratings in hopes of avoiding government censorship. The AAMA (American Amusement Machine Association), representing the video game industry, created this ratings system in the hope that its own controls would avoid government laws:

C: for children

E: for everyone

T: for teens

M: for mature

AO: for adults only

Ratings don't mean much if any youngster can buy any game. The National Institute on Media and the Family sent young boys and girls to stores to see if they could buy M-rated games. Girls were able to buy the games about once in 12 tries. Boys could buy the games half the time.[14]

Supreme Court Decision

The U.S. Supreme Court in 2011 struck down a California law to limit violent games, saying the ban went too far to limit free speech. On the other hand Senators Joseph Lieberman and Sam Brownback asked this: "Defenders of these games say that they are mere fantasy and harmless role-playing, but is it really in the best interest of a child to play the role of a murderous psychopath? Is it all just good fun to positively reinforce virtual slaughter? Is it truly harmless to simulate mass murder?" The senators led hearings that industry executives chose to avoid.

According to one witness, the more time spent playing electronic games, the lower the school performance. Teens who played violent games did worse in school than teens who did not. Boys and girls who preferred violent video games were more likely to get into arguments with their teachers. They were more likely to get into physical fistfights.[15] Eugene Provenzo, a University of Kentucky professor of education who called video games "a teaching machine," added, "When violence is stylized, romanticized and choreographed, it can be stunningly beautiful and seductive. At the same time, it encourages children and adolescents to assume a rhetorical stance that equates violence with style and personal empowerment."[16]

Military games, such as the World War II *Call of Duty* series, with intense, realistic and brutal action, are best sellers. The Army has used video games as training material for recruits. For example, *Full-Spectrum Warrior* teaches maneuvers in an urban environment along with hand-eye coordination and "muscle memory." Skill at the joystick may aid future pilots as well as assassins. *America's Army*, a training and recruiting game supported by the U.S. Army, had more than six million registered players in 2006. *Time* magazine, referring to the potential of this cross between *The Sims* and *Doom*, called it a "killer app."[17] The British army trained troops with a version of another military game, *Half-Life*. One of its developers noted that the commercial version of the game had to be altered for military use to remove some of its fantasy. In combat, the soldier who is shot doesn't simply get up and continue to fight.

Online Multiplayer Games

It has been said that our storytellers determine our culture. Radio, television and movies have been our latter day storytellers. Television airs programs that are talked about at the office water cooler and on the phone the next day. If storytellers do indeed determine our culture, we must consider the cultural impact of storytelling video games.

As of 2011, choosing among about two dozen languages, an estimated 12 million players worldwide of *The World of WarCraft* surrounded themselves with reference books, maps and one or two computers for daily or all-night adventures in a medieval fantasy world where the player/ avatar can make friends or slay enemies. The game combines sexy images plus dragons and sword fights with player teamwork. To participate in such online games, each player pays about $15 a month. This has led to friendships being created and solidified, to relationships that bloom into marriages. A survey reported that the average age of *EverQuest* players was twenty-five. About one in six players was a woman, two out of three were single, and one player in five had children. One person in three said making friends was the most important reason for playing.[18]

Multiplayer gamers send text or voice messages to each other while they battle assorted demons or other players, or try to avoid battle altogether. Friends and fellow workers take supporting online roles in team play. For them, cooperation is more important than conflict and that attracts women to the game. If your character meets another character in the game, you can just sit around and chat while other players look for players to slaughter. One way or another, players can reach out and touch someone without actually touching. Social get-togethers online have sometimes expanded to get-togethers in real life. People in the same community have established clubs and luncheon groups. Some players have met for dates. A few who met in game play have

A knight from *Lineage: Goddess of Destruction* wearing celestial heavy armor and holding an enchanted Spectre Dualsword. Both have significant value in real world money.

In 2011 the parent company NCSoft shut down its North American websites for the game, citing financial reasons.

Image courtesy: NC Soft

Entropia Universe, **run by MindArk in Sweden, takes place on the planets of a fantasy future world. Project Entropia dollars (PED) can be exchanged for U.S. dollars at the fixed rate of 10 to 1, so they have real value and so do the virtual objects and properties that players buy and sell to each other. In 2010 one player sold a virtual resort for US$635,000.**

Courtesy: MindArk

married. It has been said that the players have taken the game over from the designers.[19]

While conservative Christian groups have argued that the Dungeons & Dragons games encourage worship of the occult, violent behavior and suicides, Christian-themed games are commonly sold.[20] *Left Behind: Eternal Forces* was in the genre of the *Left Behind* books that imagine a world in which the elect are lifted into Heaven and the rest suffer the eternal penalties of the damned. The game has fighting, suspense and romance, along with Biblical references. Critics say it promotes intolerance and religious warfare. In 2008, the game was given away free, a kind of Gideon Bible for the new century.

A different complaint about all online games comes from social scientists who think it is not healthy for a nation that so many of its citizens—and voters—are so wrapped up in an ideal but artificial environment that they neglect our messy, real world.

Real Money Changes Hands

Players advertise on game websites that they own certain virtual (not real) game items that are hard to win in the game. These are for sale for real dollars; in some cases, thousands of dollars. Starting with an investment of $9.95, Ailin Graef, born in China and living in Germany, earned more than $1 million U.S. dollars buying, building, selling and trading virtual property.[21] She is not alone in playing to accumulate an online treasure to sell for real money. *EverQuest* hosts a site, "Station Exchange," where players can buy or sell—for real money—weapons, play money, or entire characters. After learning that the game generates several million dollars each month—real dollars—in game economic activity, a Congressional subcommittee met to consider taxing those who have prospered from the sale of these fantasy assets

Playfish, a maker of online games, reported selling 90 million virtual items a day to players of its games on Facebook, MySpace and other social websites, and on iGoogle and iPhone platforms.[22] These players tend virtual farms, look after pets, or enjoy being virtual gangsters with virtual guns. Game play is free. The virtual products demand real cash.

Why would people pay real money for imaginary property? One reason is that it takes many hours of game play to accumulate the virtual goods; paying cash is a shortcut. As for how much something is truly worth, the law of supply and demand operates.

An industry has sprung up to help frustrated players negotiate their way through games. The player who cannot figure out how to cross a bridge, enter a room, or get past a troll can find the answers in books that supply either hints, which many players prefer, or actual directions. These guidebooks are known as "hint books," "walk throughs," or "cheat sheets." They are the *SparkNotes* and *CliffsNotes* of the video game world. Some games contain their own "cheats," built-in codes that give the players a boost. They can also be found on the internet.

Are these games? If you think of a game as a contest that has an ending, a winner and a loser, probably the online virtual worlds are not games. One game designer said the modern online D&D games are "chatrooms with a game attached." Some of the newest games allow modification by the players, building choice as players let their imaginations flow about the persons they would like to be and what they would like to own. Something of the same motivation is true for video games of professional sports and the assembling of dream teams.

Summary

Wherever you look, video games have entered into the activities of ordinary life. Military forces and corporations use them for training. Educators design them for teaching at the college level. Kids learned math and vocabulary from *Reader Rabbit* and geography from *Carmen Sandiego*. Faith-based games impart religious values. The Wii games and *Dance Dance Revolution* provide physical exercise. Surgeons and pilots have even reported improved hand-eye coordination.

Meanwhile, dreamers encounter other dreamers at online communities. Once again, by their choices the users dictate the direction that a communication medium takes.[23] From these choices has arisen a culture.

Timeline

1952: Game written for Harvard doctoral dissertation played on EDSAC computer.

1958: At Brookhaven Lab, nuclear physicist designs a video game, "Tennis for Two."

1960: PLATO educational system looks for ways that video games can teach.

1961: *Spacewar* at M.I.T. is first interactive computer game.

1968: Ralph Baer produces games played on television sets.

1971: *Computer Space* is the first video arcade game.

1972: Atari's *Pong*, a hit in arcades, taverns, starts video game industry.

1974: Arcade video game *Tank* uses ROM chips to store graphics.

1975: 100,000 coin-operated video games were played in the U.S. alone.

      Gunfight uses a microprocessor instead of hardwired circuits.

1980: *Zork* attracts players to adventure games.

1981: *Pac-Man* and *Donkey Kong* dominate the arcade video game world.

      Some games use holograms.

1982: Disney's *Tron* game earns more that *Tron* movie.

      U.S. Surgeon General calls video games evil.

1985: Kids can't get enough of *Super Mario Brothers*.

      Tetris is developed by a Russian programmer.

1986: *Gauntlet*, a multi-user dungeon (MUD) game for up to four players.

1989: Research blames video games for poor physical fitness of U.S. schoolchildren

      Nintendo's hand-held Game Boy sells for $109.

1994: Total annual sales of video games: $3 billion.

      Senate probe of video game violence results in rating board, rating system.

      Sony PlayStation is released in U.S., a huge hit.

1998: Sony's *Everquest* multiplayer online game attracts tens of thousands worldwide.

1999: Video games bring in more money than movie box offices do.

      Columbine H.S. killings blamed partly on *Doom, Duke Nukem* fixation.

2000: *The Sims* is a big hit with families.

2001: From Microsoft: Xbox game player. From Nintendo, the GameCube.

2003: 239 million computer games are sold.

2004: More than half of all Americans play video games.

   *Grand Theft Auto: San Andrea*s sells two million plus copies in first week.

2006: *World of WarCraft* has 6 million online players worldwide.

   Nintendo game controller Wii responds to hand, body movements.

2007: Of video game players, more are adult women (30%) than boys under 18 (23%).

   China combats online game addiction; cuts points in half after three hours play.

   More than six million "residents" of *Second Life*, but not all are active.

2009: *Wii Sports* breaks video game records with more than 40 million sales.

2010: New motion-sensing video games compete with Wii.

14. Persuasion

What in human interaction is so common as the effort to convince? If nothing else is consistent in history, you can count on the desire of almost everyone to try to persuade someone else of something. The push to win over others has traveled across the centuries on a parallel track with informing others. It operates through essays, drawings, photos, slogans, advertising, public relations, government propaganda and blogs. The media used to inform and entertain you are also used to convince you of something. So is this paragraph.

Teaching the art of persuasion dates back at least to the ancient Greek and Roman rhetoricians who sought not only to convince but lectured and wrote about the means of doing so. The classical rhetoricians identified the appeals to *ethos* (ideals), *pathos* (emotion) and *logos* (reason). Rhetoric was taught from ancient times through the Middle Ages and well into the 19th century as one of the *trivium*, along with grammar and logic, the foundation of a liberal education. Among the most famous writers on rhetoric were Gorgias, Isocrates, Plato, Aristotle, Cicero and Quintillian.

The Start of Advertising

In ancient Greece and Carthage a whitewashed board announced a gladiatorial contest. The ruins of Pompeii reveal a terra cotta image taking the place of words for an illiterate population.

Advertising mosaic in Ostia, the ancient port city of Rome.

In the Roman world, a sign of a goat signified a dairy. A boy being whipped signified a school.

Advertising signs and street criers grew more common as medieval town populations increased. Like the ancient ads, these fall in the category of information rather than persuasion. The spread of printing in Europe brought the posting of printed handbills listing books for sale, a logical activity because printers of handbills also printed books. A few 16th century posters survive, again basically informational. The 17th century saw the start in England and France of public registers, government publications where buyers and sellers could post notices. It was also the century of the first newspapers and the first newspaper ads.

Shakespeare and the King James Bible used the word "advertisement" to mean "warning" or "notification." The term "siquis" from the Latin si quis ("if anyone"…desires) meant a notice. It was replaced when the words "advices" and then "advert' and "advertising" gained currency. Also used were the pejorative terms "puff" and "puffers," from which 'puffery" derives.[1] Handbills became fancier, with woodcut illustrations, hand lettering and border designs. The 18th century introduced the billboard.

The governments that controlled newspapers also controlled advertising. Britain imposed a tax on each page of a newspaper and a heavier tax on each advertisement. Censors were ever present to look for anything smelling of sedition or blasphemy. The powerful guilds watched for any sales effort that might encroach on their control of trade. Nevertheless, as trade grew so did notices of goods for sale. In Paris, *Les Petites Affiches* (*Little Notices*) reported the sale of property and goods, currency exchange rates and new books. Germany, England and the American colonies developed their own newspapers devoted to commerce and notices for auctions, houses for rent, spices for sale and other merchandise just arrived by ship, plus rewards for runaway horses or runaway apprentices. Before the Civil War, notices of slaves for sale were common.

Persuasion crept more forcefully into 19th century advertising with notices of patent medicines guaranteed to cure a long list of ailments. These ads followed what advertising leader Rosser Reeves argued was a basis of advertising: if you buy this product, you will get that specific benefit.[2] Since patent medicines failed to cure anything except the thickness of wallets, a certain skepticism arose. The conjoined twins of advertising claims and public skepticism have been together ever since.

Advertising Agencies

For mass production of goods there must be mass demand. This requires mass information and persuasion. Mass advertising began during the Industrial Revolution, which supplied advertisers with such improved printing methods as rotary presses, paper from trees and mass mailing.[3] Factories turned out goods and needed customers. Workers received cash wages that they could spend on what the factories produced.

As production of a variety of goods and mass distribution grew it was inevitable that mass marketing would become part of the process, for the goods had to be sold. That brought out advertising beyond simple notices. Advertising did more than keep factories running and stock home larders with food and closets with clothes. It affected our morals, manners, customs and the other elements of our culture.[4]

Entrepreneurs, first in France and then in the United States, spied an opportunity in the need for factories to advertise in newspapers. They created the first advertising agencies. Based on bargaining, not on fixed rates, the entrepreneurs bought space in bulk from the publications and sold it piecemeal to the producers of goods. They found a typical niche as middleman in a wholesale-retail operation, where they dispensed advice as needed, at first offering no other services.

Their role as ad space brokers took on added value when they could cut rates for national businesses that advertised in several dozen newspapers at the same time with the same ad. The brokers also revealed actual circulation figures, which differed from the puffed up numbers of publishers who were reluctant to disclose the true numbers. Some publishers regarded the acceptance of ads directly from advertisers as beneath their dignity. Asked by an advertising agent for circulation figures, *Harper's Magazine* executives responded by rejecting his advertising.

Gradually the space brokers became full-service advertising agencies. They created the ads, wrote the copy, designed the illustrations and handled ad budgets. Advertising expanded into campaigns managed by agencies. Out of this came slogans, branding, trademarks and the Audit Bureau of Circulation that produced verifiable circulation figures instead of publishers' myths. At the beginning of the 20th century, magazines were the natural vehicle for national advertising of factory goods, starting with a campaign for the Columbia brand of a new means of transportation, the bicycle.

The combination of mail order catalogues and brand names led to the decline of an American tradition, the traveling salesman who carried his battered case to small towns around the country, giving a personal touch and a human face to selling. A writer for the Lord & Thomas agency said that ad agencies were not selling space or slogans, but salesmanship in print. It wasn't the same.

Using Psychology

As advertising agency pioneer J. Walter Thompson noted, "The purpose of advertising is to sell goods to people living at a distance." That raised issues of trust, for buyer and seller could not look each other in the eye or shake hands in the time-honored way of closing a deal. Historian Richard Ohmann observed that in transactions generated only from advertising no one could say, "'My word is my bond.' The seller is a stranger; buyers are masses; anonymity prevails."[5]

Shopping for the home changed and so did the packaging of goods. Before advertising campaigns in magazines and newspapers, customers did not ask for a brand. Soap flakes were ladled out of a grocer's barrel. To sell a pickle, the grocer rolled up his sleeve and plunged his arm into a barrel of brine. Butter and lard were scooped from large tubs. The druggist squirted soft-drink syrup from a bottle and mixed it with carbonated water. Customers bought what the grocer had in stock without wondering who manufactured it. Advertising of brand names changed all that and introduced packaging for food and household staples. Flour was just flour until it became Gold Medal Flour or Pillsbury Flour. Tea and coffee were just that until it mattered that they were Lipton's and Maxwell House. The iconic cracker barrel around which men sat around to talk really existed until the National Biscuit Company began its advertising campaign for Uneeda Biscuits. This campaign convinced housewives that crackers were better for their families if they arrived wrapped in wax paper inside a cardboard box than if they were pulled out by the grocer's unwashed hand from a barrel or a bin.

Brand Loyalty

To create a human face for printed ads, agencies invented icons to symbolize products, such as the Morton Salt girl with an umbrella, the sleepy boy holding a Fisk tire, Aunt Jemima, Betty Crocker and Nipper, the dog listening to a Victor record. Today it is a gecko, chipmunks, a monkey galloping on a dog and the ageless Betty Crocker. Product testimonials were once sought from opera stars, boxers and explorers.

Advertisers tried to build "brand loyalty" in consumer purchasing decisions. *Printers' Ink*, published for the advertising industry, said in an 1895 editorial that the ad writers would have to study psychology because "The advertising writer and the teacher have one great object in common—to influence the human mind."[6]

Research grew in scope and included studies of human behavior managed by psychologists with PhD degrees who examined subtle differences in motivation and consumer activity. For instance, pursuing the psychology of fear, advertisers created campaigns that ran for years, promising protection against such previously overlooked bodily demons as halitosis, gingivitis and "B.O." (body odor).

The growing advertising industry managed to survive a reputation for fraudulent practices during scandals revolving around rigged lottery schemes and worthless patent medicines. *The Ladies' Home Journal* took the lead in publishing chemical analyses of widely advertised nostrums, revealing that alcohol and cocaine were added. Morphine was an ingredient in a soothing syrup for babies. The government stepped in by passing the Federal Food and Drugs Act in 1906. Truth-in-advertising was codified into law, starting with New York State. The pharmaceutical industry itself tried with mixed success to set ethical standards.

The early 20th century brought more ads based on a naked appeal to emotions. For example, at the start of World War I, the British government needed soldiers for the brutal trench warfare that would take so many lives. Its advertising included such questions as, "What will you answer when your children grow up, and say, 'Father, why weren't you a soldier, too?'"

With its jingles, slogans, theme songs, comedians' jokes and a persuasive voice, radio further humanized the products that were advertised. The commercials themselves were often the target of radio humor, but not the product. Television commercials would join the effort.

Advertising for a Mate

The advantages of advertising were not lost on those seeking to improve their romantic relationships. Long before Facebook the personal ad offered a break from the tradition of arranged marriages, introductions by friends, and other conventional ways of connecting with prospective mates.

Starting in the 19th century, potential suitors advertised themselves. A man regarded as an "adventurer" wrote that he wanted to meet a younger woman with property. A woman was more likely to appeal for a potential mate by identifying herself as "upstanding, virtuous," adding that no adventurers need apply. Today's lovelorn ads continue that tradition of longing for romance and finding unblushing exaggeration.

Advertising for love and companionship through the media grows exponentially. In the most personal way, mediated communication has replaced the tradition of centuries of family involvement in marriage selection. Even the traditional marriage broker has been replaced by the mediated match.com.

Advertising Spreads

During the Depression of the 1930s, advertising was an obvious target for a nation's discontent. Yet it survived, expanded and embedded itself not only in the United States but in every country of the world, including those that had nothing good to say about capitalism. The outcome? Advertising today is everywhere in the world, including the government-run media of the communist countries that once damned it.

Winston Churchill once wrote enthusiastically of advertising, "It sets before a man the goal of a better home, better clothing, better food for himself and his family. It spurs individual exertion and greater production. It brings together in fertile union those things which otherwise would never have met."[7]

During much of the 20th century newspapers dominated mass communication. First radio then television chipped away at their financial base. In the new century internet ads cut deeply into newspaper revenue. Craigslist, a network of classified ad websites, has been accused of starving metropolitan newspapers of a main income source.

We are little more aware of most ads than we are of the air around us. One researcher estimated that the average American sees or hears three thousand ads a day.[8] The inevitable result of such an assault is a numbness to ads that advertisers try to break through. Another result of this saturation, critics allege, is that an increasingly materialistic public has learned to define happiness in terms of ownership: never satisfied, always wanting.

Advertising has stirred emotions, changed attitudes, created appetites, made people want what they do not have and dissatisfied with what they do have. Yet when something is gained, such

Paying to Run for Office

In a perfect world, advertising would be an example of how mediated commun-ication signals a democratic, egalitarian society, for everyone could advertise to everyone else. Yet we live in an imperfect world, where some people are more able than others to spread their opinions.

The advantage to political candidates who can afford to advertise is frequently commented upon, overshadowing fitness for office. In politics, candidates with deep pockets can buy more advertising than candidates with small budgets.

Despite the accepted doctrine that money buys political power, the former CEO of eBay, Meg Whitman, lost in 2010 after spending $142 million of her own money ($46.91 per vote) in the race for governor of California. In Connecticut, professional wrestling executive Linda McMahon spent $100.07 of her own fortune per vote and suffered the same fate.

as a hankering for certain advertised products, it replaces something else, such as a yearning for simplicity. Advertising has given values to the public but these values, such as a standardization of judgment and taste or the belief that purchasing certain goods will bring happiness, are not always in accord with the values taught in the home, in the school or in the pulpit. Mountains of credit card debt and the notorious American paucity of saving for old age may indicate that advertising has been more successful than is healthy for the nation.[9]

Public Relations

Keeping pace with advertising, public relations via mediated communication tries to persuade us on business matters of public interest and on political issues, especially the demerits of opposition candidates. Negative advertising is increasingly damned as counter-productive public relations, but increasingly used because negativity, in a word, works. Public relations were developed into an art form by the circus impressario P.T. Barnum during the post-Civil War years. Using trickery and exaggeration with gusto, Barnum planted newspaper stories to get the public excited about Buffalo Bill, Tom Thumb and the "Swedish Nightingale" Jenny Lind.

When Theodore Roosevelt and the "muckrakers" (Roosevelt's derogatory term) attacked big business and big finance in magazine exposés, a public relations industry arose in their defense. Over time it expanded to include government and other corporate and private organizations. Edward L. Bernays, who styled himself the "father" of public relations, laid out the goal in frank terms. It was "manipulation."[10] Public relations executive Ivy Lee explained its necessity, "The crowd is now in the saddle. The people now rule. We have substituted for the divine right of kings the divine right of the multitude." Lee argued forcefully and usually successfully that public relations should be candid in presenting facts, not hiding them.

The 1930s saw political polls and marketing surveys to examine public opinion as tools of public relations advisors. The Public Relations Society of America was created in 1948. University schools of journalism teach P.R. methods. The modern philosopher Jürgen Habermas analyzed the rise of publicity and public opinion in his influential book, *The Structural Transformation of the Public Sphere.*[11] Today, public relations is a craft taught widely in universities alongside journalism, advertising, and other forms of mediated communication.

Political Persuasion

William Randolph Hearst's jingoism in the run-up to the Spanish-American War is well documented. Through his newspapers he pushed for American involvement in Cuba and the Philippines. By the advent of the First World War, a huge reading public had come into existence. Propaganda led Americans into drum-beating patriotism and the conviction that their armies would quickly carry the day against the wickedest enemy the world had ever known. Government censorship was hardly necessary when publishers considered it more of a duty to raise public morale than dispassionately informing the public.[12] That attitude has carried on in war after war.

The wish to persuade readers to a point of view that will make itself felt at the ballot box continues to be a part of newspaper journalism. Newspapers were joined during the 1930s by radio journalism and commentary, later by television journalism and, at times, situation comedies and now, in the 21st century, by internet blogs. People naturally gravitate to others who share their views. That certainly holds for those with extreme views. Before the blogosphere, to share your views with like-minded thinkers you had to at least get dressed and go out to where they were. Now you can stay home in your pajamas while you share your thoughts, vicious or benign. One research study concluded that putting together people who think alike polarizes them even more. Hawks become more hawkish, doves more dovish and racists more racist.[13] Accepting that this is valid for the general population, the study points to a more polarized electorate and

A Price for Opinions

Expressing political opinions via mediated communication in the hope of swaying opinion has a long history. The first broadsheets, newsbooks, and newspapers in Europe did not differentiate between news and opinion, but most did not stray from what the government would approve, for the printer's freedom and perhaps his neck were at risk.

Printers were forbidden to publish without permission, evidence that even in the age of the divine right of kings those in power were aware of the potential for mischief of political expression in print. Yet, a few printers dared to defy authorities. At least one printer in Protestant-controlled Elizabethan England, William Carter, was hanged, drawn, and quartered for printing pamphlets that supported the Catholic cause.

less communication between groups with opposing viewpoints. Recent elections bear this out.

Because of easily available modern communication tools, anti-intellectualism thrives. Ill-informed communicators are able to reach out through media channels to large numbers of people who seem predisposed to being ill-informed. In addition, the blogosphere and other tools give everyone a voice; knowledge doesn't matter. In a more genteel past only a small percentage of people ever engaged in intellectual public discourse. The change currently evident comes from the powerful communication tools that are now widely available.

Opinions and Objectivity

Even before the appearance of mass-media during the Industrial Revolution, mediated persuasion at a relatively simple level was used to foment revolution, peaceful and otherwise. That was true when Martin Luther's theses were translated into the German vernacular, printed and distributed. It continued to be true when Thomas Paine published his pamphlets in American colonial times. Today the small media of blogs are making serious inroads into the information monopoly of established large media.

In the mid-19th century, penny press newspapers were sold with the primary goal of entertaining, but dispensing opinion was not far behind. The raffish penny press reached readers who enjoyed the scandal and crime news that filled its columns and were not at first particularly interested in political opinions.

That did not last long. Most notable for early political commentary was the *New York Tribune* of editor Horace Greeley. Along with his eye-openers he supported the working man and the formation of unions, equal pay and full civil rights for women, temperance, agrarian reform, a greater share of material wealth for common people, the abolition of imprisonment for debt and the abolition of slavery.

The growth of wire services like the Associated Press brought objectivity in its wake for sound business reasons rather than as a moral imperative. The AP chose a neutral approach to controversial events because it did not want to alienate its publisher customers, who had widely divergent political views. Over time, some newspapers adopted a timid version of the AP way. Even their editorial pages took neutral stands on issues that mattered, a policy dismissed as "Afghanistanism," which meant you could print what you liked about distant events, but don't say anything about our controversial mayor.

During the 20th century, outside of the editorial page and the op-ed page (the page opposite the editorial page), objectivity became a newspaper standard. *Fairness* in presenting information was important to build circulation among readers who held a diversity of viewpoints and to impart at least a sense that the news they were reading had not been colored to encourage a conclusion even if a political slant crept in.

Nevertheless, the wish to persuade readers to a point of view that would make itself felt at the ballot box continues to influence journalism, although most of those who use media to express political opinions preach to echoing choirs. Newspapers with a point of view were joined during the 1930s by radio journalism and commentary, later by television journalism and even television situation comedies. If any single thread runs through the tapestry of television, it may be that persuasion is at its most effective, at least in the United States, when it entertains. Inevitably, attack shifted from the issues themselves to those who expressed opinions.

Persuading by Radio

The history of the United States is peppered with political violence. Yet during the "golden age" of radio in the 1930s and 1940s, the streets were comparatively quiet. Part of the reason: most Americans chose to listen. They stayed home close to the radio and looked forward each evening to news and opinion from a favorite commentator, a span of fifteen minutes that put an exclamation point on the day.

These were the times of the Depression, then gathering war clouds follwed by World War II. Radio delivered the ready answers from left and right. Whether or not you agreed with what you heard, the explanations from a familiar voice may have had a "we're-in-this-together"

Edward R. Murrow

Of the journalists in the past century, no one stood taller than the broadcaster who convinced without hammering his argument. He let his surroundings convey his message.

Reporting from London during the early days of World War II, Edward R. Murrow made it clear that England needed America's support. He did so indirectly because CBS did not allow him a more direct option.

Murrow's baritone spanned the Atlantic Ocean night after night through the "Blitz," but he spoke like the neighbor next door. He let American listeners hear German bombers over the city each night and the footsteps of Londoners resolutely trudging to work the next morning.

For his listeners, the world shrank. No voice may have done so much to bring ordinary American people to sympathize with ordinary British people and ultimately support America's involvement on Britain's side, no sure thing.

effect even when this was not what the commentator intended to convey. The best of these "excess prophets"[14] had a folksy manner, taking advantage of the apparent intimacy of the radio medium. (*See chapter 9, Radio: Helping Us Through the Rough Years.*)

President Franklin Delano Roosevelt recognized this intimacy with considerable success in his radio "fireside chats." CBS television anchor Bob Schieffer observed that other successful presidents knew how to use the dominant medium of their times. John F. Kennedy was elected because he understood television in 1960 and Richard Nixon did not. In 2008 Barack Obama displayed a feeling for the internet that John McCain failed to grasp.[15]

Expressing a station's political opinions during broadcasting's first two decades was routine. In fact, the right to air opinions was not given much thought until a challenge to a station's license, which included the charge that it editorialized, led to the FCC's Mayflower Decision in 1941 that broadcasts must not take political positions. Broadcasters who wanted a newspaper's freedom of choice to say anything, as embodied in the First Amendment, rebelled. They pressed the FCC to reverse the ruling.

Eight years later, the FCC did just that, but went further than the broadcasters intended. In 1949, in its Fairness Doctrine, the FCC said not only that stations *may* offer political opinions, but also that they *must* do so, seeking out matters of importance to a community. This hardly satisfied broadcasters. They wanted the same freedom of choice that newspapers enjoyed.

Meanwhile, the Fairness Doctrine was a catalyst in ending tobacco advertising on television. A successful petition to allow anti-smoking commercials as a counter to cigarette commercials frightened the tobacco industry into calling for a law that banned all broadcast advertising related to tobacco. Broadcasters bridled at the hypocrisy of support for this law by magazines and newspapers that continued to reap millions from tobacco ads. After strong criticism from broadcasters who argued that the Fairness Doctrine chilled free speech, the FCC abandoned most of its provisions in 1987 and wiped out the rest in 2011.

Political Cartooning

Images also persuade. Drawing or sculpting figures for lampooning, which led to political cartooning, traces back to the ancient Chinese, Egyptians, Greeks and Romans. We can't knowfor sure if the pot-bellied Chinese gentlemen who survive in carvings were being ridiculed. Nor is it known if any of the foxes, lions, dogs and monkeys behaving like humans in Egyptian carvings represented actual people. Nevertheless, the comic touches are undeniable. Did tweaking the powerful with these ancient images have an effect? Human nature being what it is, a smirk or two would not be out of the question. (See also chapter 7: *Photography: Personal and So Much More.*)

French artist Honoré Daumier went to jail for this cartoon showing King Louis-Philippe as a pear.

Greek caricaturists seemed to be poking fun at the gods in images on

pottery. Graffiti artists drew and carved satirical sketches on a variety of media that survive in Rome and Pompeii. During the Middle Ages, when cathedral windows told Biblical stories to the illiterate faithful, sketch artists chose religious images such as the devil and the Grim Reaper. Their work in prayer books displays a high degree of artistic skill.[16]

The late Middle Ages, the Age of Enlightenment and the Victorian Age brought forth artists willing to risk official displeasure. In England, the brilliant William Hogarth's sketches showed the moral decay of the city. George Cruikshank exposed the foibles of society and, in a pamphlet that went through forty printings in six months, attacked government corruption. James Gilray did not hesitate to caricature leading political figures. In France, Honoré Daumier took aim at government incompetence. In 1832 he went to prison for six months for his caricature of King Louis-Philippe.

In the United States, Thomas Nast's cartoons (example at right) helped to bring down the corrupt Tweed Ring in New York. One cartoon that found its way to Spain led to the recognition and arrest of Boss Tweed, who would die in prison. Nast used his artist's pen to support the abolition of slavery and to protest the plight of Native Americans and Chinese immigrants. But he also used his artistry to express bias against Irish Americans and the Catholic Church. One of Nast's cartoons was credited with the reelection of Abraham Lincoln. He has been called the father of American political cartooning, although some historians bestow that credit to Benjamin Franklin, whose pre-Revolutionary War sketches stirred patriotic fervor.

Clash of Cultures

The 9/11 airplanes were hijacked in part to send a message through mass media. Suicide bombers seek a global audience. David Kilcullen, an Australian expert on guerrilla warfare, held that insurgents did not blow up a Humvee "because they want to reduce the number of Humvees by one. They did it because they wanted spectacular media footage of a burning Humvee." Kilcullen regarded the wars in Iraq and Afghanistan as, in part, information wars that the United States and its allies were not only not winning, but are barely competing in.[17] British Prime Minister Margaret Thatcher spoke of "the oxygen of publicity."[18]

Through books, magazines, pamphlets, internet blogs, radio and television broadcasts, the enemy is demonized. Yet using Western tools does not mean adopting Western culture, a vital distinction. Reportedly operating even from such remote locations as caves as well as urban houses, the leaders of Al Qaeda continue to produce audio and videotapes. Media tools are weaponized as never before for today's information war.

Georgetown University terrorism expert Bruce Hoffman observed, "Al Qaeda may have 7th century ideas, but they have 21st century acumen for communication."[19] Jihadist websites offer videos that are widely viewed. Attacks on Americans reportedly get the strongest responses.

Among others, both al Qaeda, leader Ayman al Zawahiri and the dean of the graduate school of journalism at Columbia University, Nicholas Lemann, have characterized the conflict as, in part, "a media war."[20] Gilles Kepel, a prominent Arabist and professor at the Institut d'Études Politiques in Paris, commented, "One can say that this war against the West started on television."[21] A Middle East newspaper editor called it "digitized combat."

At the same time, by communication satellites and student backpacks, by CDs and iPods, American and other Western influences have been spreading to far corners of the globe where governments now use the same media tools for their own communication. The asymmetrical and global nature of the internet has changed warfare. There are no front lines. Modern communication has created a strong sense of identity among diaspora nationalities and religions.[22] Audio and video cassettes disseminate sermons across international boundaries and influential speakers reach distant audiences.[23] As *New Republic* writer Robert Wright said, it is "much easier for small groups to rally like-minded people, crystallize diffuse hatreds and mobilize lethal force. And wait until the whole world goes broadband."[24]

The clash of cultures that disturbs much of the world today is not altogether new. The conflicts date back beyond the attitudes of cultural and racial superiority that drove German and Japanese armies during World War II, before the 19th century opening of Japan and the savaging of China, further back beyond the European colonizing of Asia, Africa and the Western Hemisphere starting in the 15th century, still further beyond the Crusades since the end of the 11th century, beyond the invasions of the Vikings, the Mongols, the Muslims, the Roman Empire and no doubt beyond the spread of the Egyptian, Sumerian and Chinese empires at the expense of the lesser tribes around them. The invading army persisted until it dominated the field and usually imposed its culture along with its control.

Unlike previous clashes of cultures involving nations, the present one is not dominated by infantry front lines. Western media rather than foot soldiers invade traditional cultures. In terms of societal change, the results are little different from those centuries when Roman or Chinese or Arab or British or French culture was imposed by the conqueror. Sometimes it was accepted grudgingly by the conquered. Sometimes the conqueror's culture was resisted with bloody results, as when the Hebrews rejected Roman religion or the Hindu and Muslim sepoys in the Bengal army rose in 1857 to slaughter the British who were trying to impose Christian values.

The Iranian revolution that brought the Ayatollah Khomeini to power in 1979 made effective use of audio cassettes of Khomeini's speeches. The Shah, who held power, had control of the newspapers and the broadcast stations—the big media. Audiotapes and mimeographed sheets— the small media—won the streets.

The shoe was on the other foot as moderates and liberals took to the streets in 2009, a generation later, to protest what appeared to be a rigged presidential election. The government of Iran shut down opposition mainstream media. Again, small media spread the opposition's messages. Threatening bloggers with death failed to silence them. Rebellious Iranians cranked up Facebook and YouTube. They tweeted and sent news and pictures. Foreign journalists might be confined to their hotel rooms but thousands of Iranian citizens could not be fully confined in the digital age. Importantly, the tweets reached Iran's cities beyond Tehran as well as going global. The tweets went where, a generation earlier, audio tapes helped usher in the rule of the ayatollahs. A government can block all internet servers, all landline and cell phone connections, but how would the public react if all business and personal communication were stopped?

Secretive nations like Myanmar and North Korea continue to enjoy success at limiting the flow of information both to their own people and to the world outside, but as the cell phone pictures of the streets of Tehran have shown on YouTube since the 2009 election, controlling information is getting harder. The uprising that toppled governments during the Arab spring of 2011 gave evidence that suppressing information borders on the impossible.

The Danish Cartoons

In 2006 European newspapers reprinted a dozen cartoons from a Danish newspaper, *Jyllands-Posten*, that depicted Arab Muslims and the prophet Mohammed in a negative way, such as wearing a bomb in place of a turban. To the democratic West, these political cartoons were free speech. To fundamentalists in the Islamic world, they were an insult and an invitation to idolatry. Islam rejects idol worship in any form and caricatures of the prophet are a sacrilege. Pursuing their anger, Muslim imams in Copenhagen circulated not only the twelve published cartoons but three cartoons they called "even more offending" from another Danish newspaper plus several additional offensive cartoons never published anywhere but sent anonymously to further stir up rage.[25] Some were republished in a leading Egyptian newspaper, *Al Fagr*.

News of the cartoons raced through the Muslim world, releasing among religious fundamentalists a pent-up fury against the West. Crowds took to the streets shouting "Death to Denmark" and "Death" to specific other nations whose newspapers reprinted the cartoons. Danish flags were removed, Danish a dairy burned. Merchants pulled products

Angry British Muslims demonstrate outside the Danish embassy in London over the publication of cartoons of the Prophet Mohammad February 3, 2006. The cartoons, which first appeared in a Danish newspaper, sparked outrage across the Islamic world.

Courtesy: Reuters/ Stephen Hird

from their store shelves. Fires were set at the Danish embassies in Syria, Lebanon and Iran. Stone throwing, hate messages and death threats against editors added to the response. Demonstrators demanded that the cartoonists' hands be chopped off. It did not matter that political cartoons in their own newspapers were at least as demeaning in their depictions of the West. In Nigeria, what began as an anti-cartoon demonstration erupted into religious killing.

Muslim leaders demanded apologies from European nations and censoring of newspaper content. European government spokesmen responded that a government cannot apologize for what appears in a newspaper. Deeply held cultural values had confronted each other: the principle of free speech on one hand and respect for faith on the other.

One of the Copenhagen imams gave both sides their due, "In the West, freedom of speech is sacred; to us, the prophet is sacred."[26] Francis Fukuyama, author of *The End of History*, added that the religious believer "grows angry when the dignity of what he holds sacred is violated. The nationalist believes in the dignity of his national or ethnic group, and… grows angry if that dignity is slighted."[27]

Earlier Arab Media

Arabs once led the world in cultural development. They fell behind during the periods of the Enlightenment and the Industrial Revolution, after the West broke its medieval shackles and moved ahead in education, political equality, personal freedoms and economic opportunities. Yet there was progress in Turkey and Arab lands, accelerated by three major developments in communication. According to Middle East historian Bernard Lewis, they were:

1. Printing. The establishment and spread of printing presses. (However, Muslim religious opposition to printing continued for centuries, especially to printing the Koran. In Istanbul, Christians and Jews had printing presses, but not Muslims.)

2. Translation. Books, primarily on practical topics, but also some literary works, were translated into Turkish, Arabic, and Persian.

3. Newspapers. The first were produced by foreigners. Then came locally produced business newspapers, then general newspapers. The telegraph spread news and other information through public and private channels throughout the Middle East in unprecedented ways. According to Lewis, the coming of the telegraph to the Middle East was a watershed event, "a change of immense significance, and transformed Middle Eastern peoples' perception both of themselves and of the world of which they were part." In modern times, television and satellite, fax, and internet have brought a new openness, and are beginning to undermine the factors that sustain autocracy.[28]

No clearer example could be given of a clash of cultures brought about through mediated communication as these tools of communication became weapons in an ongoing struggle between good and evil, with each side convinced of its own goodness. Those who may have thought the reaction to the Danish cartoons was an isolated event would have that illusion shattered a few months later by the furious reaction to the publication of a speech by Pope Benedict in which he quoted a medieval ruler critical of Mohammed. Mass protests were mounted in several countries, churches were firebombed and several Christians were killed.

Media Across Cultures

To adopt a new means of mediated communication is always an exchange, giving up the way that we have managed our affairs until now for the promised improvement that the new tool will deliver. Not everyone in the course of history welcomed such an exchange, if not for themselves, then for others. As an example, consider the objection by men to female literacy. In some parts of the world today, opposition to female literacy remains strong, even fierce. Men have died to prevent women from learning to read. Consider, too, the opposition that exists to motion pictures, television, the internet, and even basic, non-religious education for any children. *Time*[29] quoted an Afghan tribal leader. "The Taliban walk through the streets shouting the children shouldn't go to school because they are learning modern subjects like math and science." He added, "But we want to be modern."

If there were no communication media, geographically separated cultures with opposing values might coexist with less conflict, as they did in so many places for centuries. What is new and more dangerous now? A century ago hardly anyone had ever seen a movie and no one had heard a radio or TV broadcast. Most people were illiterate. Some were unaware even of the existence of newspapers, magazines, or books. As historian Ian Morris noted, information processing is critical to social development.[30]

It is unlikely that most people who lived in what are now called developing countries had ever seen a visitor from Europe or North America. Many barely educated people were born, lived and died unaware that populations unlike themselves existed. Wealthy merchants, government officials and scholars knew of the cultural and religious differences of others, but were untroubled by them. Today, through mediated communication, awareness of the cultural divide has become obvious to everyone. Some people sense a cultural invasion and may be agitated to the point of violence.

Western media offer blatant evidence of shamelessness. If shameless behavior in sexual matters can be seen in films and on magazine covers, if women are permitted to display themselves, then in traditional non-Western thinking shamelessness can more or less be taken for granted everywhere else.[31] In 2002 a rampage left more than one hundred dead in Kaduna, Nigeria, where the Miss World contest had been scheduled. Certainly, many Americans have complained of the coarsening of culture in movies, television and tabloid magazines, but do little to stop it. The Nigerians did stop it. The venue was moved to London.

In addition to displaying its women, Hollywood, by portraying government officials and business leaders as villains, grinds out massive amounts of anti-establishment film. Screen images of nasty non-Westerners and corrupt foreign government and religious figures sit badly in a hierarchical, autocratic world of leaders and followers. Films depicting a relative lack of respect for parents and other authority figures, films espousing such uncomfortable ideas as the equality or even the superiority of women and blatant sexual imagery are a serious affront to many cultures.

In 2007 when an American hit film, *300*, depicted the Greek-Persian battle of Thermopylae 2,500 years ago, the government of Iran expressed outrage. An Iranian newspaper headlined, "Hollywood Declares War on Iranians."

The Hollywood Product

The world sees an industrialized West peopled by gangsters, prostitutes, monsters and morons. Secretary of State Hilary Clinton observed, "If you look at American TV as much as the rest of the world does, you would think that we all went around wrestling and wearing bikinis."[32] Yet images of sex, violence and horror that require little translation are in demand around the world. The tawdry stuff that many educated Westerners themselves ignore travels better than culturally bound humor and thoughtful drama.

An Editorial in Thailand

Annoyance with media is hardly limited to the Muslim world. You can hear many complaints in the West, especially from conservative Christians. And here is an editorial in a Thai weekly, *Matichon*; Thailand is predominantly Buddhist:

What's wrong with our young people these days? The parents of families living in the country's bigger cities are complaining more and more that their children are becoming addicted to computer games and fast food.

In addition, Thai children are paying less attention to their family affairs and social problems. They are increasingly pursuing activities for nothing more than their own pleasure.

Young Thais are no different from their foreign counterparts in this respect. They chat on the internet, eat fast food, talk on their mobile phones and listen to the same kind of music as youngsters living overseas. They also see the same violence in video games, and react violently when being faced with problems in their daily lives.

It is high time that government agencies concerned with youth policies look closely into the changing behavior of young Thais. If globalization is partly to blame for this problem, then corrective and preventive measures must be taken to enable our young people to cope with the changes.[37]

Movies and television are blamed if moral slippage is perceived at home, such as a boy seeing a girl outside the strict confines of a traditional society.[33] At the same time the complaining viewers might be enjoying *Desperate Housewives*. The Hollywood product that is specifically sought for its sex and violence is also bitterly attacked for undermining tradition, decency and social cohesion. The hypocrisy seems to go unnoticed. The West is not the only source of the guilty secrets. Indian soap operas, widely watched and widely condemned, show lavish settings, fast living and much cleavage. Bollywood plots regularly deal with divorce, adultery and the children of unmarried parents.

That *Baywatch* is popular in the Third World not only fails to convince the upholders of traditional values that it is acceptable, it proves to them that Western entertainment, particularly American, is a conscious effort to undermine the values held by billions in the rest of the world. A Hezbollah leader in Lebanon said that seeing people dressed in American-style clothes is "seeing the bullets of the West."[34] Armed attacks become a justifiable defense against this Western aggression. According to Bernard Lewis, the emancipation of women is a mark of Westernization. But, both for traditional conservatives and radical fundamentalists, such emancipation is neither necessary nor useful. It is noxious, a betrayal of true values.[35] The mufti in India who threatened to smash all television sets in his village correctly identified his village's television sets as the carriers of values different from those traditional values he espoused. Historian Siva Vaidhyanathan made this pithy observation about the cultural divide: "In the United States, Homer Simpson is a unique character, interesting for how he deviates from American behavioral norms. In Europe, he is a typical American: fat, rude, stupid and provincial."[36]

Differences in News

Cultural differences extend to news as well as to entertainment. Like the unbalanced flow of entertainment programs from West to East and North to South, news flows daily from Western developed countries. AP, BBC, Reuters, CNN, Deutsche Welle and Agence France-Presse are major news suppliers to the world. Many countries have complained that Western values distort the news they get from these agencies and the news that other countries get about them. Most of what Kenyans and Bolivians learn about each other is fed through Western news services and their Western-educated editors.

What difference can this make? In much of the world, news is primarily about government leadership, national economic growth and police activity shown in a positive light. In the United States, news, especially local television news, features violent crimes, the sexier and gorier the better: "If it bleeds, it leads." Accusations are true that news reports of troublesome events emphasize conflicts. News reflects what interests and concerns people. Gossip, which glories in troublesome events and conflicts, has always done so. To Western journalists the Yangtze River flooding was about villages swept away and people killed or left homeless. The comparable Katrina tragedy got the same treatment. To Chinese journalists, all too familiar with tragedy, the news slant was about the heroic efforts of soldiers to stem the Yangtze flood and to save lives.

Government pressure influenced the coverage, but the news judgment was nonetheless valid.

Western broadcast satellites that beam directly into people's homes have clearly not been greeted with unalloyed joy. These communication satellites rekindled old quarrels about cultural imperialism.

The 1991 Gulf War and the 2003 invasion of Iraq saw a public glued to their television sets watching the effects of the newest weapons technology. General Norman Schwarzkopf, feeling it necessary to remind everyone during the Gulf War that real blood was being shed, said, "War is not a Nintendo game." Yet that is how it appeared. Viewers sitting comfortably at home watched as real missiles rained down on real targets.

As a counter, Arab media enjoy a wide following in the Middle East and can be seen in many parts of the world. Al Jazeera and Al Arabiya news networks, based in the Arab Gulf nations of Qatar and Dubai respectively, are hugely popular (Al Jazeera broadcasts throughout the world) and has earned a reputation in many quarters as a more reliable source than either government or Western stations.

In Saudi Arabia, a younger generation has access to the internet and satellite dishes through which they receive a far different picture of the world than what their government-controlled media allow them. Affordable pizza-sized satellite dishes on rooftops have given millions of Egyptians a new outlook on a world previously blocked from their view by their government.

Governments everywhere act to insure retention of power, so the appearance of satellite dishes on modest houses is not without political undertones. Home satellite dishes at one time or another have been banned in Iran, Syria, Saudi Arabia, Lebanon, Qatar, Iraq, Vietnam and Singapore, though the bans have not always been enforced. The military junta ruling the largely Buddhist nation of Myanmar (Burma), which dealt with unwanted programming by a prohibitive license fee on satellite dishes, went further when it declared that just watching a certain BBC soap opera was a treasonable offense.

Timeline

1477: In England, an advertising poster.

1666: After the Great Fire in London, merchants advertise to win back customers.

1704: In the American colonial city of Boston, newspaper ads.

1742: Benjamin Franklin's *General Magazine* prints ads.

1832: Honoré Daumier imprisoned for caricatures of France's king.

1835: P.T. Barnum begins career by exhibiting an old slave who said she was 161.

1842: Barnum opens the American Museum in New York City; shameless fraud works.

1849: The term "advertising agency" is used by Volney B. Palmer.

1867: Double-column advertising appears in newspapers.

1868: Thomas Nast begins cartoon attacks on corrupt Boss Tweed ring.

   In Philadelphia, N.W. Ayer & Son begins a full-service advertising agency.

1873: Advertising agents convene in New York.

1880: "Advertising copywriter" becomes an occupation.

1893: *Munsey's Magazine* sells below production cost; depends on advertising.

1898: Uneeda Biscuits seeks brand loyalty with million dollar ad campaign.

1904: Advertising discovers hard-sell.

1905: Popular actors are used to advertise a product, Murad Cigarettes.

1906: Pure Food and Drug Act requires listing ingredients on product labels.

1911: Sex appeal appears in an ad for Woodbury Soap. The concept works.

1917: The American Association of Advertising Agencies, a trade association, is formed.

1920: Stanley and Helen Resor introduce psychological advertising research.

1922: A commercial is broadcast on radio for real estate near New York City.

   Walter Lippmann's *Public Opinion*, is a seminal study of opinion formation.

1923: A sponsored radio program, *The Eveready Hour*.

1928: Edward Bernays, "father" of public relations, writes book about it, *Propaganda*.

1932: George Gallup's opinion poll learns what Americans are thinking.

1941: First television ads; a Bulova watch ticks for a full minute.

1947: American television viewers watch commercials.

1948: The Public Relations Society of America is created.

1949: The Fairness Doctrine requires broadcast advocacy.

1957: Vance Packard's best-selling *The Hidden Persuaders* attacks advertising.

1958: The National Association of Broadcasters bans subliminal ads.

1965: British ban televised cigarette advertising.

1971: U.S. Congress bans radio and television cigarette commercials.

1976: The Supreme Court grants advertising First Amendment protection.

1987: The Fairness Doctrine is repealed.

1990: World Wide Web opens a new universe of persuasion opportunities.

1991: Gulf War TV reports shows government learned Vietnam War propaganda lessons.

2006: Arab street riots in response to Danish newspaper cartoons.

2010: Supreme Court blocks a ban on corporate political spending.

2011: "Arab spring" shows that social networks can compete with government propaganda.

15. We Are Different

Living in a World of Change

Media change our lives in subtle ways. Tourists from cities in developed nations who visit slums from Bogota to Calcutta quickly discover that these poor streets, parched but no longer empty of media, are teeming with family and neighborhood life. Observing such vibrant social interaction, Western travelers may feel a twinge of sadness that something is missing from their own lives. At home their own streets are all but deserted in the evening as people opt to spend their time indoors with television, computers, video games, recorded music and other media. Apartment residents in modern cities may hear sounds of a television program or music, but have no idea who lives next door. Without thinking about it, we made a trade. To live as we choose in a media-rich environment, we do not—*cannot*—live as poor villagers do. An hour with a magazine or television program or video game is an hour not mingling with neighbors.

We never simply acquire a new means of communication. We replace what currently exists, whether it is old equipment or a method or activity we know well. What we have replaced had value to us. There is always an exchange of one way of doing or living for another. Socrates understood this when he opposed the teaching of writing because he thought it would lead to a loss of memory.[1] It has been understood by book and movie censors concerned about political views and social standards, and it is understood by angry, tradition-bound people who regard media content as an invasion of their culture by those who would substitute their own culture.

Streets Paved With Gold

The ragged poor of the world watch television programs for more than the plots. In the stories and the commercials they see how people live in other places. You cannot fault them if they want to go there, either into the big cities of their own country or outside its borders.[24] They see nice houses, new clothes and tempting food on the table. In traditional societies young women watch stories of seeming fantasy in which women marry for love and are not treated as chattel. North Koreans face death if captured escaping into China with the dream of going to South Korea, but pay the "snakeheads" and flee. Why? *The Economist* explains: "In recent years illegally copied DVDs from China have flooded the country, enabling citizens of the world's most repressive state to see how sumptuously their southern cousins live."[25]

All over the world, movies and television have left people with the sense that others enjoy better lives than they do. That awareness is fuel for revolution. It has also created in the minds of many a resolve to improve their own lives and the lives of the families they leave behind. Desperate people climb the barbed wire fences built specifically to keep them out. Seeking a better life, they set sail on overcrowded, leaky boats, risking death from drowning or pirates to enter countries where they are less than welcome. Some governments encourage emigration. Remittances sent home by family members have become a significant source of national income for Mexico, the Philippines and other developing countries.

It is almost axiomatic that television and movies significantly drive the current mass migrations. Historian Paul Kennedy speaks of "new media... breaking state monopolies of information, permeating national boundaries, allowing peoples to hear and see how others do things differently. Modern media have also made richer and poorer countries increasingly aware of the gap between them and has stimulated legal and illegal migration."[26]

Hussein Amin, chairman of the journalism department at Cairo's American University echoed this, predicting profound transformations as illiterate viewers in conservative and highly traditional rural villages gain knowledge about the outside world.[27] A Pakistani science teacher who once lived in a now troubled border village said of his former home, "Soon the last educated villagers will be gone, leaving an illiterate people in the hands of narrow-minded mullahs."[28]

Thousands of Mauritanians on the west coast of Africa, joined by families from Senegal and Mali and Nigeria, crowd onto small, leaky fishing boats to embark on perilous Atlantic Ocean journeys of five hundred miles from Mauritania to reach the Spanish-owned Canary Islands as a first step to entering Europe. Many drown but others keep coming. Families in North Africa gamble everything to reach Italy. Families in Myanmar gamble to reach Thailand. Families in Mexico and Central America sell what they own to scrape together the sums that the "coyotes," smugglers of this human cargo, demand to move them across the Rio Grande. Families from Turkey to Afghanistan pay out life savings, borrow more and risk their lives to reach Germany. And they come from the former Soviet Union and Eastern Europe with dreams that fuel an international sex trade, with children sometimes knowingly sold by complicit parents.

What Has Changed?

This mass migration is one of the most significant political stories of this millennium, dwarfing the legal migration to Ellis Island a century ago. But why now? After all, poverty and misery, disease and famine have stalked these lands for centuries. For the answer, think again of communication. In the 19th century occasional letters from America spurred emigration. The émigrés had relatives and friends in the United States who told them exactly where to go and how to get to the jobs waiting for them.

What has changed? Today's émigrés are more likely to receive cell phone calls from relatives who went first. They have seen the newspapers, the magazines and the letters with reports of salaries

Watching a Better Life

Aalo Maity barely remembers life before her tiny Indian village got its first television set. She only remembers that after, life seemed unbearable. Every night she would gather with other villagers in a hut to watch soap operas that showed people in pressed clothes strolling while savoring ice cream from pretty cups.

"In my hut we ate soggy rice and lentils and I wore darned saris," Maity recalls, "I wanted a better life." So she and her husband, Gaurang, leased out their land and found jobs in New Delhi.

Newsweek[23]

beyond belief for the same work they now do for a pittance. When they watch television and movies they see the cars, the houses, the clothes, the food, and a different way of life. For those who decide to uproot, media also lessen the pain.

One writer noted, "A 19th -century Russian emigrant might never see or speak to his family again. A 21st-century migrant can Skype them in the taxi from the airport."[29] Added an *Economist* reporter, "A century ago, a migrant might board a ship, sail to America and never see his friends or family again. Today, he texts his mother while still waiting to clear customs. He can wire her money in minutes. He can follow news from his hometown on his laptop."[30] And easy email access to the people they left could lead to more insularity in the new country.

Today's social change will be familiar to anyone who has lived in countries filled with the media-delivered advertising, sights and sounds of America, Western Europe and Japan. Advertising tempts even those who do not buy, but simply notice—cannot help noticing—the brand names, the pictures, the proffered delights, the sharp reflections of life as it is lived by the more fortunate.[31] Deprived people see a living standard they want for themselves and their children.

When they can manage it, one of their first goals is to acquire the tools of mediated communication for themselves. When Saddam Hussein fell in 2003, thousands of Iraqis rushed to buy satellite dishes, some primarily for entertainment programming, others for news, all of them for information about the lands beyond their borders.[32]

That the developing, non-Western world continues to come to the West either to seek a better life, as the poor do, or to send their sons and daughters for education, as the wealthy do, does not mean acceptance of Western culture.[33] According to historian Meic Pearse, many non-Westerners regard Westerners "as rich, technologically sophisticated, economically and politically dominant, morally contemptible barbarians."[34] Parents who send their children to Europe or the United States for an education may in fact try to limit internet use at home, limit the use of English and generally control personal communication with the West.

In their adopted countries, confined by necessity or choice in a Little India or a Little Istanbul, unable to find adequate salaries, or pleasant working conditions, or even any work at all, and with their media-fueled dreams crushed, the immigrants or their sons, daughters and grandchildren can become a sullen, aggrieved proletariat. Thousands of rock-throwing, car-burning young protesters, mostly in North African and African immigrant neighborhoods, took to the Paris streets in 2005. They expressed frustration at high unemployment and police harassment. The riots spread to other French cities. In 2010 young protesters joined others protesting, of all laws, an extension of the retirement age.

Migrating Within Borders

Enticements lie within national borders as well as beyond them. Poor Chinese have seen not only Western films but films from Hong Kong and Shanghai; the Chinese government must deal with the problem of mass internal migration. Similar stories of internal population shifts are common in India, the Philippines, Indonesia and other developing countries. City populations are swelling faster than they can be counted as country dwellers seek the promising rewards of urban life. Although the division between haves and have-nots has always existed within countries, modern media expose that difference more quickly and more widely than ever before.

With information floating on every breeze, more intense migration may lie ahead. Historian and futurist Ian Morris predicted, "Global warming threatens to make even the most lurid fears of anti-immigrant activists come true by the 2020s. Tens of millions of the world's hungriest, angriest and most desperate people may be fleeing the Muslim world for Europe, and Latin America for the United States. The population movements could dwarf anything in history."[35]

Storing Knowledge

Of all the rewards that media have brought us since the invention of writing, the most valuable is the expansion of knowledge. Nearly all of it is stored outside the brain, to some extent at the expense of what is stored in memory. Because of those first scratches on clay and all the means of mediated communication that followed, the store of human knowledge is beyond comprehension. Because we can look up information, we can derive endless benefit from what others have done and thought.

The more educated we are, the more we rely on mediated communication to bolster our knowledge. We do more. We entrust people who have specialized information—the physician, the pilot, the automobile mechanic—with our lives because they know what we do not.

Beyond writing have come all the subsequent means of storing information and entertainment: photography, movies and a variety of audio recording media. So have the means of acquiring distant information: mail, telegraph, telephone, radio, television, the internet. Once printing took root, those who could read had access to more information than memory could hold. Printing exponentially expanded available information.

With the expansion of information has come knowledge specialization and segmentation. The tip of that iceberg is visible in any library, bookstore, or large magazine rack. This too has been part of communication history. The study of the growth of libraries lies beyond what can be reasonably taught in a course on communication history, just as the history of public education does, yet both of these areas of study are integral to literacy and therefore to an understanding of how we are changed by mediated communication.[2]

Surprising Directions

Today the information highway offers cheap and easy access to unlimited stores of information, but its direction seems to lead us less to the public library or the news office than to the cinema and the shopping mall. Our society might wish it otherwise, but tastes and behavior have proven stubborn attributes. Information is pouring out at exponential rates and the ways it reaches us are changing just as fast. To collect a market audience of 50 million, it took radio 38 years, television 13 years, the internet 4 years, the iPod 3 years and Facebook 2 years.[4]

Among the hardest things to predict is how new communication methods will be used. Inventions by themselves have scant value until they attain a social use. That social use may be neither intended nor anticipated by the inventors. Gutenberg could not have imagined how his invention of movable type would affect the world in future centuries. French innovators Niépce and Daguerre could hardly have imagined what photography would accomplish. Nor did the university researchers who first exchanged email messages guess its future.

Some communication media began their public existence beyond anyone's understanding of how they could have any meaning in daily life, yet as they were diffused into society, the public found that meaning. Some communication media were intended solely for government and business, not for personal use. The computer, a means to process numbers quickly, went through a period of government support but little public awareness. The telegraph had a similar history. It took years before the copier was considered to be anything more than a complicated, expensive and unnecessary substitute for a perfectly adequate sheet of carbon paper. The typewriter, the telephone, the phonograph, the radio, audiotape, videotape, facsimile machine and, of course, the computer, were initially considered for their military or commercial applications. Who would have thought that tens of millions of ordinary people would one day want to take them into their homes?

Where Communication Blossoms

Mediated communication has been particularly effective at the nexus of newer technologies. Movable type printing combined with the new (to Europe) medium of paper, not the old papyrus or parchment. Recorded sound joined recorded motion photography. Technology merged the home computer and connective media like cable and satellite with the end-user media of cell phones, digital photographs, books and television. Cell phones and cameras met in the iPhone. The potential for new ways to communicate is making itself felt in public entertainment and in news reporting by ordinary citizens.

Another mark of the symbiosis of our mediated communication has been the political pattern of their growth. Although they may have been born in absolute and settled autocracies, they do not blossom there. Mediated communication grows best where there is intellectual ferment, not where life is controlled. The reason should be obvious. A communication invention finds a wide social use where it improves upon what exists. That brings change, and change is frequently egalitarian, spreading knowledge, encouraging democracy and opening economic opportunities.

The wide-ranging potential of writing blossomed in the troubled, independent ancient Greek cities, not in the controlled empires of Babylonia, Persia and Egypt. Printing with movable type did not spread across China for several reasons, not the least of which was a controlled society where literacy continued to be limited to those with a measure of power. Nor did it spread across feudal Korea despite the invention, contemporaneous with Gutenberg in Germany, of both movable type and the simplified Hangul alphabet. Yet literacy grew in Western Europe in the midst of political, economic and religious turmoil.

The breathless emergence of one communication device and method after another comes out of the free, competitive and frequently turbulent industrial belt stretching in the Northern

The Global Village

Concerning that popular metaphor of our era, the "global village," Marshall McLuhan foresaw technology that would permit most of humankind to share information. *The Gutenberg Galaxy: The Making of Typographic Man*, written a generation before the internet, predicted the computer's potential to retrieve and organize vast amounts of information.

His vision of the world as a single village presumes that radio, television and other "electric technology" are returning us to an oral culture. Today we have not only that oral culture but also a enlarged written culture that includes many kinds of media content delivered instantaneously, including information and entertainment via the written underpinnings of oral media.

If there is a culprit undermining the concept of a global village it is, once again, the quantity of communication available in industrialized societies, translated into the variety of choices of reading, viewing, and listening. On rare occasions, such as a lunar walk, the Olympic games, the World Cup, or the Iraq War, the world ventures together into the shared space of a global village. For the most part, we are more likely than we once were to watch different programs or engage in different activities, going our separate ways.

It is worth noting that McLuhan did not believe that a Global Village would bring peace and harmony to mankind. Division was a more likely outcome, he believed.[3]

Hemisphere west from Finland across two continents and two oceans to Japan and South Korea. Autocratic regimes that try to stifle social unrest use communication products but contribute little or nothing to their improvement.

More Openness

Where societies are not free, the yearning to communicate is no less strong. It is not necessary to go back to the medieval burning of printers along with their books to find people who willingly risked their lives to express themselves through media. Jails today are full of dissidents who have used media to declare their frustrations. Look along the margins of controlled societies during recent history for examples. Underground "samizdat" media were a factor in overthrowing the Soviet Union, their authors risking arrest or worse. The internet and a growing film industry have been nudging China toward a more open society. "Small media" like smuggled pamphlets and audiotapes assisted risk takers in shaking off the shah in Iran, and there are signs that new media may yet contribute to shaking off the theocracy that has replaced the shah. Consider the 2009 post-election demonstrations in Tehran using Twitter to get the message out. And an Iranian film industry is taking tentative steps.

At one time, revolutionaries seized railroad terminals and factories. Today they are likely to seize television stations as they did in Lithuania in 1991. Alternatively, they may produce provocative videos that television stations will display, as al Qaeda has done. Sad to say, the world has in recent years been assaulted with horrific examples of this going to extremes. And journalists are being killed in record numbers.

Open expression is often crushed but inevitably the introduction of new means of mediated communication leads to greater dispersal of information over more and more channels and to considerably greater quantities of information. Content not only deepens but broadens. What is new is the capacity of mediated communication in anyone's hands to send information to the furthest reaches of the world, including places that block free expression. The information is delivered with pictures and sound, edited to show what is most inflammatory.

The fertile ground of a society where people are free to experiment with communication lends itself not only to the spread of information but also to improvements in the technology and to fresh uses. With free media and free society, the relationship is reciprocal. As more people are able to communicate ever more freely to wider and wider audiences, they will take advantage of all the available means to do so and keep seeking even newer means.

Yet as communication has improved, so has the ability to manipulate it and to bury us under its flow. This overload of information includes much of dubious value. And misinformation is just a click away. The public is not totally oblivious to this. Popular distrust of newspapers has grown in recent years and the condition extends to cable, the internet, digital photographs, advertising in any form and all other types of content.

Too Much Choice?

What began with Gutenberg shows no sign of flagging. Quite the opposite. As the centuries have rolled along and new communication technologies have emerged, more providers have delivered more content over more media to an ever-growing world of media content consumers. This observation almost sums up the history of communication. Just about every means of communication has participated in this reality. New means of mediated communication continue to expand our choices, dispersing greater quantities of information over more channels.

Yet questions have been raised about whether such a great increase of media content is good for society as a whole. Psychologist Barry Schwartz speaks of the "paradox of choice": "As the number of choices keeps growing, negative aspects of having a multitude of options appear until we become overloaded. At this point, choice no longer liberates, but debilitates. It might even be said to tyrannize."[5] People living in an age of plenty may suffer what Gregg Easterbrook, an editor of *The New Republic*, calls "choice anxiety," when they have so many options that choice becomes a source of anguish.[6] Certainly, given a choice between more or fewer channels to watch, more or fewer magazines to choose from, one community newspaper or three, one video game or many, we vote with our wallets for more.

Today, everywhere from major cities to isolated farmhouses, people enjoy information and entertainment choices of a staggering variety. The more choices we have, the less we have in common with one another and the more we become communities of strangers. The process can be seen clearly in movie rental options like Netflix, a far cry from just a few decades ago when at-home video offered just three television networks and a smattering of local stations. When TiVo staffers could send along new fare based on their judgment of a viewer's tastes, this "choice without choosing" seems to come at the expense of some privacy, but added choice wins out for many viewers.

The video rental shop has gone the way of the drive-in movie theater. Downloading and shop-

Changes on the Island of Atiu

Consider this observation of Sinoto Yoshiko, renowned expert on Eastern Pacific cultures, speaking to author Paul Theroux:

"I was working there and as recently as 1984 Atiu (one of the Cook Islands in the Pacific) was totally traditional. Everything was intact. I returned for several years, and then in 1989 the culture was gone. It was finished, just like that. How did it happen so quickly? You know what caused it? The video. I don't know why the government doesn't regulate videos. They are terrible. Rape. War. Violence. Drinking. They give bad ideas to young people, and they destroyed the culture in Atiu, which had lasted for over a thousand years."[12]

Annika (left) and Lucy Pellant, glued to the TV. The older sister keeps firm control of the remote.

by-mail video rental services like Netflix offer far more choices than any store can stock. Media that offer more choices have hurt the broadcast networks and even the cable channels. The expanding number of radio stations that advertise their unique "sound," including multi-channel satellite radio and the expanding number of cable channels are less-than-mute testimony to fragmentation and the desire for choice.

More production sources are turning out more films and television programs at lower costs to smaller audiences. A curious downside of all this is that pretty good films—but not blockbusters—must endure more competition and suffer the results. That is also true of pretty good books, magazines and television programs. The blockbusters—*Avatar, American Idol, Harry Potter*—still make a profit, but everyone else faces a struggle of limited budgets. One consequence has been a race for the intellectual bottom to reach the largest possible audience. And inevitably, the star system gives way to more journeymen actors who work for smaller wages than stars command. Even the star system is decaying in the face of the inexorable mathematics of expanding choice.

Content sold on paper and plastic is now being replaced by electronic content. Telephone wires are following telegraph wires. Computer hard drives are going to the cloud. All this meets our wishes for lower costs, a smaller footprint and more choice. Yet there are cynics who say we are not spending less on media or sparing the environment or having true content choice.

Media Growth

Consider the growth of media:

• Today, in the developed world, libraries and bookstores repeatedly confront the problem of what to do with too many books.

Hikikomori

In Japan, concentration on mediated communication has a name: "hikikomori." It means social withdrawal. Hikikomori refers to the state of anomie estimated to afflict more than one million young Japanese.[19]

Socially withdrawn kids typically lock themselves in their bedrooms and refuse to have any contact with the outside world. They live in reverse: they sleep all day, wake up in the evening and stay up all night surfing, watching television, or playing video games.

Many have few or no friends. Their funk can last for months, even years in extreme cases. How kids who grew up playing electronic games for hours each day will fare in the real world is now playing itself out. No official statistics are available, but it is estimated that more than one million young Japanese suffer from the affliction.[20]

• Cable television executives speak of a 500-channel universe, which is shorthand for an unlimited number of channels, constrained only by demand.

• Urban newspapers have suffered reader attrition, but the phenomena of desktop publishing and desktop video are exponentially increasing the ranks of publishers of books, newsletters and magazines, and producers of films.

• The internet has seen rapid growth in every direction. No one can accurately count the number of websites, website "hits," or emails. We are drowning in email.

• Video news stories and podcasts flow through thousands of openings. YouTube alone receives tens upon tens of thousands of uploaded videos daily.

• Industrial societies are awash in mediated content contained in downloads, DVDs and videotapes.

• New videogames seem to emerge daily. Demand for popular games continues to soar.

• Meanwhile, despite the competition, television still attracts viewers throughout the world although newer media in the more developed countries have dragged down newspaper readership.

• No one can accurately guess how many photographers are using how many cameras, let alone gauge how many photographs are taken daily in this digital age, and how many of these are transmitted along telephone networks to distant friends and relatives.

• No one in this age of the cell phone can accurately measure how many phone calls are made each minute.

• In industrial societies it has been true for some time that anyone can own a book. Now, anyone can own a movie. And many more people can make a movie. In 2011, a film called *Night Fishing* was shot in South Korea solely with iPhones.

Separation and Connection

Media separate us from those near us even as they connect us with those living far away in space or time. The book reader shuts out immediate surroundings to focus on the open page as readers have been doing for centuries. The headphone-wearing jogger shuts out surrounding birdsong and traffic noises, perhaps along with a fire engine bearing down.[7] We embrace cell phones to distraction. At home, preferring to roam in a mediated fantasy, the video game player shuts the real world out for hours at a stretch. Call it a Faustian bargain. Knowing the time could be spent in more productive ways, the stubborn player plunges on. More than one divorce has cited a spouse's addiction to video games. Grandma gets an occasional phone call from her son. By calling, he discharges his filial duty in a way that avoids actually visiting his mother. However, from her distant location the slogan "Reach out and touch someone" is not hollow. Grandma gets a real social benefit. She appreciates what connection the telephone brings and she recalls the plight of her own grandmother on a typical American farm, for whom the arrival of the four-party telephone line was a godsend.

Examining the America of the 1920s and 1930s, the eye-opening sociological Middletown studies blamed radio, movies and the automobile for breaking down such established social behavior as attending church and interacting with neighbors.[8] More than a half-century later, *Bowling Alone* identified the ways that isolated behavior cracks old patterns of social cohesion.[9]

A 2007 Nielsen Research television study reported that rich people and poor people watch different programs.[10] Given a choice, people choose what appeals to them based on education, culture and experiences. As one writer put it, "...late-night viewers belong to a different demographic from prime-time viewers: they are younger and better educated; they have higher incomes; they are more likely to have white-collar jobs. Most of them don't have to get up at six to milk the cow or open the store. They expect something edgier and more sophisticated than *The Beverly Hillbillies.*"[11] We also expose ourselves to different political messages. Obviously that has implications for a functioning democratic society.

Television brings the outside world to a rural Bangladeshi family thanks to solar power.

Photo: USAID/Grameen Shakti

The phenomenon of media-related separation, as old as reading itself, has markedly increased in our media-heavy world. Yet, sensing that something is missing, at the same time we have seen an almost atavistic use of many types of media as a means of self-expression to let others know that we exist, how we exist and what we think about. Diaries and photographs have been supplemented by blogs, tweets and the entire growing tapestry of social networking that are part of Web 2.0. There is a reason that YouTube, Twitter and Facebook became part of our culture virtually overnight.

The Trade-Off

It is a familiar scene in family sitcoms. Children absorbed in multitasking with computer-based communication ignore parents returning home at the end of the day. The fully plugged-in family shares a roof but not much else. It can be argued that multitasking mediated communication has made the family dysfunctional. Columnist George Will speaks of an increasingly infantilized society besotted with graphic entertainments.[13] Multitasking has led to easily distracted students who are less able to concentrate on such long-term activities as reading an entire book.[14]

Without thinking about it, we make a trade of time in order to receive communications. There is always a trade-off. The yearning for "the simple life" sends us to the countryside for a two-week holiday with the resolve to "get away from it all," but it is too hard to leave a cell phone, a laptop or a BlackBerry behind. Our dependence upon mediated communication is just too strong. Columnist Thomas Friedman recalled an hour-long taxi ride during which he and the driver occupied themselves with phone, video, laptop and iPod, but did not speak to each other. "It's a pity. He probably had a lot to tell me," Friedman reflected.[15]

The baby in the crib of a modern family can now hear recorded or broadcast sounds and watch televised moving pictures for hours each day. The trade? The bustling sounds of a parent going about the household chores, the noise of a brother or sister, the silence to think infant thoughts. A 2007 University of Washington study reported that forty percent of three-month-old American infants watch television regularly. By age two, it's ninety percent. Conditioning begins early in life to consider mediated communication as a reward. In return for certain behavior, the older child is promised a film, a favorite TV program or a video game. A few decades ago, it was the promise of a radio program. A few decades before that, a book. Like the unruly convict who is denied access to television or reading material as punishment, the child discovers that mediated communication, independent of content, plays a role in being happy. A few years later, that child, now a teen, lives more fully each day in the world of mediated communication.

Of a daily average 6.5 hours with all media, the American child spends more than 4.5 hours daily in front of a screen watching television, playing video games, or surfing the internet.[16] That is more time than is spent with parents or listening to a teacher. Much of that time is spent media multitasking, listening to iTunes, watching a DVD and tweeting friends all at the same time.[17] Edward Hallowell and John Ratey, experts on attention deficit disorder sees the hours with electronic media as a possible source of the disorder: "Raised on a diet of sound bites and electronic stimulation, children can lose the ability to carry on an extended conversation or listen to one, whether or not they have ADD."[18] The extent to which mediated communication actually contributes to ADD or ADHD (Attention Deficit Hyperactivity Disorder) among the "video game generation" has not been established, but it is a topic of academic inquiry.

The Facebook Phenomenon

A study of American teenagers found that during junior and senior high school, both girls and boys were spending less time being physically active and more time on the computer, not counting schoolwork. They were also watching more television than spending time at exercise and computers combined.[21]

Comparing surveys in 1985 and 2004, a team of sociologists reported a one-third drop in the number of people with whom the average American could discuss "important matters." The average number of close friends had dropped; one in four said they had no close friends. Isolation assumes many shapes. The "ME generation" may have several hundred friends on Facebook and lots of people to tweet and email, but those distant conversations are likely to be shallow.[22]

The old are following the young. Planned by young people, led by Mark Zuckerberg and initially devised for use by college students, Facebook has seen unexpected and astonishing growth among the middle aged and elderly. They are more likely than their juniors to have traveled and to have lived far from where they now live. Many of their friends and former co-workers may be far away. Especially if age and circumstance have shrunk the number of nearby friends they see regularly, these distant connections are precious to the elderly as Facebook dulls the sharp sting of loneliness.

Grandma by definition looks back on more years than her son does and may know more people in distant places because she or they have moved. With the telephone, email and social media the people that she knew when she was younger may just be a few clicks away. That could matter deeply. As she reminisces about her life, it has become easier than ever to reach out. For her, as William Faulkner put it, the past isn't dead. It isn't even past.

Keeping What We Have

The well-known author Dr. Andrew Weil has argued that heavy media use can lead to depression: "We are deluged by an unprecedented overload of information and stimulation in this age of the internet, email, mobile phones, and multimedia, all of which favor social isolation and certainly affect our emotional (and physical) health."[36] Yet it is most unlikely that you will want to give up any form of mediated communication. No one who is literate wants to be illiterate. No one wishes that the alphabet had never been invented or that printing would just vanish. Although some people do without television or movies, the overwhelming majority of us would not willingly give them up. You may have worked hard to save up to pay for a large HDTV, a cell phone contract or a powerful sound system. You would resist parting with them.

If you wish sometimes that you could "get away from it" to a simpler life, ask yourself if mediated communication is something you want to get away from. Our connection with media is like an old tangled love affair that takes up a lot of our time, much of it pointless, but we may not be able to imagine life without all of what we have. We are too comfortable with what we have to give up any part of our love affair with media. And all in all, like any love affair it has its rewards.

Our dependence upon mediated communication has become almost as intrinsic as breathing and eating. Our attachment is, in many ways, a reward for labor, and it is more central to human lives today than ever before. How a particular kind of mediated communication has made a difference in life is not always clear, but we sense that it has altered the human experience. We may not recognize that what we lost in the shift to new media once had value to us, but we should recognize that a simpler life went out the door when the first television set was carried in. It was not long ago that people lived in a narrower world. Many still do, but the benefits of mediated communication, exchanged for that simpler life, overwhelm any awareness that we surrendered something. Few of us truly prefer the simpler life.

Mediated communication has been entwined in human life for many centuries and is now entangled more than ever. The media matter to us. The more educated we are, the more media matter. Mediated communication is not something we can easily take or leave alone and leaving media alone is not really an option in a modern world. We will not allow ourselves to be deprived of mediated communication. We would vigorously resist any attempt to reduce what we have. If nothing else, that is worth our attention.

Further Reading

1. Writing: *Gathering Knowledge*

Allen, Marti Lu, *The Beginning of Understanding: Writing in the Ancient World*. Ann Arbor: Kelsey Museum of Archaeology, 1991.

Daniels, Peter T. and William Bright, eds., *The World's Writing Systems*. New York: Oxford University Press, 1996.

Delaporte, L., *Mesopotamia: The Babylonian and Assyrian Civilization*. New York: Columbia University Press, 2004.

Fischer, Steven Roger, *A History of Writing*. London: Reaktion Books, Ltd., 2001

Gnanadesikan, Amalia E., *The Writing Revolution: Cuneiform to the Internet* Oxford: Wiley-Blackwell, 2009

Graff, Harvey J., *Literacy and Historical Development*," Carbondale: Southern Illinois University Press, 2007

Hooker, J.T., ed., *Reading the Past: Ancient Writings from Cuneiform to the Alphabet*. Berkeley: University of California Press 1990.

Houston, Stephen, ed., *The First Writing: Script Invention as History and Process*. Cambridge University Press, 2004.

Martin, Henri-Jean, *The History and Power of Writing*. Trans. Lydia G. Cochrane. Chicago: University of Chicago Press, 1994.

Schmandt-Besserat, Denise, *Before Writing* Austin: University of Texas Press, 1992.

2. Printing: *Reaching More of Us*

Briggs, Asa and Peter Burke, *A Social History of the Media: from Gutenberg to the Internet*. Cambridge, UK: Polity Press, 2002.

Eisenstein, Elizabeth, *The Printing Revolution in Early Modern Europe*. Cambridge University Press, 1983.

Emery, Michael, Edwin Emery, and Nancy Roberts, *The Press and America: An Interpretive History of the Mass Media*, Ninth Edition. Boston: Allyn & Bacon, 2000.

Finkelstein, David, and Alistair McCleery, *An Introduction to Book History* New York: Routledge, 2005.

Howsam, Leslie, *Old Books and New Histories: An Orientation to Studies in Book and Print Culture*. Toronto: University of Toronto Press, 2007.

Kapr, Albert, *Johann Gutenberg: The Man and His Invention*, tr. by Douglas Martin. Aldershot, England: Scolar Press, 1996.

Kozol, Jonathan, *Illiterate America*. Garden City, N.Y.: Anchor Press, 1985.

Manchester, William, *A World Lit Only by Fire: The Medieval Mind and the Renaissance*. Boston: Little, Brown and Company, 1992.

Martin, Henri-Jean, *The History and Power of Writing*. Trans. Lydia G. Cochrane. Chicago: University of Chicago Press, 1994.

Nicolson, Adam, *God's Secretaries: The Making of the King James Bible*. New York: HarperCollins, 2003.

Ravitch, Diane, *The Language Police: How Pressure Groups Restrict What Students Learn*. New York: Alfred Knopf, 2003.

Stephens, Mitchell, *A History of News: From the Drum to the Satellite, 3rd ed*. New York: Oxford University Press, 2006.

Vincent, David, *Literacy and Popular Culture*. New York: Cambridge University Press, 1989.

Winship, Michael, *American Literary Publishing in the Nineteenth Century*. New York: Cambridge University Press, 2003.

3. Mail: *The Snail That Could*

Bowyer, Matthew J., *They Carried the Mail: A Survey of Postal History & Hobbies*. Lincoln, NE: iUniverse.com, 2000.

Bruns, James H., *Mail on the Move*. Polo, IL: Transportation Trails, 1992.

Fuller, Wayne E., *Morality and the Mail in Nineteenth-Century America*. Champaign, IL: University of Illinois Press, 2003.

Henken, David M., *The Postal Age: The Emergence of Modern Communications in Nineteenth Century America*. Chicago: University of Chicago Press, 2006.

John, Richard R., *Spreading the News: The American Postal System from Franklin to Morse*. Cambridge, MA: Harvard University Press, 1995.

Kielbowicz, Richard B., *News in the Mail: The Press, Post Office, and Public Information, 1700-1860s*. New York: Greenwood Press, 1989.

Starr, Paul, *The Creation of the Media: Political Origins of Modern Communications*. New York: Basic Books, 2004.

4. Telegraph: *Uniting the United States*

Beniger, James R., *The Control Revolution*. Cambridge: Harvard University Press, 1986.

Coe, Lewis, *Telegraph: A History of Morse's Invention and Its Predecessors in the United States*. Jefferson, N.C.: McFarland & Co, 2003.

Czitrom, Daniel J., *Media and the American Mind*. University of North Carolina Press, 1982.

Oslin, George P., *The Story of Telecommunications*. Macon, GA: Mercer University Press, 1992.

Sloan, William, James Stovall and James Startt, *The Media in America*. Worthington, OH: Publishing Horizons, 1989.

Standage, Tom, *The Victorian Internet: The Remarkable Story of the Telegraph and the Nineteenth Century's On-line Pioneers*. New York: Walker Publishing Co., 1998.

5. Telephone: *Reaching Without Touching*

Beniger, James R., *The Control Revolution* Cambridge: Harvard University Press, 1986.

Brooks, John, *Telephone: The First 100 Years*. New York: Harper & Row, 1976.

Czitrom, Daniel J., *Media and the American Mind*. University of North Carolina Press, 1982.

Fischer, Claude, *America Calling: A Social History of the Telephone to 1940*. Berkeley: University of California Press, 1992.

Marvin, Carolyn, *When Old Technologies Were New*. New York: Oxford University Press, 1988.

Oslin, George P., *The Story of Telecommunications*. Macon, GA: Mercer University Press, 1992.

Prescott, George B., *Bell's Speaking Telephone: Its Invention, Construction*. New York: Arno Press, 1972.

Shirer, George, *The Telephone: An Historical Anthology*. New York: Arno Press, 1977.

Shulman, Seth: *The Telephone Gambit: Chasing Alexander Graham Bell's Secret*. New York: W.W. Norton, 2009.

Sloan, William, James Stovall and James Startt, *The Media in America*. Worthington, OH: Publishing Horizons, 1989.

6. Recording: *Beyoncé Sings Better Than Our Sister*

Butterworth, William E., *Hi Fi: From Edison's Phonograph To Quad Sound*. New York: Four Winds Press, 1977.

Chanan, Michael, *Repeated Takes: A Short History of Recording and Its Effects on Music*. New York: Verso, 1995.

Gronow, Pekka, and Ilpo Saunio, *International History of the Recording Industry*. Tr. Christopher Moseley. London: Cassell, 1999.

Hollander, Richard S., *Video Democracy*. Mt. Airy, MD: Lomond Publications, 1985.

Levy, Steven, *The Perfect Thing*. New York: Simon & Schuster, 2006.

Litman, Jessica, *Digital Copyright: Protecting Intellectual Property on the Internet*. Amherst, NY:Prometheus, 2001.

Marty, Daniel, *An Illustrated History of Phonographs*. New York: Dorset Press, 1981.

Marvin, Carolyn. *When Old Technologies Were New*. New York: Oxford University Press, 1988.

Oslin, George P., *The Story of Telecommunications*. Macon, GA: Mercer University Press, 1992.

Sterling, Christopher H., and John M. Kittross, *Stay Tuned: A Concise History of American Broadcasting*. Belmont, CA: Wadsworth Publishing Co., 2nd ed., 1990.

7. Photography: *The Effects Are Personal and More*

Broecker, William L., ed., *Encyclopedia of Photography*. New York: Crown Publishers, 1984.

Buckland, Gail, *Fox Talbot And The Invention of Photography*. Boston: D.R. Godine, 1980.

Gernsheim, Helmut, *The Origins of Photography*. New York: Thames and Hudson, 1982.

Jeffrey, Ian, *Photography: A Concise History*. New York: Oxford University Press. 1981.

Newhall, Beaumont, *The History of Photography*. New York: Museum of Modern Art, 1982.

Rosenblum, Naomi, *A World History of Photography*. New York: Abbeville Press, 1989.

Spira, S.F., *The History of Photography: As Seen Through the Spira Collection*. New York: Aperture Foundation, 2001.

Turner, Peter, *History of Photography*. New York: Exeter Books, 1987.

8. Movies: *Made by More of Us*

Bowser, Eileen, *The Transformation of Cinema, 1907-1915*. University of California Press, 1994.

Coe, Brian, *History of Motion Picture Photography*. New York: Zoetrope, Inc., 1981.

Ellis, Jack C., *A History of Film*, 2nd ed. Englewood Cliffs: Prentice-Hall, 1985.

Hansen, Miriam, *Babel and Babylon: Spectatorship in American Silent Film*. Cambridge: Harvard University Press, 1991.

Jarvie, Ian C. *Hollywood's Overseas Campaign: The North Atlantic Movie Trade, 1920-1950*. Cambridge University Press, 1992.

Koszarski, Richard, *An Evening's Entertainment: The Age of the Silent Feature Picture*, 1915-1928. University of California Press, 1994.

Lardner, James, *Fast Forward*. New York: W.W. Norton, 1987.

May, Lary, *Screening Out the Past: The Birth of Mass Culture and the Motion Picture Industry*. Chicago: University of Chicago Press, 1980.

Musser, Charles, *The Emergence of Cinema: The American Screen to 1907*. Berkeley: University of California Press, 1994.

Nasaw, David, *Going Out: The Rise and Fall of Public Amusements*. New York: Basic Books, 1993.

Shipman, David, *The Story of Cinema*. Englewood Cliffs: Prentice-Hall, 1982.

Thomson, David, *The Whole Equation: A History of Hollywood*. New York: Vintage Books, 2006.

Walsh, Frank, *Sin and Censorship: The Catholic Church and the Motion Picture Industry*. New Haven: Yale University Press, 1996.

9. Radio: *Helping Us Through the Rough Years*

Barnouw, Erik, *The Sponsor*. New York: Oxford University Press, 1978.

Beniger, James R., *The Control Revolution*. Harvard University Press, 1986.

Douglas, Susan J., *Inventing American Broadcasting, 1899-1922*. Baltimore: The Johns Hopkins University Press, 1987.

Fang, Irving, *Those Radio Commentators!* Ames: Iowa State University Press, 1977.

Halper, Donna L., *Invisible Stars: A Social History of Women in American Broadcasting*. Armonk, N.Y.: M.E. Sharpe, 2001.

Hilliard, Robert L., and Michael C. Keith, *The Broadcast Century and Beyond: A Biography of American Broadcasting*. Woburn, MA: Focal Press, 2001.

Keith, Michael C., *The Radio Station: Broadcast, Satellite, and Internet*. 7th ed. Boston: Focal Press, 2007.

Lenthall, Bruce, *Radio's America: The Great Depression and the Rise of Modern Mass Culture*. Chicago: University of Chicago Press, 2007.

Lewis, Tom, *Empire of the Air: The Men Who Made Radio*. New York: HarperCollins, 1991.

Pease, Edward C., ed, *Radio: The Forgotten Medium*. New York: Columbia University, 1993.

Schiffer, Michael Brian, *The Portable Radio in American Life*. Tucson: University of Arizona Press, 1991.

Sterling, Christopher H., and John M. Kittross, *Stay Tuned: A Concise History of American Broadcasting*. Belmont, CA: Wadsworth Publishing Co., 3rd ed., 2002.

Weightman, Gavin, *Signor Marconi's Magic Box*. London: HarperCollins Publishers, 2003.

10. Television: *Pictures in Our Parlors*

Abramson, Albert, *The History of Television, 1942 to 2000*. Jefferson, NC: McFarland & Company, 2003.

Barnouw, Erik, *The Golden Web: 1933-1953*. New York: Oxford University Press, 2001.

Barnouw, Erik, *The Image Empire: A History of Broadcasting in the United States: From 1953*. New York: Oxford University Press, 2001.

Baughman, James, *Same Time, Same Station: Creating American Television, 1948--1961*. Baltimore: Johns Hopkins University Press, 2007.

Briggs, Asa, and Peter Burke, *A Social History of the Media: From Gutenberg to the Internet* Cambridge, UK: Polity Press, 2002.

Downie Leonard Jr., and Robert G. Kaiser, *The News About the News*. New York: Alfred A. Knopf, 2002.

Edgerton, Gary, *The Columbia History of American Television*. New York: Columbia University Press, 2007.

Inglis, Andrew F., *Behind the Tube: A History of Broadcast Technology and Business*. Focal Press, 1990.

Magoun, Alexander, *Television: The Life Story of a Technology*. Westport, CT: Greenwood Press, 2007.

Postman, Neil, *Amusing Ourselves to Death*. New York: Viking Penguin, 1985.

Roman, James, *From Daytime to Primetime: The History of American Television Programs*. Westport, CT: Greenwood Press, 2005.

11. Computers: *Beyond Calculation*

Berners-Lee, Tim, *Weaving the Web*. San Francisco: Harper, 1999.

Campbell-Kelly, Martin, and William Aspray, *Computer: A History Of The Information Machine,* 2nd Edition. New York: Basic Books, 1996.

Castells, Manuel, *The Information Age: Economy, Society, and Culture*. New York: Oxford University Press, three volumes, 1996-98..

Ceruzzi, Paul, E., *A History of Modern Computing*, 2nd ed. Cambridge, MA: M.I.T. Press, 2003.

Ifrah, Georges, *The Universal History of Computing: From the Abacus to the Quantum Computer*. New York: John Wiley & Sons, 2001.

Levy, Steven, *Crypto*. New York: Penguin Books, 2001.

_____, *Hackers: Heroes of the Computer Revolution*. Sebastapol, CA.: O'Reilly Media, 2010.

Okin, J.B., *The Information Revolution: The Not-for-dummies Guide to the History, Technology, And Use of the World Wide Web*. Winter Harbor, ME: Ironbound Press, 2005.

O'Regan, Gerard, *A Brief History of Computing*. London: Springer-Verlag, 2008.

Sellen, Abigail, and Richard Harper, *The Myth of the Paperless Office*. Cambridge, MA: MIT Press, 2002.

Swedin, Eric, and David Ferro, *Computers: The Life Story of a Technology*. Westport, CT: Greenwood Press, 2005.

12. The Internet: *The World at Our Fingertips*

Abbate, Janet, *Inventing the Internet*. Cambridge: MIT Press, 1999.

Banks, Michael, *On the Way to the Web: The Secret History of the Internet and Its Founders*. New York: Springer-Verlag, 2008.

Berners-Lee, Tim,*Weaving the Web*. San Francisco: Harper, 1999.

Castells, Manuel, *The Information Age: Economy, Society, and Culture*. New York: Oxford University Press, three volumes, 1996-98..

Ceruzzi, Paul, E., *A History of Modern Computing*, 2nd ed. Cambridge, MA: M.I.T. Press, 2003.

Haffner, Katie, and Matthew Lyon, *Where Wizards Stay Up Late: The Origins Of The Internet*. New York: Simon & Schuster, 1996.

Levy, Steven, *Crypto*. New York: Penguin Books, 2001.

Naughton, John, *A Brief History of the Future: From Radio Days to Internet Years in a Lifetime*. Woodstock, NY: Overlook Press, 2000.

Okin, J.R., *The Information Revolution: The Not-for-dummies Guide to the History, Technology, And Use of the World Wide Web*. Winter Harbor, ME: Ironbound Press, 2005.

Ryan, Johnny, *A History of the Internet and the Digital Future*. London: Reaktion Books, 2010.

Van Schewick, Barbara, *Internet Architecture and Innovation*. Cambridge: MIT Press, 2010.

13. Video Games: *Leaning Forward*

Anderson, Craig A., et. al., *Violent Video Game Effects on Children and Adolescents: Theory, Research, and Public Policy.* New York: Oxford University Press, 2007.

Bissell, Tom, *Extra Lives: Why Video Games Matter.* New York: Pantheon Books, 2010.

Calvert, Sandra, Amy Jordan, and Rodney Cocking, eds. *Children in the Digital Age: Influences of Electronic Media on Development* New York: Praeger, 2002.

Donovan, Tristan, *Replay: The History of Video Games.* East Sussex, England: Yellow Ant, 2010.

Egenfeldt-Nielson, Simon, et. al., *Understanding Video Games: The Essential Introduction.* New York: Routledge, 2008.

Gee. James Paul, *What Video Games Have to Teach Us About Learning and Literacy.* New York: Palgrave Macmillan, 2004.

Greenfield, Patricia Marks, *Mind and Media: The Effects of Television, Video games, and Computers.* Cambridge: Harvard University Press, 1984.

Herz, J.C., *Joystick Nation.* Boston: Little, Brown and Company, 1997.

King, Brad, and John Borland. *Dungeons and Dreamers: The Rise of Computer Game Culture from Geek to Chic.* New York: McGraw-Hill/Osborne, 2003.

Poole, Steven, *Trigger Happy: The Inner Life of Video Games.* London: Fourth Estate, 2000.

Wolf, Mark J.P., ed., *Video Game Explosion: A History from PONG to PlayStation and Beyond.* Westport, CT: Greenwood Press, 2008.

14. Persuasion: *The Push Never Stops*

Cutlip, Scott, *Public Relations History: From the 17th to the 20th Century: The Antecedents.* Hillsdale, NJ: Lawrence Erlbaum Assoc., 1995.

Emery, Michael, Edwin Emery, and Nancy Roberts, *The Press and America. An Interpretive History of the Mass Media,* 9th ed. Boston: Allyn and Bacon, 2000.

Fox, Stephen, *The Mirror Makers: A History of American Advertising and Its Creators.* New York: Morrow, 1984.

Friedman, Thomas L., *The World Is Flat.* New York: Farrar, Straus, and Giroux, 2005.

Fukuyama, Francis, *The End of History and the Last Man,* 2nd ed. New York: Free Press, 1993.

Hoff, Syd, *Editorial and Political Cartooning.* New York: Stravon Educational Press, 1976.

Lears, Jackson, *Fables Of Abundance: A Cultural History Of Advertising In America.* New York: basic Books, 1994.

Lewis, Bernard, *What Went Wrong: Western Impact and Middle Eastern Response.* New York: Oxford University Press, 2002.

Pearse, Meic, *Why the Rest Hates the West: Understanding the Roots of Global Rage.* Downers Grove, IL: InterVarsity Press, 2004.

Pincus, Stephane, and Marc Loiseau, *A History of Advertising.* Cologne, Germany: Taschen, 2008.

Roy, Olivier, *Globalized Islam: The Search for a New Ummah.* New York: Columbia University Press, 2004.

Sivulka, Juliann, *Soap, Sex, and Cigarettes: A Cultural History of American Advertising*. Belmont, CA: Wadsworth Publishing, 1997.

Tungate, Mark, *Adland: A Global History of Advertising*. New York: Kogan Page, 2007.

Tye, Larry, *The Father of Spin: Edward L. Bernays and The Birth of Public Relations*. New York: Henry Holt, 1998.

15. We Are Different: *Living in a World of Change*

Briggs, Asa, and Peter Burke, *A Social History of the Media: From Gutenberg to the Internet*. 3rd ed. Cambridge, UK: Polity Press, 2009.

Easterbrook, Gregg, *Progress Paradox: How Life Gets Better While People Feel Worse*. New York: Random House, 2003.

Hallowell, Edward M., and John J. Ratey, *Delivered from Distraction*. New York: Ballantine Books, 2005.

Johnson, Steven, *Everything Bad Is Good for You*. New York: Riverhead Books, 2005.

Keeley, Brian. *International Migration: The Human Face of Globalization*. OECD (Organisation for Economic Cooperation and Development), 2009.

Putnam, Robert, *Bowling Alone: The Collapse and Revival of American Community*. New York: Simon & Schuster, 2000.

Qualman, Erik, Socialnomics *How Social Media Transforms the Way We Live and Do Business*. Hoboken, NJ: 2009.

Schwartz, Barry, *The Paradox of Choice: Why More Is Less*. New York: HarperCollins, 2004.

Web Resources

1. Writing: *Gathering Knowledge*
http://www.historian.net/hxwrite.htm
http://www.historyworld.net/wrldhis/PlainTextHistories.asp?historyid=ab33
http://www.krysstal.com/writing.html
http://groups.ku.cdu/~stl/historyofliteracy.htm
http://www.wisedude.com/history/alphabet.htm
http://inventors.about.com/library/weekly/aa100197.htm
http://research.ncl.ac.uk/egwest/test/test/egwest/pdf/education%20and%20the%20state/
Literacy%20and%20the%20Industrial%20Rev.pdf
http://mises.org/daily/1425

2. Printing: *Reaching More of Us*
http://inventors.about.com/od/pstartinventions/a/printing.htm
http://www.sas.upenn.edu/~traister/hbp.html
http://bubl.ac.uk/Link/p/printinghistory.htm
http://www.historicpages.com/nprhist.htm
http://www.wan-press.org/article2821.html
http://www.mediahistory.umn.edu/
http://www.well.com/~art/maghist01.html
http://www.internetcampus.com/frtv/mag1.htm
http://www.bl.uk/collections/early/victorian/intro.html

3. Mail: *The Snail That Could*
http://inventors.about.com/od/mstartinventions/a/mail.htm
http://inventors.about.com/library/inventors/blmailus1.htm
http://www.usps.com/postalhistory/
http://www.bbc.co.uk/dna/h2g2/A1082558
http://www.postalhistory.org/

http://en.wikipedia.org/wiki/Postal_history
http://www.postalhistoryfoundation.org/

4. Telegraph: *Uniting the United States*

http://www.telegraph-history.org/
http://inventors.about.com/od/tstartinventions/a/telegraph.htm
http://historywired.si.edu/detail.cfm?ID=324
http://eh.net/encyclopedia/article/nonnenmacher.industry.telegraphic.us
http://www.unitedstatesmilitarytelegraph.org/
http://www.wrvmuseum.org/morsecode/morsecodehistory.htm

5. Telephone: *Reaching Without Touching*

http://www.pbs.org/wgbh/amex/telephone/timeline/timeline_text.html
http://www.telephonetribute.com/timeline.html
http://www.corp.att.com/attlabs/reputation/timeline/27atlan.html
http://inventors.about.com/library/weekly/aa070899.htm
http://library.thinkquest.org/04oct/02001/home.htm
http://cellphones.org/cell-phone-history.html

6. Recording: *Beyoncé Sings Better Than Our Sister*

http://www.recording-history.org/
http://www.videointerchange.com/audio_history.htm
http://www.aes.org/aeshc/docs/audio.history.timeline.html
http://www.audiohistory.com/
http://www.ehow.com/about_5380379_history-car-audio.html
http://www.soc.duke.edu/~s142tm01/history.html

7. Photography: *The Effects Are Personal and More*

http://www.rleggat.com/photohistory/
http://photo.net/history/timeline
http://photography.about.com/od/famousphotographersbios/
famousphotographersandfamousphotographs.htm
http://www.historyplace.com/unitedstates/childlabor/
http://www.all-art.org/history658_photography1.html
http://www.huntfor.com/arthistory/C20th/photography.htm

8. Movies: *Made by More of Us*

http://www.filmsite.org/
http://dmoz.org/Arts/Movies/History/
http://www.classicmovies.org/articles/aa030799.htm
http://www.cln.org/themes/history_film.html
http://vlib.iue.it/hist-film/journals.html
http://arts.columbia.edu/film/film-studies-international-film-history-1930-1960
http://eh.net/encyclopedia/article/bakker.film

9. Radio: *Helping Us Through the Rough Years*

http://www.pavekmuseum.org/
http://earlyradiohistory.us/
http://www.old-time.com/toc.html#contents
http://www.oldradio.com/
http://radiohistory.org/
http://www.museum.tv/
http://www.bls.gov/oco/cg/cgs017.htm

10. Television: *Pictures in Our Parlors*

http://www.pavekmuseum.org/
http://library.duke.edu/digitalcollections/adaccess/?keyword=Television
http://library.thinkquest.org/18764/television/history.html
http://inventors.about.com/library/inventors/bltelevision.htm
http://www.classic tv.com/
http://www.tvhistory.tv/
http://www.ncta.com/About/About/HistoryofCableTelevision.aspx

11. Computers: *Beyond Calculation*

http://www.computerhistory.org/timeline/
http://www.hitmill.com/computers/computerhx1.html
http://www.google.com/search?hl=en&source=hp&q=computer+history+museum&aq=1&aqi=g10&aql=&oq=computer+history
http://www.computersciencelab.com/ComputerHistory/History.htm
http://www.computerhope.com/history/
http://inventors.about.com/library/blcoindex.htm

12. The Internet: *The World at Our Fingertips*

http://www.zakon.org/robert/internet/timeline/

http://www.nethistory.info/History%20of%20the%20Internet/email.html

http://www.let.leidenuniv.nl/history/ivh/chap3.htm

http://www.isoc.org/internet/history/

http://www.walthowe.com/navnet/history.html

http://www.netvalley.com/cgi-bin/intval/net_history.pl?chapter=1

13. Video Games: *Leaning Forward*

http://www.gamespot.com/gamespot/features/video/hov/

http://users.tkk.fi/~eye/videogames/index.html

http://www.designboom.com/eng/education/pong.html

http://www.pbs.org/kcts/videogamerevolution/history/

http://www.thegameconsole.com/

14. Persuasion: *The Push Never Stops*

http://xroads.virginia.edu/~MA96/PUCK/part1.html

http://www2.truman.edu/parker/research/cartoons.html

http://advertising.about.com/od/history/History_of_Advertising_and_Public_Relations.htm

http://scriptorium.lib.duke.edu/eaa/

http://www.grady.uga.edu/reports/PRHistory.CommYrbk.pdf

http://changingminds.org/techniques/propaganda/propaganda_history.htm

http://www.pbs.org/now/politics/propaganda.html

http://www.globalpolicy.org/globaliz/cultural/2003/0304clash.htm

http://www.arabview.com/articles.asp?article=176

http://www.crosscurrents.org/Mileswinter2002.htm

15. We Are Different: *Living in a World of Change*

http://blogs.business2.com/business2blog/2006/03/the_downside_of.html

http://www.columbia.edu/~ss957/vanguard.html

http://blackfriarsinc.com/totm.html

http://www.uky.edu/~drlane/capstone/mass/

http://www.rdillman.com/HFCL/TUTOR/Media/media1.html

Endnotes

Introduction

[1] *Newsweek*, 14 March 2011: 71.

[2] Clive Thompson, "Watching the Watchers," *Wired*, July 2011: 52.

[3] See John B. Thompson, *The Media and Modernity: A Social Theory of the Media.* (Stanford: Stanford University Press, 1995) 24-31. Thompson offers a number of reasons to argue that "mass communication" is now a misleading term. Like the author, Thompson prefers "mediated communication."

1. Writing: *Gathering Knowledge*

[1] Socrates relates a conversation between two Egyptian gods, Theuth, the inventor of letters, and Thamos, the ruler of Egypt. When Theuth said the use of letters would make Egyptians wiser and give them better memories, Thamos replied, "...this discovery of yours will create forgetfulness in the learners' souls, because they will not use their memories; they will trust to the external written characters and not remember of themselves. The specific which you have discovered is an aid not to memory, but to reminiscence, and you give your disciples not truth, but only the semblance of truth; they will be hearers of many things and will have learned nothing; they will appear to be omniscient and will generally know nothing; they will be tiresome company, having the show of wisdom without the reality." *Phaedrus*, trans. C.J. Rowe, 2nd. (corrected) ed. (Warminster, England: Aris & Rowe, 1988).

[2] For a thoroughgoing comparison of chirographic (writing-based) and oral societies, see Walter J. Ong, *Orality and Literacy: The Technologizing of the Word* (London: Methuen, 1982).

[3] Marshall McLuhan, *The Gutenberg Galaxy: The Making of Typographic Man* (Toronto: University of Toronto Press, 1962) 22.

[4] Ong 78.

[5] Ong, 51, describing research by Aleksander Luria, *Cognitive Development: Its Cultural and Social Foundations* (Cambridge: Harvard University Press, 1976).

[6] Robert Scribner, "Oral Culture and the Diffusion of the Reformation," in Harvey J. Graff, *Literacy and Historical Development*," (Carbondale: Southern Illinois University Press, 2007) 161.

[7] Denise Schmandt-Besserat, *Before Writing* (Austin: University of Texas Press, 1992) 1.

[8] Schmandt-Besserat 178ff.

[9] Adolf Erman, *Life in Ancient Egypt* (London, 1894) 328, mentioned in Will Durant, *Our Oriental Heritage* (New York: Simon & Schuster, 1936) 170.

[10] Robert K. Logan, *The Alphabet Effect: The Impact of the Phonetic Alphabet on the Development of Western Civilization* (William Morrow and Co., 1986) 82.

[11] Amalia E. Gnanadesikan, *The Writing Revolution: Cuneiform to the Internet* (Oxford: Wiley-Blackwell, 2009) 143.

[12] Gnanadesikan 144-45.

[13] Jack Goody, *Literacy in Traditional Societies* (Cambridge: Cambridge University Press, 1968) 3.

[14] Durant, *Our Oriental Heritage* 106.

[15] Henri-Jean Martin, *The History and Power of Writing* (Chicago: University of Chicago Press, 1994) 46.

[16] Eric Havelock, *A Preface to Plato* (Cambridge: Belknap Press of Harvard University Press, 1963) 41.

[17] Havelock 200.

[18] Havelock 205, 208.

[19] A letter from a 16th century English gentleman declared, "I swear by God's body I'd rather that my son should hang than study letters. For it becomes the sons of gentlemen to blow the horn nicely, to hunt skillfully and elegantly, carry and train a hawk. But the study of letters should be left to the sons of rustics." In Lawrence Stone, "The Thirst for Learning," in Norman Canton and Michael Werthman, *The History of Popular Culture* (New York: Macmillan, 1968) 279.

[20] Tamara Plakins Thornton, *Handwriting in America: A Cultural History* (New Haven: Yale University Press, 1996) 13-14.

[21] Thornton 4-12.

[22] Thornton 56.

[23] Ian Morris writes of "more effective organization and widespread literacy" before 200 BCE: *Why the West Rules—For Now* (New York: Farrar, Straus and Giroux, 2010) 279.

[24] Hangul now uses fourteen consonants and ten vowels.

[25] Gnanadesikan 203.

[26] Gnanadesikan, 133-42.

[27] Ronald E. Seavoy, *An Economic History of the United States: From 1607 to the Present* (New York: Routledge, 2006) 48.

[28] Seavoy 28.

[29] Farley Grub, "Growth of Literacy in Colonial America: Longitudinal Patterrns, Economic Models, and the Direction of Future Research," in Harvey J. Graff, *Literacy and Historical Development*, (Carbondale:

Southern Illinois University Press, 2007) 274-77.

[30] Lucien Febvre and Henri-Jean Martin, *The Coming of the Book: The Impact of Printing 1450-1800*. Trans. French edition 1958 (London: Verso Editions, 1984) 210-11.

[31] Seavoy notes that a few heartless mill owners who employed fathers and children threatened to fire them all if one of the children was removed to attend school, 115.

[32] Reported in Susan Jacoby, *The Age of American Unreason* (New York: Pantheon Books, 2008) xviii.

[33] The knowledge gap theory was first proposed in 1970 by Philip Tichenor, George Donohue, and Clarice Olien, University of Minnesota.

[34] 6 June 2008.

[35] See Clive Thompson, "The New Literacy," *Wired*, September 2009 48.

2. **Printing:** *Reaching More of Us*

[1] *New Advent Encyclopedia*, citation for Berthold of Henneberg, online at http://www.newadvent.org/cathen/02520b.htm.

[2] Thomas F. Carter, *The Invention of Printing in China and Its Spread Westward*, 2nd ed. (New York: Ronald Press, 1955) 112.

[3] Jixing, Pan, *History of Chinese Science and Technology: Papermaking and Printing* (Beijing: Kexue, 1998) 22-23.

[4] De Lamar Jensen, *Renaissance Europe: Age of Recovery and Reconciliation*, 2nd ed. (Lexington, MA: D. C. Heath and Company, 1992) 222.

[5] Jensen 423.

[6] Lawrence Stone, "The Thirst for Learning," in Norman Cantor and Michael Werthman, *The History of Popular Culture* (Macmillan, 1968) 279.

[7] Natalie Zemon Davis, "Printing and the People: Early Modern France," in Harvey J. Graff, *Literacy and Historical Development* (Carbondale: Southern Illinois University Press, 2007) 142.

[8] R.R. Bolgar, "The Greek Legacy," in M.I. Finley, ed., *The Legacy of Greece*. (Oxford University Press, 1984) 452.

[9] Albert Kapr, *Johannes Gutenberg, The Man and His Invention*, tr. by Douglas Martin (Aldershot, England: Scolar Press, 1996) 15.

[10] Albert Einstein, *Short History of Music* (New York: Vintage Books, 1954) 20, 45.

[11] Benedict Anderson, *Imagined Communities: Reflections on the Origin and Spread of Nationalism* (London: Verso, 1991) 44.

[12] For a discussion of this point, see Asa Briggs and Peter Burke, *A Social History of the Media: from Gutenberg to the Internet* (Cambridge, UK. Polity Press, 2002) 85 ff.

[13] According to Harold A. Innis, *The Bias of Communication* (University of Toronto Press, 1951) 24-29.

[14] It was first called *A Weekly Review of the Affairs of France.*

[15] *Worcester Magazine,* III, 181 (first week, July 1787).

[16] James P. Wood, *The Story of Advertising* (New York: Ronald Press, 1958) 444.

[17] Adam Nicolson, *God's Secretaries: The Making of the King James Bible* (New York: HarperCollins, 2003) 236-37.

[18] William Gray and Ruth Munroe, *The Reading Interests and Habits of Adults* (New York: Macmillan, 1929) 149.

[19] Ann Haugland, "Edward L. Bernay's 1930 Campaign Against Dollar Books," in Ezra Greenspan and Jonathan Rose, eds., *Book History*, vol. 3. (University Park: Pennsylvania State University Press, 2000) 233.

[20] *The Economist*, 27 February 2010, 72-3.

[21] See, for example, Evan Smith, "The Texas Curriculum Massacre," *Newsweek*, 26 April 2010, 34-5.

[22] Ravitch, 21.

[23] The argument and eye-opening examples of excess zeal are offered by Diane Ravitch, *The Language Police: How Pressure Groups Restrict What Students Learn* (New York: Alfred Knopf, 2003)

[24] *Tech & Learning*, July 2011. URL: http://www.techlearning.com/editorblogs/40408.

[25] Henri-Jean Martin, *The History and Power of Writing.* Trans. Lydia G. Cochrane (Chicago: University of Chicago Press, 1994) 266.

[26] William A. Mason, *A History of the Art of Writing*, 454

[27] Reverend Enos Hitchcock, *Memoirs of the Bloomsgrove Family* (Boston: Thomas and Andrews, 1790).

3. Mail: *The Snail That Could*

[1] For some opinion, see Alvin F. Harlow, *Old Post Bags* (D. Appleton, 1938) 7.

[2] The Silk Road Foundation website, http://www.silk-road.com/artl/marcopolo.shtml.

[3] Herodotus, *The History* 8:98.

[4] Wayne E. Fuller, *The American Mail* (Chicago: University of Chicago Press 1972) 4.

[5] Marshall McLuhan, *Understanding Media: The Extensions of Man* (New York: McGraw Hill, 1964) 100.

[6] William Manchester, *A World Lit Only by Fire: the Medieval Mind* (Boston: Little, Brown, 1992) 61.

[7] Shakespeare's phrase was used as the title of a postal history, George Walker's *Haste, Post, Haste* (New York: Dodd, Mead & Co., 1939).

[8] For a fuller examination of the postal service in the early years of the republic, see Richard R. John, *Spreading the News: The American Postal System from Franklin to Morse* (Cambridge, MA: Harvard University Press, 1995).

[9] Siva Vaidhyanathan, *The Anarchist in the Library* (New York: Basic Books, 2004) 102.

[10] Richard B. Kielbowicz, "Post Office and the Media," in Margaret Blanchard, ed., *History of Mass Media in the United States* (Chicago: Fitzroy Dearborn Publishers, 1998) 57.

[11] Mauritz Hallgren, *All About Stamps* (New York: Alfred A. Knopf, 1940) 47.

[12] The human side of Britain's postal reform is described in Laurin Zilliacus, *Mail for the World* (New York: John Day Co., 1953).

[13] Rowland Hill, "Post Office Reform: Its Importance and Practicability," pamphlet, 1836.

[14] David Vincent gives greater credit to the first postcard: "The subsequent arrival of the telephone and cheap road transport merely completed the transition which was set in motion not by the Penny Post but by the halfpenny postcard." David Vincent, *Literacy and Popular Culture.* (Cambridge: Cambridge University Press, 1989), 52.

[15] H.W. Hill, *Rowland Hill and the Fight for Penny Post* (London: Frederick Warne & Co., 1940) 20.

[16] Hill, 37.

[17] James H. Bruns, *Mail on the Move* (Polo, IL: Transportation Trails, 1992) 89.

[18] Daniel J. Boorstin, *The Americans: The Democratic Experience* (New York: Random House, 1973) 135.

[19] Gerald Cullinan, *The United States Postal Service* (New York: Praeger Publishers, 1968) 192-93.

4. Telegraph: *Uniting the United States*

[1] George P. Oslin, *The Story of Telecommunications* (Macon, GA: Mercer University Press, 1992) 16.

[2] Tom Standage, *The Victorian Internet* (New York: Walker and Co., 1998) 52.

[3] In the United States, it is known as Reuters, not Reuter, due to the erroneous title of a popular Hollywood movie, *A Dispatch from Reuters.* Life sometimes imitates art.

[4] Standage, 167.

[5] Daniel J. Czitrom, *Media and the American Mind* (University of North Carolina Press, 1982) 18.

[6] William Sloan, James Stovall and James Startt, *The Media in America* (Worthington, OH: Publishing Horizons, 1989) 204.

[7] Edward Cornish, "The Coming of an Information Society," *The Futurist*, April 1981: 14.

[8] Francis Williams, *Transmitting World News* (UNESCO, 1953) 19.

[9] James R. Beniger, *The Control Revolution* (Cambridge: Harvard University Press, 1986) 253.

5. Telephone: *Reaching Without Touching*

[1] George P. Oslin, *The Story of Telecommunications* (Macon, GA: Mercer University Press, 1992) 220.

[2] George Basalla, *The Evolution of Technology* (Cambridge University Press, 1988) 98.

[3] Marion May Dilts, *The Telephone in a Changing World* (New York: Longman's Green, 1941) 11.

[4] George P. Oslin, *The Story of Telecommunications* (Macon, GA: Mercer University Press, 1992) 227.

[5] John Brooks, *Telephone: The First Hundred Years* (New York: Harper & Row, 1976) 94.

[6] Before email and Twitter became so widely used, the author asked students to identify the one communication device in the home they would be most reluctant to lose; invariably it was the telephone.

[7] Dilts, 15.

[8] A few years ago the fire department of the upper income Los Angeles suburb of Bel Air for a time had an unlisted number.

[9] Oslin, 281.

[10] Thomas L. Friedman, *The World Is Flat* (New York: Farrar, Straus, and Giroux, 2005).

[11] James R. Beniger, *The Control Revolution* (Cambridge: Harvard University Press, 1986) 285.

[12] For the scene in India, see Anand Giridharadas, "A Pocket-Size Leveler in an Outsize Land," *The New York Times*, 10 May 2009, WK3.

[13] *Newsweek*, 20 March 2006: 80.

[14] Reported on *ZD Net* 12 May 2011, http://www.zdnet.com/blog/gadgetreviews/can-you-bzzzz-me-now-study-says-cell-phones-are-killing-honey-bees/24673

[15] CNN report, 4 August 2003.

[16] For a discussion of these changes, with examples, see *The Economist*, 26 September 2009, special section following page 58.

[17] *The Economist*, 26 September 2009, special section, 8.

[18] *The Economist*, 9 January 2010, 72.

[19] *The Economist*, 26 September 2009, special section, 6.

[20] *Newsweek*, 11 October 2010: 45.

6. Recording: *Beyoncé Sings Better Than Our Sister*

[1] Marshall McLuhan, *Understanding Media: The Extensions of Man* (McGraw-Hill Book Co., 1964) 283.

[2] George P. Oslin, *The Story of Telecommunications* (Macon, GA: Mercer University Press, 1992) 227.

[3] Daniel Marty, *An Illustrated History of Phonographs* (New York: Dorset Press, 1981) 71.

[4] B.L. Aldridge, *The Victor Talking Machine Company.* (Camden, NJ: RCA Sales Corp., 1964), 118.

[5] Carolyn Marvin, *When Old Technologies Were New.* (New York: Oxford University Press, 1988), 203.

[6] *Harper's Magazine*, September, 1893, 726.

[7] Andrew F. Inglis, *Behind the Tube: A History of Broadcast Technology and Business.* (New York: Focal Press, 1990), 19-20.

[8] Christopher H. Sterling and John M. Kittross, *Stay Tuned: A Concise History of American Broadcasting* (Belmont, CA: Wadsworth Publishing Co., 2nd ed., 1990) 339-41.

[9] David Lander, "Technology Makes Music," *Invention and Technology*, Spring/Summer, 1990: 63.

[10] J.M. Fenster, "How Bing Crosby Brought You Audiotape," *Invention and Technology*, Fall 1994: 58.

[11] "John (Jack) T. Mullin (1913-99) Recalls the American Development of the Tape Recorder," at http://community.mcckc.edu/crosby/mullin.htm.

[12] *The Wall Street Journal* 19 September 1989, B1.

[13] Timothy J. Mellonig, "DCC and MD," in Grant, August E., and Kenton T. Wilkinson, eds., *Communication Technology Update, 1993-1994* (Austin: Technology Futures, Inc., 1993) 191-96.

[14] For an interesting discussion of this point, see Gary Gumpert, *Talking Tombstones and Other Tales of the Media Age* (New York: Oxford University Press, 1987) 91.

[15] Steven Levy, *The Perfect Thing* (New York: Simon & Schuster, 2006) 34.

[16] Richard S. Hollander, *Video Democracy* (Mt. Airy, MD: Lomond Publications, 1985) 132.

[17] Levy, 207.

[18] *Time*, 5 May, 2003: 61ff.

7. Photography: *Personal and So Much More*

[1] *100 Photographs That Changed the World* (New York: Life Books, 2003) 7.

[2] For a fuller description read Richard G. Tansey and Horst de la Croix, *Art Through the Ages* (Harcourt Brace Jovanovich, 1986).

[3] Geoffrey Batchen, *Each Wild Idea* (Cambridge: MIT Press, 2001) 4.

[4] Daniel J. Boorstin, *The Americans: The Democratic Experience* (New York: Random House, 1973) 398.

[5] An earlier photographer, Richard Beard, had taken daguerreotypes in London streets that were used for illustrations in another sociological study of the travails of the London poor. Henry Mayhew, *London Labour and the London Poor*, 1851: 62.

[6] Found at http://www.spartacus.schoolnet.co.uk/IRhine.htm.

[7] Richard Hofstadter, *The Progressive Movement*, 1900-1915 (Simon & Schuster, 1963).

[8] It is also a cheaper way to acquire good photos and videos than hiring staff photographers. See Jeff Howe, "The Rise of Crowdsourcing," *Wired*, June 2006:177-83.

[9] *Time*, 25 December 2006: 63-64.

[10] Wikipedia entry, http://en.wikipedia.org/wiki/Photo_manipulation.

[11] *Newsweek* not only placed Martha Stewart's head on a model's body, but in the accompanying article freely admitted doing so and saw nothing wrong with such a "photo illustration."

[12] Giving other examples, Arthur Goldsmith wrote, "With the new technology we can enhance colors or change them, eliminate details, add or delete figures, alter the composition and lighting effects, combine any number of images, and literally move mountains, or at least the Eiffel Tower, as one magazine did to improve a cover design. *TV Guide* didn't even stop at decapitation—it placed Oprah Winfrey's head on Ann–Margret's body." Arthur Goldsmith, "Reinventing the Image," *Popular Photography*, March 1990: 49.

8. Movies: *Made by More of Us*

[1] More than a half-century ago, Leo Rosten wrote, "The American press is read only where English is read; the American radio is heard only where English is comprehended; but the American movie is an international carrier which triumphs over differences in age or language, nationality or custom. Even the Sumatran native who cannot spell is able to grasp the meaning of pictures which move, and he can love, hate or identify himself with those who appear in them." Leo Rosten, *Hollywood, the Movie Colony and the Movie Makers* (Harcourt Brace & Co., 1941) 7-12.

[2] Speech at the American Museum of the Moving Image, 24 February 1994.

[3] For an early take on this, see Leo Rosten, *Hollywood, the Movie Colony and the Movie Makers* (Harcourt Brace & Co., 1941) 7-12.

[4] Ian C. Jarvie, *Hollywood's Overseas Campaign: The North Atlantic Movie Trade, 1920-1950* (Cambridge University Press, 1992) 299.

[5] David Nasaw, *Going Out: The Rise and Fall of Public Amusements* (New York: Basic Books, 1993) 167.

[6] Harry M. Geldud, *The Birth of the Talkies: From Edison to Jolson* (Indiana University Press, 1975) 28.

[7] One excited Parisian newspaper exulted: "With this new invention, death will no longer be absolute, final. The people we have seen on the screen will be with us, moving and alive after their deaths." David Shipman, *The Story of Cinema* (Englewood Cliffs: Prentice-Hall, 1982) 18.

[8] Lloyd R. Morris, *Not So Long Ago* (New York: Random House, 1949) 29-35.

[9] 12. Simon Patten, *Product and Climax* (New York: B.W. Huebsch, 1909) 18-19.

[10] Hansen 117.

[11] Nasaw 152-53.

[12] Daniel J. Boorstin, *The Image, or What Happened to the American Dream* (New York: Atheneum, 1961) 127-8.

[13] Raymond Fielding has argued that silent films were seldom truly silent. "The systematic use of... live performers during motion picture presentations began at least as early as 1897... and during the first decade of the century a number of professional actors companies were founded to provide such services to theaters on a regular basis.... In fact, then, the 'silent film' is a myth. It never existed. Furthermore, the term was rarely used prior to 1926—only afterwards." Raymond Fielding, "The Technological Antecedents of the Coming of Sound: An Introduction," in E.W. Cameron (ed), *Sound*

and the Cinema (New York: Redgrave Publishing Co., 1980) 5.

[14] Ellis, Jack C., *A History of Film*, 2nd ed. (Englewood Cliffs: Prentice-Hall, 1985) 152.

[15] http://www.filmsite.org/index.html

[16] Miriam Hansen, *Babel and Babylon: Spectatorship in American Silent Film* (Cambridge: Harvard University Press, 1991) 63.

[17] Faith Popcorn, *The Popcorn Report: The Future of Your Company, Your World, Your Life* (New York: Doubleday, 1991).

[18] *Time*, 14 August 2006 75.

[19] For an extensive discussion, see Robert Putnam, *Bowling Alone: The Collapse and Revival of American Community* (New York: Simon & Schuster, 2000). It should be noted that the decades following World War II saw an upsurge in social club and community activity. It was the heyday of Lions, Elks, Moose, Rotarians, Shriners, and veterans organizations.

[20] David Denby wrote, "...even people who like going to movies alone don't necessarily go to be alone. In a marvelous paradox, the people around us both relieve us of isolation and drive us deeper into our own responses." David Denby, "Big Pictures," *The New Yorker*, 8 January 2007. 56, 62.

[21] An interesting examination of this point can be found in the *New York Times*, 10 December 2006: Sec. 2:30.

9. Radio: *Helping Us Through the Rough Years*

[1] "Like graphics but unlike the printed word, radio could influence illiterates (6 percent of U.S. adults in 1920) and preliterate children, so that Ipana toothpaste, for example, could make its radio pitch for "the one in the red and yellow tube." James R. Beniger, *The Control Revolution.* (Harvard University Press, 1986), 367.

[2] "If the ultimate goal stops being about capturing an audience's attention once, and becomes more about keeping their attention through repeat viewings, that shift is bound to have an effect on the content." Steven Johnson, *Everything Bad Is Good for You.* (New York: Riverhead Books, 2005), 159.

[3] Bruce Lenthall, *Radio's America: The Great Depression and the Rise of Modern Mass Culture.* (Chicago: University of Chicago Press, 2007) 56. An inexpensive RCA set cost $37.50 in 1931. An inexpensive RCA set cost $49.95 a decade later.

[4] Gavin Weightman, *Signor Marconi's Magic Box.* (London: HarperCollins Publishers, 2003), 56.

[5] Stephen N. Raymer, "Fessenden Revisited," *Pavek Museum of Broadcasting Newsletter*, Vol. 4, #4, 1993: 5.

[6] Susan J. Douglas, *Inventing American Broadcasting, 1899-1922.* (Baltimore: The Johns Hopkins University Press, 1987), 15.

[7] Doubt has been cast upon the generally accepted report that the broadcast took place on Christmas Eve. It may have occurred a few days earlier, on December 21, 1906. Similar doubts were not raised about the content of the transmission. See: Donna L. Halper and Christopher H. Sterling, "Fessenden's Christmas Eve Broadcast: Reconsidering an Historic Event," *AWA Review* 19. (2006).

[8] Erik Barnouw, *The Sponsor*. (New York: Oxford University Press, 1978), 16.

[9] Speech to the Third National Radio Conference, October 1924.

[10] *Printers' Ink*, 27 April 1922.

[11] Ithiel de Sola Pool, *Technologies of Freedom*. (Harvard University Press, 1983), 122.

[12] George P. Oslin, *The Story of Telecommunications*. (Macon, GA: Mercer University Press, 1992), 283.

[13] Douglas, 308.

[14] Robert W. McChesney, "Press-Radio Relations and the Emergence of Network, Commercial Broadcasting in the United States, 1930-1935" *Historical Journal of Film, Radio & Television*, vol 11, issue 1, 1991:41.

[15] Christopher H. Sterling and John M. Kittross, *Stay Tuned: A Concise History of American Broadcasting*. (Belmont, CA: Wadsworth Publishing Co., 2nd ed., 1990), 239.

[16] Robert L. Hilliard and Michael C. Keith, *The Broadcast Century and Beyond: A Biography of American Broadcasting*. (Woburn, MA: Focal Press, 2001), 57.

[17] According to the FCC's tally as of September 30, 2010, there were 4,784 AM stations, 6,512 commercial FM stations, and 3,251 FM educational stations, a total of 14,547 radio stations. For television: 1,022 UHF commercial TV stations, 370 VHF commercial TV stations, 284 UHF educational TV stations, and 107 VHF educational TV stations, for a total of 1,783 television stations in the United States. This and other data can be found online at http://fjallfoss.fcc.gov/edocs_public/attachmatch/ DOC-302349A1.doc

The National Cable & Telecommunications Association 2008 Industry Overview listed 64,900,000 basic cable customers, or 52.5% of the total homes passed by cable video services. It also listed 35,600,000 high-speed Internet customers. There were 1,212 cable operating companies and 565 national cable networks. These date can be found online at http://i.ncta.com/ncta_com/PDFs/NCTA_Annual_ Report_05.16.08.pdf

[18] Michael Wusterhausen, "AM Stereo Radio," in Grant, August E., and Kenton T. Wilkinson, eds., *Communication Technology Update, 1993-1994*. (Austin: Technology Futures, Inc., 1993), 121.

[19] *The Economist*, 7 May 2011: 66.

10. Television: *Pictures in Our Parlor*

[1] "Television is different because i encompasses all forms of discourse. No one goes to a movie to find out about government policy or the latest scientific advances. No one buys a record to find out the baseball scores or the weather or the latest murder. No one turns on radio anymore for soap operas or a presidential address (if a television set is at hand). But everyone goes to television for all these things and more, which is why television resonates so powerfully throughout the culture." Neil Postman, *Amusing Ourselves to Death* (New York: Viking Penguin, 1985) 92.

[2] Asa Briggs and Peter Burke, *A Social History of the Media: From Gutenberg to the Internet* (Cambridge, UK:

Polity Press, 2002) 252.

[3] *The Economist*, 13 February, 1994: 12.

[4] Edmund Carpenter, *Explorations in Communication* (Boston: Beacon Press, 1960) 165.

[5] The concept is credited to Paul Klein of NBC.

[6] Todd Gitlin, "Flat and Happy," *Wilson Quarterly*, Autumn, 1993: 48.

[7] Bruce Lenthall, *Radio's America: The Great Depression and the Rise of Modern Mass Culture* (Chicago: University of Chicago Press, 2007) 57-8.

[8] Speech to the 1961 convention of the National Association of Broadcasters.

[9] According to 2009 statistics generated by TVB, which represents the commercial television industry, men on average spent 4 hours 54 minutes watching television daily, women spent 5 hours 31 minutes, teens spent 3 hours 26 minutes, and children spent 3 hours 21 minutes. The television set in the average household was on 8 hours 21 minutes. These data are available online at http://www.tvb.org/media/file/TVB_FF_TV_Basics.pdf. They do not include watching DVD rental movies, downloads or video games on the television screen.

[10] WCCO-TV used that comment as the title of a documentary about the experience.

[11] Vern Boerman, "Potholes on Sesame Street," *The Banner*, 20 October 1986. Reprinted online at http://www.catapultmagazine.com/saturday-morning/article/potholes-on-sesame.

[12] Christopher Sterling and John Kittross, *Stay Tuned*, (Belmont, CA: Wadsworth, 1990) 418.

[13] George A. Wiley, "End of an Era: The Daytime Radio Serial," *Journal of Broadcasting*, Spring, 1961: 110.

[14] Christopher H. Sterling and John M. Kittross, *Stay Tuned: A Concise History of American Broadcasting*. (Belmont, CA: Wadsworth Publishing Co., 2nd ed., 1990) 582,

[15] Sterling and Kittross 582,

[16] Survey by Oliver Quayle and Company, 1972.

[17] Delivered by Vice President Spiro Agnew in Des Moines, IA, 13 November 1969

[18] Matt Stump and Harry Jessell, "Cable: The First Forty Years," *Broadcasting*, 21 November, 1988: 42.

[19] Lloyd Trufelman, Cable Television Advertising Bureau.

[20] For a deeper discussion about news preferences, see Leonard Downie Jr. and Robert G. Kaiser, *The News About the News* (New York: Alfred A. Knopf, 2002) 172.

[21] E.B. White, *Harper's Magazine*, October, 1938, written when television began to attract public notice for its future potential.

[22] For further thought on this, read Richard Ohmann, *Selling Culture: Magazines, Markets, and Class at the Turn of the Century* (London: Verso, 1996) 11-12.

[23] Marshall McLuhan, *Understanding Media: The Extensions of Man* (McGraw-Hill Book Co., 1964) 195.

11. Computers: *Beyond Calculation*

[1] Will Wright, "Dream Machines," *Wired*, April, 2006: 112.

[2] The abacus is used in villages and cities by clerks and merchants throughout Africa and in much of Asia. The user is sometimes known as an abacist. (http://dictionary.reference.com/browse/abacist). It is also a valuable counting tool of the blind. (http://www.aph.org/tests/abacus.html).

[3] James Redlin, "A Brief History of Mechanical Calculators." (http://www.xnumber.com/xnumber/mechanical1.htm)

[4] Management historians Daniel A. Wren and Arthur G. Bedeian write that Lady Lovelace "expressed his ideas better than he could." (*The Evolution of Management Thought*, John Wiley and Sons, 2009) 68. Stronger opinions on this subject can be found at: http://en.wikipedia.org/wiki/Ada_Lovelace.

[5] Martin Greenberger, ed., *Management and Computers of the Future* (Cambridge: The MIT Press, 1962) 8.

[6] A number of websites review the history of desktop publishing. Go to Google: desktop publishing. Two of the better sites are: http://www.brighthub.com/multimedia/publishing/articles/1912.aspx and http://www.tsd.state.tx.us/cte/careertech/desktoppublishing/historyDTP.HTM.

[7] Abigail Sellen and Richard Harper, *The Myth of the Paperless Office* (Cambridge, MA: MIT Press, 2002) 13.

[8] Peter Leyden, "Teleworking could turn our cities inside out," Minneapolis *Star Tribune*, 5 September, 1993:1A, 16A.

[9] Marcia Kelly, "Work-at-home," *The Futurist*, November/December 1988: 32.

[10] John Matthias and James Twedt, "TeleJustice—Videoconferencing for the 21st Century," 1997, at http://ctl.ncsc.dni.us/bbsfiles/ctc5_rom/208.htm.

[11] Alvin Toffler, *The Third Wave* (New York: William Morrow, 1980) 210-23.

[12] Irving Fang, *A History of Mass Communication: Six Information Revolutions* (Newton, MA: Butterworth-Heinemann, 1997).

[13] See Manuel Castells, *The Information Age: Economy, Society, and Culture* (New York: Oxford University Press, three volumes, 1996-98.)

[14] *The Economist*, 31 December 2011-6 January 2012: 46.

12. The Internet: *The World at Our Fingertips*

[1] *Time*, 15 December 2010, cover story.

[2] The URL of the site is: secondlife.com.

[3] Nathan Shapira, et. al., "Problematic internet use: Proposed classification and diagnostic criteria," *Depression and Anxiety*, 17:4, 2003: 217.

[4] http://www.caslon.com.au/addictionnote.htm.

[5] "The Secret World of Lonelygirl15," *Wired*, December 2006: 236-39.

[6] Published in *Communication Systems, IEEE Transactions*, March 1964 (Vol. 12:1) 1-9.

[7] Michael Hauben, "The Social Forces Behind the Development of Usenet." http://www.columbia.edu/~rh120/ch106.x03. Also in *Netizens* (Los Alamitos, CA: IEEE Computer Society Press, 1997) 48.

[8] Michael Dertouzos makes the point in his foreword to Tim Berners-Lee, *Weaving the Web* (San Francisco: Harper, 1999) ix.

[9] For a detailed description, see Tim Berners-Lee, *Weaving the Web* (San Francisco: Harper, 1999).

[10] See, for example, *Wired*, August 2005: 96.

[11] Jones, Sydney, and Susannah Fox, "Generations Online in 2009," *Pew Internet and American Life Project*, January 28, 2009. Information can be found at: http://www.pewInternet.org/~/media//Files/Reports/2009/PIP_Generations_2009.pdf

[12] Stanford University Professor B.J. Fogg reported that older women join Facebook to "friend" their younger family members, then stay on to connect online with their peers. The Facebook organization, on its Inside Facebook site, reported on April 13, 2009, that 1.5 million women over 55 had joined, a 550% increase in six months. Total membership at the time was 200 million, a larger user base than the population of any country except China, India, the United States, and Indonesia. http://www.cnn.com/2009/TECH/04/13/social.network.older/index.html?iref=t2test_techmon

[13] Pew Internet & American Life Project, 2005.

[14] See Hauben 123.

[15] For a take on this point see Steven Johnson, *Everything Bad Is Good for You* (New York: Riverhead Books, 2005) 120.

[16] Fallows, Deborah, "How Women and Men Use the Internet," *Pew Internet and American Life Project*, December 28, 2005. http://www.pewInternet.org/~/media//Files/Reports/2005/PIP_Women_and_Men_online.pdf.pdf

[17] *The Digital Futures Report, Year Four* (Los Angeles: Annenberg School, USC, 2005) 97.

[18] For a discussion of Usenet, see Michael Hauben, "The Social Forces Behind the Development of Usenet." http://www.columbia.edu/~rh120/ch106.x03. Also in *Netizens* (Los Alamitos, CA: IEEE Computer Society Press, 1997) 48.

[19] Kevin Kelly, "The New Socialism," *Wired*, August 2009, 116-121.

[20] Steven Levy, *Crypto*. (New York: Penguin Books, 2001), 1.

[21] Niall Ferguson, "The Mash of Civilizations," *Newsweek*, 18 April 2011: 9.

[22] The King James Bible (2000) translates Matthew 5:45 as "That you may be the children of your Father who is in heaven: for he makes his sun to rise on the evil and on the good, and sends rain on the just and on the unjust."

13. Video Games: *Leaning Forward*

[1] The Economist presented a broad analysis of the video game industry in a special report, 10 December, 2011, 1-12.

[2] James Paul Gee. *What Video Games Have to Teach Us About Learning and Literacy* (New York: Palgrave Macmillan, 2004) 13, 204.

[3] In an interview with *MacWorld*, 2004.

[4] http://www.videotopia.com/intro.htm

[5] Ted Friedman, "Making Sense of Software: Computer Games and Interactive Textuality," in *Cybersociety*, ed. Steven G. Jones (Thousand Oaks, CA: Sage Publications, 1995). Taken from: http://www.duke.edu/~tlove/simcity.htm.

[6] *Nursing Spectrum*, 3 January 2005. Online at http://nsweb.nursingspectrum.com/NurseNewsEzine/item.cfm?ID=1710.

[7] James C. Rosser, Jr., et. al., "The Impact of Video Games on Training Surgeons in the 21st Century," *Archives of Surgery*, Vol 142 no. 2, February 2007: 181-86.

[8] B. De Waal, "Motivations for Video Game Play." MA Thesis, School of Communication, Simon Fraser University, 1995.

[9] J.C. Herz, *Joystick Nation* (Boston: Little, Brown and Company, 1997) 172.

[10] Reported at http://www.zdnet.com/blog/gadgetreviews/study-tetris-wipes-out-bad-memories-heals-trauma/771.

[11] K.E. Scheibe and M. Erwin, "The Computer as Altar" *Journal of Social Psychology* 108 (1979) 103-9.

[12] Study headed by Dr. Vincent Mathews, Indiana University School of Medicine, reported by *Newsweek*, 28 November 2006.

[13] Kaveri Subrahmanyam, Patricia Greenfield, Robert Kraut, and Elisheva Gross, "The Impact of Computer Use on Children's and Adolescent Development," in Sandra Calvert, Amy Jordan, and Rodney Cocking, eds. *Children in the Digital Age: Influences of Electronic Media on Development* (New York: Praeger, 2002) 24-25.

[14] David Walsh, president, National Institute on Media and the Family, at the 1993 Congressional committee hearing reported in Kent, Steven L. *The Ultimate History of Video Games* (New York: Three Rivers Press, 2001) 471ff.

[15] Steven Kent, *Minneapolis Star Tribune*, 6 November, 2004: E1,

[16] Testimony at the 1993 Congressional committee hearing reported in Kent 471ff.

[17] *Time*, 28 February 2005: 43.

[18] Brad King and John Borland. *Dungeons and Dreamers: The Rise of Computer Game Culture from Geek to Chic* (New York: McGraw-Hill/Osborne, 2003) 224-25.

[19] King and Borland 170.

[20] King and Borland 72.

[21] *Business Week*, 1 May 2006, cover story.

[22] Daniel Lyons, "Money for Nothing," *Newsweek*, 29 March 2010: 22.

[23] Will Wright, "Dream Machines," *Wired*, April, 2006: 112.

14. Persuasion: *The Push Never Stops*

[1] Philippe Schuwer, *History of Advertising* (London: Leisure Arts, Ltd., 1966) 42.

[2] http://www.ciadvertising.org/student_account/spring_01/adv382j/ootvas/paper2/hardsell.htm.

[3] James R. Beniger, *The Control Revolution* (Cambridge: Harvard University Press, 1986) 18.

[4] James Playsted Wood, *The Story of Advertising* (New York: Ronald Press, 1958) 342.

[5] Richard Ohmann, *Selling Culture: Magazines, Markets, and Class at the Turn of the Century* (London: Verso, 1996) 106.

[6] *Printers' Ink*, October 1895, cited in James Playsted Wood, *The Story of Advertising* (New York: Ronald Press, 1958) 6-7.

[7] Wood, 13.

[8] Barry Schwartz, *The Paradox of Choice: Why More Is Less* (New York: HarperCollins, 2004) 53.

[9] For a fuller discussion, see C. Edwin Baker, *Advertising and a Democratic Press* (Princeton: Princeton University Press, 1994) 4 ff.

[10] He wrote: "The conscious and intelligent manipulation of the organized habits and opinions of the masses is an important element in democratic society. Those who manipulate this unseen mechanism of society constitute an invisible government which is the true ruling power of our country... It is they who pull the wires which control the public mind." Edward L. Bernays, *Propaganda* (New York: Horace Liveright, 1928) 9-10.

[11] Translated from the German (1962) and published by the MIT Press, 1989.

[12] G.J. Meyer, *A World Undone: The Story of the Great War, 1914 to 1918* (New York: Delacorte Press, 2006) 434.

[13] Elizabeth Kolbert, "The Things People Say," *The New Yorker*, 2 November 2009, 110-14. This topic is considered more extensively by Cass R. Sunstein, head of the White House Office of Information and Regulatory Affairs, in five books: *Republic.com* (2001), *Infotopia* (2006), *Republic.com 2.0* (2007), *Going to Extremes: How Like Minds Unite and Divide* (2009), and *On Rumors: How Falsehoods Spread, Why We Believe Them, What Can Be Done* (2009).

[14] A term coined by one of their own, Quincy Howe.

[15] Jonathan Alter made this point in a column: *Newsweek*, 5 June 2006: 35.

[16] See Syd Hoff, *Editorial and Political Cartooning* (New York: Stravon Educational Press, 1976) 16-26.

[17] David Kilcullen, quoted in David Packer, "Knowing the Enemy," *The New Yorker*, 18 December 2006: 64.

[18] Speech to the American Bar Association, London, 1985.

[19] Bruce Hoffman, Georgetown University terrorism expert, *Newsweek*, 3 September 2007.

[20] See a statement attributed to Ayman al Zawahiri, reportedly the al Qaeda second-in-command, "We are in a battle. And more than half of this battle is taking place in the battlefield of the media." in Lawrence Wright, The Master Plan," *The New Yorker*, 11 September 2006:53; and an observation

regarding the Israeli-Hamas conflict by Columbia Dean Nicholas Lemann, "It isn't just a war. It's a media war. Public opinions outside the region are very important, and they're shaped by the press coverage." in Clark Hoyt, "Standing Between Enemies," *New York Times*, 11 January 2009:WK10.

[21] *The New Yorker*, 2 August 2004: 49.

[22] Samuel P. Huntington, *The Clash of Civilizations and the Remaking of World Order* (New York: Touchstone, 1996) 175-6.

[23] Barbara Daly Metcalf, "The Comparative Study of Muslim Societies," *Items*, 40 (March1986) 3.

[24] Robert Wright, *Nonzero*, quoted in the *New York Times*, 29 June 2003, op-ed page column by Thomas Friedman.

[25] Niels-Jacob Andersen, news editor, Danish Broadcasting Corp., private communication, 23 March 2007.

[26] Quoted by David Brooks, *Minneapolis Star Tribune*, 11 February 2006: A17.

[27] Francis Fukuyama, *The End of History and the Last Man*, 2nd ed. (New York: Free Press, 1993) 214.

[28] *Matichon Weekly*, Bangkok 24 February 2003.

[29] Bernard Lewis, *What Went Wrong: Western Impact and Middle Eastern Response* (New York: Oxford University Press, 2002) 52-54.

[30] *Time* 2 April 2007: 31.

[31] Ian Morris, *Why the West Rules—for Now* (New York: Farrar, Straus and Giroux, 2010) 149.

[32] Meic Pearse, *Why the Rest Hates the West: Understanding the Roots of Global Rage* (Downers Grove, IL: InterVarsity Press, 2004) 48.

[33] Interview on an Australian television program, 9 November 2010.

[34] As an example, see Amy Waldman, "Sarendhi Journal," *New York Times*, 28 March 2003, A4.

[35] Pearse, 35.

[36] Lewis, 73.

[37] Siva Vaidhyanathan, *The Anarchist in the Library* (New York: Basic Books, 2004) 78-9.

15. We Are Different: *Living in a World of Change*

[1] Plato, *The Phaedrus*.

[2] Media have played a part—but only a part—in the development of civilization. To that extent to focus on it is a technologically deterministic act, and here it is unapologetically so. But technological changes are entangled in social changes. Marshall McLuhan put this well at the start of *The Gutenberg Galaxy*: "Far from being deterministic, however, the present study will, it is hoped, elucidate a principal factor in social change which may lead to a genuine increase of human autonomy." *The Gutenberg Galaxy: The Making of Typographic Man* (Toronto: University of Toronto Press, 1962) 3.

[3] Marshall McLuhan, *The Gutenberg Galaxy* (University of Toronto Press, 1962) 31. See also Gerald Stearn, *McLuhan Hot & Cool* (New York: Penguin Books, 1968), 314.

[4] Sony reported these numbers at an executive conference in 2009, along with the startling assertion that the number one English speaking country in the world will soon be China. Presented by Karl Foch, Scott McLeod, Jeff Bronman, http://www.youtube.com/watch?v=cL9Wu2kWwSY.

[5] Barry Schwartz, *The Paradox of Choice: Why More Is Less* (New York: HarperCollins, 2004), 2-4.

[6] Gregg Easterbrook, *Progress Paradox: How Life Gets Better While People Feel Worse* (New York: Random House, 2003) xviii.

[7] See Richard Hollander's *Video Democracy* (Mt. Airy, MD: Lomond Publications, 1985) for comments about portable audio equipment.

[8] Two books by Robert Lynd and Helen Lynd, *Middletown: A Study in Modern American Culture*, published in 1929, and *Middletown in Transition : A Study in Cultural Conflicts*, published in 1937.

[9] Putnam, Robert D., *Bowling Alone: The Collapse and Revival of American Community* (New York: Simon & Schuster, 2000).

[10] For example, a study by Nobel Prize-winning behavioral economist Daniel Kahneman reported that people earning less than $20,000 annually spent more than one-third of their time in such passive leisure as watching television; people earning more than $100,000 annually spent less than one-fifth of their time this way (Washington Post, 23 June, 2008: A02).

[11] Lewis Menand, "Talk Story," *The New Yorker*, 22 November 2010:132.

[12] *The Happy Isles of Oceania* (New York: G.P. Putnam's Sons, 1992) 492.

13 George Will column, 21 June 2001. Located at: http://www.townhall.com/opinion/columns/georgewill/2001/06/21/165862.html.

[14] "Digital Nation," *Frontline*, 8 February 2011.

[15] *New York Times* column, reprinted in the *Minneapolis Star Tribune*, 6 November 2006: A9.

[16] Study by the Annenberg Institute of the University of Pennsylvania, 1999.

[17] See *Time*, 27 March 2006, for a 2005 report by the Pew Internet and American Life Project.

[18] Edward M. Hallowell and John J. Ratey, *Delivered from Distraction* (New York: Ballantine Books, 2005) 157.

[19] *Time,* Asia edition, at http://www.time.com/time/asia magazine/2000/0501/japan.essaymurakami.html

[20] ibid

[21] Melissa C. Nelson, et. al. "Longitudinal and Secular Trends in Physical Activity and Sedentary Behavior During Adolescence," *Pediatrics*, Vol. 118 no. 6, December 2006: e-1627-e1634.

[22] Lynn Smith-Lovin reflects on this in an article in the *Washington Post*, 23 June 2006: A03.

[23] *Newsweek*, 20 October 2003: E36.

[24] Nayan Chanda, reported by Thomas Friedman, *New York Times*, 6 June 2004, WK 13.

[25] *The Economist*, 20-26 November 2010: 50.

[26] Paul Kennedy, *Preparing for the Twenty-First Century* (Toronto: HarperCollins Publishers Ltd., 1993) 333.

[27] Reported in the *Minneapolis Star Tribune*, 1 December 2005: A20.

[28] *Newsweek*, 16 June 2008: 43.

[29] In a book review of *Exceptional People: How Migration Shaped Our World and Will Define Our Future* by Ian Goldin, Geoffrey Cameron and Meera Balarajan. (Princeton University Press, 2011). *The Economist*, 28 May 2011:87.

[30] *The Economist*, 19-25 November 2011: 72.

[31] James P. Wood, *The Story of Advertising* (New York: Ronald Press, 1958) 342.

[32] Richard Oppel, *New York Times*, 10 August 2003.

[33] For a discussion of this, see : Samuel P. Huntington, *The Clash of Civilizations and the Remaking of World Order* (New York: Touchstone, 1996).

[34] Meic Pearse, *Why the Rest Hates the West: Understanding the Roots of Global Rage* (Downers Grove, IL: InterVarsity Press, 2004) 34.

[35] Ian Morris, *Why the West Rules—For Now* (New York: Farrar, Straus and Giroux, 2010) 603

[36] Andrew Weil, "Don't Let Chaos Get You Down," *Newsweek*, 7&14 November 2011: 9.

Index